CRIME
WITHOUT PUNISHMENT

CRIME
WITHOUT PUNISHMENT

HOW CASTRO ASSASSINATED PRESIDENT KENNEDY AND GOT AWAY WITH IT

Dr. Carlos J. Bringuier

authorHOUSE®

AuthorHouse™ LLC
1663 Liberty Drive
Bloomington, IN 47403
www.authorhouse.com
Phone: 1-800-839-8640

Published by AuthorHouse 12/20/2013

ISBN: 978-1-4918-4336-9 (sc)
ISBN: 978-1-4918-4335-2 (hc)
ISBN: 978-1-4918-4334-5 (e)

Library of Congress Control Number: 2013922826

TABLE OF CONTENTS

Introduction vii

Chapter 1   Roots 1
Chapter 2   Education On Communism 25
Chapter 3   Exile In Cuba 32
Chapter 4   Guatemala (1960) 69
Chapter 5   Argentina (1960-61) 72
Chapter 6   Guatemala—Miami (1961) 81
Chapter 7   New Orleans (February 1961-July 1963) 85
Chapter 8   Lee Harvey Oswald (August 1963) 108
Chapter 9   The Assassination Of President John F. Kennedy 152
Chapter 10   New Orleans (1964-1967) 241
Chapter 11   The Garrison "Investigation" 266
Chapter 12   New Orleans (1968-1995) 314
Chapter 13   Miami, New Orleans, Alabama (1995-2005) 382
Chapter 14   The Woodlands, Texas (2005-Present) 385
Chapter 15   Commercial Activities 389
Chapter 16   Lies, Lies And More Lies 396
Chapter 17   The Verdict 431
Chapter 18   Conclusions 438

INTRODUCTION

The date of November 22, 1963 will be an historic mark forever in History. When Lee Harvey Oswald fired the shots in Dallas it was not only a President who had been killed it was the spirit of a Nation who was, at the moment, the leader of Freedom in the world.

After John F. Kennedy was assassinated, the United States of America initiated a radical change to the left. The Great Society was instituted creating generations of Americans depending on welfare, food stamps and other government give-a-ways. Senator Barry Goldwater, Republican candidate for the 1964 presidential elections and a serious threat to President Kennedy attempt to win a re-election was swept by a country mourning the Democrat President.

The eyes of the United States were suddenly moved from Cuba, a real menace 90 miles away, to the jungles of Viet-Nam, thousands of miles away. Working like termites the red ideologists started to spread a socialist vision of the world. In some cities anarchism broke out and with the help of the liberal press the criminals that were out to destroy the United States were portrayed as idealist pacifists. Narco-traffic from Colombia and Cuba became rampant.

Generations of young American brains were damaged in order to destroy our youth and our future.

In the meantime, as a Cuban born attorney, I was trying to initiate a new life in this Nation waiting for a prompt return to my native Country. When I arrived to the United States on February of 1961 I never dreamed that I would become part of the History of this great Nation.

I was *in god's hands* when I met Lee Harvey Oswald during the summer of 1963 in New Orleans, Louisiana and in this book I explain truthfully the activities that transpire during that period. Many lies and distortions of the truth have been published about those incidents, with my law-school background I confront and clarify each one that I have been aware off.

God gave me the opportunity to meet, among others, Lee Harvey Oswald, New Orleans District Attorney Jim Garrison and movie director Oliver Stone. God is my witness that I write the truth in this book. It is time for the United States public and the World public to learn the truth about *HOW CASTRO ASSASSINATED JFK*. With my Lawyer background I always study the background and credibility of a witness, in this book you have the opportunity to do so. At the same time you also will be reading events and anecdotes never published before. Here you have also the opportunity to know me, where I come from, and you can judge if I am a credible witness. This book has all the legal ingredient for the indictment and conviction of Fidel Castro for the assassination of President John Fitzgerald Kennedy.

Chapter I

Roots

In 1958 something more dangerous than a tropical storm was threatening the isle of Cuba. A category 6 political upheaval was very close to transform a tropical paradise in a horrendous hell.

I, personally, was in a very uncomfortable situation because I could not identify myself with any of the groups fighting for power. Families became divided and mine was not an exception.

Which Country who had suffered a civil war, no matter the fact that our, was more of words than of bullets, have not seen its sons divided in totally opposed camps?

In Havana of 1958 the last name Bringuier was recognized instantly. My father, Julio Bringuier Laredo, had been a Correctional Judge for over 20 years. In 1958, for a brief period of less than 2 months he was President of the "Tribunal de Urgencia de la Habana" (Tribunal in charge to judge terrorists) and after suffering a real coup d'état from the Secretary of Justice, he ran, in judicial competition, and gained the position of Magistrate of the Second Criminal Court of Havana province.

My uncle, José Enrique Bringuier Laredo had been a Senator from Camagüey province until Batista's coup on March 10, 1952.

My father's uncle, Federico Laredo Bru, uncle "Fico", a veteran Colonel of the Independence War had been President of Cuba from 1936 to 1940. Uncle "Fico" was a very honest man and while President he tried to convert Batista, the military man, to Batista, the civilian politician. At the time of Laredo Bru presidency Batista was Chief of the Army and

1

was attempting to dictate the government from the Columbia barracks but was confronted with the intelligence of Laredo Bru. Most of the time when Batista prepared a decree to be signed by the President, uncle "Fico" was returning the decree, unsigned, to Batista based on judicial issues.

During his presidency uncle "Fico" was confronted with the economic stagnation preponderant in Cuba following the Great Depression and he also had to confront the odyssey of the ship "St. Louis", loaded with 937 Jews refugees and sent on May 1939 from Germany by Nazi Minister of Propaganda Joseph Goebbels with a double mission: 1) Trying to discredit the Jews internationally by portraying them as "undesirables" and 2) Trying to accomplish a secret espionage mission.[1]

Federico Laredo Bru major concern was the wellbeing of the Cuban people. He considered that Cuba was a very small country, a country less than 40 years as a Republic, with an economy in very bad shape and that Cuba could not afford to receive the 973 refugees and the others that would be following in other ships like the English "Orduna" and the French "Flandre". He was a firm believer that the United States of America was the indicated country to receive the refugees.

On May 27, 1939 the German ship "St. Louis" arrived to Havana. President Laredo Bru had already promulgated decree 937 which forbade them entry to Cuba. For several days there were negotiations trying to make Laredo Bru change his mind, but he was set in his idea: Cuba was too small of a Country to receive those refugees, it was the United States of America the Country that should receive them.

One night General Manuel Benítez summoned my uncle José Enrique Bringuier Laredo, who at that moment was Secretary of the Presidency, to the Presidential Palace. José Enrique went to the Palace with his son, José Enrique, Jr. (Cucú). When they arrived it was almost midnight. General Benítez was waiting with a suitcase containing $1,000.000.00 (One million US$) in cash and as my uncle José Enrique was the only person authorized to wake up President Laredo Bru at his house in the middle of the night, Benítez requested that José Enrique call the President and inform him that the one million US$ were for him if he would authorize the Jews refugees to land in Cuba. As my cousin "Cucú" described the incident to me, José Enrique told "Cucú" to open the

---

[1]   "Voyage of the Damned", by Gordon Thomas/Max Morgan, pages 18 & 19.

suitcase and take a look at the amount of cash because maybe, never in his life, he would be able to see an amount of cash like that. José Enrique then called President Laredo Bru to his house and told him what was going on. President Laredo Bru could not believe what General Benítez was trying to do and he furiously told José Enrique:

"Tell General Benítez to immediately return that money and that when I will arrive in the morning I want to see over my desk his resignation and also tell him that I will not send him to prison because he was my comrade during the Independence War".

On June 2, 1939 the "St. Louis" departed Havana and eventually disembarked the refugees, some going to France, England or Belgium. The secret mission was accomplished as an agent working for Goebbels went ashore and brought back to the ship, microchips, diagrams and other information about USA defenses that had been brought to Cuba from the USA with the purpose of doing sabotages in case of war.

One of the most importance legacies of Federico Laredo Bru was the 1940 Constitution, the most advanced Constitution in Hispanic America. To achieve that, President Laredo Bru exercised his intelligence to the max. In his farm, 'Párraga", in the town of Wajay, it was orchestrated the accord to bring about the elections for members of the assembly to write the new Constitution. Then he managed to make shake hands two bitter enemies, Fulgencio Batista Zaldívar and Ramón Grau San Martin. It was his 1940 Constitution the one that was violated on March 10, 1952 by Fulgencio Batista with his coup and it was this 1940 Constitution the one that Fidel Castro Ruz pledged to restore during his revolution, pledge ignored by Castro who just used it to ambush the naiveté of the Cuban people.

For us those were very nice years. It was a great event when the President car stopped in front of our house to visit us. The neighbors gathering around the car to see and cheer the President, and he coming inside our house to greet us. I was very young but I have been told that he used to sit in our dining room and place me in his lap asking me if I wanted to be a President like him, according to my family my answer always was the same: No.

But now it was 1958. Let's go back to our roots and see from where we came from.

My mother's maiden name was Vicenta María Expósito Alfonso[2]. She was born on October 10, 1894 in the town of Chambas, Camagüey province. She studied Art in Havana at the famous school of San Alejandro, and did her grammar and high school at the Mariana Lola School for girls. Her mother was Gertrudis Alfonso, born November 16, 1857 in Arroyo Blanco, Camagüey province. Her father was Alonso Casimiro Expósito born March 4, 1856 in Guadalupe, Cáceres province, Spain. Alonso Expósito came to Cuba as part of the Spaniard Army and, before the war ended, he left the Army and decided to remain in Cuba. Gertrudis and Alonso met when she was working as a seamstress and he was bringing his uniforms to be fixed. After their marriage Alonso and Gertrudis went to the town of Tamarindo where he excelled in business. Alonso was a peddler bringing items, on his horse, from the town to the peasants and bartering for chickens, pigs, etc., which items he brings with him and sold in town, afterwards buying more things and doing the same bartering again. Eventually some bandits, whose leader last name was Mirabal, captured him inquiring where he was hiding his gold. Alonso refused to answer being brought to a tree where he was going to be hanged. Finally, with the rope around his neck, he gave away his gold.

Alonso and Gertrudis moved to the city of Morón and started doing business there.

First they started as a mom & pa general store and grocery. Eventually, the customers, afraid of being robbed were depositing money with Alonso for safeguarding. After some time, the intelligent Spaniard opened his own bank. During the depression there were only two banks in Cuba that didn't go in bankruptcy, Alonso's bank was one of them. In 1908, only 6 years after Cuba's independence, Alonso Expósito, the former Spaniard soldier and now Cuban citizen, was elected as Mayor of the city of Morón. As Mayor he served until 1912. Due to his hard work and intelligence Don Alonso Expósito, at one time, owned almost half of the city of Morón real estate.

History shows us the animosity, and sometimes hate, between the Spaniards and the Frenchmen. In my case I am a result of the opposite. The first Bringuier to arrive to Cuba was a Frenchman, Henri Bringuier, who escaping the revolution in Saint Domingue (now Haiti) arrived

---

[2]   In Hispanic America the person uses 2 family names the first one from the father the second from the mother.

4

in a small boat to the eastern coast of Cuba around 1794. Henri had a brother, Paul, who had died fighting at the side of Napoleon Bonaparte and Napoleon had designated both of them the title of Marquis.

After a while Henri traveled to the western province of Pinar del Río and settled in the town of Artemisa where he started a coffee plantation.

In 1809 the Spaniards were threatening to expel the Frenchmen from Cuba and Henri married a Cuban lady wedding that automatically exempted him from deportation. In May 1809 the Spaniards finally expelled the Frenchmen from Cuba sending them from Santiago de Cuba, Baracoa and Havana to New Orleans. By 1810 more than 10,000 Frenchmen had arrived to New Orleans from Cuba. It is said that those Frenchmen were the ones who really civilized New Orleans bringing there the first newspaper and the opera.

Henri had three sons and each of them decided to settle in a different city. One went to Havana, another to Cárdenas and the other to Remedios. From the one that choose the city of Cárdenas is from where my ancestors came. Basilio Bringuier, my grandfather was born in Cárdenas, his father was Enrique Bringuier and his mother Manuela Corrales.

As I am writing these lines I feel proud of my ancestry. That is one of the things that I have over Fidel Castro Ruz. He was born as a result of an adulterous affair of his father and the servant cook in his house. That is the reason why Fidel Castro was not baptized until his father's wife had died.

Basilio Bringuier married María Laredo Lapeyre. María was the daughter of José Bernardo Laredo and Irene Lapeyre. In 1868, at the beginning of Cuba's Ten Year War, because of their sympathies for Cuban independence José Bernardo Laredo and Irene Lapeyre were forced to leave Cuba and went in exile to New Orleans where my grandmother María Laredo Lapeyre was born and where almost a hundred years later I would have a rendezvous with History.

Basilio and María had two sons. José Enrique Bringuier Laredo and Julio Salvador Teodoro Bringuier Laredo. Basilio only met one of them, the older, José Enrique. With María pregnant of Julio, Basilio joined other *mambises*[3] and took to the hills to fight for Cuba's independence.

---

[3]   Freedom fighters

Eventually in a section called Lomas de Magulla he confronted death without having the opportunity to meet his soon to be born son Julio. It is ironic that at the same time Fidel Castro's father was killing Cubans who were fighting for Cuba's independence.

It was so much the involvement in the struggle for independence of the Bringuier, Laredo, and Lapeyre families that the new born was baptized Julio Salvador Teodoro. The name Julio was given for a Cuban independence hero, July Sanguily; Salvador, for Salvador Cisneros Betancourt (Marquis of Santa Lucía) first President of Cuba in Arms in 1895; and Teodoro for the great American hero Theodore Roosevelt.

During their youth the two Bringuier children were first raised by their mother, and when her health failed, their maternal aunts Rosa and Carmen Laredo Lapeyre took care of them. Rosa Laredo Lapeyre was also born in New Orleans and was the first woman to graduate at the University of Havana as Doctor in Pedagogy.

During those years it was normal that the first-born child receives all the benefits, and Rosa and her husband were not different. They decided that José Enrique was going to go to the University of Havana and become a lawyer, and that Julio, the youngest one, was going to be a merchant. Julio didn't like the idea and one day he escaped from the house arriving at Havana penniless and enrolling at the Law School in Havana University.

There is an anecdote in our family that is of historical importance. My grandmother María had another sister besides Rosa. Her name was Carmen and she was a real beauty.

Carmen Laredo Lapeyre had also been born in New Orleans and when the family returned to Cuba from their exile, in 1878 after the Ten Years War, she became a fervent admirer of Cuba's independence. At one time she was engaged to be married. Her sweetheart was a Spanish Captain in charge of the city of Remedios. Suddenly, and after serious consideration, Carmen sent a messenger to the Spanish Captain. When his sweetheart arrived she returned to him her engagement ring telling him: *"We can't get married, you are a Spanish captain and I am a "Mambi"*[4] with those words the engagement ended.

When Generalissimo Máximo Gómez advanced with his troops to the western section of Cuba in his liberation march he arrived to the

---

4   Cuban Freedom Fighter.

city of Remedios. The town welcomed him with a ball, "Liberty Ball", at the Lyceum. Rosa and Carmen attended the ball with the whole town. Máximo Gómez, attracted by her immense beauty, approached Carmen and asked her to dance. Carmen responded: *"I don't dance but with you my General I will be delighted to do so"*. So they danced and by the end of the ball Máximo Gómez gave my great aunt Carmen a scarf (in reality a small Cuban flag) that he used at his neck to cover a scar left by a bullet.

Many years later, after Castro's Revolution, the scarf, Paul Bringuier uniform, a picture of Generalissimo Máximo Gómez signed with a message to Carmen and many other memorabilia were lost. Carmen never married. One day, years later while in the city of Remedios, trying to protect my cousin José Enrique Bringuier (Cucú) she fell from a very high sidewalk and suffered a severe lesion in one of her legs which had to be amputated. She died in Havana in her eighties.

When my father left the city of Remedios to attend Law School at the University of Havana he suffered hunger and had to go walking to the University because he didn't have money for the street car. He survived doing some construction work. Eventually he moved to a boarding house where there were some other students, among them Juan Expósito Alfonso, a student of Pharmacy and his future brother-in-law.

My uncle José Enrique graduated as a lawyer and Julio, instead of becoming a merchant, also graduated as a lawyer. Havana was a tough city to start a career without money and without been known, Julio decided to move to the interior and as his friend Juan Expósito Alfonso was also graduating as a Doctor in Pharmacy and was going back to his city of Morón, Julio decided to move to Morón.

When Julio arrived to Morón he opened his office as a lawyer but in the beginning, as it was tough to start, he used his experience in the construction area and started to build small houses and then selling them for a profit. In the meantime, Juan introduced him to his family and that is how he met my mother. They said it was love at first sight.

Julio was tall, around six feet, and Vicenta was short, around five feet five inches. In those days courtship was kind of difficult and my father told me how he managed to kiss Vicenta for the first time. They were outside in the backyard at Vicenta's house and Julio pointed high up to a branch in a tree saying: *"Look, what a beautiful bird."* Vicenta raised her head to look at the bird and Julio inclined his head and deposited the first kiss that Vicenta had ever received in her lips.

Then on July 19, 1919 Julio and Vicenta celebrated their wedding in Morón, Camagüey province, Cuba. That day they promised each other that they were going to be together for the rest of their lives and in eternity.

It was in that way, with honest love, that our family was form. In the other hand, Fidel Castro and two of his brothers were born bastards as a result of an affair among his married father and the maid of the house.

In 1934, the year I was born (and I was born because I was *in God's hands* (due to the fact that I was children #6 and my mother was reaching the age of no more child births), my father was appointed Judge of the town of the city of Zulueta and in 1935 he was transferred to the city of Camagüey, capital of the province of Camagüey. While in there, *God's hands* showed in my life for the second time.

During an election my father was designated to be in charge of the city's Electoral College and a group tried to bribe him in favor of one of the candidates. He refused the bribe and after returning one night to the house, while everybody went to sleep, some vandals placed a bomb by the front door. He heard some people yelling *"You have a bomb"* and then somebody rang the bell. My father ordered everybody to go to the last room and while gathered over there they realized that they had forgotten me. At one year of age I was sleeping on a crib in the front room. My father ran, picked me up, and when he arrived back to the last room the bomb exploded. A chunk of material from the ceiling landed on my crib.

In 1936 my father was transferred as Judge of the city of Sagua la Grande in Las Villas Province. It was there where my sister María del Carmen fell in love with her future husband Jorge Medina Núñez.

In 1937, with my great uncle Federico Laredo Bru as President of Cuba, my father was appointed Judge of the Second Night Court in Havana' and a few months later he became Judge of the Eighth Correctional Court of Havana.

At our arrival to Havana my parents rented a house on Paseo Street in the El Vedado section of Havana. In 1939 we moved renting a house at Calzada 255 between J and I streets also in El Vedado. The first school that I attended was Colegio Añorga and in 1941 I entered into first grade at Belén School in Marianao, at the other side of the Almendares River in Havana.

On December 7, 1941, while Pearl Harbor was suffering the devastation of the treacherous Japanese attack, I was receiving my first communion at Belén School.

My father loved all members of his immediate and extended family. For him his family was his treasure. Around this time the Cuban government was going to follow the United States steps in regard to enemies during World War II. In the United States President Roosevelt ordered the Japanese to be interned in concentration camps. Cuba had decided to do likewise, intern the Germans residing in Cuba. My mother's family became nervous. One of my mother nieces, Teresa Bray, was married to a German, Henry Pfister, and they asked my mother for help. Henry Pfister was a real gentleman and my father moved his influences and managed to obtain permission for Henry and Teresa to leave the country which they did going to Argentina where they spend the happiest days of their lives. Teresa and Henry always appreciated what my father had done for them.

Either in 1942 or 1943 *God's hands* again took care of me. While crossing Calzada Street I was struck by a car and brought unconscious to a Hospital located three blocks away from my house. When I recovered consciousness I didn't have any broken bones or any other injury.

I really enjoyed my youth at Calzada Street. I had a lot of friends among them Tony Copado, Luisito Roca, Reinaldito González, the Pujals brothers, Bobby Marichal, Villito Sánchez Ocejo, the brothers Raúl and Néstor Domínguez, Luisin Nóbregas, Pedro González, Miguelito Grau, another was a very nice black kid that hanged around with us and who was so black that we called him "negative", a black shoe shine youngster by the nickname of "Winche" and others whose names escape my memory at this time. Among the girls were María Luisita González, Mariita Grau, Milagritos Estébanez, Natalia Cervantes, Lyda Jiménez, Ana Cecilia Pando, Martica Cambó, the sisters Rosita and Margot Albear, Nuria Alfonso, Gladys Soto, Ofelita Gassó, Heidi Alvarez, Enid González, Astrid Navarro (daughter of a Mexican diplomat), Clarita and others whose names also escape my memory.

In those years when we return from school the first thing that we did was going outside to play. No Nintendo or Play Station. No computer or text messages. One of our favorite games besides "hide and seek", was "El taco" game. We used to play it on I street in between Calzada Street and the José Martí Park. It consisted of a broom stick and a cork taped all over. It was kind of a baseball game and we had a lot of fun with it.

When I was a teenager I disliked been called the son of the Judge. I didn't want to feel special but just to be like everybody else, no matter the fact that some days during vacation from school, my father was bringing me to his court and I was sitting next to him and the Secretary, watching the trials.

We joined a club, Casino Español de La Habana, where I practiced baseball, squash, bowling, rowing and swimming. My baseball coach was Johnny Jaén and he was a great coach. In that club my best friends were Tony Huerta, Rafa Inclán, Clemente (Machito) Inclán, Gustavo Laffite, Matalobos, Javier Varona, Pedro Bacallao, Jorge Ledo, Carlos Padial, Pedro Julio Martínez Fraga and others. Among the girls in the club I remember among others, Macucha Baños, Purita Fernández Ichaso, Enid Turró and Baby Inclán.

During my teenage years we used to rent a house, during summer months, at Tarará Beach. At that time Tarará was a very special beach and the club had been founded by an American: Royal Webster. There I kept practicing my swimming, squash, volleyball, rowing and baseball. My friends over there were among others, Tony Copado, the Casellas brothers (Tony and Rogelio <Muñeco>), Rafael (Piquete) del Cerro, Isidro (Chilo) Borja, Fiquín Cano, Manolito Mellado, Flaquelito, Alberto Morató, Wilbur Clark, the Muller brothers (Juan Antonio y Alberto), Benito del Cueto, Pompeyo Durán, the Webster family (Edward, Willy, Medora, Helen, Susan and Chata), Willy Borroto, Julito González Rebull, Alfredo Izaguirre, Juan A. Michelena, Bernabé Peña, Akika Rodríguez, the Mesa sisters (Gladys and Nora) who were in charge of the telephone office, the Sowers brothers, Silvia Domínguez, Magda Díaz, Martica Cambó, María Inés Bergnes, the sisters María Elena and María del Carmen Fernández del Collado, Felo Etchezarreta, Teresita del Cueto, Manolito Cueto and Mari Paz Someillán.

Tarará was a very exclusive club and Castro resented it no matter the fact that his wife's family was bringing his son, Fidelito, to Tarará where I met him when he was a child. Now Tarará is even more exclusive. Only the hierarchy of the government or tourists with euros or dollars are allow to have access to it.

My mother was a very devout catholic, she was a saint. My father was the most intelligent person that I have ever met. He had a tremendous memory and he was very honest. He didn't drink. He smoked a lot of cigars, he had a great personality and he was very strict in his courtroom.

I remember one time when I heard in Havana that my father was going to the Courthouse drunk. The stupid ignorant person who was saying that didn't knew my father. Since very young my father suffered from asthma and almost every night he had to burn and inhale the fumes of some small incense rocks which helped him to breath. On some nights he was unable to sleep and the next morning he had to go to the Courtroom, sometimes with red eyes, due to the lack of sleep. In my house we never had a bottle of rum, whiskey or any other alcoholic beverage. Only during the Christmas season we had Cider bottles. But that is the stupidity of making false accusations. Later on, when Castro took over, stupidity would become a pandemic.

Carlos Bringuier and friends at Tarará Beach, Cuba.

In 1950 we improved a lot, economically. An aunt of my father, Aurelia (Aunt Lela) Lapeyre Letamendi, born in New Orleans but living in Cuba, passed away and left her fortune to my father. In that year we stopped renting the house in Calzada Street because we bought it. My father loved animals and he bought a couple of farms in San Antonio de los Baños around 32 kilometers from Havana, each one of them was about 20 acres each, in reality not large farms. The farms were named "San Julio" and "Santa Vicenta" and my brother Juan installed in one of them a dairy by the name of "El Crisol".

In March 10, 1952, Senator Fulgencio Batista Zaldívar took over the government in a bloodless coup that the great majority of the population accepted as fait accomplished. I still remember my brother-in-law Jorge Medina asking himself, at the entrance of the Calzada house, how everything was going to end.

My other brother-in-law, Rolando Peláez, was a true believer of Batista and in the morning he went to the Columbia barracks to offer himself to help Batista, his friend. Rolando who had been a Colonel in the Cuban Navy was not reintegrated to the Navy but was appointed as Under Secretary of Defense, post that he held until January of 1959. Rolando was not reintegrated to the Navy because he was an honest man and the small group around Batista didn't want him in the Navy. That small group was the one that caused Batista's downfall with their treachery and corruption.

On September 1952, I was enjoying my youth, nothing could stop me. I had a lot of fun and I never indulged in drugs. To us, at that time, the ones using marihuana were the scum of society. I saw some of them with their brains destroyed by drugs, but the ones using it were the lowest of society. That year I graduated from High School at Belén and from the Marianao Institute. After graduation my father gave me a brand new 1953 Buick Special. The only thing that I regret is that I did paid more attention to having fun than to my studies. In September I entered Law School at the University of Havana attending it in the morning while at night time I also attended Commercial Science (CPA).

My father with his fame as a hard line Judge, was designated Special Judge to investigate the corruption during the government of deposed President Carlos Prío Socarrás.

During a few months my father conducted the investigation and one day had an interview with the Secretary of Justice. My father explained that yes, he had found loose threads that proved corruption existed during Prío's presidency but that following those threats he had found also proof of corruption during the presidency of Dr. Ramón Grau San Martín (1944-48) and that following those threads he had found also corruption during the previous presidency of Fulgencio Batista Zaldívar (1940-44). The Secretary of Justice response was that next day my father was notified that he had been dismissed as Judge of the special case. My father returned to his Judgeship at the Correctional Court.

While at Law School I became involved in University politics and joined the group CRU (Candidatura de Renovación Universitaria) whose leader Albertico Hernández was promoting a clean, democratic and anti-Communist student body. Among my friends at Law School were Jorge Marbán Leiva, José (Pepe) Puente Blanco, José (Pepé) Fernández Cossío, Carlos R. Busquets, René Maresma, Elsa Márquez, Silvia Valdés Figueroa, Abel Holtz, Rosita Nieman, Juan Nuiry, Pedro Maseda, Rodolfo Nodal, René Anillo, Miguelito Alfonso, Osmel Francis, Ramonín Martínez, Orestes Vázquez, Raoul García Cantero, José Auñón, Gisela Campos, Enky Capetillo, Rubén D'Toste, Ana María Planiol, Sarita Portela, José Raúl Rodríguez Brito, Otto Vilches, Fermín Fernández and many others.

In 1953 I participated in student marches against the Batista government. The great majority of students were well inspired. A small group was with other ideas in mind. In one of those marches a student, Rubén Batista (not related to Fulgencio Batista), was killed by a bullet. Immediately the government was blamed for the killing. The burial was another march from the stairs of the University to the cemetery. I participated in that march. After the burial, while still at the cemetery a small group of students, with their own agenda, started to riot on 23rd Street in El Vedado. The police arrived and dispersed the march. After the march finished I learned that some shots have been fired "from" the University trying to cause victims within the marchers.

That same year I ran as Delegate candidate from CRU in one of the studying subjects. My opponent was a mulatto by the name of Roberto Santiesteban. I took an early advantage and a few weeks before the election the opposite group dropped Santiesteban from the slot and substituted him with a more powerful candidate. The day of the election each candidate selected a personal inspector to help supervise the voting. I was *in God's hands* when I selected as my representative a friend of mine from the Casino Español de la Habana whose name was Fermín Fernández. I lost the election by 3 votes and I learned that my friend and inspector was asking different students to vote against me. When I lost that election, and the way in which I lost it, caused me to alienate myself from University politics.

During the month of May 1954, I was appointed Officer of the 5th Criminal Court of Havana becoming the youngest person ever occupying that position in Cuban history. At that moment I had to take a decision: which career I was going to follow? I decided to continue Law School using a special type of academic course that allowed me to study without attending the faculty.

A year later, on May 1955 while I was at the portal of the Calzada Street house when the phone rang. It was not *God* but I am sure that *His hands* directed my friend Virgilio (Villito) Sánchez Ocejo to call me. Villito's parents owned an apartment building across the street from their house barely two blocks away from my house and Villito was asking me if I wanted to meet a beautiful Argentine girl who had moved to one of their apartments.

I always had dreamed with Argentina and at my 21 years of age I was very popular. 15 minutes later I was at Seventh Street been introduced to María del Carmen (Pochi) Pearce Ferrari. Villito was right and the Argentine girl was indeed a beauty but she was showing her Argentine prepotency and we made the wrong connection. After a few months she was my girlfriend and in December 24, 1955, I was formally asking for her hand to get married.

On December 13, 1955 our family received a strong blow. My sister Vicenta María (Vicentica), during a big bout of depression committed suicide at our house. The impact almost killed my mother. It took years for her to overcome her grief.

On December 31, my future wife and her family departed for Buenos Aires, Argentina. Her father, Héctor Pearce Balochi, who was working at the Argentinean Consulate in Havana, had gone back to his country (at his own request because he wanted to see if we would break off our engagement) and we started preparing everything to get married in Buenos Aires.

Finally on April 14, 1956 we got married at the Church of Nuestra Señora de las Victorias (Our Lady of Victories Church). I went alone to Buenos Aires because my father didn't like to travel overseas or go in an airplane. At the time there was a great polio epidemic in Argentina and even my brother Julio was advising me not to go there and instead to get married by power of attorney.

The idea was ridiculous to me. I took a small pox vaccination shot (as required in those days for international travel) and arrived to Buenos Aires in March of 1956. After our honeymoon in Mar del Plata, Rio de Janeiro and Miami we returned to Cuba and I continued working at the Criminal Court. The first night that we arrived to Rio de Janeiro we stayed at the Hotel Serrador. Around 6:00 a.m. Pochi woke me up saying that she was smelling smoke in our room. I went to the window and she was right. There was a fire in the second floor (we were staying in the 14th floor), the fire was in a night club named "Night and Day". We had to descend, in pajamas the fourteen floors with our two pieces of luggage passing a few feet from the flames by the second floor and finally we were able to make it safely to the street. That night we went to the movies and we saw our faces in the news reel. Next day the local paper Diario da Noite showed our picture in the front page with the caption: *"Argentinean couple escaping by fire in honeymoon."*

After returning to Cuba we installed our home at an apartment on Calzada Street right across my parents' house. On February 2, 1957 our first child was born. We baptized him with the names Carlos José. He was born at 9 months of pregnancy. I continue working at the Criminal Court but after work I was moonlighting at a second job as co-manager of my brother Julio's Shell service station in Linea Street at the corner of E Street in El Vedado.

After some months we moved close to my brother Julio in the neighborhood on La Víbora at 418 Heredia Street and finally we bought a house, with my parent's help, at 426 San Francisco Avenue in Alta Habana. In order to do that my mother sold a house that she had in Morón inherited from her father. On February 27, 1958 our daughter María del Carmen was born. She was born at 8 months of pregnancy. As a coincidence the day that she was born bloomed our first rose in the front yard of the new house and as a rose she has enlighten us with love during our life.

In the meantime the political situation in Cuba was growing from bad to worse. Our family was becoming deeply divided. As mentioned before, my sister María Gertrudis (Totó) was married to Rolando Peláez Bosch who had graduated from the Cuban Naval Academy, later on became Director of the Naval Academy and during the years of the Second World War a Cuban Navy Attaché in Washington, D.C. Rolando was a very honest person. He saw in Batista a man for the poor and when Batista left power in 1944, Rolando was forcefully retired as Colonel in the Navy. He became a farmer growing gladiolus in Havana, owning the "Tebenque Farm" and became the larger grower of gladiolus in Cuba. When, on March 10, 1952, Batista did the coup d'etat he appointed Rolando as Under-Secretary of Defense.

My uncle José Enrique despised Batista and after the coup he refused to participate in politics to undermine Batista's legitimacy. José Enrique for years was a Senator from the province of Camagüey. In 1954 when Batista called for new elections he contacted my uncle and offered him $100,000 US dollars to run for the Senate and participate in the elections. José Enrique refused to play Batista's game. With Fidel Castro in the Sierra Maestra my uncle José Enrique contributed with $50,000 US dollars to help the revolution. In the meantime his son, Cucú, who owned shrimp boats, used them to bring arms to the rebels.

A couple very good friends of my parents, Mario González and his wife Blanca Secades were confronting a problem. Their daughter Blanca María was engaged to a revolutionary member of a very famous Cuban family. His name was Manolito Hevia. My parents' friends were concern that Manolito Hevia was going to be killed by the Batista police and requested help from my father. My father asked them to bring Manolito to his house and Manolito lived there until my father managed to obtain permission for him to leave the country. During the mornings, when my father was leaving for his Courthouse he was bringing Manolito with him to assure his safety. My father even contacted Cardinal Arteaga and obtained dispensation for Manolito and Blanca María to get married, in a hurry, before their departure from Cuba.

My father was appointed President of the Tribunal to judge the political detainees. Two other Magistrates were appointed to join him at the Court. They were Dr. Raúl Delgado Perera and Dr. José Piña Varona. My father lasted in that job less than two months.

Different things affected our family in those moments. My parents were still living at their house in Calzada Street. It was a very large house consisting of a wide portal, a large living room. Another small living room, six bedrooms, two baths, dining room, large walk-in pantry, a large open pantry, a large kitchen, a garage for 5 automobiles and over the garage two bedrooms and two bathrooms for the servants. With my parents were living my sister María del Carmen, her husband Jorge Medina Núñez and their children. The house had two stories and the upper story also consisted of six bedrooms and two baths and it was rented for $180.00 a month. My father had me in charge of collecting that rent and keeping it to financially help me and my family.

When my father took over the position as President of the Tribunal de Urgencia he confronted the problem that his daughter, María del Carmen, and her family were against the government and for the Revolution. My father, trying not to hurt them economically decided to move out of the house, leave them living there without paying any rent and with my mother they moved first to my brother Julio's house but after a few weeks they decided to move and live at my house in Alta Habana.

We both were working in the same building: "The Judicial Palace" (which after the triumph of the Revolution Castro has converted into his Presidential Palace). Some revolutionary lawyers (the William Kunstlers of Cuba) started to create problems on my father's court. Among them was a Syrian-Lebanese named Alfredo Yabur Maluf. One day, after I finish my work at my court I went to the side of the building were my father's court was located. I was present when Alfredo Yabur Maluf told my father that he was scared that the police was going to arrest him and kill him. My father told Yabur that if at any time he was arrested to have instructions given to his family to contact my father and that he (my father) will take care that nothing will happen to him.

There were several attorneys going to my courtroom. Among them Carlos Rafael Mencio (the best criminal attorney in Cuba), José Sánchez Boudy (who I used to call "Pepito"), Luis I. Rosas Guyón, José Antonio Suárez de la Fuente and others. One day I was approached by José Antonio Suárez de la Fuente who was asking me to become a partner in his law firm. His proposal was that as I could not practice law while working for the Criminal Court I could become his partner. According to his proposal he would take care of cases of political detainees I could obtain their freedom through my father and then we would divide the legal fees 50/50.

My response was: *"Tony, you know that I don't take money in my courtroom how come would you think that I would take money in something related to my father's courtroom? If you or any of your relatives is detained then I will be willing to help you for free, because of our friendship".*

One day, while my parents were living in my house in Alta Habana, one of the sons of Pelayo Cuervo Navarro went to see my father at the Judicial Palace. Pelayo Cuervo Navarro, a prestigious lawyer, had been assassinated on March 13, 1957. His corpse with 8 bullet wounds has been found on March 14 and it was presumed that he had been killed by Batista's police as a reprisal for the failed assassination attempt against Batista that same day of March 13, when opponents to Batista assaulted the Presidential Palace.

Pelayo Cuervo's son was coming from the Sierra Maestra as an emissary of Fidel Castro with a list of detainees which Castro wanted my father to set free. My father studied the list, check the names with the crimes allegedly committed by them and told Fidel Castro's emissary: *"I am sorry, but the people whose names appears in this list are accused of killing policemen and of terrorist acts and placing bombs in Havana. Tell Fidel Castro that I can't set them free."* Within 72 hours my father received another visitor. This time it was Bernardo Caramés Camacho, Secretary of Justice of the Batista government. Bernardo Caramés presented my father a list of persons that the government wanted to set free. My father was surprised when he realized that the list in question contained the same names previously presented to him by Fidel Castro's emissary.

My father, who had a strong temper, was furious. He told the Secretary of Justice: *"The people in this list are accused of killing policemen and of committing terrorist acts exploding bombs in Havana. Those are crimes punished by our Penal Code. If the government want to set them free I will do so, but I will free all political detainees because in good conscience I can't let some go free while others stay in jail while all are accused of the same crimes."*

Bernardo Caramés Camacho, Secretary of Justice, left the Judicial Palace knowing how strict my father was. Next day, the three Magistrates of the Havana Tribunal de Urgencia were deposed by the Secretary of Justice. My father returned to his courtroom at the Eighth Correctional Court of Havana but I have never see him so angry.

That afternoon we were playing Canasta in the living room of my house, my father and my mother against Pochi and me, when at a moment he exploded saying: *"Even if get blind I would like to see them dragged by the streets."* He was referring to the circle of corrupt people surrounding Batista. When I told him not to say anymore nonsense he was shocked and asked me what I was meaning. My response to him was: *"Papá, remember that if you get blind you will not be able to see them dragged by the streets."* His response was: *"Carlitos, you always with your ironies."*

Later on, after a few days, my father recovered from his sense of humiliation and entered in a judicial competition to obtain a vacant place as Magistrate of the Audiencia of Havana, position that he won. My parents bought a house a few blocks from my house and my father dedicated himself to his new court, his wife, his birds and his farm.

In the meantime the opposition to Batista was growing. One day I saw a friend of mine from the Casino Español, Javier Varona, passing by the hall in front of my courtroom. I knew that Javier was a member of the July 26th Movement. I called him and we started talking. My point was that those who carried the assault against the Presidential Palace in March 13, 1957 were right. The only thing that Cuba needed was a political change not a revolution. In my view the only thing that Cuba needed was democracy and an honest government. His answer was: *"Carlitos, you are wrong. We don't want Batista killed or out so soon. We need Batista to stay longer in power because now we don't have the political power to take over the government. We need more hate and more time to consolidate our power. Cuba needs to be changed, from bottom to top, 100%, we need to start a new Republic."*

Thinking about my nephew Jorge Medina Bringuier who had become so involved with the revolutionary ideas that my sister and her husband had sent him into exile to the USA, I asked Javier Varona about the people that were dying on both sides of the power struggle. His answer was: *"Carlitos, we don't care about the ones who die defending Batista and in regard to those that could die opposing Batista let me tell you . . . in all revolutions there are mentally unbalanced people that joint the struggle and it is better that they die now as martyrs and not that we will have to kill them later."*

After lunch I went to talk to my sister, María del Carmen, and repeated to her the conversation. Javier Varona never dreamed that just a few years later, with the Revolution in power, he himself would be assassinated at the G2 offices. There is another version that, disenchanted by Fidel Castro, he committed suicide at the G2 offices. Whatever is the truth, Javier Varona's life was another young life sacrificed by the ambition for power of the Castro brothers.

Another day a friend from Law School came to visit me at my courtroom. He was Pepé Fernández Cossío and he was requesting my help. Pepé took part in an anti-Batista demonstration at the stadium of baseball in Havana and he wanted to leave the country without asking for political asylum in an embassy but he was confronting the problem that there was a pending order for his arrest at the courtroom under which jurisdiction the incident had occurred. The courtroom in question was my father's courtroom. As we were good friends I brought him to my father's courtroom and after I spoke to my father the order for his arrest was lifted and he was free to leave Cuba through the airport as an average citizen, which he did.

When we left the courtroom I never dreamed that with the triumph of the Revolution Pepé Fernández Cossío was going to become a very important person. Among other achievements he became Ambassador to Canada, Ambassador to the United Nations and Ambassador to Mexico. While he was Ambassador to Mexico was when it was initiated the Chiapas revolt that catapulted Sub-Comandante Marcos to international publicity. What not everybody knows, as I was informed, the Mexican government requested from the Cuban government, that Pepé, as Cuban Ambassador, be returned to Cuba because if not the Mexican government would expel him. Apparently the Mexican government had proof that the weapons to the "Zapatistas" had been supplied by the Cuban government through its Embassy in Mexico.

Around the middle of 1958 one afternoon I left the Palace of Justice and was driving my 1956 Mercury Montclair on Rancho Boyeros highway and when I was approaching a street light it changed to the red light. Two cars that were ahead of me stopped and I managed to do the same but a bus that transport passengers to the airport could not manage to stop and hit my car from behind. I steered the wheels to the right trying to avoid the car in front of me but my reaction made me leave the highway and my car, *in God's hands* drop by a cliff several meters deep. The car flew over a wire fence, went in between two trees and finally stopped at a place where the car could not be seeing from the highway, I escaped unscathed. My Mercury was a total loss.

As a result from this accident Cuban Airlines (Compañía Cubana de Aviación) gave me, as part of the settlement for the damages to my car, a free ticket to fly from Havana to Buenos Aires via LAN Airlines.

When the 1958 November elections approached I decided to cast my vote for Carlos Márquez Sterling, the opposition candidate for the Presidency, and I did so at the electoral precinct located at José Martí Park in El Vedado.

We started preparing a trip to Argentina and I decided that when we would return in January 1959 I would resign my job at the Courtroom and will open my own law firm. In Cuba, different than in the United States, if you worked in the court system you could not practice your Law career because it was considered that then you would have an advantage over the other lawyers.

On November 1, 1958 a tragic event struck our family. I have a cousin "Chichita" Bray married to a pilot, Ruskin Medrano, who worked with Cuban Airlines. It was reported that his plane had crashed at Nipe Bay, Oriente province. The night of the funeral, what we called "Radio Bemba" (Radio Gossip) at the funeral house was spreading the word that the airplane tried to defect going to the Sierra Maestra to join Castro's forces when the Batista government had shot it down.

The real truth was that the plane leaving Florida, USA to Varadero Beach, Cuba, had been highjack by a group of members of the July 26th Movement, under orders of Fidel and Raúl Castro. They had boarded the plane in the USA, ordered my cousin pilot Ruskin Medrano to fly to the Sierra Maestra and when Ruskin refused alleging not enough fuel to reach the Sierra Maestra, then the revolutionaries stabbed him to death. The co-pilot attempted to comply the orders of the revolutionaries and directed the plane toward Oriente province but before reaching the Sierra Maestra the plane ran out of fuel crashing in the Bay of Nipe.

Several innocent people died in the high jacking, including my cousin, pilot Ruskin Medrano, but some passengers and revolutionaries survived the crash. After the triumph of the Revolution, Bohemia Magazine, published an article interviewing several of the revolutionaries, then working for the Castro government. One of those revolutionaries was recently interviewed in Miami, FL by "EL Nuevo Herald" and he was reported as living in Coral Gables, Florida. As the writing of this book none of the participants in the highjack have been charged in any court of the United States and obviously the masterminds behind the deadly act, Fidel and Raúl Castro neither had been charged no matter the fact that the plane originated its flight in the USA and the terrorist boarded the plane in the USA. As far as I know, Murder is not a crime that prescribe. But several Senators and Congressmen had traveled to Cuba to shake hands with those murderers. Even ex-President Jimmy Carter (always hiding behind an hypocrite smile), the same one who had occasioned so many dead among American soldiers when he betrayed the Shah of Iran, turning our former ally into an extremist Islamic terrorist Country, had been a visitor of Dictator Fidel Castro, even playing baseball with him.

The presidential election passed and Batista's candidate won in a landslide something that just showed the ineptness of Batista committing fraud at the elections and not paving the way for a peaceful outcome of the political crisis.

Batista was not the solution for Cuba. The Revolution neither. I realized that for Batista sympathizers I was becoming a revolutionary and for the revolutionaries I was becoming a Batista sympathizer. To me both groups were wrong. Batista should have facilitated a peaceful solution accepting the electoral victory of the opposition. The Revolution was not healthy, for me, neither for my family, or for Cuba.

I knew that Fidel Castro was a gangster and that his brother Raúl was a Communist. A cousin of mine, Manolo Castro (not related to Fidel Castro) had been assassinated on February 22, 1948 at the corner of San Rafael and Consulado streets in Havana. One of his murderers was Fidel Castro Ruz. On the other hand I had knowledge that an Argentine who was with Castro in the Sierra Maestra, Ernesto Guevara, was also a Communist. The fact that my father-in-law, Héctor Pearce Balochi had worked at the Argentinean Consulate in Havana had given me the opportunity to learn that the Argentinean government gave orders to not provide any help to Guevara who was considered a Communist.

I feared for my father and I asked him to prepare his passport in the event of the downfall of the government in which case he should leave Cuba for a while in the meantime that the tempers cool down. My father rejected the idea. He didn't like to take an airplane and besides he said nothing was going to happen. Just in case, I contacted my cousin Jorge Ernesto (Necho) Rey, who also was a lawyer, and asked him to prepare the passport for my father.

A friend of mine, Angel Francisco Belvedere was the diplomatic courier of the Argentinean Embassy and I requested from him the assurance that in case that the government was overthrown my father would be granted political asylum at the Embassy of Argentina. Belvedere was married to Mercedes Sorhegui and they had married in Havana the same day that Pochi and me got married in Buenos Aires, and he was a very good friend of mine.

At the end of November 1958, Pochi, our son Carlos, our daughter María del Carmen and I left Cuba for Buenos Aires, Argentina. That day when I looked the view of Havana from the airplane it was the last time that I saw a free Cuba.

CHAPTER II

---====◉====---

EDUCATION ON COMMUNISM

Few days after our arrival at Buenos Aires I realized that Batista downfall was imminent and unavoidable. It is incredible how when we are out of a country, without the passionate daily living, you can acquire a much better interpretation and panoramic view of the facts.

Before the end of December the Cuban Ambassador to Argentina gave possession of the Embassy to the 26th of July Movement. On television I could see Batista's relatives arriving to the United States.

On December 30, 1958, I could not contain myself any longer and I called my brother Julito inquiring if Necho had finally obtained what I had requested from him in regard to my father. Julito didn't knew what I was talking about. I remembered that my father had told me to forget about a passport for him. I was confident that he had changed his mind.

As Julito didn't understand what I was trying, in a veiled way to tell him over the phone, I decided to be blunt: *"Julito tell papá to leave the country immediately because the situation there is crumbling down and Batista will not last in power 72 hours."* Neither my father nor Julito believed that what I was saying was going to happen.

Next day, the last day of the year 1958, in New Year's Eve, we had a gathering of relatives of Pochi's family. At midnight I rose to my feet and toasted for Batista to leave Cuba. In my mind, gone Batista, Cuba's political problems would be solved. I was young and naïve. When I finished my words, my father in law, Héctor Pearce Balochi, a very wise diplomat, also rose to his feet and said: *"Carlitos, I hope that you never would have to repent of your toast, a bad government eventually will pass, but we never know what a Revolution could bring us."*

At those very moments, thousands of miles away, coincidently Batista was getting ready to leave Cuba. Events were happening in my country that would change forever the destiny of my life, of my family, of Cuba's history, of millions of Cuban people and of Humanity.

Batista was leaving Cuba. Now the road was open for the opposition to take over the power. In Cuba everybody knew that if Batista leaves the power nobody could stop the opposition. What is was not widely known was that the opposition was going to be unable to stop Castro's ambition for power. We didn't know that Fidel Castro was in reality a tool of the Fabian Illustrated Marxists to take over Cuba and pave the way for Socialism to triumph in the United States of America. The dice was cast.

Early in the morning of January 1st, 1959, my mother in law, Zafira Ferrari Pertine, woke me up telling me that over radio and television the news was that Batista had fled Cuba.

As soon as I was dressed and ate my breakfast I hurried up to the offices of the Cuban Embassy in Buenos Aires.

When I arrived you could feel the sentiment of euphoria which was spreading throughout the place. Among others I met well known Cuban newsman Agustín Tamargo; also a man whose last name was Beruff and who was the representative of the 26th of July Movement in Buenos Aires; an aunt of Ernesto "Che" Guevara; a blonde model who I recognized because of the advertisements in TV of Edén cigarettes (the famous "Girls from Edén" ads in Cuba's TV); and an Argentine with the last name of Rojo.

I introduced myself to Beruff and when we shook hands I told him: *"I was not a Fidelista before, I am not a Fidelista today, and I am not going to be a Fidelista tomorrow but as you have the power I pray to God that you do what is best for our Fatherland."* After a few minutes I departed.

A couple of days later I was able to establish telephone contact with my brother Julito inquiring about our father. Julito informed me that my father had obtained political asylum in the Argentinean Embassy. The news calmed me down because we have been getting information on TV about the executions been carried out in Cuba by rebels who were the government now and were creating a blood bath never before experienced in Cuba.

I had, naively expected, that the traditional political parties would reach an agreement to share the power. But no, Fidel Castro was now the power in Cuba and as he knew what he had in mind for the future he started planting the seed of Terror. With the first news of the executions I thought that they would be sporadic cases, but it turned out that the executions increased with the veiled effort to seed Terror among the population. And you know what happens when you seed Terror? When you seed Terror what you harvest is Blood and Fear. And now, for the first time in our history the Cuban people was learning what really means Terror and Fear.

A few days later I read in the La Nación newspaper that the first Cuban exiles had arrived to Buenos Aires. They were: Dr. Gustavo Gutiérrez, Dr. Alejandro Herrera Arango and Eusebio Mujal Barniol. The first two were Secretaries of Commerce and Finance in the deposed government. Mujal was the General Secretary of the Confederation of Cuban Workers (CTC). According to the newspaper they were staying at Hotel Crillón.

As fast as I could I went to downtown Buenos Aires reaching the Hotel Crillón. When I arrived I located them at the dining room having breakfast and when I introduced myself they immediately recognized my last name and invited me to sit down with them and join them for breakfast. I wanted to know about my father's condition and they assured me that my father was safe and in good health.

For a few days I visited them at the hotel but the one who gave me the most profound impression was Mujal. I remember how in one opportunity that we were chatting, Gustavo Gutiérrez and Herrera Arango entered to the room and Mujal exploded. They have been shopping and they were delighted with some bargains that they have obtained. Mujal, turning toward me, told me: *"Look Bringuier that is why what happened to us happened to us. Look at this stupid pair buying silk shirts and they still don't realize what is coming to us."*

During the days that Mujal and I got together he gave me a really first class education in communism. He was a great teacher, he started his career as a workers representative as a Communist. He knew how Communism works. Also he made me laugh with anecdotes that took place at the Embassy of Argentina during his stay there.

According to Mujal, on the night of December 31ˢᵗ, 1958, after he became aware of Batista's flight (Mujal, in his own words, considered Batista to be semi-senile, a traitor and a coward) he started to locate friends that could be persecuted, make them aware of the situation and bringing them to different Embassies to obtain political asylum. At the end he took refuge at the Embassy of Argentina.

Mujal was feeling deep respect and admiration for Mrs. Paloma Amoedo, wife of his Excellency, Ambassador Julio Amoedo. Mujal related to me that in one of the first nights at the Embassy, shots were heard close to the building and rumors started flowing that revolutionary forces were going to assault the Embassy in order to capture Mujal.

Among the noises provoked by the shots, coming down the stairs, he saw the figure of his Excellency Ambassador Amoedo, who hysterically and almost in tears was shouting: *"Majul, Majul, please surrender to them because if not they are going to kill all of us."*

Mujal refused the idea of committing suicide by surrendering and all of the sudden he counted with the support of Mrs. Paloma Amoedo.

The same degree of his admiration toward Mrs. Paloma Amoedo was the same degree of contempt that he felt for his Excellency Ambassador Julio Amoedo. As expressed by Mujal to me, Paloma Amoedo had comported herself more manly than her husband. She had, no matter the fact that she was a beautiful woman, more male attributes than her husband.

Mujal also related to me that after the moments of suspense when they had been waiting for an assault to the Embassy one of the refugees, Cuban actor Otto Sirgo could not be found. Finally Otto Sirgo was discovered hidden in one of the tanks of water.

Now in Buenos Aires, with the passing of the days, Mujal was becoming more cautious every day that passes. Just by looking at his eyes I could notice how nervous he was becoming. I was becoming concern about his mental wellbeing.

Another visitor that I encountered several times while visiting with Mujal was Mr. Lara, the Cuban Consul in Buenos Aires who was still occupying his Consular post.

Mujal selected a code that we had to use to knock at his door. He explained to me that his political origin was as a member of the Partido Socialista Popular (Cuban Communist Party) and that as he knew all the Communists that were with Castro, and no matter the fact that years ago he had broken his ties with the Communist party, as he knew that the Communists had taken over the power in Cuba, Castro will order his assassination in order to silence him. Mujal had good connections with some political figures in the USA and also with labor leaders but what Mujal ignored was how deep the Fabian Socialists had invaded the State Department, the Legislative body and the executive body of the USA.

At the beginning I thought that Mujal nerves were reaching their limits. To make it worse the new President of Cuba, Manuel Urrutia Lleó, was trying to invoke into this hemisphere a new diplomatic doctrine called "Urrutia Doctrine" by which persons who obtain political asylum in an Embassy, when they arrive to the country giving them asylum would have to stay in that country for at least 30 days so the Cuban government would have time to initiate extradition proceedings against the refugee.

With that new "doctrine" the Cuban Revolutionary government now in power was trying to destroy the historic bastion of political asylum. The right to political asylum had been highly respected up to that time in all Hispanic America.

One day, at the verge of a nervous breakdown, Mujal called me. When I arrived at the Hotel, I used the code at the door and he let me in. During several days Mujal had been giving me an education on Communism. He explained to me how the Communists are like fanatics working 24 hours a day to destroy us and in the meantime what we want to do is stay with our families, enjoy some sports, watch TV or go to the movies. For the Communists, according to Mujal, their best sport is to do something that could help destroy society as we know it. A family nexus is not important, what it is important is the Revolution. Now Mujal, the former Union leader, was not attempting to teach me anything. He was fearing the Communists moving against him. Terror was shown on his face.

He gave me his passport and enough money to buy a one-way ticket Buenos Aires to Miami, Florida. He also asked me to go to the Department of Federal Police and obtain for him a permit to leave the country. I managed to obtain both of his requests.

In Cuba I never considered Mujal a very intelligent person but now that I knew him personally he proved to have a brilliant brain. Mujal was able to identify with first names and last names the new Communist hierarchy now in power in Cuba. I remember that one of the times when he looked more worried was when he told me: *"Bringuier, what it is in power in Cuba is not an autochthonous Communism, it is controlled by Moscow."*

As his last days in Buenos Aires were bringing him closer to his dreamed departure to the United States, Mujal increased his nervousness almost by the hour. Now he was convinced that he would be killed before having a chance to leave the country. During those days it was declared a union general strike in Buenos Aires and that event produced another deep emotional impact on him. Mujal assured me that he could not travel in a taxi to the airport because the taxi driver would kill him. I thought that Mujal was in the verge of paranoia, felt sorry for him and decided to talk to my father-in-law about it. We devised a plan to help Mujal.

If my recollection of the facts is right, Mujal was scheduled to take his flight to Miami in a Sunday. That day we went to pick him up at the Hotel Crillón with my father in law driving his car. We covered Mujal's head with a hat, put some dark glasses on him and the three of us arrived at the suburb of Liniers, the section of Buenos Aires were my in-laws were residing. After lunch we brought Mujal to the Ezeiza airport. If I am not wrong his plane was also boarded by a famous wrestler named Antonino Roca. Eusebio Mujal Barniol left Buenos Aires alive and in good physical health, he was going to a friendly land, bastion of freedom, where he could unmask the Communist that he so well knew.

A couple of days after Mujal's departure I received a phone call from Cuban Consul Lara, the same one that usually visited Mujal at the Hotel Crillón. It is good to mention here that I first met Consul Lara in 1956 when I went to Buenos Aires to get married. Consul Lara was one of the guests at my wedding. Now the Consul was worried about Mujal; he stated that he had been trying to contact Mujal but has been unable to do so and inquired if I knew something about his whereabouts. Using my good Jesuit education of mental restriction I told him that there has been a couple of days in which I have not seeing Mujal. Finally Consul Lara confided that he was seriously concern about Mujal's security and relay to me a message to Mujal in case that I was able to contact him: *"Tell Mujal that while I was at the Consular office I overheard a conversation among two individuals that just arrived from Uruguay with orders to kill Mujal."*

In my mind a veil had been removed and my ideas became clearer. The long arm of Fidel Castro had reached Buenos Aires trying to kill Eusebio Mujal Barniol, as Mujal has feared; luckily for Mujal he had been a Communist and he knew how the Communists operate. His knowledge saved his life. Now he was far away. Something strange and new came alive inside me, I enjoyed the satisfaction to have helped to prevent that assassination ordered by Fidel Castro Ruz.

By the end of January 1959, together with my wife and our two children, Carlos and María del Carmen, we boarded a plane at Ezeiza airport to bring us back to Cuba. But the one returning to Cuba was not the same one who had arrived two months earlier. During January 1959, in Buenos Aires, I had received an extensive education in what Communism was all about. My professor had been Cuban Union Leader Eusebio Mujal Barniol. From him I learned how Communism operate, their theories and principally the fact that Communists never relax in their endeavor to destroy us. Mujal's experience showed to me that assassination was one of Communism's favorite tools to deal with their enemies.

Now, with my return to Cuba it would be my chance to study, personally and directly, the practical side of how that dangerous and lethal system works.

CHAPTER III

———◈———

EXILE IN CUBA

It was still daytime when the plane landed on the José Martí International Airport in Rancho Boyeros, Havana, Cuba. The date: January 26, 1959.

Waiting for us at the airport was my brother Julito. We were ready to go to our house at 426 San Francisco Avenue in the Alta Habana subdivision. Then Julito told me something that made me change our plans. Our house had been taken over by the newly created Ministry of Recovery of Misappropriated Properties. Militiamen of that Ministry were in possession of my house.

We accepted Julito's offer to go to his house at Vista Alegre 72 in the "La Víbora" subdivision. That night I slept with Pochi, Caki and Miri in a little apartment in the basement of my brother's house.

Next day I went to work to my courtroom. Immediately I noticed the change. Before, I was the son of the Magistrate Julio Bringuier Laredo, now I was the son of the ex-Magistrate Bringuier who was under political asylum. Many friendships went sour. That was how my first year on internal exile started. A different kind of exile, many idiots were trying to rise up in the new government some others were trying to survive but they turned their backs on me, just to eventually ending also in exile in Miami or some other cities. But that is the nature of the human being. Mine was a different kind of exile. At that time it didn't cross my mind the idea of leaving Cuba. The traditional political parties surely were going to stop the Communist from taking full power. If that fail, then the United States of America and the Organization of American States would not allow the new Communist regime to remain in power. There were diplomatic accords to prevent that, and also, it was in the best interest of the United States to prevent that, because that, was a cancer which could do metastasis and invade the whole hemisphere including the United States of America. This was an internal exile, that could last a few months, but in which I saw dear relatives take different paths and some of them jump into a Revolution that eventually will devastate all of us. Some friends will turn their backs and others will betray me.

In the afternoon, with the Titles and Act of Sales of my house and my parent's house in Alta Habana, I entered into the Capitol building, now converted into the headquarters of the newly created Ministry of Recovery of Misappropriated Properties in order to plead my case and try to obtain the return of both properties.

I was *in God's hands*, that the person who was in charge of our case was an old man who felt a lot of respect for my father. He helped me to fill the documents reclaiming my house and the house of my parents located at #330 K Street in the same Alta Habana subdivision. The old man explained to me that I would have to go with an employee of the Ministry, take an inventory of whatever was inside both houses, return to the Ministry and then they could be returned to me, as depositary, while both cases were investigated.

I had a glimpse of hope when I recognized walking into the office an ex student from Belén School who had played baseball with me at the school and also at the Casino Español de la Habana. His name is Yamil Emedán who resulted to be working for that Ministry. When I explained to him my situation he showed interest in the case. Emedán explained to me that he was also working at the American Embassy but that after he finish his work at the Embassy he comes to the Ministry to work for the Revolutionary government. He volunteered to go with me to Alta Habana and do the inventories in the two houses.

We arrived first at my parent's house. Unfortunately, there I met the real Emedán. As soon as we entered the house his personality totally changed and turning toward the militiamen that came with us, told them: *"This is the house of the man that we are interested in, I want it searched inch by inch. We have to find something that could incriminate him."*

After a couple of hours of the fruitless search we proceeded to do the inventory.

It was dark when we arrived to my house. With us was a Captain of the Ministry Police, Captain Carlos Eloy Hernández, who was in charge of the intervention of both houses. To have access to the house we had to wait a few minutes because after ringing the bell we became aware that the militiaman in charge, was making love to a militiawoman on our bed. When they managed to get dressed we stepped in and did the inventory. When the inventory was finished Emedán asked me to surrender to him the Titles and Act of Sales that I had brought with me. I refused alleging that they were mine, that I had come with them and that they were not subject to the inventory. He threatened me stating that now they were inside a house being investigated. I repeated my refusal telling him that I would be willing to let the Ministry decide the issue when we would return there. The stalemate lasted for a few seconds, finally Emedán blinked first.

Luckily when we returned to the Capitol building the old man who respected my father was still there. Emedán talked to him in private and then left. I was called to the office and the old man congratulated me saying that I have done the right thing, that I should keep the documents and use them in any other procedures that I would have to do and finally he advised me to be very cautious with Emedán whom he qualified as a dangerous man. After he filled some documents he gave me possession of both houses, as depository, and responsible of the inventory while the investigation continue.

It was the last time that I saw Yamil Emedán in person. Eventually he left Cuba, and if my information is right he resides in Coral Gables, Florida. I don't know when, or if, he severed his ties with the Communist government of Fidel Castro and if he mentioned his work at the Communist Ministry of Recovery of Misappropriated Properties when he entered into the USA.

Next day, after work, I returned with my family to our house in Alta Habana. At the time of the inventory I have noticed that several items had been stolen from the house, some of them of value like jewelry, but unbelievable many of them almost of no value at all. From the missing items the one that impacted us the most was the movie of our wedding in Buenos Aires. Still today I ask myself, what kind of imbecile, what kind of cretin would steal a movie of a wedding? Maybe that imbecile is living today in Miami. I rechecked the inventory list and, to my surprise, I found that a piece of cloth material that had been listed the night before now was missing from the house.

Knowing that Captain Carlos Eloy Hernández had his office at an occupied house in the Casino Deportivo subdivision, next day after work, I went directly there to confront him.

In his office I explained to him that I didn't want to cause harm to the Revolution, but as since the previous night I was given, as custodian and as depositary, everything that was listed in the inventory of my house I was responsible for each one of the articles listed in it. If one item was missing then I could be held responsible for it, and in order to protect myself I would have to report to the Ministry of Recovery of Misappropriated Properties the theft of the article. Then I confronted him that the piece of cloth material listed in the inventory was missing when I returned to my house. Captain Carlos Eloy Hernández, without looking at my eyes, opened one of the drawers of his desk and returning to me the piece of cloth material said: *"Bringuier, you don't know how ashamed I am at this moment."*

These were the saviors of the Fatherland. These were the kind of excrement that worked for the Ministry of Recovery of Misappropriated Properties and there I was, recovering a "misappropriated" property stolen the previous night from me. A sad future laid ahead for Cuba.

In the way back to my house I stopped at my parent's house and, as a precautionary measure, I took with me items that were easy to steal. Among the items taken by me, to be under my protection in my house, were the window screens that protected the house from insects, mosquitoes, etc. I still don't know what moved me to take those window screens.

For a few days I dedicated myself to go and have lunch with the militiamen at the house serving as office for Captain Carlos Eloy Hernández. My intention was to try to find and recover some of the items stolen from my house.

My effort paid benefits. One of the stolen items was an am/shortwave radio Phillips with "magic eye". Repeatedly Captain Hernández had told me that when he took over my house the radio was not there. One day, when I was alone and searching his office, bingo, I found it. To verify that it was my radio I checked that it had the same defective button like mine.

After I found the radio, a militiawoman who had finished her lunch, walked into the office. I explained to her who I was and that the radio was my radio. She did not denied that, accepting that it was my radio and explaining to me that during the first days of January, Captain Carlos Eloy Hernández had taken the radio out of my house in order to be able to hear the speeches that Fidel Castro was delivering from different Cuban cities. I sat in front of a typewriter, proceeded to redact a document returning the radio to me. The militiawoman signed it and I recovered my radio. During several days I was able to recover other items stolen from my house including some law books. One of the books had my father's signature on it. I don't know how many Cubans had the opportunity to recover "misappropriated" properties from the Ministry of Recovery of Misappropriated Properties, but I did it.

One of the Revolutionary laws that most affected me directly was Law #11. I had been studying law until the University of Havana was closed during the Batista government. At that time there were created other Universities among them, José Martí University, University of Las Villas and the University of the Norte de Oriente. This last University was located at the City of Holguín in Oriente province. After the closing of Havana University I continued my studies under the supervision of a tutor who worked at the Library of the University of Havana. His last name was Génova and he had a brilliant legal mind. After I passed some subjects at the José Martí University, and as I did not like the environment there, I decided to take my last three tests at the University of the Norte de Oriente.

After I enrolled there I took three trips by train to Holguín in order to take my exams.

While in Holguín I always stayed at the Royal Hotel. The three exams that I had to take were:

Obligations, Successions, and Contract. The Dean of the University was Pedro Peñaranda Díaz. Two of my professors were openly against Batista. One of them, the one from Obligations had confronted a difficult situation with a son of a Secretary of the Batista government who had failed his exam. I took my exam with him, returned to Havana and after a few days returned back to Holguín to take another exam.

At the Royal Hotel I went to the bar and found there the professor of Obligations, satdown with him and started chatting. He explained to me what had happened with the Secretary's son. The professor explained that he was not rich and that the only thing of value that he had was his profession and that he would not prostitute his profession for all the gold in the world. After a while he congratulated me saying that he had given me a grade of Notable in my test and that he wanted me to know that my grade had been the highest that he had given since he became a professor of Obligations. If my memory doesn't fail me his name was Juan Mir.

Afterwards some other people tried to obtain their Diplomas like Fidel Castro had obtained his: with a gun in his hand. Dean Pedro Peñaranda Díaz was a just an honest man, he refused to sign the Diplomas of those intellectual gangsters. Trying to keep his good name he signed the Diplomas obtained academically correct, he refused to sign the corrupt ones and left the Country going into exile. My Diploma has the signature of Dean Pedro Peñaranda Díaz.

With the triumph of the Revolution Fidel Castro implanted not only the physical "paredón" to assassinate opponents (and seed the Terror) but also implanted a poisonous intellectual "paredón". This intellectual "paredón" was Law #11 by which the Revolutionary government annulled all Degrees obtained after the closure of the University of Havana during the Batista government. Later on Fidel Castro was going to ignore all academic principles and award degrees just for climbing the Pico Turquino (most famous mountain in the Sierra Maestra). Making the Cubans the people with more University degrees in our hemisphere. Where else could you find so many taxi drivers, peddlers and prostitutes with University degrees?

Both "paredones" were imposed thanks to the resentment, envy and low level intelligence of those that thought that bringing someone else down would make them become higher. The Cuban people would have to pay dearly for their un-Christian attitude.

If they would have seek justice, they would have established University Tribunals to study each individual case, but no, in those moments they were not looking for justice, they were blinded by their desire for vengeance. It was not important to affect honest students together with dishonest ones. Law #11 was a clear cut example of the low morale and pigmy mentality of those that even calling themselves Christians allowed to be dragged by hate, envy and rancor. Sometime later many of those who approved Law #11 were affected by new Revolutionary laws. We can't forget: "Revolution devours his own children."

The Castro Revolution became what some Cubans started to call: "The Revolution of the stepped on corn", which meant that today the State would step on my corn and nobody would say anything because "it was on my corn not in their corn". Tomorrow the State would step on somebody else corn and nobody would pay attention because it was not their corn and the State would continue stepping on corns until everybody ended up jailed, in exile, at the paredón or becoming a slave of a sadist feudal master, the State (Fidel Castro).

José Martí, the Apostle of our independence thought with unbelievable premonition that something like this could happen one day in Cuba. For those wretched souls who enjoyed themselves with the promulgation of Law #11 and the law instituting the death sentence in Cuba, I repeat here this thought of José Martí: *"Anyone who doesn't look for the human rights of his neighbor as his own deserves to lose his own human rights."*

In the meantime the stay of my father at the Embassy of Argentina was been prolonged due to the spirit of the "Urrutia Doctrine". While at the Embassy I visited him every day before his departure. He had been given a room separated from the main building by a floral garden. During normal times it was the servant's room.

My father recounted to me that when he learnt about Batista's flight he went in hiding at Julito's house, from there he went to the Belvedere's apartment and for several days he was changing his hiding place around the houses of different relatives. Finally Julito and Belvedere coordinated a plan for my father to enter the Embassy of Argentina. At a specific day and time the door of the gate of the Embassy would open and my father would be able to enter the building. The Embassy was located on 5th Avenue in Miramar subdivision and it was surrounded my militiamen. On January 7th, at the prearranged hour my brother Julito drove his car in front of the door, the door opened, and my father also opened the door of the car, and ran for his life inside the Embassy before the militiamen could be able to react. Now inside the Embassy my father requested political asylum.

It was *God's hands* that had directed my friend Virgilio (Villito) Sánchez Ocejo to call me in May 1955 to ask me if I wanted to meet a beautiful girl from Argentina. Four years later my father's life had been saved because I married that beautiful girl from Argentina. Not only had my father's life been saved but also the lives of his three sons. Another

Magistrate, Arístides Pérez Andreu, who occupied the same position as my father but as President of the Tribunal de Urgencia in Pinar del Río province, had been apprehended and assassinated at the paredón. If my father would not have been able to receive political asylum at the Embassy and would not have been able to escape and, after apprehended, was going to be executed at the paredón I am sure that together with my brothers Julito and Juanito the three of us would have perished trying to kill Fidel Castro.

Because of what he did, that undoubtedly saved the life of my father, I will always be grateful to Angel Francisco Belvedere.

My father had many friends and was respected by many functionaries of the Batista government. He also had many friends and was respected by many functionaries of the new Revolutionary government. The new Prime Minister José Miró Cardona was also a friend of my father. The new Secretary of Foreign Relations Roberto Agramonte, President of the political party, Partido del Pueblo Cubano (Ortodoxo) also respected my father.

While my father was waiting for his safe conduct to leave the country he received a message from Secretary Agramonte: *"Dr. Bringuier is in total freedom to leave the Embassy of Argentina and if after that, he decides to leave Cuba, he can do that freely without the necessity of asking for political asylum."* Secretary Agramonte was giving his word of honor and we knew that he was an honest person.

My father contemplated the idea of accepting the offer from Secretary Agramonte. We had a meeting at the Embassy at which meeting together with my brothers Julito and Juanito we decided to refuse the offer received. Secretary Agramonte, surely in good faith was guaranteeing the offer, but who could guarantee Secretary Agramonte? Which means, Secretary Agramonte, honestly believed that he had authority to guarantee my father's life but what Secretary Agramonte didn't realize was that the real authority in Cuba was Fidel Castro not the Secretary of Foreign Relations. We could not jeopardize our father's life. We decided not to take the risk.

Until he received the safe conduct my father stayed at the Embassy and finally, together with my mother, he started the road to an exile, expected to be short, but an exile that didn't allowed him to return alive to Cuba. They left Cuba with less than $5,000.00 US dollars. Luckily they had in Buenos Aires my wife's family with whom they stayed.

In the Bohemia magazine No.6, dated February 8, 1959 appeared an interview with the new Secretary of Justice Alfredo Yabur Maluf. Yabur was virulently attacking my father for his strong position as President of the Tribunal de Urgencia. This was the same lawyer that my father, in front of me, had offered protection during the Batista government. It was like having put William Kunstler as Secretary of Justice of the United States.

In another issue of Bohemia magazine appeared an article about the hijacking of the Cuban Airlines airplane in which on November 1st 1958 had died the pilot Ruskin Medrano, incident to which I previously narrated. But I would like to mention that with the murder of my cousin Ruskin Medrano, Fidel Castro closed a circle initiated on February 22, 1948 with the assassination of my cousin Manolo Castro. Fidel Castro, closing the circle, had made widows two sisters. Manolo Castro's widow was my blood cousin María Gertrudis (Nena) Bray; Ruskin Medrano's widow was my blood cousin Narcisa María Valentina (Chichita) Bray. Both, Nena and Chichita, were sisters and their husbands were assassinated by Fidel Castro.

On February 13th 1959 we suffered another blow from the Revolution. At 8:00 a.m. Orlando Cambas Pulgarón, Commissioner of the Ministry of Misappropriated Properties; his assistant, Manuel Macías Díaz; typist Vicente Iglesias; and witness José Pita González, appeared at the "San Julio" farm, located at the Govea subdivision in the municipal term of San Antonio de los Baños doing an inventory of the furniture, all other items and the animals. They occupied all documents and money sending them to the Ministry for investigation.

The "San Julio" farm had approximately 20 acres and had been acquired by my father in 1951 and in 1955 was donated to my brother Juan.

When the inventory was done a document was redacted assigning provisional custody to my brother Juan who was therefore responsible for the care and maintenance of the farm and he was not allowed to take from the farm any movable items, objects or animals without a written order from the Ministry.

The "Vicenta" farm that was located in the opposite side of the highway and that had been acquired by my father in 1950 was confiscated by the Revolutionary government without any investigation or trial.

It was sad to see how the Revolution rushed forward against a property legally bought by my father with inherited money. Like us, many other Cubans started to become victims of the new regime.

Meanwhile the vast majority of Cubans kept hypnotized by the revolutionary orgy. They started moving against freedom of the press. Newspaper like Diario de la Marina, Información, Avance, El Crisol, Prensa Libre and others where becoming under siege by the Communists and the useful idiots following them. It was not important if human rights were violated, the Revolution was above all and Fidel was portrayed as a new Jesus; Commander Camilo Cienfuegos's beard made previously circumspect ladies fall in love with him.

Today, after so many years in exile, I still remember an advertisement of a popular Cuban beer, Polar beer. It used to say: *"Polar Beer, the beer of the people and the people never make mistakes."* But in Cuba's case it was wrong. The people made a disastrous mistake that still is paying for and will need generations to come in order to bring Cuba forward to the economic and social status of December 31st, 1958.

At the Judicial Palace we could feel a nervous uneasiness. The Revolutionary government decide to carry on a depuration of the Magistrates, Judges and employees of the Judicial Power. By information received from persons who were present, when my case came up a difficult situation was confronted.

The depuration was supposed to be carried out by the Magistrates of the Supreme Court. The Magistrates of the New Supreme Court already had been extracted by the Revolutionary government from within the Judicial Power. But there was a person who wanted to dictate his decision to the court. That person was former Magistrate and now President of the Revolutionary government, Manuel Urrutia Lleó.

President Urrutia advocated for my destitution. In my defense rose, non-other than Emilio Menéndez, President of the Supreme Court, who inquired about the motives to fire me. The President of the Supreme Court explained that there were 3 reasons to fire an employee: 1) that the employee was inept and incompetent to occupy his position; 2) that the employee was corrupt and takes bribes; 3) that the employee didn't attend his job and just picked up his salary (deadhead).

Magistrate Emilio Menéndez stated that it was well known that I was competent in my job; that it was also well known that I did not accept bribes and that I was a worker who was at my job during all time required. He stated that if the reason to ask for my firing was because I was the son of ex-Magistrate Julio Bringuier then he wanted to know until what degree of blood connection they were going to be vindictive.

The point of view of the President of the Supreme Court prevailed and I was not fired from my job at the Criminal Courts. A very well-known Cuban attorney, Luis I. Rosas Guyón, was the one who brought me the news that I had been saved from the depuration. In the meantime I was able to see how some Cuban people was awakening of their siesta and President Urrutia started to be known by the nickname of "Little spoon President" ("Cucharita") because he didn't pinch (like a fork) neither cut (like a knife).This was a man full of hatred and rancor who ended been depurated by Fidel Castro when Castro decided it was not more use for him, as a useful idiot, and forced Urrutia to ask for political asylum at a foreign Embassy. Luckily for Urrutia, the "Urrutia Doctrine" was not applied against him.

One of the things that impressed me the most, during the beginning of the Revolutionary government, was the denaturalization of the character of great part of the Cuban people.

By idiosyncrasy the Cuban people was noble, friendly, witty, willing to help, frank and open. Now, with the triumph of the Revolution, a large majority of the Cuban people became ungrateful, disloyal, inflexible, cunning, envious and unjust. Every day at the Judicial Palace I had the most tangible prove of what I am saying.

I remember that one morning, while I was glancing at the morning paper "El Crisol" I saw the picture of a young man accusing a former policeman, Pedro Ramos Lugo, of the assassination of his father. There it was in the paper the moving figure of a young son fingering a henchman of the previous government in front of Revolutionary Tribunal. According to this victim of the deposed tyranny his father had been assassinated because his father was involved in revolutionary activities.

But I remembered the face of the young accuser. Yes, he was the son of a vendor of hamburgers ("fritas"). During the previous government there was a case that we had under Secretary of the Court Amalia Cuéllar. The assassination happened in front of the new Sports Arena known as Sport City. The young man appearing in the photo had declared in front of me and under oath, that his father had been killed because of a problem involving women. He had given the license plate of the car occupied by the assassins who were living in the city of Banes,

Oriente province, and we have written an exhort to the criminal court of the city of Banes to depose the occupants of the car. Now, with the triumph of the Revolution it was becoming profitable to establish yourself as a revolutionary and as a victim of the Batista government.

That human excrement in the photo, was asking for "paredón" to the ex-policeman Pedro Ramos Lugo. With the newspaper in my hand I opened the door of the Judge office. At that moment the Judge was Ismael López de Villavicencio Balbona, a very distinguished man, but who was starting to show the weight of the years. After apprising the Judge of the situation I urged him to go, both of us, to the Revolutionary Tribunal in order to clarify the situation. The Judge response was: *"Bringuier, you are young and full of spirit, but I am an old man and what I want is not to be involved in problems. Let's wait. If Pedro Ramos Lugo is sentenced to death then I will decide what I am going to do."*

In this case, Pedro Ramos Lugo was spared the death sentence. He was sentenced to only ten years in jail for a murder that he had not committed. I was shocked because I knew Pedro Ramos, he was one of the policemen in his precinct investigating cases of robberies and as such he was visiting our court almost every week.

Around those days I felt the urge and obligation to write a sign that I displayed on top of my desk in a way that those who appear to testify had to see it. The sign said:

Ser Justo es ser Hombre	*(To be Just is to be a Man)*
Ser Injusto es ser Bestia	*(To be Unjust is to be a Beast)*
¿Qué eres?	*(What you are?)*

I also witnessed at my Criminal Court another anecdote that reflects the vindictive spirit that took over many Cubans. But before going into it I would like to refer to a slang going on at the time. The slang was: *"Throwing the towel."* This slang was derived from boxing when one of the boxers was been beating-up and his seconds noticed that he was hurt but the referee was not stopping the bout and from the corner of the hurt boxer come flying a towel. The act of throwing the towel was a humanitarian act to stop somebody from receiving unnecessary harm. Throwing the towel was to protect someone. Before Castro raise to power the Cubans loved to throw towels to everybody in need.

The acting Judge during this incident was Oscar Pina Hernández, righteous and dignified like many other Judges in the Cuba of those days. I had met Judge Pina from other occasions when he had been acting Judge in my Criminal Court and I remembered him mostly because of an incident which had occurred during the Batista regime. Every Friday, the Criminal Judicial Courts paid a visit to a prison located at the Prince's Castle[5] in order to give the detainees an opportunity to address the Judiciary for any grievances, complaints or questions that they would like to present. There we gathered Magistrates, Judges and Secretaries.

Ideologically Judge Pina was an opponent of the Batista government. One Friday, when we finished the visit to the imprisoned, Judge Pina rose from his seat and asked the Magistrates to proceed and pay a visit to the section of the prison that was occupied by "political" detainees. The Magistrates agreed and we moved in that direction. In the meantime the Chief of the Prison, Colonel Dámaso Montesinos made his appearance and joined us in our inspection.

There, in a big room we found the political detainees; we saw a big Cuban flag attached to a big wall. They had a radio from where they received the latest news and music. We strolled among them and Judge Pina was inquiring from them how they were been treated. The general consensus of the political interns was that the Prince's Castle was like an oasis for them. They related how the most serious danger for them was while they were detained at the police precincts and how they felt protected as soon as they arrived to the Prince's Castle and that Colonel Montesinos, in several occasions, had personally intervene to prevent the police from taking back some detainees already under his custody.

After the visit ended, we walked outside the Prince's Castle toward where our cars were parked. There, from where we were seeing a beautiful panoramic view of Havana, Judge Pina congratulated Colonel Montesinos for his laudable attitude toward the detainees. We were talking, the three of us for about one hour. Colonel Montesinos also had words of appreciation about me for been the son of my father.

But now the Revolution had triumphed. The ex-detainees were in power. Colonel Montesinos had been apprehended and sentenced to many years in jail. Judge Pina had returned as acting Judge in my court.

---

5   Castillo del Príncipe

While I was in my office studying the case of a little girl that had been killed by an errant bullet fired by a nervous policeman of the Ministry of Recovery of Misappropriated Properties the bailiff of our court, Pedro Touzet, informed me that the Chief of Police of the Ministry was outside and wanted to talk to me. I ordered him in and learned that what he wanted was to talk to the Judge. I lead him into the Judge's office and introduced him to Judge Pina. The Judge with a smile in his face shook hands with the Chief of Police. The Chief explained to Judge Pina that he had come to see him because he was interested in justice to be done, that it was just an accident and that the policeman never had the intention of firing a shot. Judge Pina looking straight at the eyes of the Chief of Police told him: *"Look, why you are not frank with me and tell me the real purpose of your visit which in reality is that you have come to throw a towel to your friend."*

The military man, with a cold and emphatic voice, answered that he had not come to throw a towel to anybody.

Judge Pina, with his face red by indignation, rose from his chair and with a firm voice stated: *"What is happening is that you and your people are very cruel. The great majority of you would not be alive if it would not have been for all the towels that were thrown to help you during the previous government, but tell me, what is wrong with throwing towels? What is wrong with helping people? What is wrong with helping your neighbor? No, for you and your kind there should not be any towels thrown, a person have to be hard, inflexible, without mercy.*

Ok, let me tell you this, I conspired against President Machado, I conspired against President Batista and if this would continue in the way that it is going . . . "The Chief of Police of the Ministry of Recovery of Misappropriated Properties interrupted him saying: *Please Judge, do not continue because I would have to arrest you."*

Judge Pina, immutable and courageous continued: *"If this continue in the way that it is going I would have to conspire against Fidel . . . Ah, and as we are not friends, and as you are not the defendant's lawyer, and as you have not come to ask for a towel to be thrown in favor of the defendant, you have nothing to do here, then please do me a favor and just leave."*

After the Chief of Police of the Ministry of Recovery of Misappropriated Properties left the room, Judge Pina complained to me about the barbaric way that the new government was establishing in Cuba.

Years later I learned that Judge Pina became involved with "Operation Peter Pan" (a Catholic operation that transported out of Cuba thousands of children to save them from Communist indoctrination) and he was apprehended. Judge Pina was an avid collector of musical records, mainly real old records, and he was considered as the owner of the largest collection of musical recordings in Cuba. While in jail, his wife didn't tell him that following his arrest the revolutionary police had gone to their apartment at the López Serrano Apartments Building and confiscated (stole) all his musical recordings. When Judge Oscar Pina Hernández was freed, he returned to his apartment. Next day he died of a heart attack. Another honest Judge who paid with his life for the thirst of power of Fidel Castro.

All this time several Cuban publications and newsmen were asking the question: Where is Mujal? Some Cuban newsmen like Mario Kuchilán were placing him in the Republic of Panamá; others located him in some other countries in Hispanic America. All were wrong. I knew were Mujal was. My father in law had received a postcard from Mujal thanking us for what we had done for him while he was in Buenos Aires. In the postcard Mujal explained that when he arrived to the United States his visa was revoked and he was forced to continue to Europe. Mujal was another victim of the honeymoon going on with the Eisenhower administration, the fourth floor of the State Department and the Communist now in power in Cuba. Eventually Mujal was able to come to the United States and for years resided in Washington, D.C. Finally he died in this Country. One of the most important lessons that I learned from Mujal was something that he told me in Buenos Aires remembering that he started his career as a member of the Cuban Communist Party: *"Bringuier, the disadvantage that we encounter is that we want to enjoy a normal life, while we are with our family, while we enjoy watching a baseball game, or a movie, in the meantime the Communists are working 24 hours a day to destroy us."*

Kuchilán, José Pardo Llada, Bohemia Magazine, Carteles Magazine and all of the other intellectual henchmen of the Communist elite now in power could continue asking a thousand times where Mujal was. From my lips they didn't found out. For years that secret was kept by 4 persons: my parents-in-law, my wife and me.

I was young and naïve, I could not realize that the revocation of Mujal's visa was due to the Communist moles that had infiltrated the

State Department since before World War II. Communist moles that had not only infiltrated the State Department but the US Congress and the Executive Power.

I had several encounters with acquaintances and friends that helped me solidify my ideas about the new regime. Most of them occurred at the Judicial Palace. One day, while I was in my office, entered José Miguel Pérez Lamy, a well-known lawyer and member of the Cuban Communist Party. When he saw me he smiled and embracing me said: *"Bringuier, finally I see Cuba as I always dreamed."*

In another occasion, when a high officer of the Revolutionary Armed Forces was deposing in front of me, he said: *"Secretary, before two years Latin America will have to tip its hat to Emperor Castro."*

Still in another opportunity I encounter, at the Judicial Palace, José (Pepe) Puente Blanco who previously was attending with me University of Havana's Law School and who had been President of Students Federation (FEU). We embraced with happiness and I asked him what position he was going to get in the government. He moved me a little to the side, and almost close to the wall next to the elevators, telling me: *"Carlitos, I want nothing from these people. This is no good."* Pepe Puente Blanco was right. Years later, in 2002, we had in Miami a reunion of those of us who had entered Law School at the University of Havana in 1952. I was talking to a couple relating this incident. I have not recognized that the one that I was talking to was Pepe Puente Blanco and he didn't remember that encounter.

One day I had the visit at my courtroom of José Antonio Suárez de la Fuente, the same lawyer who had offered me to go with him 50/50 while my father was President of the Tribunal de Urgencia de la Habana. Now he was Lieutenant Suárez de la Fuente, prosecutor in the Revolutionary Tribunals where he had earned the nickname of "poodle of blood."[6] Tony was dressed in his military uniform, had a pistol at his waist and an escort who was carrying a rifle. I asked the escort to leave the room and closed the door. Turning to Tony I told him: *"Tony, with you uniform, your pistol and your bodyguard you are an imbecile. You can send a defendant to jail and he, and his family, has the hope that one day he would be free but when*

---

6   "Charco de sangre."

you send somebody to the paredón[7] that person and his family and friends know that there is no return from there and that there is no hope."

Tony answered that he knew that I was right in everything that I was telling him. He stated that he had tried to resign his job but that he had been subjected to investigations and threatened to be sent, himself, to the paredón.

When I was already out of Cuba I read in a magazine that Tony Suárez de la Fuente had escaped in a boat and had asked for political asylum in Venezuela.

Another who visited my courtroom was also a prosecutor in the Revolutionary Tribunals, Captain Pelayo Fernández. He was an acquaintance from the club Casino Español de La Habana. At the time I was working as Officer[8] under Secretary Raúl Luya García and also working with us were Osvaldo Vázquez and Emma Lamas. Now Pelayo Fernández had earned the nick name of "Pelayito Paredón", because of the amount of Cubans sent by him to the execution wall. He had become an accomplice of the G2 to exterminate those who were dangerous to the government or at some other times when the government wanted to seed Terror.

"Pelayito Paredón" had come to our office to say hello to us. After shaking hands with Luya and Vázquez he turned toward me and extended his hand with a smile on his face. And I left him like that, with a frozen smile in his face and his hand extended. I rose from my chair, turned toward the door and left the office. After he was gone I returned to the office and I still remember Luya's face when he asked me how I dared to do what I had just done. I told Secretary Luya, who was a good person, that to me it was impossible to shake hands with a murderer like "Pelayito Paredón."

Since the triumph of the Revolution my brother-in-law, Jorge Medina Núñez had been assigned to work as Secretary in the Revolutionary Tribunals. One day, I believe that it was on March 13, 1959 Jorge called me asking for a favor. He had loaned his car, a 1956 Ford Fairline, to his son Jorgito who, without his permission, had taken the car to the city of Cárdenas for an act in memoriam of José Antonio Echevarría, a student leader who had died the day of the frustrated assault to the Presidential

---

[7]   Execution wall
[8]   Oficial

Palace in 1957. Jorge's car ran into mechanical problems while in Cárdenas and Jorge was requesting that I give him a ride to that city. We went in my 1958 Peugeot and during the trip Jorge explained how worry he was with Jorgito. He said that Jorgito was one day with groups pro-Castro and some other days with anti-Castro groups. His concern was that Jorgito would end up with both groups trying to kill him. My poor brother-in-law didn't knew how close he was to the truth.

In the night of August 7, 1959 another blow hit my family. My cousin Cucú Bringuier was apprehended with more than one hundred persons in a conspiracy against Castro betrayed, among others, by Commanders Eloy Gutiérrez Menoyo, William Morgan and Jesús Carreras. It was called the Trujillista conspiracy. Cucú was sentenced to years in jail, and his father my uncle José Enrique Bringuier Laredo, had to obtain food in bags to bring him to prison. That man, my uncle, who was affable, lovable, good politician, who had contributed thousands of dollars for the Revolution saw his life completely changed, completely ruined. Now, the only thing that he could do was to find food for Cucú.

Less than a year later Majors William Morgan and Jesús Carreras got involved in a real conspiracy against Castro and Castro do not forgive those who conspire against him. Morgan and Carreras were executed at the "paredón" on March 11, 1961.

Writing about my uncle it comes to my mind another anecdote showing how stupid the Communists were. The city of Morón, Camagüey province, was well known not only because of it beautiful train station, it's delicious pastry carrying it name, the parochial festivities of "La Candelaria" but also for the famous saying: *"Like the rooster from Morón, without feathers but still crowing."* No matter the fact that this saying doesn't had anything to do with our city of Morón. The city had erected a monument to honor the rooster and inside the statue they had put a recording with the crowing of one my uncle's roosters. José Enrique was an avid breeder of fighting roosters and considered one of the best in Cuba. Well, the cretin Communists decided to apply the paredón to the statue of the rooster and they prepared a firing squad to execute the Statue and dragged it by the streets of Morón, Incredible but true.

The following month of Cucú's arrest, while at my courtroom, I received a call from my sister-in-law Anita Lancho. She was informing me that some policemen were searching their house and to contact my brother Julito and tell him not to go to the house. I could not locate my brother, left the courtroom and went to their house. My brother was already there.

After an exhaustive search, the security forces found, and confiscated, some bottles of Champagne, an empty safe, and some clothes. All of them belonging to Carlos Guas Decall, son of former Cuba Vice-President Rafael Guas Inclán. Carlos Guas was a good friend of my brother Julito and before entering an Embassy to ask for political asylum he had left those items in my brother's house. The security forces asked Julito to follow them in his car, to the Technical Department of Investigations at its office in the city of Marianao, in the house of former Chief of Police Rafael Salas Cañizares.

My brother owned a 1959 Chrysler and the security forces told him to drive his car, in that way, after questioning, he would have transportation to return to his house.

In those days that was a typical trick of the Communists and I was well aware of it. When they would arrive to the Technical Department of Investigations they will keep him in jail for several days. In the meantime they will steal his car and when they will free him he would be so terrorized that he would not fight for his car. I knew of hundreds of people that had gone through the same shameful sting. Been aware of this trick I told my brother what it was going to happen and that I will go with him, in that way when he would be notified that he was under arrest I will be able to drive his car back.

Julito agreed with my way of thinking. When we arrived at the Technical Department of Investigations the first person that I saw there was a revolutionary policeman by the name of Armando Hernández Ponce who inquired what I was doing there.

I personally knew the now revolutionary policeman Armando Hernández Ponce. In my courtroom, with Amalia Cuéllar acting as Secretary, we had a case in which he had been indicted for blackmail and he had been weekly signing in front of me while he was out on bail. When I informed him what was going on he immediately disappeared.

Julito underwent questioning by Lieutenant Silvio Sanabria while I sat on a chair in a nearby office reading a newspaper. During the interrogatory, full of threats, at one point Lieutenant Sanabria told my brother: *"I am a son of a bitch and I will make you confess."* When he finished questioning Julito, he ordered his arrest under the charge of contraband of weapons. No weapons had been occupied at my brother's house and my brother had never been involved with weapons. Later, my brother said that Lieutenant Sanabria glanced at me and inquired who I was. When informed, he ordered my arrest.

While we were waiting I was approached by a militiaman who told me that my brother was going to remain and that why I didn't leave. I decided to play ignorant because I suspected that it was a trap to have the opportunity to shoot me and state that I was trying to escape. I informed him that I would stay with my brother until his detention become official. Then, another officer came into the room and told us that we were officially arrested.

We were brought to a larger room where there was a militiaman with a machine gun. Also, detained there, was an old man that when we entered he was drinking water from a cloudy bottle and who, seeing us, turned his head in our direction extending his arm with the bottle and inviting us to drink some of the dirty water. Politely we declined his offer then with a smile in his face he told us: *"Wait a few days and you will see if you drink the water or not."* We found out that he had been arrested at the airport trying to leave Cuba with dollar hidden in his luggage.

At midnight we heard that the person in charge of the Technical Department of Investigations Captain Mario Gil González had arrived. We heard that he was with two women picking up the bottles of champagne confiscated at Julito's house and we saw some militiamen trying on some of the clothes occupied at my brother's house. We overheard that they were going to a sex party.

I knew who Captain Mario Gil González was but I had never met him personally. At my courtroom we had a case against him for murder. In times of the previous government he used to go into a bus, if a policeman was a passenger in the bus, he becomes a death policeman because a few blocks later Mario Gil González would signal the bus to stop and in his way out he would shoot he policeman and leave. There were several victims of his" heroic" acts as a revolutionary. Now we were under his jurisdiction.

When the lights of the sun started to appear I told Julito that I will not stay there without doing something to get out and that as still at that moment part of the press was free I would declare myself in hunger strike. Julito response was that if I wanted to jump the bearded militiamen and grab his machine gun he would second me but not in a hunger strike, Julito was an avid eater.

At 7:00 a.m. Captain Mario Gil González returned and approached us. I apprised him of my decision and declared myself in hunger strike telling him that I preferred to die there now and not to lose my job at the courthouse if I didn't show up in a couple of hours. Captain Gil approached me and putting of his arms over my shoulder told me: *"Bringuier, you are too skinny and if you put yourself in hunger strike you will be dying here pretty soon, look, go to your courtroom and I will take care of the rest. Your brother will be free in a few days."*

I left driving my brother's car, a 1959 Chrysler, which Julito was able to sell before he eventually left Cuba. I visited some of my brother's friends asking for help. After three days my brother was freed. He related to me that after I was freed by Captain Mario Gil González an incident occurred between Captain Gil and Lieutenant Sanabria because Sanabria was angry with Captain Gil for him setting me free. But what Lieutenant Silvio Sanabria did not realize was that I was *in God's hands.*

Sometime after I left Cuba I heard that one day the Technical Department of Investigations was surrounded by policemen and militiamen. Captain Mario Gil González was arrested, submitted to a revolutionary trial and sentenced to 20 years in jail.

It is good to show how common criminals had become now enforcers of the law. After a few months of the triumph of Fidel Castro some persons started using a nickname for the Revolution: *"The Revolution of the stock up toilet"* which meant that the shit had overflowed the toilet. The shit was now in power in Cuba. And that could happen to any country in the world including the United States of America.

A typical example of the theory of the "Stock up toilet" was the case of "Tomeguín", his nickname, he had as center of operations the Fraternity Park near the Manhattan Hotel in Havana. When he was known as "Tomeguín" he was a fervent believer in free enterprise no matter the fact that he was not shoe shinning neither selling newspapers in the street. "Tomeguín" also had a very peculiar concept of what was private property. He lived in room No.31 of Arcade 17 in the Vapor Plaza.

After been apprehended several times he transferred his activities to the corner of Monte and Angeles streets. Finally he started to operate at the corner of J Street and 23rd Street in El Vedado subdivision, which was in my father's jurisdictional correctional court district. It was in this corner where he got acquainted with students attending the University of Havana. In two occasions, when he was arrested for purse snatching, he was brought in front of my father then Judge of the Correctional Court #8 in Havana. My father gave him two prison terms, the first time 60 days, the second, as a repeat offender, 180 days.

Now that we had the "stuck up toilet Revolution" in power, "Tomeguín", the purse snatcher, was in power. Now Efigenio Almejeiras Delgado, aka "Tomeguín" had been named Chief of the National Revolutionary Police.

On November 14, 1959 I went with my wife to a night club/casino in Havana. My wife was pregnant and we were laughing because while I played roulette she deposited her big belly on top of the green carpet at the table trying to bring me good luck. Next day we had to go running to the hospital and Pochi gave birth to our third child, a beautiful girl. My wife's pregnancy this time had lasted only 7 months. Next day, the pediatrician approached us with very bad news. Our daughter had born with a problem that was called hyaline membrane. It was explained to us that her lungs had not developed sufficiently. At the time the prognosis was that the survival rate was only 20%. One child of John F. Kennedy died of the same problem.

We spent the day crying. Our friend Mercedes Sorhegui (Angel Belvedere's wife) brought us some water from "Lourdes" which was considered miraculous by large amount of Catholics and we put a few drops in her mouth while she was in the incubator. I drove to my former school, Belén and asked a priest, father Mata, to come with me to the hospital in order to baptize our daughter. At the baptism we named her Ana María.

Ana María struggled and managed to survive and became a precious beautiful girl.

Slow but sure, the Fidelista government was suffocating the freedom of the Cuban people. Eventually my brother Julito managed to sell his Shell service station and left Cuba with his family to Guatemala. I decided to move to his house and rent my house in Alta Habana.

A few days before we moved I visited some of my neighbors in Alta Habana to tell them where we were moving. One night the next door neighbor came to visit me. He was a Spaniard (Catalán) already retired, by the last name of Rifé.

That night he narrated to me the history of his life. In his youth he had left Spain as a stowaway, in a ship bounded to Mexico. While in Mexico and traveling in a train it was attacked by Pancho Villa troops who proceeded to execute in front of his eyes all well-dressed passengers. The only thing that he was able to save was a ten cent coin and some aspirins that he hid under his belt. In Mexico he starved and one night, while he was sleeping on a bench in a park, he woke up when someone was trying to steal his shoes. With a big stone that he used as a pillow he hit the Mexican in the head killing him. That night Rifé told me how much he suffered in the Mexican jails and how eventually the Spaniard Consul managed to get his freedom and he was deported back to Spain. The ship bringing him back to Spain stopped in Havana and Rifé managed to disembark escaping from the ship. He traveled to Oriente province where he started working at a bakery. He worked harder than anybody else. On Sundays, while the other workers were enjoying walks around the park, he stayed at work perfecting an idea that he had in his mind. He experimented for some months and finally, with his invention in his brain, he left Oriente province and went to Havana. His invention was a certain kind of cracker for mealtime.

Rifé started his little factory and because there was not any other cracker similar to his, he baptized them with the name of "La Unica" ("The only one"). That small factory grew to a large emporium and Rifé dedicated his life to his family. He didn't drink alcohol, he didn't gamble and he was not a womanizer. He was residing next door to me with his daughter, his son-in-law and his grandchildren.

When he finished narrating his story he was crying. He had retired and he had bought some apartment buildings with the honest money product of his efforts and sacrifices. Fidel Castro had just finished delivering a speech where he was accusing the owners of apartment houses of vampirism. No, now Rifé, was not an honest Spaniard who with his intelligence and sweat had helped Cuba to become one of the richest and more advanced countries in this hemisphere. Now, Rifé had become a "blood sucker", a vampire who exploited the people in need. To Rifé the worst was to see people believing in Fidel Castro and looking at him as a parasite. That night Rifé cried in front of me like I had never see a man crying before.

Like Rifé, thousands of Spaniards lost their fortunes in Cuba. I would like to mention here that the Cuban people, before Castro, never had any bad sentiments against the Spaniards, genetically the vast majority was of Spaniard ascent. The only Cuban who I heard expressing hatred against the Spaniards was a Communist relative of Mercedes Sorhegui who once told me: *"The big mistake of Cuba was not to have killed all the Spaniards after the Republic was established."* Proof that he was in a very small minority was the election of Don Alonso Expósito (a Spaniard), my grandfather, as Mayor of the city of Morón a few years after the establishment of the Republic. This shows you how Socialism works, building hate among the classes.

While living in my brother's house in Vista Alegre #72 in "La Víbora" suburb my wife and I heard a speech delivered by Fidel Castro that really impressed us. Castro was forecasting how Cuba's future would be one of richness and abundance. With his childish verbal diarrhea characteristic of him, like a visionary Santa Claus, he was predicting the material and economic achievements that the Cuban people could expect from the Revolution. Remembering him at that time, speaking of hope and change, with a brilliant future for the youth now it comes to my mind that he spoke like a white Barack Hussein Obama.

It was one of those endless verbal paranoid deliriums of the Commander in Chief who was bombarding and brainwashing the population in a daily bases. During that particular speech Fidel Castro stated that the government was going to increase the production of milk to such level that in the future the Cuban people would be able to open a faucet in their houses and milk would be coming out. And the gullible Cuban people applauded. I named that speech the speech of the "milk duct".

After January 1st 1959 we invented in Cuba what I called the "brain meter". According to this revolutionary invention you could judge the mental capacity of a person according to the time needed to become disillusioned with the new Socialist regime of Fidel Castro. During that time also started to circulate and expressions a little like a syllogism: *"Not all Fidelistas are stupid but all stupid are Fidelistas."*

The only thing that we had to do for a scientifically verification of this syllogism was to analyze among our acquaintances to see who were the ones that we considered stupid. The experiment never failed, it had a 100% scientific verification.

One day appeared at my courtroom Ernesto. He was the grease man at the former Shell service station of my brother Julio and he was the union's representative. Ernesto explained that as we had been very good employers, the employees didn't want to move against us, but that now that my brother had sold the business they wanted my legal advice in how they could move against the new owner and take over the service station. Diplomatically I explained to Ernesto that I was working in the criminal court and could not give them any advice.

With Julito in Guatemala we suffered another blow from the government. Militiamen of the National Institute of the Agrarian Reform, heavily armed, showed up at "San Julio" farm. Pointing a pistol to my brother Juan they threw him out of the farm into the highway from where he had to walk 32 kilometers to Havana. A few days later my brother Juan followed my brother Julio into exile in Guatemala.

I established legal appeals at the Ministry of Recovery of Misappropriated Properties requesting the return to us of the properties taken away by the government including my house in Alta Habana.

In the meantime things were turning dangerous in my courtroom. I had escaped a second depuration of the Judicial Power. I had been appointed in my courtroom to take part of a Tribunal created to admit new employees to our courtroom. But Secretary of Justice Alfredo Yabur henchmen were keeping an eye on me.

An attempt to recruit me to work for the Revolutionary government came from Raulito Amaro, son of a former Judge Raúl Amaro Vallejo who had been fired for corruption. Raulito Amaro was an Oficial in another courtroom, had joined the government and he came to invite me to organize with him the militias of the Judicial Power. He was offering me to join the Socialist government of Fidel Castro. If I would have accepted the government would have delighted and I am sure that I would have escalated good positions in it. But I knew that the government was a Communist one. I could not betray my God, my country, my father, my family and my heritage. It would have been great for Fidel Castro to have a Bringuier creating the militias of the Judicial Power but as a Bringuier I refused to do so. Raulito Amaro organized the militias and years later became President of the Assembly of Popular Power.

Later on while I was absent of my courtroom two policemen from the Secretary of Justice took two signs that I had over my desk and went to the Judge accusing me of been a counter revolutionary. Judge Villavicencio, after reading the signs, turned to them saying that he didn't see anything counter revolutionary in them, and that he believed that those signs were very revolutionary.

One of those signs I had mentioned before, the other was a sign that I had prepared when I was expecting José Pardo Llada[9] to depose before me. Pardo Llada never appeared but I left the sign there anyway. It read:

> "There are men that are like reptiles
> Who dragging themselves and with their venom
> Want to poison us, without realizing
> That they live at the expense to be crushed
> By someone stepping on them."

The environment at the courtroom was becoming more vicious day by day. The employees avoided talking politics because we didn't knew who was who.

Secretary of Justice Alfredo Yabur send additional new employees to each courtroom whose real work was as informers. The Judges said one thing privately and another in public. Intimidation was rampant. One day a police Captain went into the office of Judge Villavicencio and verbally assaulted him; in another opportunity when our bailiff went into a police precinct to serve a summon for a policeman to appear in our court the bailiff was expelled from the police precinct and the policemen told him that neither him, the bailiff, nor the Judge were man enough to indict any revolutionary.

Another incident that really impacted me was the case of the son of the policeman of our court, Ceferino Carpintero. Still today I clearly remember the affable smile in the face of that good man who was Ceferino Carpintero. He was the policeman assigned to my courtroom and he was decent, correct, honest, likeable and always willing to help. He had a son who was the dream of his life. During the Batista government he managed to have his son accepted as a policeman who started working in a police precinct.

One day, while assigned to guard the front entrance of the police precinct, a common thief was brought in. When the thief was inside the precinct the thief punched a policeman and tried to escape through the

---

9   José Pardo Llada was a very popular newsman and avid defender of Fidel Castro and Communism.

front door. Other policeman and the Sergeant in charge started yelling *"Shoot him", "Don't let him escape"*. Young Carpintero shot the thief who died outside the police precinct. Nobody claimed the body of the thief.

With the triumph of the Revolution, now young Carpintero had been accused of murder. The thief was now a "revolutionary". Young Carpintero was assassinated at the execution wall (paredón). His father, with a broken heart, followed his son after suffering a heart attack.

In the meantime the majority of the Cuban people kept chanting *"Paredón", "Fidel, this is your house" and "Yankee go home"*.

One morning while I was at my office I received a call from Amado Hernández Ponce the same policeman that I had encounter at the Technical Department of Investigations the day my brother Julito was arrested. Hernández Ponce had been benefited by an amnesty declared by the Revolutionary government. His case for kidnapping was closed as well as another for continuous fraud in another courtroom. Now he was calling me with an invitation. Amado Hernández Ponce had obtained the position of Chief of a prison in Havana. He was going to celebrate that night with an orgy at the prison and he was inviting me to join them in the sexual festivity. I declined thanking him for remembering me.

In another occasion I received a call from attorney Agapito Cabrera, son of the Judge Herminia de Zalba. Agapito, a lawyer, was now working with the Ministry of Recovery of Misappropriated Properties but he was a gentleman and a decent person.

He informed me that there was a big problem because my parents' house at #330 K Street in Alta Habana had been turned over to the parents of Captain José Abrahantes Fernández. I sensed in his voice deep concern for me and he explained that Captain Abrahantes wanted to order my arrest because there were some items missing from the house. Agapito had asked Captain Abrahantes not to order my arrest for the moment and he was asking me to go immediately to his office located in "La Rampa" section of the subdivision of El Vedado. Luckily again I was *in God's hands.*

When I arrived, Captain Abrahantes was furious and told me: *"I was ready to order your arrest for the items that you have taken out of the house but you have to thank lawyer Cabrera who convinced me to wait. Where are the items that you took?"*

I stayed cool and answered: *"Captain, you can order my arrest if you want but at the same time I would accuse you of violating the order of the Ministry who named me as depositary of the house and the items in it. I have not been officially notified that I have been relieved of my duties from the original order, therefore, neither you nor any other person have the right to put a foot inside the house until I am notified and sign acknowledgment of my termination as custodian of the house and its contents."*

Thanks to the friendly intervention of lawyer Agapito Cabrera the incident ended there. In the afternoon I proceeded to return to my parents' house the items that I had removed for safekeeping to my house, and there I discovered why Captain Abrahantes had been so furious. I met his mother who was in the kitchen and she was bleeding on the arms and legs. I calculated that she had more than 100 mosquito bites. In my hands were the metallic screens to cover the windows.

What at the time I was ignoring was that Captain Abrahantes' father, José Antonio Abrahantes Orgas was an old militant of the Cuban Communist Party who after the triumph of the Revolution was sent as a Union Attaché to the Cuban Embassy in Moscow. At the moment I also ignored that Captain Abrahantes had been born in Mexico in 1932 and that at the time of this incident he was personal bodyguard of Fidel Castro and Chief of the Department of State Security, having earned the nickname of "sure shot".

Thirty years later, on July 31, 1989, José Abrahantes was deposed as Chief of State Security and sentenced to jail during the trial where General Ochoa was executed. José Abrahantes knew too many things and while in prison he died of a "heart attack". This was the same Abrahantes who was personally responsible for the assassination of 400 persons as reprisal for the death of Fidel Castro's physician Major Manuel "Piti" Fajardo. This is the same Abrahantes who later on, in 1961 ordered a brutal repression in the city of Cárdenas where 43 persons were executed and more than 500 were sent to prison. No questions in my mind: I was *in God's hands.*

Another person started to create problems to me at the Judicial Palace. His last name was Pozo and he was an Official of the 6th District Criminal Court. During mid-morning we used to go to a coffee break to the bailiff's house in the basement of the building. Every time that he had an opportunity Pozo was trying to confront me and to make me talk against the Revolutionary government. To talk against Fidel Castro could had been like committing suicide.

I always based my arguments attacking Communism. Castro was swearing that he was not a Communist. Fidel Castro had sentenced to long years in jail Commandant Huber Matos because Matos tried to alert about the Communist take-over. I kept verbally attacking the Communists. I remember that one day I exasperated Pozo when I said: *"Pozo, Communism is to society like syphilis it to medicine. A Communist is a mental syphilitic."* At the same basement I saw Judges praising Castro. I remember Judge Federico Justiniani stating that Fidel Castro was a prophet from God. During those days it was incredible to watch so many people, with a supposedly elevated intellectual capacity, men and women, falling in love with "Fidel".

In 1959 there was another incident that is worth to mention. My nephew Jorge (Jorgito) Medina Bringuier had enrolled in an expeditionary force that was going to invade Nicaragua. The leader of this military expedition was a Nicaraguan named Chester Lacayo Lescalles. But there was a problem; the leader was not a Communist. The Castro government imparted orders to stop the invaders before their departure from Cuba and to arrest everybody involved. That afternoon I arrived to the house at Calzada 255 in El Vedado where my sister María del Carmen was living with her husband and their children. I found that everybody was looking for Jorgito, the "internationalist" youth. Apparently they had their training camp somewhere in Pinar del Río province. There, in that nice house where I grew up I saw again the Argentinean with the last name of Rojo who I had met at the Embassy of Cuba in Buenos Aires on January 1st, 1959.

Now Rojo was a Lieutenant or Captain of the Revolutionary Armed Forces. He told me not to worry about my nephew because the young people involved would be freed but that the one that was going to have a big problem was their leader Chester Lacayo Lescalles because he, Rojo, had instructions to bring him to La Cabaña prison after giving him *"some kicks in the ass."*

They were apprehended. The young people were let go free after been informed of presenting themselves next day at La Cabaña. Next day they were gathered together and Raúl Castro addressed them saying: *"We congratulate you for your internationalist spirit but this is neither the moment nor the leader for such an invasion. Don't worry we will call on you, in its moment and with our leaders, Nicaragua will be ours."*

With my parents and my two brothers out of Cuba, sensing that a circle was enclosing me an idea started to grow in my brain. I would have to leave Cuba in order to protect my wife and my three children.

Julito had left with me a list of people that owed him money from the time he owned the Shell service station. One person in the list was a friend of mine from the Casino Español de La Habana, Pedro Julio Martínez Fraga. We made an appointment to meet at a restaurant by the name of "El Jardín" located on Linea Street across from the Parochial church of El Vedado Pedro Julio related to me how during the Batista government he was head of a revolutionary cell and as such he expelled from his group a man who was a Communist. When Batista left, Pedro Julio was put in charge of the G2, but that lasted just a few days. As soon as Raúl Castro arrived to Havana the Communist man he had expelled entered into the offices of the G2 and was surprised to see Pedro Julio in charge of it. The man, now working directly with Raúl Castro, asked Pedro Julio what he was doing there. Immediately Pedro Julio was fired from his position.

Pedro Julio confided to me that now he was involved in a conspiracy against Castro and he invited me to join him. I declined the invitation stating: *"Pedro Julio, if they catch me in a conspiracy, with my last name, they are going to execute me; and the ones who are going to ask "paredón" for me are not going to be only the Communists but the plebs, the ones who are sitting in these other tables around us and who think that they have the power. I have a duty to protect my wife and children and I plan to eventually leave Cuba, in which way they would not have to suffer the vicissitudes that are coming to Cuba. I will be going out of Cuba to watch all these stupid people sitting in this restaurant, who yell phrases praising the government following me later on. Pedro Julio, 80% of the Cuban people is stupid and sympathizes with Fidel Castro."*

I was *in God's hands* when I declined to join Pedro Julio Martínez Fraga in his conspiracy. A month later I called his house and was told that he had been apprehended. He had to suffer many years in a Castro's jail. Thanks to an acquaintance connected to the G2, I learned that in the conspiracy the government had placed an informer and when the group was apprehended, one of the conspirators cowardly divulged everything to the G2. This man is now, or at least until recently, a well-known anti-Castro activist in Miami.

During the whole year of 1959 I continued presenting appeals to the Ministry of Recovery of Misappropriated Properties requesting the return of our properties. I presented different documents showing that those properties had been obtained with money honestly earned (remember Aurelia Lapeyre Letamendi's inheritance to my father in 1950). Even I traveled to the city of Morón to obtain proof that my mother had sold a house inherited from her father and that money was used to buy my house in Alta Habana. I was lucky, the person who had bought the house in Morón still had the cancelled check which was used to pay my mother and my mother had endorsed the check and giving it in payment toward the house in Alta Habana. I also presented names of persons that my father had helped as Judge or Magistrate.

While I was gathering all the above information I heard that Manolito Hevia's mother, the same Manolito Hevia who my father had sheltered in his house, she was now slandering my father saying that my father was taking Manolito with him to his courthouse trying to provoke the police to kill Manolito. I went to the apartment where Manolito Hevia was living with his wife Blanca María González confronting him with that information. I noticed in his eyes that he was a coward and he ended up apologizing and offered to present testimony helping my father. I included his name in the list of people helped by my father.

It is good to know that with the years Manolito Hevia left Cuba coming to the United States and according to him he started working with the Central Intelligence Agency (CIA), because at least that is what he declared when he returned to Cuba. In reality Manolito Hevia was a double agent working for the Castro government to infiltrate the CIA.

On March 8, 1960 it was published in the Gaceta Oficial[10] pages 5771 and 5772, Resolution No. 2576 of the Ministry of Recovery of Misappropriated Properties. By this resolution the Communist government was justifying the confiscation of properties to persons that the regime could not prove had used corrupt money. Machiavelically they based the confiscation in the fact that all of the persons named in the above mentioned Resolution No. 2576 had left the country.

In one of those paragraphs the Resolution stated: *"Whereas, to be absent of the national territory, either by way of exile, or by any other abnormal way of the persons named in this Resolution, determine by itself the admission of the defendants of the charges formulated against them."*

Criminal legal outrage! In reality what it meant was that as the Communist government could not prove charges against the defendants, the government was declaring them guilty and confiscating their properties because they had left the country. For the first time that happened in Cuba's history. And the stupid people kept chanting "Viva Fidel".

The names of those affected by Resolution No. 2576 was: *"Carlos Márquez Sterling, José de Jesús Larraz Sorondo, Roberto Fiat Cura, Roberto Ortega Chomat, Elpidio García Tudurí, Mario Ariel Machado Pacheco, Onelia Luzardo Dopico, Antonio Angel Hernández Estrada, Ernesto López Valdés, Facundo Pomar, **Julio Bringuier Laredo**, Cándido Alfonso Baeza, Gustavo Alemán Simó, Francisco Javier Zayas Ayala, Jorge Navarro Gómez. José I. Orúe Falcón, Alfredo González Durán, Miguel Borell Navarro, Orestes Ferrer Hernández, Dagoberto Darías y del Castillo, Ramiro Amor Chirino González, Oscar Salamea Valdés, José Marcos Cabezón Feito, Carmelo Pozo del Puerto, Loreto Armando Lemus Castillo, Salvador Ziegenhirt Menéndez, Octavio Acosta J.R. Costa Blanco, Francisco José de Arce Araús, Pedro Armengol Valdivia, Pedro Norta Butari, Javier Bolaños Pacheco, Juan González, Eduardo Fernández de Velazco, Oscar González Rodríguez, Adalberto Ferrer García, Humberto Machado Pacheco, José Saif Yapor, Antonio Lamas Parra, Carmela Batista Diéguez, José Luis Pujol Hernández, Rogelio Rojas Lavernia, José Ramón Cabezas Clavelo, José Antonio Cabargas Saínz, Rolando Pozo Jiménez, Mario Lamar Pitaluga, Dámaso Ayuso Quintana, Juan Payret Veitía, José Martínez Alegría, Roberto Acosta González, Patrocinio Bravo Moreno, Rubén Labastilla Zigler, Carlos Manuel Pirri Llorea, Remigio Fernando Salas Humara, Antonio SánchezMena, Raúl Acosta Rubio, Artemio Pérez Díaz, José Hernández Toraño, Guillermo Corvo Alzamora, Luis Rodolfo Castroverde Mecalling, René Luis de Jesús Scott, Bertha Ziegenhirt, Nereida León Blanco, and Luis Fernández Pinelo.*

Immediately I presented an appeal at the Ministry of Recovery of Misappropriated Properties.

At the beginning of 1960, Ernesto "Che" Guevara as Secretary of Industries, with the idea of extorting money from the Cuban people, developed the idea of taking money from the workers by asking them to "volunteer' 4% of their salaries for the "Industrialization" of the country. Anyone who didn't want to "volunteer" had to send a letter to the Ministry under which his job was qualified, expressing that they refused to contribute.

On April 5, 1960, by certified mail No.1361, I notified the Minister of Justice, Alfredo Yabur Maluf my refusal to contribute "voluntarily" 4% of my salary. I was the only employee of the Cuban Judicial Power who did so.

I was summoned to appear in front of the Secretary of Justice to ratify my negative, but the person who received me was a former acquaintance from Law School, Pedro Maseda. I knew Maseda from the University of Havana, he was a very good friend of Juan Nuiry, Maseda had married a friend of mine from Law School Silvia Valdés Figueroa, and he was now the Paymaster of the Ministry of Justice. Maseda invited me to drink coffee and after chatting for a few minutes I signed the paper ratifying my decision to refuse to "voluntarily" contribute to Ernesto "Che" Guevara's request of 4% of my salary.

I also refused to contribute in another campaign launched by the government to buy "weapons and airplanes". Another campaign to extort money from the Cuban people.

I had decide that we had to get out of Cuba. In my mind something was going to happen to put an end to the Castro government and I didn't want my family to be there when that would happen. But how we would be leaving? I could not ask at my courthouse for vacation time because it would be going to be denied to me. I started preparing our way out by requesting a needed government authorization to leave the country as a tourist. Normally that request, at that moment, was granted in less than 72 hours. Mine took more than a month to be granted and I had to go in person to pick it up at the same office of the Technical Department of Investigations where I had been detained over-night.

At the time the government was allowing to exchange up to three hundred pesos for three hundred dollars for those tourists going out. When I went to my bank, Pujol Bank, located in Linea Street in El Vedado, the teller was creating problems to me. Finally, the Manager of the bank called me aside and told me that the teller was asking that I should not be given the dollars because he was sure I was not going to return to Cuba. The Manager told me that he wished his teller was right and wishing me good luck handed the dollars to me.

My niece María del Carmen (Carmucha) Medina Bringuier had married her sweetheart Drago (Draguito) Stoyanovich. They were sympathizers of the Revolution and Draguito was a friend of Rolando Díaz Aztaraín who, at the time, was Secretary of the Ministry of Recovery of Misappropriated Properties. In the middle of April of 1960 Draguito went with me to see Secretary Rolando Díaz Aztaraín. We went to the Secretary's office and discussed with him the legal claims and appeals that I had presented.

At my courtroom I had not asked for vacation time and nobody knew that I was leaving Cuba. I was taking the risk of been stopped at the airport but I had bought tickets living early in the morning to Guatemala, from Guatemala to Buenos Aires and I also had bought return tickets from Argentina to Cuba. In case that I was not allowed to leave Cuba I would return to work at the courtroom as if nothing had happened in the meantime of obtaining political asylum at the Argentinean Embassy. At least that was my train of thought at the time.

On April 18, 1960 it was published in the Gaceta Oficial[10], (pages 9464, 9465 and 9466) Resolution #3410 of the Ministry of Recovery of Misappropriated Properties. By it the government was returning to us the following properties and items:

1) The house located at #426 San Francisco Highway, Alta Habana.
2) Movable items and animals at "San Julio" farm.
3) The house located at 255 Calzada Street in El Vedado returned to the children of Dr. Julio Bringuier Laredo and his wife.

As I repeat before, I believe that I was the only Cuban who managed to receive property back from the government. I had everything prepared for leaving Cuba on May 4, 1960 and as the day for our departure was approaching I was confronted with a couple of difficult situations in my courtroom. Before the festivities of May 1st 1960, International Labor Day, Official Pozo of the 6th Criminal Court came to my office to invite me to participate in the activities of May 1st. He wanted me to march on that day but I rejected his invitation. He argued that it was a revolutionary act and that all of us must be present at the march, to which reasoning I countered explaining that the Judicial Power was an

---

[10] Official Journal

autonomous Power of government and therefore could not be involved in politics. Pozo then alleged that it was a march of the union workers and I countered saying that the Judicial Power was not affiliated with the Confederation of Cuban Workers (CTC).

Pozo left my office looking at me with a threat in his eyes. I don't know what could have happened to him. He could be alive or he could be dead. If he is still in Cuba or if with the years he came to the United States and now he is collecting his check and his food stamps in this land of "Yankee Imperialism" as he was calling his hated United States of America.

With almost everything ready for our departure came into my office a young man who identified himself as a detective of the Technical Department of Investigations. He explained that he had been assigned to investigate a Homicide case that was in my courtroom and gave me the case number. When I located it I was highly surprised.

During the government of Batista we had initiated this case at the Secretary of Amalia Cuéllar, while I worked there as an Official. The case consisted in that a person who was in custody at the rooftop of the 10th Police Precinct had thrown himself to the street dying of the impact. At the moment almost everybody suspected that the poor man had been pushed to his death. The widow had deposed in front of me, at that moment she declared that she didn't have any prove to present to the court. The case went to our archives.

Now, the case had been reopened and it was pending for the result of the investigation from the man that I had in front of me. The detective of the Technical Department of Investigations informed me that he had been able to locate three other revolutionaries who were at the rooftop at the time the man jumped and that they had corroborated the information to him. Nobody had pushed the young dead man. According to the witnesses the young man had asked permission to use the restroom and when he got up from his chair he became like crazy and ran yelling incoherent words and jumped to the street. The three witnesses were now occupying positions in the Revolutionary government.

I asked the investigator what the problem was.

The young Detective, maybe a few years younger than me, answered: *"Secretary, the problem consists in the situation that for this same case, but in a Revolutionary Court, they executed former Captain of Police Evelio Mata. I would like you to tell me what I should report in my investigation."*

For a few seconds I meditated my answer. I didn't know if everything was a provocation from the government to entrap me or if this was an honest young man looking for guidance. Finally I told him: *"You should render your investigation according to your conscience and the truth of the facts."*

After the young Detective left my office I was glad that I had everything prepared to leave Cuba. Justice had disappeared.

I had already sold my 1958 Peugeot and while riding in a bus I saw Roberto Santiesteban, my former political rival at the Law School elections. Now he was wearing a military uniform. I didn't dream at the moment that the next time that I would see his face was when later on he became an infamous terrorist and his picture appeared in a New Orleans newspaper.

On May 3, 1960 I was summoned to appear, in the early morning, at the Ministry of Recovery of Misappropriated Properties to legally receive possession of the properties returned to us. I was surprised when they even returned to us the rents collected during the period of investigation. I left that money with my sisters.

It was an ephemeral victory but it was a victory. There, in all those documents it was attached a certified copy, requested by me, of each Judgeship in Havana certifying that there have not been a single claim or accusation filed against my father.

In the afternoon I went with a truck to take the furniture out of the "San Julio" farm. I was surprised to find out that there was a peasant living there with his wife and children. If I proceed to take the furniture with me they would have to sleep on the floor. I apprised the peasant of the situation, told him that I would be coming back in two weeks to implement the order and that in the meantime he should go to the National Institute of the Agrarian Reform for them to provide new furniture for him and his family. He was very pleased with my attitude and having gain confidence on me, he stated: *"I am not from Havana. I was put here to plant seeds and grow different vegetables but this farm is full of stones and is not good for that. The only way that this farm could be productive is for what your brother had it: as a dairy farm. But they give me the seed, the house and they pay me a salary, if they are stupid that is their problem"*

At night time we went to dinner at my sister Totó's house. Her husband Rolando and I had bought two similar dictionaries and we were going to use them to communicate in code. Rolando was giving me advice of what he considered was ahead of us. Their son, Rolandito was already attending LSU University in Baton Rouge, Louisiana where he had been studying Agronomy for the last couple of years. It never crossed our minds Rolandito would end up as Professor of Economics at Houston University.

On May 4, 1960, Pochi, Caki, Miri, Ana María and I went early in the morning to the airport. I had left with my brother-in-law Jorge Medina Núñez my letter of resignation to my job that he was going to present to the Judge when the plane had arrived to Guatemala.

At the airport I put myself again *in God's hands*. At my courtroom nobody knew that I was leaving since I had not asked for vacation time. The Technical Department of Investigations wrongly assumed that I had a permit from my courtroom to be absent.

The only two relatives that attended our departure were my uncle José Enrique Bringuier Laredo and my brother-in-law Rolando Peláez Bosch.

When the employees at the airport looked at the Secretary of the Court pin that I was wearing in my coat they assumed that I was with the government and they even didn't check my luggage. In my pocket was all my capital $700.00 US dollars.

When the plane departed I was glad that I had been able to take my wife and my three children out of the hell Cuba was going to become, my children would have the opportunity to live in a free country and to grow up to be free persons and do whatever they would want to do. I know that all of them appreciated what we did.

I expected a short absence from Cuba, kind of a vacation. I was convinced that the Cuban people eventually would revolt and bring down the Castro government. I was also convinced that a Communist government could not survive 90 miles from the United States of America.

Undoubtedly I still had a lot to learn.

CHAPTER IV

GUATEMALA (1960)

Our arrival to Guatemala City was a mix of happiness and sadness. To leave Cuba was not an easy decision. But what made it more palatable was the idea that it was going to be only something temporary, only for a few months and we will be back.

The principal happiness was to be able to embrace once more my parents and my brothers. As soon as Julito had arrived to Guatemala he coordinated the fly for my fathers to go from Buenos Aires to Guatemala and start living with him.

After we passed immigration and the baggage inspection we departed for my brother's house at Avenida Independencia 11-30, Zona 2.

While we were having lunch we received the visit of two police agents in civilian clothes. They took me to a police office to question me. According to them I was traveling with propaganda of the Castro government. Everything was clarified when I discovered that their problem was the two Official Journals referring to our properties in Cuba. Nothing happened, the case was closed and I returned to Julito's house. At the time the President of Guatemala was Miguel Ydígoras Fuentes.

While in Guatemala I had long conversations with my father. He was exasperated with the continental inactivity to confront Castro's crimes. He told me of an incident that happened to him while in Argentina. As both, my father and my father-in-law, suffered from asthma they decided during the Argentinean winter of 1959 for the two couples to expend some-time in the City of Formosa, located in the north of

Argentina because the weather was better there. They took a ship to bring them there and during the trip my father engaged in an argument with an officer of the ship who was a Communist. That night, due to the nervousness caused by the argument, my father suffered an asthma attack. To make things worse it happened that the officer involved in the argument was the physician aboard the ship. The Communist physician refused to attend to my father. Eventually the Captain of the ship ordered the physician to take care of my father.

On May 18, 1960 after reading an article in Visión magazine, I, for the first time in my life wrote a letter as an exile, refuting the propaganda in Castro's favor.

During our stay there my father insisted that we should stay in Guatemala and don't waste our money going to Argentina because the down fall of Castro was around the corner. According to him, the Monroe Doctrine of the United States of America would not allow a Communist regime to exist 90 miles from the United States, and on the other side the Pact of Río de Janeiro explicitly forbidden the existence of a Communist regime in this hemisphere and Cuba's situation would make this problem a multilateral one and our brothers in Latin America were legally forced to repel the existence of a Communist government in this hemisphere. My father was convinced that Castro's end would come within six months. My father was using common sense but was ignorant of how deep the Communist infiltration had reach inside the United States government.

Among the people that I met there I remember a Cuban newsman, Luis Manuel Martínez, who at the time was very active against Castro. Luis Manuel had been a political protégée of Batista and eventually, after many years in exile I was told he had become a political protégée of Fidel Castro. Another was Don Anolio Martínez who was trying to help in the fight against Castro.

We used our time there to sightseeing Guatemala City, we also paid a visit to the city of "La Antigua" and to a beach of black sand.

A few days after our arrival we had a small crisis. Our daughter Ana María developed a fever. A Guatemalan physician discovered that she had a kidney infection and after been treated she was cured. It was our first scare in exile.

On May 21, 1960 I wrote another letter this time refuting an editorial of the Cuban magazine "Carteles". In its editorial "Carteles" stated that now Cuba was free at last, that now Cuba was a peaceful and progressive nation, that the Fatherland was solidifying its independence. My letter appeared published in the Guatemalan newspaper "Flash de Hoy" on June 17, 1960.

Against my father's advice we left Guatemala City on June 3rd 1960 in a plane that brought us to the city where we had gotten married four years before.

CHAPTER V

———◆———

ARGENTINA (1960-61)

Our arrival to Buenos Aires brought a lot of happiness to my in-laws there. We were received with a lot of love and we went to reside with Pochi's parents at their house at 257 Las Bases in the Liniers subdivision.

Our impression when we arrived was as if we were there in a vacation. In a few months the Communist government would be deposed and we would be able to return to a free Cuba. Therefore we spent the first month visiting relatives and doing two of my favorite sports while in Buenos Aires: Go to theaters and go to restaurants to eat good bifes and parrilladas[11]. What I didn't knew was how deep was the Communist infiltration inside the United States and how they would protect Castro from falling down.

After the first month we decided that I should find a job and my father-in-law started to help me to search for one. The alternative for me was to go to the University of Buenos Aires and become a lawyer there, something not appealing to me because I considered a waste of time. My future was in Cuba.

One day I found in a newspaper a note about a mass that was going to be held at the Santo Domingo Church for the victims of Communism in Cuba. The day of the mass I was there. I introduced myself to the priest officiating the service and who was in charge of that particular church, his name was Father Pinto.

---

[11] Steaks and barbecues.

Father Pinto introduced me to several young men who attended the church regularly. They were very interested in listening to what I had to say about what was going on in Cuba and when the mass finished they invited me to meet the leader of their organization. To me it was good news to be able to talk with young anti-Communists Catholic youngsters in Buenos Aires. I accepted the invitation and a few nights later we got together.

Their organization was an extreme right-wing one. The name was "Tacuara" and later on I found out that it was considered a pro-Nazi inclined organization. After meeting their leader and chatting with him for about one hour we ended the reunion and talking outside with the two young men who had invited me there I told them that I was sorry to have to tell them but that I was convinced that their leader in reality was a Communist. To me it was not a surprise, I had learned how the Communist expertise is to infiltrate the opposition, and if they manage to move those groups to do extreme irrational things the group would lose their appeal to the masses.

They were surprised by my conclusion. They were practicing Catholics and practicing anti-Communists. When they become aware of a Communist gathering they attended a special mass at the church, received the communion and after the mass they picked up pipes with rubber coverings making themselves present at the Communist gathering and start hitting heads of Communists with their pipes. I lost contact with them until one day when I was traveling in a bus, back from work, and a group of youths was having a demonstration in the street throwing pamphlets into the air. One of the pamphlets flew into the bus and landed on my lap. They were announcing that they were splitting from "Tacuara" because they had discover that some of their leaders were Marxists. Another pamphlet was announcing the formation of a new anti-Communist organization called "Guardia Restauradora Nacionalista."

My father-in-law had contacted a relative, Roberto Fraga Patrao, who was the OwnerDirector of a magazine that reproduced legal cases and jurisprudence in the Argentinean courts. The name of the magazine was "La Ley"[12]. I was interviewed and offered a job as an assistant proof reader. Reluctantly I accepted the offer and after a few days found out

---

[12] The Law.

that in reality I was doing the proof reader work. I remember the last name of two of my co-workers: Pinillos and Eroles. My salary was the equivalent of $45.00 US dollars a month.

I met other Cubans residing in Buenos Aires among them the former Cuban Ambassador to Argentina, Alberto Espinosa Bravo and a young Cuban couple formed by José Manuel Lamela Castro and his wife Noelia. I had met Lamela when we received the visit in Buenos Aires of a very important Cuban, former Castro's Prime Minister José Miró Cardona. Also in Buenos Aires was another Cuban, designated as delegate of the Frente Revolucionario Democratico[13], Angel de Jesús Piñera Guevara.

We tried to cooperate with Piñera who liked to attend the meetings dressed in black and red (the colors of the 26th of July Movement) and whistling the song "Adelante Cubanos"[14] the official hymn of the 26th of July Movement. With Piñera I had my first ugly encounter with what was to be our worst enemy in our struggle for the liberation of Cuba: Stupid personal ambitions. As Delegate of the FRD Piñera maneuvered things with personal ambitions (later on I became aware that his ambition was to become Secretary of the Interior in a post Castro government). In a letter dated January 7, 1961, I complained to my former teacher from Belén School, José Ignacio Rasco about the political maneuvers of Piñera. At that moment I was unaware of the political maneuvers going among the leaders of the FRD where everyone wanted to get the largest piece of the pie. A pie that was in the sky and that they will never will be able to get. But I was naïve, I didn't have any political ambitions, the only thing that I wanted was to see Castro out, a free Cuba and open my own Law office. But with my last name a lot of Cubans suspected me of having political ambitions.

Around this time I was approached by some of the extreme right-wingers who I had previously met and they presented me an offer. They were willing to help us and they were willing to bring to the "paredón" an Argentinean Communist for each anti-Communist Cuban executed by Fidel Castro. We turned them down. We were anti-Communist, willing to fight, but we were not going to be involved in murders. They came back with another offer, this time they wanted to kidnap the Cuban Ambassador to Argentina and leave him at the "Obelisco[15]", the

---

[13] Revolutionary Democratic Front.
[14] Forward Cubans
[15] National landmark in 9th of July Avenue in Buenos Aires

Ambassador was going to be left there naked and covered with red paint. Again their offer was refused.

It was in the middle of October 1960 that a prominent Cuban arrived to Buenos Aires. Former Prime Minister of the Revolutionary government, José Miró Cardona had broken his ties with Fidel Castro and after seeking political asylum at the Argentinean Embassy in Havana was now in Buenos Aires with his son Pepito.

They were staying at the Hotel Crillón and I appeared there in the morning. They were eating breakfast at the restaurant of the hotel and I introduced myself to them. José Miró Cardona, a lawyer, had been professor of Penal Law at the University of Havana, was a friend of my father, and his son Pepito was an acquaintance of mine from Cuba. They invited me to sit down and join them in the breakfast. There was a young Cuban with them by the name of José Manuel Lamela Castro who later on became my friend in Buenos Aires.

During the conversation I told Miró Cardona how the ironies of life work, how the year before while he was Prime Minister of the Revolution, I had been at this same Hotel sitting at the same restaurant with Eusebio Mujal, Gustavo Gutiérrez and Alejandro Herrera Arango. Miró Cardona told me that we, all Cubans including him, were guilty of what happened to Cuba saying at the end: *"We are all guilty because we all gave electroshocks to this monster, this new Frankenstein who is now in power."*

During his stay José Miró Cardona was invited to give a conference at the offices of the Democratic Conservative Party and on Tuesday October 18, 1960 he delivered his dissertation. There he stated that his disillusionment with Fidel Castro came when Castro refused to held elections. He explained how tragic was the Cuban situation when workers had lost the right to free unions, how Cubans had lost the right to freedom of the press, how the government was against religion principally against the Catholic Church, is dressing the children with military uniforms and giving weapons to them. Next day the La Prensa newspaper published an article about the presentation with a photograph of Miró Cardona taken while he was delivering the speech and over Miró Cardona's right shoulder appeared my figure.

After José Miró Cardona left Buenos Aires he went to Miami and became the leader of the Frente Revolucionario Democratico (FRD) who appeared as the Cuban organization preparing the Bay of Pigs invasion.

His son, Pepito, was captured at the Bay of Pigs and spent some time in Castro's jails. After the debacle of Bay of Pigs José Miró Cardona felt betrayed and his heart could not take it any longer. He never saw his dream realized of seeing a free Cuba. He died in exile.

While in Guatemala my father received a letter from Jorgito Alonso Pujol, son of a former Cuban Vice-President Guillermo Alonso Pujol. Jorgito Alonso Pujol was a close friend of my brother Julito and now Jorgito Alonso Pujol was involved with the Frente Revolucionario Democratico (FRD) in Miami. My father had offered his services to go to fight in Cuba and in that letter Manuel Antonio (Tony) de Varona was thanking my father for his disposition to go to Cuba to fight. In the same letter Jorgito Alonso Pujol communicated to my father that my brother Juanito had arrived at Miami, from Guatemala, and already had joined the Cubans in the training camp. Juanito was one of the first Cubans training for the invasion.

Meanwhile in Buenos Aires I was aware, through my father, that the invasion was been prepared.

On November 11, 1960 the Catholic Church organized the First Inter-American Marian Congress with a living silent rosary for the Church of Silence in which the Catholic Church wanted to honor and remember the Church that was subjugated by the Communists behind the iron fence. I had the honor to be designated to participate in it by praying one Holy Mary at the end of the fifth mystery. Right next to me was a Russian Cossack who prayed for his country. The act was held at the Ferrocarril Oeste Stadium. All the persons who formed the living silent rosary held two flashlights that were lighted at the moment each person started his prayer. At 10:30 p.m. the Archbishop of Buenos Aires, Monsignor Antonio Caggiano, made his entrance to the stadium filled with more than 30,000 persons. I don't have to tell you that at my age, 26 years old, I could not contain myself and broke crying when after finishing my prayer I heard those more than 30,000 persons yelling: *"VIVA CUBA"* in support of the Cuban people suffering under Communism. It was a very impressive ceremony. Next day all newspapers in Buenos Aires carried the news about the event. In the newspaper La Nación, on page 3, appeared a photo of the event.

During all this time I was convinced that the end of the Communist regime in Cuba was approaching. We didn't want to continue in Argentina and I decided that we should go to the United States. My wife supported me all the way. The economic situation in Argentina was not the best. The high inflation denied us the opportunity to save money and be able to make economic plans for the future, in the other hand moving to the United States would bring us closer to Cuba and it would make it easier for us to return there as soon as Cuba was liberated. Pochi was pregnant with our fourth child due to be born by April 1961. We went to the USA Consulate in Buenos Aires and filled all necessary documents to request our Immigrant visas as permanent residents. We followed all legal and required procedures like medical exams in order to migrate to the United States.

On December 16, 1960 my sister Totó and my brother-in-law Rolando Peláez took a flight from Havana to Miami. They took whatever they could carry in two small suitcases. They were gone for good. But while in the United States, Rolando contemplated the idea of him returning to Cuba to take some other things of value and bring them back from Cuba. The problem that he confronted was his son Rolandito who refused to allow him to return to Cuba. Rolandito told his father: *"If you return to Cuba I will enroll in the training camps for the upcoming invasion."* Rolando desisted of his idea and decided to stay in New Orleans where they were living. Their decision to live in New Orleans was based in something very simple, it was based not on a master CIA plan. Rolandito was attending LSU in Baton Rouge and their daughter Martha, who had been previously sent to New Orleans, was working at the office of the Pan American Insurance Company. Liberal-leftist-conspiracy-lovers take note of this: No CIA involvement in the establishment of that part of the family in New Orleans.

On January 11, 1961, I had my final interview with the Consul of the United States in Buenos Aires and our visas as legal residents of the USA were granted.

Among the visitors to Buenos Aires were members of the Cuban student organizations among them Abel de Varona and Joaquín Pérez. Joaquín was also active with Catholic Action, an organization that was very active against Communism.

On December 11, 1960, I wrote a letter to Mr. Leo Frade, 18 No. 113, La Habana, Cuba who had published a letter in the magazine O'Cruzeiro asking to establish contacts with boys and girls (from 15 to 17 years old) from Latin America who were interested in the "Union of Latin American Republics". After reading his letter I was convinced that the name Leo Frade was a fictitious one and that it was someone from the Castro government trying to recruit Latin American youngsters. But I was wrong, Leo Frade existed and I was going to meet him personally some years later in New Orleans.

Before the end of December we received another visitor to Buenos Aires, it was former President Carlos Prío Socarrás, he stayed at the Plaza Hotel. After having been deposed by Batista, Prío had reportedly given money to Fidel Castro to buy the Granma[16] and had been a vocal supporter of the Revolutionary government. On December 28, 1960 I went to the Plaza Hotel with the hope of talking to ex-President Prío who had been an acquaintance of my father. Prío was not at the Hotel when I arrived and then I left a letter for him in which letter I was asking him to break his ties with the Castro regime.

What I didn't knew at the time was that Piñera was able to meet with Prío without letting us know what he was going to do. Prío departed Buenos Aires returning to Cuba where, for some time, he continued to praise Castro until eventually he found an opportunity to leave Cuba for good and came to the United States. Many years later, apparently disheartened about the Cuban situation he put a gun to his head and committed suicide.

That same day of December 28, 1960 we had a meeting of five Cubans in Buenos Aires to establish a "Management Committee" in order to organize the Cubans presently living in Argentina as well as the ones that could arrive in the future. We met at No.1160 President Roque Saenz Peña, eight floor, apartment B. There we signed a document explaining our four main topics of agreement:

1) The overthrow of the regime of Fidel Castro.
2) Reestablishment of the Cuban Constitution of 1940.
3) Establishment of a Provisional Government who should call for immediate free elections in Cuban territory.
4) Reincorporate Cuba to the Inter-American system with total dignity and sovereignty.

---

16   The boat used by Castro to land in Cuba from Mexico.

The ones signing the document were: Alberto Espinosa Bravo, José Manuel Lamela, Oscar Pérez, Jr., Carlos Bringuier and Mario Urquía de la Torre.

During my stay in Buenos Aires I also had been able to establish contact with several student leaders at the University of Buenos Aires, among them some members of the Movimiento Universitario de Centro[17] which was, as his name imply, neither to the left nor to the right. They had a newspaper "Programa" and in the December issue they published an article written by me. The title was "Consumatum est" in which I was referring to the recent assassination at the "paredón" in Cuba of Porfirio Ramírez, President of the Federation of Students at Central University of Las Villas. I ended the article with these words:

"Argentinean student, today was Porfirio Ramírez, tomorrow could be you, you can't allow the Communist advance; fight, because with your fight you will be defending the three basic pillars of our civilization: <Freedom, Justice and Democracy>.
Remember that Communism could execute men, but not ideas."

Our lives in Liniers had been going in a quietly way. We made a lot of friends in the nice neighborhood but there was only one, a young lady across the street who never became friend. We discovered through some of the other neighbors that she was a Communist sympathizer.

On January 20, 1961 my wife and I decided to do some sightseeing and we took a boat ride around the Tigre River. The boat left us, for a few hours, in a little island to enjoy a nice lunch. Next day, Pochi started to have the symptoms of been ready to give birth. Her family couldn't believe it, she was less than seven months pregnant, in reality around six months. With the acquired experience of her previous deliveries when our son Carlos Jr., (Caki) had survived an almost miscarriage during Pochi's first pregnancy, María del Carmen (Miri) had survived her premature (8 months) arrival because of her strong will, Ana María (Ani) had overcome her terribly fight when she was born at 7 months of pregnancy with not well developed lungs and suffering from hyaline membrane, now this fourth one was going to establish a record fighting for survival at 6

---

[17]   University Movement of Center

months of pregnancy. To Pochi's family surprise Pochi gave birth to a girl weighing 2 pounds and with her lungs underdeveloped. But that fourth girl, like the other children was a real fighter. She was put in an incubator and we were told that even when my wife would be authorized to leave the hospital, the new born girl, María Elena (Marlena) would have to stay in the hospital for several weeks.

We were forced to make a quick decision in regard to our forthcoming trip to the United States. I talked to the USA Consulate and they told me not to worry, that when my wife's visa was granted she was already pregnant and that the visa included the new born girl. Pochi and I decided that I would be leaving first, Pochi would have chance to recover as well as the new born María Elena. I would be able to find a job in the United States and prepare everything for their arrival. We set a day for my departure which was January 31, 1961.

The night before my departure, January 30, 1961, we had a family reunion at the house in Liniers and when it finished, almost at midnight, we went out to say goodbye to those relatives that have come. It was a big surprise that the Communists were giving me also a goodbye. Painted in the walls at the front of the house, with black paint, were slogans like: *"Traitor to the Paredón"* and *"Viva Fidel"* I had gained their hate, apparently they had noticed the work that I had been doing in Buenos Aires against them. When I saw the sign *"Viva Fidel"* I could not have dreamed that 2 ½ years later I would see, in New Orleans, the same words hanging from the neck of Lee Harvey Oswald.

CHAPTER VI

─══◉══─

GUATEMALA—MIAMI (1961)

At my arrival to Guatemala I encountered my family full of hope. My father was seeing an imminent return to Cuba. Finally the Eisenhower administration had waked up and the Americans were training the Cubans to overthrow Fidel Castro. My brother Juan was being trained at Retalhuleu as a paratrooper. Spirits were high.

During the few days that I stayed in Guatemala City we kept talking about family issues and the coming downfall of Castro.

I wrote a series of articles entitled "Fidel vs. Fidel" in which I was confronting Castro's promises against Castro's deeds. The false Castro who promised free elections, restoration of the 1940 Constitution, no more political prisoners versus the real Castro who brought no more free elections, who embraced Communism and threw away the 1940 Constitution, thousands of Cubans assassinated at the paredón and the creation of a great prison as large as the Island where tens of thousands of Cubans were already suffering the real Castro. The articles were published in the newspaper "La Hora" on three consecutive days: February 14, 15 and 16 when I was already in the United States.

I arrived to Miami on February 8 and went to the Monroe Hotel. My intentions at my arrival was to find a job, rent a house and wait for Pochi and the children to arrive.

I had just a few relatives in Miami during those days. One that I remember was Mario Medina Núñez brother of Jorge my brother-in-law. Mario was working in a company that makes plastic items. Mario and his wife were living at Ocean Dr. 202 in Miami Beach. One night I went to visit them and I brought a record that I had bought: "Volvió la Noche" ("The Night Returned") by Father Jaime de Aldeaseca and while we listened to it we finished crying all of us.

I got in touch with several Cubans friends of my brother Julito inquiring for a job but at the moment the economic situation in Miami was stagnant. On the other hand you could smell in the air the patriotism to join the forthcoming invasion. I was swept by the smell and decided to join the forces that were getting ready to liberate Cuba.

On a morning of February 1961, I arrived at the recruitment office and underwent a physical examination that was done to me by Dr. Juan Rodríguez Pintado who, by coincidence, was the forensic physician assigned to my old courtroom in Cuba. There I also encountered a friend of my brother Julito, Jorgito Alonso Pujol. Jorgito Alonso Pujol was the one who gave me the enrollment paper that I had to fill and vouched for me. My file number was 1569.

Something incredible happened. Since my father was appointed as President of the Tribunal de Urgencia I had been affected by a discomforting stomach problem. I had been treated in Cuba, by Dr. Ottón Madariaga and in Argentina by another physician and it had been diagnosed as "nervous colitis". The day that I signed to go in the invasion my "nervous colitis" disappeared. Apparently I had reached the point of no return.

I was sent to a motel on Biscayne Boulevard and I was given a room. My roommate was from Sagua la Grande and he knew the Medina last name. Jorge my brother-in-law was from Sagua la Grande. The name of the Cuban was Carlos Elcoro.

The first thing that I did when I decided to join the invasion was to write a letter to my wife informing her of my decision. In that letter I explained to her what I had been taught in Belén School. No.1 was God; No.2 was the Fatherland and No.3 was the Family. I had an obligation to defend God who was under attack by the evil forces of Communism; at the same time my Fatherland was been destroyed by the regime of Fidel Castro. I told her that I had been a member of a privileged class and that now I will have to pay my dues, that I was going to put at risk my life in order to be able to have a free Cuba where our children could grow up. At the end I said: Good bye.

On one evening of February it was scheduled a big concentration of Cubans at the Bayfront Park. Before I went to the meeting at the park I stopped at the house of my second cousin José Alberto Crespo Grasso who had invited me to dinner. José Alberto had been a member of the Cuban Air Force and during the Batista government he took a military airplane and escaped from Cuba to the United States. When Castro took over, José Alberto returned to Cuba and rejoined the Cuban Air Force. A few months later, disillusioned with the Communist control of the government he took another military airplane and returned to the United States. Now he was a member of the Rebel Air Force been trained in Guatemala and he had come to Miami to meet his son who had been recently born and to say goodbye to his wife.

We were chatting and he told me that the skies were going to be ours. That we were going to count with the best air force on earth. He explained that by dominating the air, the invasion will be victorious because Castro's forces would be unable to make massive attacks against the Brigade because then our Air Force would annihilate the Communist forces. During our conversation he told me that my brother Juan had already been informed that I had joined to go in the invasion and that as the Air Force was going to be the strongest and the safest place to be he was going to get me a place in his plane. After the dessert and the Cuban coffee José Alberto drove me to Bayfront Park.

Next day I went to the liquor store of Carlos Guas Decall, the son of another former Cuban Vice-President and friend of my brother Julito. When he learned that I had signed to go in the invasion he was furious and he was trying to convince me to forget about the invasion. He told me: *"Carlitos, with your name and my name, they will kill us by shooting us from our back."* He begged to me not to go in the invasion. At the time I didn't knew about it but later on I learned that immediately he wrote a letter to my brother Julito in Guatemala asking him to make me stop in my decision of joining the invasion.

I am fortunate that during those days the post office was run with accurate efficiency.

For several days I had been at the motel waiting to be transported to the training camps in Guatemala. I remember that at lunch time they made a delicious soup and the cook was a famous police Captain by the name of Caramés. One morning I received a letter from Argentina and I opened it thinking that it was from my wife. But no, it was from my father-in-law Héctor Pearce, the Argentinean diplomat who wrote to me in very undiplomatic terms.

Héctor was asking me how come I had married his daughter, procreate four children with her and now I was going to embark in such foolish adventure and leave my wife a widow with four kids. His writing woke me up from my idyllic and patriotic dream of liberating Cuba. I took my luggage and walked out of the motel going to the Greyhound Bus Station to take a bus to New Orleans where my sister Totó was living with her family. I don't have any doubts that, once again, I was *in God's hands.*

After I had signed for the invasion and after I had decided to walk out of the motel I felt uncomfortable staying in Miami and that was the reason that moved me to decide to go to New Orleans.

There have been scavengers, and pro-Communist writers who had inferred that I was under the control of the CIA and that the CIA had sent me to New Orleans. Here I had related the truth. I never met a CIA agent until December 1963 in an unrelated case.

CHAPTER VII

——◆◇◆——

NEW ORLEANS (FEBRUARY 1961-JULY 1963)

At my arrival to New Orleans I went to live with my sister Totó. She was staying at Parkchester Apartments with her husband Rolando Peláez and their daughter Martha. They had rented an apartment at 4436 Paris Avenue Apt. D. Rolando was working with Mr. Levy, owner of "California Redwood Fences" and Martha was working at Pan American Life Insurance Co.

They were very happy to see me but the apartment, a two-bedroom one, forced me to occupy a small bed in my sister's bedroom. The first few days were tough because it was hard to find a job. Some acquaintances of my sister try to land me a job as an assistant to Representative Hale Boggs.

Attorney W. Ford Reese wrote the following letter to U.S. Representative Hale Boggs:

> *March 2, 1961*
> *Honorable T. Hale Boggs, M. C.*
> *New House Office Building*
> *Washington, D. C.*
>
> *Dear Hale:*
>
>   *I am taking the liberty of writing you about Mr. Carlos Bringuier who is a lawyer and who has left Cuba because of his*

disagreement with the policies and theories of the present Cuban government. He left Cuba with his family, moved to Buenos Aires because his wife was from Argentina, left Buenos Aires and came to Louisiana. I was impressed with him in an interview in my office and feel that with his background he can be of considerable benefit to our State and to our country.

It would be keenly appreciated if you could arrange time to interview him in Washington and he assures me that at your convenience he will be there. I feel certain that you will arrange for him to see the people in the government service where he is best fitted to serve.

My deep appreciation for any courtesies which you may be able to show. My kindest personal regards to you and Lindy.

Sincerely,
W, Ford Reese
Dr. Carlos J. Bringuier—
WFR/la
Cc: Mr. Carlos Bringuier 4436 Paris Ave., Apt. D
New Orleans, La.

Then on March 17, 1961 Mr. Reese prepared the following letter:

March 17, 1961
Honorable Hale Boggs, M. C.
New House Office Building
Washington, D. C.

Dear Hale:

I enclose application for Federal employment which has been filled in and signed by Mr. Bringuier.

He will, as previously stated, be glad to come to Washington at your convenience.

I appreciate very much your courtesies and am

With kind personal regards,
W. Ford Reese

Unfortunately Representative Hale Boggs response was negative, he was not able to help me. Now, after the years, I understand that it was God's desire that I would stay in New Orleans, He had other plans for me, and I was *in God's Hands.*

If I would have go to Washington I would have never met Lee Harvey Oswald and God wanted me to meet him.

The first Cubans that I met in New Orleans were Otto Blanco and his wife; Ernesto Bascuas and his wife (Chea); and a friend of my brother-in-law, Colonel Orlando Piedra who was a former Chief of the Bureau of Investigations of the Cuban police under the Batista government. There were other Cubans living in Parkchester and it became a "little Cuba".

The first money that I earned in the United States was a two days job unloading wooden fences from a railroad wagon; my pay was $20.00 from Mr. Levy.

Sometime in March, I read in the newspaper an add looking for a bilingual sales person in Casa Alejandro but when I showed up I was received by an Argentinean, Rodolfo Mesorio, who was working there and who told me that the job have been already taken.

A few days later I found a job at Macy's Discount House a clothing store owned by Abe Glazer. When I was interviewed I was asked what kind of experience I had an I stretched the truth answering in my broken English: *"I worked at the Sun of Cuba:,"* like if it was a store by that name when in reality I was referring to having worked *"under the sun of Cuba"* which was basically true. With the new job I was feeling very good no matter the fact that it carried long hours and low pay. I was working 66 hours a week and my pay was $40.00 per week.

On March 31, 1961 my former teacher from Belén School, José Ignacio Rasco, who was the leader in exile of the Christian Democratic Movement, wrote me a letter. I had been trying to see if I could be designated Delegate in Buenos Aires of the Frente Revolucionario Democratico (FRD) and Rasco, in his letter, was telling me that the FRD was going to be dissolved with the creation of the Consejo Revolucionario Cubano [18] and that it was better for me if I go through Tony Varona because at the moment, coming from him (Rasco) maybe it would be counterproductive.

---

[18] Cuban Revolutionary Council.

On April 2, 1961, I wrote a letter to Joaquín Pérez, one of the Cuban students who had visited Buenos Aires while I was living there. In my letter I was trying to find out if he could help me in my interest on the Delegation in Buenos Aires. I explained to him that I had to know pretty soon because my wife and the children had a deadline of May 11, 1961 to use their immigrant visas.

The person representing the FRD in New Orleans was a Cuban by the name of Sergio Arcacha Smith. I went to see him to offer my assistance but I noticed that his reception was not very warm.

On April 15, 1961, very early in the morning, my brother-in-law Rolando received a phone call from Orlando Piedra, informing us that Cuban airports had been bombarded. Later on the news of the attacks appeared on television. I did not know at the time that Piedra's brother "Chirrín" was one of the pilots involved in the raid but I was almost sure that my cousin José Alberto Crespo was also one of them. The Bay of Pigs invasion was ready to start.

April 17 arrived and the news broke that an invasion brigade had landed at Bay of Pigs. We expected the invasion to be a success. How it was possible it could fail when the American government had recruited them, trained them, and armed them? The prestige and honor of the American government was at stake. Now it was just a matter of days for our return to a free Cuba. What we ignored was up to what degree the American government had been infiltrated by Communist agents.

From my work, at lunchtime, I was walking to Arcacha's office to find out about the situation. My concern started to grow up when Arcacha told me that the invasion was going "as planned" and that the invaders were going to the mountains to join the guerrillas in the Escambray Mountains. That scenario didn't match with the one explained to me in Miami by my cousin José Alberto Crespo Grasso. Rolando received the real tragic news from Orlando Piedra: the invasion had been defeated, what was unbelievable had happened.

Our first reaction was shock then crying thinking in our brother Juan, our cousin José Alberto, our friends, all the members of the Brigade and what it was more important we cried for the terrible future that now Cuba was going to suffer.

I am not going to detail events about the invasion itself because there have been several good books dedicated to it. My favorite is: "Decision for Disaster" by a real American, Grayston L. Lynch. In his book Lynch mention an incident narrated to him by Richard Bissel who was one of the CIA architects of the invasion. The incident happened at the moment the Brigade 2506 was starting to see the end approaching. John F. Kennedy was attending a black-tie affair when Admiral Arleigh Burke called him out of the meeting. Admiral Burke was requesting U.S. Navy air support in order to keep the supply ships afloat and being able to deliver the ammunitions and supplies to the Brigade. Kennedy response had been: *"We just can't be involved"*. Admiral Burke's historic response was: *"Goddammit, Mr. President, we are involved. We put those people in there and promised aid to them. We can't just wash our hands of them and walk away."* Lynch's book was not published until 1998.[19]

We communicated by phone with my brother Julio in Guatemala trying to find out the whereabouts of Juanito but to no avail, he didn't knew anything about Juanito's situation. In the press started to appear names of dead ones and prisoners. Day after day we looked for Juanito's name but it did not appear anywhere. We learned that "Chirrín" Piedra was one of the dead pilots. Another of the dead pilots was my second cousin José Alberto Crespo Grasso. This is another instance where there is no questions about it, I was *in God's hands* when I decided to leave the motel in Miami. If I would have gone in the invasion I would have been going in José Alberto's airplane and I would have been killed as my father-in-law had predicted.

For days, we cried in New Orleans thinking Juanito was dead. Luckily one day we were informed that he had been captured. After his release Juanito told me, how when he had landed in the area of San Blás, they captured several militiamen and how others surrendered and joined them in the fight against Castro. What the liberal press have spiked and never said is that when Castro eventually won the battle, he ordered to be killed all his soldiers that had surrendered and showed them as killed in battle. Goebbels couldn't have done better. Juanito had run out of bullets and he managed to escape for several days surviving by eating lizards and drinking his own urine. He slept by day and walked by night. Finally one day when he awoke he was surrounded by soldiers. He was brought to Havana to a medical center at the prison. After several days he still was very skinny but he received the visit of Fidel Castro who addressed him in this way: *"Bringuier, I heard that you are trying to help the Revolution*

---

19   Decision for Disaster, by Grayston L. Lynch, page 128.

because you refuse to eat." Juanito said to me that after that encounter with Castro he started to eat the rotten food that his jailers were serving him.

I learned that several of my friends had died during the invasion. One of the ones that affected me the most was the one that I least expected to hear about. After I had left Miami going to New Orleans, Rafael Guas Inclán, former Cuban Vice-President, presented himself at the recruitment center in Miami offering himself to go in the invasion. With that gesture from the old man his son, Carlos Guas Decall, could not do less. Carlitos Guas, the same one who had begged me not to go in the invasion, now was offering his services to join the Brigade. His father's request was not accepted due to his old age, but his son's was accepted.

During the battle at Bay of Pigs, Carlos Guas Decall, knowing that he was running out of ammunition and that they would be captured and humiliated by Fidel Castro, as Castro later tried to do to several of the survivors in televised programs, Carlitos Guas preferred to die. I had been told that Carlos Guas Decall knowing that the defeat was real and imminent, charged with his rifle and shooting his last bullets when a shell from a bazooka or a mortar struck him. Another congenial and brave Cuban who died for the ambition of power of Fidel Castro.

I also have been told that José Alberto Crespo Grasso, my second cousin, after finishing flying a B-26 (Puma 1) was attacked by one of Castro's heroes of Bay of Pigs, pilot Alvaro Prendes who was flying a T-33. José Alberto's plane was badly damaged by Prendes but José Alberto managed to leave the bay and tried to return to Puerto Cabezas (a trip of around 3 ½ hours). He made radio contact with another rebel plane who was carrying a Catholic priest and he did a radio confession with the priest before his plane crashed in the sea without been able to reach Nicaragua. His plane disappeared in the dark waters of the Caribbean Sea. Next day four transport planes started a fruitless search for his plain to no avail.

With the years, Fidel Castro's hero of Bay of Pigs, pilot Alvaro Prendes escaped from Cuba to Miami.

To José Alberto's credit it has been estimated that he inflicted more than one thousand deaths among the Communist forces. His widow dedicated her life to protect orphan children in Guatemala.

After the failure of the invasion, which was not a defeat of the 2506 Brigade, but treason from those who were supposed to assure that if the

United States government was involved, as it was, there could be no other result than victory, President John F. Kennedy publicly assumed responsibility for the failure but in my opinion he was not the only one responsible. His lack of character let other sinister figures, working in favor of Fidel Castro, among them Adlai Stevenson and William Fulbright to decide Castro's victory. Years later I had the opportunity to attend a dinner with President of Guatemala Miguel Ydígoras Fuentes who occupied that position during the Bay of Pigs invasion.

The dinner was at the Brenthouse Hotel and hosted by Dr. Alston Ochsner, Sr., who was always very kind to me and that night Dr. Ochsner gave me the honor of sitting me next to President Ydígoras.

During the dinner Ydígoras wanted to know about my encounters with Lee Harvey Oswald. I asked Ydígoras that in reciprocity I wanted to know something about the Bay of Pigs invasion that I didn't know.

President Ydígoras related to me that about one month before the invasion Kennedy sent an emissary to Guatemala who told Ydígoras that the invasion was going to be cancelled and asking President Ydígoras to start dismantling the training camps. Ydígoras said that he was perplexed and his reaction was to send one of the Alejos brothers to Washington with his response. President Ydígoras message to President Kennedy was that the moment was the right moment to get rid of Castro, that if they do not achieve that, then Castro eventually would get rid of them explaining what would happen in Latin America if Fidel Castro remained in power. Ydígoras said that Alejo told him that when he finished relaying his message to Kennedy, the President of the United States started rocking his chair and turning to Alejos said: *"Mr. Alejos, tell your President that he has convinced me that he is right. That I am sorry that I do not have around me more people like him. Fetish people surround me. They are always presenting to me the wrong side of the issues. Please tell your President that the invasion is going."*

I believe that President John F. Kennedy was a victim of those "fetiches" who surrounded him. Many of them were inclined to sympathize with Fidel Castro and Castro knew in advance of the plans for the invasion. I do not know how many Ana Belen Montes where very close to John F. Kennedy. What I know is that those who formed the 2506 Brigade were the best of Cuban youth, the bravest soldiers who fought until the last bullet.

I was depressed because of the Bay of Pigs disaster and I thought that Fidel Castro and the United States could not co-exist and that Castro was going to take over Latin America and then send his people to cross the Río Grande and overwhelm the United States. In my mind, before that invasion occurred the forces against the United States would declare an economic embargo against the USA to strangled it economically and pave the way for the invasion. For this reason I wrote to some of the Argentineans that I had met in Buenos Aires and told them to be prepared because soon they would be fighting the Communists over there.

In the meantime, after the Bay of Pigs debacle, I tried to help Arcacha. I knew he was confronting problems with the increasing Cuban population in New Orleans. Arcacha called a meeting of the Cubans in New Orleans and we attended nine persons including him. Among Arcacha's friends in New Orleans was a young Cuban engineer who I had met at Belén school, his name was Carlos Quiroga. While attending Belén we used to ride in the same school bus and his father, owner of the poultry business "El Liro" was the one selling us chickens to eat.

One of the grievances of the Cubans was that Arcacha was hanging around with a distasteful looking American named David Ferrie. I asked Arcacha to introduce me to Ferrie in that way I could decide if the Cubans were right in their apprehension against Ferrie. One day we went, Arcacha, Quiroga and I to Ferrie's house. I stayed there less than 10 minutes and when we left I told Arcacha that he should not be seen with Ferrie because the guy was quite repulsive and gave the impression that he was homosexual because of the youngsters that were at his house.

During May 1961, Pochi and the four children arrived from Buenos Aires. We rented, for $83.50 a month, an apartment in Parkchester, the address was 4525 Duplessis Street, Apt. B.

Apparently the letter that I had sent to Buenos Aires, to those anti-Communists youngsters produced some effect. I received a letter from one of them enclosing clippings of the newspaper "La Prensa" relating what they have done. Che Guevara's mother was scheduled to speak at the University of Buenos Aires after an unsuccessful attempt to do the same at the University of Recife in Brazil where the Brazilian government refused to give a permit for such an event. Mrs. Celia L. de Guevara went to the Gallery Quetzal, at Buenos Aires University to deliver a dissertation about the Cuban Revolution. Around 8:00 p.m., among slogans like "Cuba, symbol of the anti-imperialist struggle is today in the School of Law" the meeting started. At 8:15 p.m. Che Guevara's mother started her speech and about 15 minutes later a blond young man lighted a smoke bomb and threw it to the floor. With that, the two bands Communists and anti-Communists, started fighting among them. Insults were shouted to Guevara's mother, windows were broken. The anti-Communists had a white handkerchief tied to their right arm. The Communists started to take out their weapons and shooting to repel the attack. The antiCommunists repelled the aggression with their own weapons.

There were shouts of *"Guevara to Moscow"*, and *"We are fed with Communists"*. Another bomb exploded. At 9:00 p.m., a truce is declared to evacuate the wounded. Guevara's mother used the truce to leave the Gallery. The Dean of Law School, Dr. Francisco Laplaza made his appearance trying to end the conflict but to no avail. The anti-Communists started to shout: *"We want to trade her for a tractor"* and then the truce disappeared and the struggle continued fiercely, pieces of bricks flew by the air, parts of chairs did likewise, new tear gas grenades and bullets created more panic. The anti-Communists set fire to the front door and soon it expanded around the Gallery. It was 9:50 p.m.

Guevara's mother managed to escape from the second floor window using a rope to reach down. The attempt to exchange her for a tractor failed but as the anti-Communist wrote me: *"our missions was 1) not to allow her to speak, and 2) put the Gallery on fire. She did not speak and the Gallery was set on fire. We were not able to exchange her for a tractor because she escaped through a window."*

The reader has to remember that after the betrayed Bay of Pigs invasion Dictator Fidel Castro offered to swap the members of the 2506 Brigade for tractors. The anti-Communists in Buenos Aires were trying to pay Dictator Castro with the same currency.

In New Orleans I also encountered a friend from the Casino Español de la Habana, his name was Jorge Ledo. Ledo also had attended Law School with me at the University of Havana. Ledo was one of the Cubans disenchanted with Arcacha. Another Cuban who had the same feelings was José Manuel Cuscó. The three of us decided to create a newsletter to try to unify the Cubans in New Orleans. We gave the name "Cruzada" to the newsletter. The first issue was published during the second half of October 1961. The response was incredible, the great majority of the Cubans in New Orleans were in our favor.

On October 10, 1961 we proclaimed the Declaration of New Orleans which was signed by more than 100 Cubans, all of us claiming for our freedom and it was sent to all Latin American Presidents having been delivered, in person, to their respective Consulates in the city.

On November 25, 1961 we organized (as called for a few days before in Cruzada) a demonstration against the Mexican Ambassador to the Organization of American States (OEA). Mexican Ambassador Vicente Sánchez-Gavito had made unfortunate statements in favor of Dictator Castro. The demonstration was held in front of the Roosevelt Hotel and more than 80 Cubans joined in the protest. Ambassador Sánchez-Gavito requested police protection but he lost the battle because the public opinion agreed with us.

The newspaper Times Picayune wrote an article on December 3 about an event prepared by Sergio Arcacha Smith. It was name "Crusade to Free Cuba". The article announced that William A. Monteleone, a New Orleans hotel executive, had been name General Chairperson of the campaign. Listing as members of the city-wide Committee the following persons: Mrs. Martha Robinson, William T. Walshe, Fritz Lindley, Robert D. Reily, Maurice Andry, Col. Provosty A. Dayries, Mrs. Philip Wogan, Mrs. Stockton B. Jefferson, Edward Brignac, J. B. McMahon, Councilman Paul V. Burke, Rudolph Vorbusch, Mrs. Sidney Schoenberger, Dr. Gilbert Mellin, Arnesto Rodríguez, the Rev. William K. Sisk, Jr., Maurice G. Maher, Charles C. Deano, Edward M. Hannan, E. A. Tharpe, Jr., Jack Yates, Manuel Gil, and Louis A. Garber.

The night of December 4, 1961 we held an Assembly of the Cubans in New Orleans at Gallier Hall[20]. More than 300 Cubans took part in the meeting. Historically, the largest meeting held up to that moment by Cubans in the history of New Orleans. The assembled democratically designated a "Comité Gestor"[21] to prepare the documents in order to organize the Cubans in the city. Carlos Quiroga went to the meeting with the intention to help Arcacha. I knew Quiroga and I was sure that

---

[20] Old City Hall.
[21] "Operating Committee".

he was a young decent man and that eventually he would realize that we were right.

Around those days it was announced that the President of Argentina Arturo Frondizi was going to arrive to New Orleans. The Cubans wanted to demonstrate asking Frondizi's help in our struggle against Fidel Castro's dictatorship. I thought that it was waste of time. I had been in Argentina and to me Arturo Frondizi was a Marxist whose brothers Risieri and Silvio were also Marxists and defenders of Fidel Castro. Later on, I learned that Arturo Frondizi, as President awarded Ernesto "Che" Guevara an Argentinean medal at a secret ceremony in the Pink House[22]. But the majority of the Cubans were in favor of the demonstration and I helped to paint the placards but I did not go because I knew it was a waste of time to ask President Arturo Frondizi for help against Castro.

While we were painting the placards, something special happened to me. Something that never had happened before. I believe in my intuition. Talking with a group of Cubans about the meetings been held to formulated the papers that would united the Cubans in New Orleans thru the "Operating Committee" I launched a salvo. I said I knew something was going on and that what was going on would exploded and when it does some people would be feeling sorry for themselves. After a while one of the Cubans present, Carlos de la Vega, called me apart and told me that he was not involved in what was going on but that he knew that our meetings were being recorded in tape without our knowledge. He claimed that he was not involved but apparently he was trying to clear himself of the wrongdoing. I did not had the slightest idea of those recording going on. I had gone fishing and caught a big one. We were meeting at the Berlitz School whose owner/manager was a Cuban name Arnesto Rodríguez. During the meetings two factions had been created, one formed by Ledo, Cuscó, Francisco Henares, others and me. Ricardo Davis, René Ruiz and Arnesto Rodríguez among others, formed the other faction. Carlos de la Vega who was also a member claimed that he was in the middle.

---

[22] Argentina Presidential Palace.

D R E   DIRECTORIO REVOLUCIONARIO ESTUDIANTIL

jose antonio echeverria con tus ideas en marcha

Miami, August 9, 1962

To whom it may concern:

        The Directorio Revolucionario Estudiantil
(Cuban Student Directorate);

        Certifies that Mr. Carlos Bringuier has
been appointed our representative in the city of New Orleans,
Louisiana.

        Mr. Bringuier, as Delegation
Chairman, has full powers in all matters concerning the
organization in the above mentioned city.

Jose Antonio Lanuza
CUBAN STUDENT DIRECTORATE

96

With the information supplied to me by Carlos de la Vega I confronted Arnesto Rodríguez. Arnesto had been living in New Orleans for years and he confessed and apologized for what he had done and promised to bring the recordings to me. Eventually one night he showed at my apartment with the tapes and at that moment Ledo and Cuscó were there. Cuscó was so angry that he threw a punch to Arnesto and I intervened.

Maybe I am wrong but when somebody sincerely apologizes to me I believe that that person deserves a second chance. After that incident Arnesto and I became friends.

On December 31, 1961 "Cruzada" cooperated with Mrs. Cuqui Henares[23], Mr. Enrique Bascuas and Elisa Cerniglia who was the Director of the Cuban Catholic Center, obtaining funds from Cubans to buy Gamma-globulin to help the members of the 2506 Brigade affected by hepatitis while in prison.

For some time Sergio Arcacha Smith had tried to organize his campaign entitled "Crusade to Free Cuba" which would be a fundraising event ending with a march of Cubans on Canal Street. The main problem that he confronted was that the Cubans in New Orleans didn't want to cooperate with him. There were rumors that he was in debt and that he needed the money that was going to be collected in order to pay those debts. I would like to clarify something here. We were not used to have leaders collecting money for different causes and then using those monies for paying personal expenses. We preferred that a person be assigned a salary and then send everything collected to the main office. We didn't like co-mingling. In reality, the best idea was that we had a job and work without salary or compensation for our group. Moreover we resented that Arcacha had named his campaign "Crusade to Free Cuba" which could confuse some people and maybe they could think that it was related to our newsletter "Cruzada".

With all the rumors floating around I nicknamed Arcacha's fundraising efforts as "Crusade to free Arcacha". At that moment Arcacha and I were not speaking terms. "Crusade to Free Cuba" was scheduled for January 20-21, 1962.

---

[23] Wife of Ramiro Montalvo a 2506 Brigade member, prisoner in Cuba.

On January 10, 1962 we sent to the Cuban Revolutionary Council in Miami, in the name of "Cruzada" a document relating our activities in New Orleans and in the last paragraph we stated:

> "8—*CRUZADA is confronting an historic dilemma. Our relations with the Delegate of the Council can't be any worse, when it had reached the point when a person had been physically attacked without respect for his home or family and the intent to defame a person*[24]. *For the coming days of the 20 and 21 of this month it is scheduled "CRUSADE TO FREE CUBA" promoted by the Delegate of the Revolutionary Council. Notwithstanding the ideological and other differences in between, on one side CRUZADA and the Cubans exiled in this city, and in the other the Delegate of the Cuban Revolutionary Council, we ask from that entity CRC a reply in writing and given to the bearer if "CRUSADE TO FREE CUBA" is endorsed and guaranteed by the Cuban Revolutionary Council or it is endorsed and guaranteed by Mr. Sergio Arcacha Smith, because if it is endorsed and guaranteed by that organism we will give our support to the American Committee that form part of "CRUSADE TO FREE CUBA" but on the contrary we will be forced to abstain from the events of such organization, we do this very conscious that our position is the only possible in cases like this."*

The response from the Cuban Revolutionary Council was to send to New Orleans Mr. Ruizsánchez (brother-in-law of its President Manuel Antonio de Varona). After conferring with us and after Mr. Ruizsánchez told us that we were right we accepted to participate in the "CRUSADE TO FREE CUBA". After the event finished Sergio Arcacha Smith was deposed as Delegate in New Orleans of the Cuban Revolutionary Council in his place was designated a long time Cuban resident of New Orleans by the name of Louis Rabel Núñez.

As everybody can imagine, if before this, Arcacha and me were not in speaking terms one with the other, now the situation was worse. After a few weeks Sergio Arcacha Smith departed from New Orleans and went to

---

[24] We are referring to Arcacha going to Jorge Ledo's house and throwing a punch to him.

live in Houston, Texas. We wouldn't talk to each other until a few years later.

When Louis Rabel organized the Delegation I was named in charge of Press and Propaganda. I lasted in that position just a few months and eventually resigned in March 21, 1962 disillusioned with the infighting within the Cubans in the Delegation.

It was at the beginning of summer that I took a small vacation with Pochi and the four children and went to visit my brother Julito who had moved from Guatemala to Miami. When Julito came from Guatemala, he stopped over in New Orleans and had surprised me with a present. It was a used 1953 Ford 2 doors, for which he paid $395.00. With that car we made the trip to Miami via Highway 90. We did not had money to spend in a motel and the trip took me 24 hours driving, stopping only for gas and to eat the sandwiches that we carry with us. My parents were also living with Julito in Miami.

While in Miami, Pochi and I went to see a play at the Martí Theatre. The principal actor was a famous Cuban called "Tres Patines" [25]. To my surprise I discovered that sitting in the row ahead of us was a former companion from Belén School and his wife. His name was Elio Más Hernández he was married to a daughter of Raúl Menocal a well-known Cuban politician.

After the show we decided to go to drink a Cuban coffee. While chatting Elio told me that he was working with the Cuban Student Directorate (DRE) and that as they didn't have a representation in Louisiana I could be the ideal candidate for that position. He was going to check with other Cuban friends of mine who formed part of the DRE and he would let me know.

Following our return to New Orleans I received the designation as Delegate of the Cuban Student Directorate [26] (DRE) in that city.

I had quitted my job on the store on Canal Street and Rolando and I were earning our living peddling to the merchant seamen that arrived to the port of New Orleans. We were buying from wholesalers and retailing aboard the ships to the seamen. We had some good weeks and some

---

[25] "Three Roller-skates".
[26] Directorio Revolucionario Estudiantil.

terrible weeks. During this time in several occasions Pochi and I went to sleep with our stomachs empty. Luckily our kids never went hungry.

There was an incident that clearly portrait the precarious situation in which we were living. One day, while we were selling clothes aboard a merchant ship we had to leave in a hurry because the ship was ready to depart. One of the seamen had not paid us $10.00 that he owed. With the ship leaving the dock, the seaman threw us the $10.00 inside an empty can. As physics indicate the paper weight less that the can and we saw the $10.00 descending slowly to the Mississippi river and the can dropping faster. For us $10.00, in those moments, was a lot of money. Rolando found a long wooden stick and we were fortunate that the river was at a high stage and there I was, hanging head down over the Mississippi river and Rolando holding me by my feet and with the wooden stick grabbed in my hands I was trying to fish the $10.00 bill. We were lucky and I was able to recover the $10.00. I had risked my life for a $10.00 bill.

One of the wholesalers selling to us was Shepard Zitler, owner of Wholesale Style Center on Decatur Street and he offered us to open a store with him. In the first moment his proposition was that it was to be a partnership. There was a store on Canal Street that went into bankrupts, the store was "L-shaped" with also an entrance by Decatur Street. The name of the store was "Grumblatt's". I explained to Zitler that the part that was of interest to us was the one with the entrance by Decatur Street and my reasoning was that the rent was less expensive that the part fronting Canal Street, besides that the part with exit to Decatur Street was better location because we were going to be across the Post Office located at the Custom House building, just across the street. We were going to cater to merchant seamen and that type of person writes a lot of letters at sea and when they arrive to port the first thing that they look for is for a Post Office in order to drop their letters.

Zitler who won the auction and got the lease for the building accepted my reasoning, but then Zitler changed his offer. It was not going to be a partnership, Rolando and I were going to be co-managers of the store with a salary of $60.00 per week. We accepted.

Then the discussions arose about the name to put to the store. Rolando and I decided that the best name was "Casa Roca". There was already a big store directed to the same customers by the name of "Casa

Alejandro" and we thought that combining the names of Rolando and Ca-rlos it would be the perfect name because Roca translated to English is Rock and the seamen would remember that name.

I wanted to clarify this about the name "Casa Roca" because later on, scoundrels launched the misconception that the name Roca was derived from the name of a well-known anti-Castro Cuban. I have never met any well-known anti-Castro Cuban with the name Roca.

In New Orleans there was a tradition to celebrate a special Catholic Mass that if my memory doesn't fail me was called "Red Mass". The celebration was at the Cathedral and the maximum leaders of the Archdioceses were there as also the Mayor, the Councilmen as well as other political leaders. I went to Jackson Square, in front of the Cathedral, to watch what was going on. I was surprised to see that there was a demonstration going on organized by a leftist group. I was there on my own, by my own decision or intuition. I was neither a CIA agent nor a FBI one, I was just *in God's hands.*

I mingle among the demonstrators and entered in a conversation with an older man. When he heard my accent he asked what was my country of origin and my answer was deceiving: *"I am Cuban but I plan to return there to support the revolution".* When he heard what I had just said he became very sympathetic to me. When the demonstration ended he invited me to drink coffee and eat doughnuts at the famous Café Dumonde.

While drinking our coffee we were chatting and I convinced him that I was pro-Castro. At one moment he told me: *"One day we are going to take the power in the US but it would be not by war. One day a President will say that we are a Communist country and when he says that a great decision would have to be made. Eighty per cent of the American people do not have brains and they would accept to live under Communism. The other 20% would be wiped out."*

The name of the person talking to me was Donald Savery a very active Quaker associated with the New Orleans Council for Peaceful Alternatives, a "Band the Bomb" organization headed by two lawyers: Benjamin Smith and Bruce Walter.

After a few weeks the same organization held a march on Canal Street. They started the march at the corner of Canal and Decatur streets. From Casa Roca I noticed that something was going on and when I saw their leftists signs I went inside the store and took with me a big placard that I had there showing the Statue of Liberty stabbed at her back with a sign saying: "Danger, only 90 miles away Cuba lays in chains."

The marchers, all members of the New Orleans Council for Peaceful Alternatives, had started moving on Canal Street in direction of the downtown area and I decided to follow them with my placard taking my place at the end of the marchers. I ruined their day. When the march ended it was disbanded right in front of Casa Roca where they started buying soft drinks from a Coke machine that we had at the entrance outside our door. When Donald Savery saw me opening the door of the store he told me: *"If I would have known who you really are I would not have paid for your coffee at the Café Dumonde."*

Now these people knew where I was working and on which side I was. That is the reason why I always have in the back of my mind that Lee Harvey Oswald was sent to me by people that knew where I was.

On August 9, 1962, José Antonio Lanuza officially sent me a letter certifying my appointment as Delegation Chairman of the Directorio Revolucionario Estudiantil (DRE) in the city of New Orleans.

At almost the end of August 1962 I received a communication from Miami directing me that on the afternoon of August 24 I should contact the New Orleans press and tell them that something big was going to happen in Cuba that night. They put it like an important broadcast would be coming from inside Cuba. I went to the New Orleans States-Item and talked to newsman Bill Stuckey. Bill heard me but apparently he was not impressed. That day nothing appeared in the newspaper.

Next day was completely different. A big article appeared in the front page where the DRE and I were featured. On the night of August 24, two boats of the DRE had departed to Havana. Leslie Nóbregas commandeered one of the boats. His boat was the larger one giving protection to a smaller one who was closer to the Cuban coastline. Exactly at 10:30 p.m., they managed to pass under the radar umbrella of the Castro's government and coasting the isle, they approached the coast of the Miramar subdivision. The smaller boat, a Bertram about 31 feet long, reached about 200 meters from the coast. They were carrying one German cannon, bought with $375.00. 2 Belgian "Fals", and a 60 mm mortar among other small weapons. When the leader of the DRE Juan Manuel Salvat gave the order to fire they did so with all their hearts. Sixteen cannon shots were fired hitting a hotel where Russian soldiers were staying, another place that received some shells was the "Cuban

Institute of People's Friendship" where a Communist meeting was being held and other shots hit the "Charles Chaplin Theatre". All in total the shelling lasted 6 minutes and as a result of the shelling it became publicly known that Soviet troops were in Cuba. Castro escaped unhurt at one of the places shelled.

Participating in that heroic event were Juan Manuel Salvat, Bernabé Peña, José Basulto, Carlos Hernández, Isidro "Chilo" Borja, Leslie Nóbregas, Rodolfo Vidal, Luis Camos, Francisco Blanco, Lesmes Ruiz, Francisco G. Calviño, Lázaro Fariñas, Alfredo Fontanills, Luis Gutiérrez, Ignacio Arjona, . . . and others whose name the DRE never notified to its cells in Cuba due to security reasons.

After the shelling and the article in the front page of the New Orleans States-Item I became a celebrity among the Cubans in New Orleans. Unfortunately, I also became a celebrity to others. If my recollection is not wrong I believe that it was after this event that I received in Casa Roca the first visit of a FBI agent. This agent apparently was in charge of the Cuban affairs in New Orleans and his name was Warren C. De Brueys. Agent De Brueys was very interested in knowing the names of the other members of the DRE in New Orleans. When I explained to him that I was the Delegate and only member of the DRE in New Orleans, De Brueys didn't believed me. Agent De Brueys became irritated and told me that it would be easy for the FBI to infiltrate my Delegation and find out what they wanted. My response was: *"You are losing your time because I am the only member of the DRE in New Orleans. You can't infiltrate the Delegation because as I am the only one you would have to infiltrate me."* Unfortunately, De Brueys was the FBI man in New Orleans to deal with Cuban affairs.

During the approximately 20 months that the members of the 2506 Brigade were incarcerated in Cuba there were several proposals from the Castro's government to exchange them for food, medicines, tractors, etc. Castro as a real pirate, was requesting ransom for his captives. As well as he knows to do it Castro moved his pawns inside the United States and the exile community became divided in 2 groups. One group wanted the members of the Brigade to be able to return to their families after they had been betrayed by those who organized, armed and sent them to the Bay of Pigs. The second group did not want President Kennedy to deal with Castro. I was in group No.1.

My idea at the moment was the members of the Brigade were the best of the Cuban youth, that a crime had been committed against them with the betrayal, because of their bravery (fighting up to the last bullet) and their mastery of war (at the beginning they had defeated Castro's forces inflicting heavy casualties to them until they ran out of ammunition) they could be the ones who could unite the Cubans in exile to get Cuba free. In my opinion, President John F. Kennedy didn't have any other option but to rescue them. He had a moral obligation with them and with the Cuban people. I believed that Kennedy was going to rescue them and find a way to get rid of Castro.

During the October Missile Crisis I got in touch with the offices of the DRE in Miami.

They were very confident that Cuba was going to be invaded as per a letter dated October 26, 1962 that I received from Zoila Díaz explaining that if the invasion occur we, the DRE, was going to support the steps taken by the United States, mentioning that the new President of Cuba would be Dr. José Miró Cardona, this was reinforced by a telephone conversations that I had with Cubans friend of mine inside the DRE. I started preparing our return to Havana. We did not count with the "fetiches" referred later on by Guatemalan President Miguel Ydígoras Fuentes. Ydígoras and Kennedy called them "fetiches" but in the first part of the fifties they would have been called something else. Now we are aware of the influence and power that Castro has infiltrating US intelligence services and how he can manipulate US actions. One of the most recent examples is that of Ana Belen Montes, chief analyst of DIA (Defense Intelligence Agency) who was first in charge of El Salvador and Nicaragua and later of Cuba. Ana Belen Montes for 16 years was passing information to Cuba's intelligence and was responsible to illustrate the Pentagon about the Cuban situation, and finally on September 21, 2001 she was arrested. On October 16, 2002 she was sentenced to 25 years in jail. How many Ana Belen Montes were advising President John F. Kennedy during the Bay of Pigs? How many "fetiches" were advising him during the October Crisis?

Another great example is the case of the American couple formed by Walter Kendall Myers, a retired employee of the State Department and known by Cuban Intelligence as "Agent 202" and his wife Gwendolyn Steingraber Myers, known by Cuban Intelligence as "Agent 123" and/ or "Agent E-634". This couple, for three decades worked for Fidel Castro intelligence's service. This traitor couple even met privately with Fidel Castro in Cuba in 1995.[27]

Finally, the agreement to pay ransom to Castro was reached and on late December 1962, I took my Ford 1953 with my son Carlos, Jr., to Miami to receive my brother Juan who was going to be set free and return to the US. With us also traveled my nephew Rolando Peláez, Jr., and a friend Raúl Valdés Fonte, Jr.

I went to the Orange Bowl stadium on December 29, 1962. I took photos and filmed, with my 8 mm camera, part of the activities. I felt proud when I saw my brother Juan and many of my friends marching there. I heard John F. Kennedy promising to return the 2506 Brigade's flag to a Free Havana. I left convinced that President Kennedy was going to fulfill his promise. He had a debt of honor with History.

While there and by chance I encountered Carlos Elcoro, the same one who had been my roommate at the motel while we were waiting to be transferred to the training camps in Guatemala. To my surprise he told me that my nephew Jorge Medina Bringuier was very active with the DRE in Cuba. I felt some discomfort, I did not trusted my nephew.

Upon my return to New Orleans I wrote a letter to my friend Isidro (Chilo) Borja inquiring about Jorgito's position with the DRE. Chilo wrote me a letter on February 1, 1963 where he stated that he was going to talk next day either to José Antonio[28] or with the person in charge of intelligence but that he would write back to me as soon as he finds out.

The following letter from Chilo was a terrible one. He was telling me that unfortunately I have one of the most despicable nephews that a person could have. He ended the letter ratifying his friendship with me. That is how I learned of the betrayal of my nephew Jorge (Mongo) Medina Bringuier.

On March 24, 1963, I mailed the following letter to President John F. Kennedy.

---

[27] El Nuevo Herald, Miami, Fl. November 20, 2009.
[28] José Antonio González Lanuza.

"Honorable John F. Kennedy
White House Washington, D.C.

Dear Sir:

I have the honor to addressing this request to you, not as President of the United States, but as a citizen of this country.

I am aware that as President of the United States of America you cannot freely contribute financially to our cause, BUT AS AN AMERICAN CITIZEN YOU MAY EXPRESS YOUR SIMPATHIES WITHOUT THE LIMITATIONS OF YOUR OFFICE. And to this citizen, responsible for his family, as a husband and a father I, as husband and as father, appeal for your assistance in the name of the New Orleans Delegation of the Cuban Student Directorate, and in the name of our common struggle against Communism.

Respectfully yours,
Carlos Bringuier
New Orleans Delegate

On May 21, 1963 Ricardo Davis presented to me an offer in regard to a boat named "Linda Lee" which boat he claimed to have an option to buy for 24 months. According to Davis the "Linda Lee" was a cruiser of 32' equipped with two Chrysler motors 115 HP each able to reach a speed of 30 miles per hour and tanks of gasoline containing 150 gallons. Davis told me that the "Linda Lee" could be bought with $3,500. As Ricardo Davis was claiming that he was the Delegate in New Orleans of the Christian Democratic Movement, I wrote a letter to Miami asking them to confirm to me if that was true. I also advised the DRE that if Davis was not the Delegate of the CDM then the CDM should appoint Davis its Delegate and convince him to turn the boat over to them. I didn't want to be involved in any dealings with Davis because I didn't like him.

On May 20, 1963 we commemorated the anniversary of Cuba independence with a large gathering at Gallier Hall where we also honored newsman Robert J. Angers, Jr., of Franklin, Louisiana for his April 23 editorial "Come to Louisiana You Cuban Patriots". Speaking at the meeting were Frank Bartés (Cuban Revolutionary Council), Bob Angers, Ernesto Bascuas (Cuban Revolutionary Council), Dr. José Manuel Cuscó and Carlos Bringuier (Cuban Student Directorate-DRE).

Next day, The Times Picayune published an article about the event Apparently the liberal newspaper was giving us good publicity but the venom showed in the first paragraph where, quoting Frank Bartés it said: *"Cubans have the feeling that they have been sold out, not only by the American people but by the American government."* You will have to remember that the Editor of The Times Picayune was none other than Mr. George W. Healy, Jr., the same Editor who had invited Fidel Castro to the USA in 1959 to speak at the National Convention of Editors of USA newspapers. What in reality Bartés had said was: *"Cubans have the feeling that they have been sold out, not by the American people, but by the American government."*

That night we went to The Times Picayune to complain. We knew that the damage had been done and we requested a retraction and a correction from The Times Picayune. They obliged and a few days later they published a small correction notice. The original, changing Bartés words in a typical liberal trick was at the top of a page in a four columns article with a picture. The correction was lost in the middle of the paper.

The summer of 1963 was approaching to the Crescent City. It was going to be the most historic summer of the City of New Orleans. Meanwhile I kept working at Casa Roca, earning a modest salary to provide for my family but always confident that we would be returning to a free Cuba.

In July 1963, I wrote a letter to all the United States Senators in regard to the dangerous situation regarding Cuba. Many of the Senators answered sympathetically.

Chapter VIII

---◆◆◆---

Lee Harvey Oswald (August 1963)

It was a hot summer, the humidity made you remember the hot summers of Buenos Aires. Walking on the sidewalks Americans, with shorts or tight slacks and shirts of vivid colors, did not realize the tragedies that were weaving in the underground of the large cities.

In one of the streets of the French Quarter there were various Latin businesses, there on Decatur Street, Spanish speaking people could find a large diversity of Spanish names like "Habana Bar", "Las Americas Bar", "Copacabana Bar", "Casa La Marina Bar" and "Casa Roca".

The first names are of some of the bars with more Latin clientele or Americans looking for good Hispanic music. The last name "Casa Roca" was a small clothing store managed by 2 Cubans and in which historic incidents occurred of which I was a witness or participant.

In the evening of August 2, 1963, 2 Cuban youths entered into "Casa Roca" asking for the location of the office of the Directorio Revolucionario Estudiantil (DRE). Immediately I told them my name and informed them that I was the Delegate of the DRE in New Orleans asking them what they wanted and how could I help them.

When they heard my name they produced a sympathetic smile and explained that one of them was from Boston and the other one from Puerto Rico and that they had been recruited by the Christian Democratic Movement to take part in commando attacks against the regime of Fidel Castro. A few days before they had arrived at the training camp located across Lake Pontchartrain and they had started their training.

According to them, the military leader of the training camp was Commander Diego Paneque and the one in charge of the civilian part was a Cuban-American named Ricardo Davis. They explained that when they arrived at the camp they expected to be doing commando attacks pretty shortly but that the training camp was not functioning as expected.

One of their problems was circulating rumors that a Castro spy was inside the camp, who now they described as a young Cuban with oriental features and who previously had been a reporter. Then they explained that now they had left the camp and wanted to return to Miami because moral was very low at the camp due to the discovery of the spy and the camp would have to close down.

Realizing that they were out of money I decided to put them in a hotel room at the Silver Dollar Hotel located on Chartres Street. I believe that the charge was about $1.00 per room. I was going to try to raise the money to send them back to Miami.

My interest in getting them, as soon as possible, out of town and out of the eyes of the press was that around those days the FBI had discovered a large deposit of weapons a few miles away from where these Cubans said was located the training camp. The FBI had stated that the cache of weapons found was worth several thousand dollars and the raid had captured front-page coverage in the city newspapers. I was also aware that the FBI casually had found a load of explosive going to Miami when one of the cases fell open from the cargo truck that was transporting them. This was still secret but I had been informed by a customer that was passing by the place where the incident occurred and who saw the agents of the FBI arriving at the location of the discovery.

Worried about the bad public image that the liberal press could portrait of the Cubans in New Orleans I immediately contacted Ricardo Davis. Davis admitted about the training camp and he told me that some Americans financed it and he asked for my help to raise money to send all of them back to Miami suggesting that I contact Mrs. Elisa Cerniglia, Director of the Cuban Catholic Center, to see if the Center could pay for their transportation. Two problems arose. One, I did not want to involve Mrs. Cerniglia and the Cuban Catholic Center in the mess created by Davis, and second, I did not trust Davis. My thought at the moment was that Davis would be asking the sponsors of the training camp for the funds to transport his men to Miami and that he wanted the Cuban Catholic Center to pay for their transportation and in that way he could pocket the money received from his American sponsors. I told him what I thought and I refused to help him in that endeavor.

During our conversation Davis confirmed that they had discovered a spy from Castro inside the training camp. Later on I learned more about the spy when the Diario Las Americas[29] reported about it. I was *in God's hands* when I did not wanted to get involved with anything related to the Christian Democratic Movement's training camp. Before the defection of the 2 Cubans who had come to "Casa Roca" asking for help, I was unaware of the existence of the training camp. Luckily, I did not became involved in trying to relocate the rest of the commandos to Miami. I never visited or even knew exactly where the training camp was located. Years later, New Orleans District Attorney Jim Garrison would try to place me there. Other scavengers, idiots or pro-Communists had tried to do the same.

August 5, 1963 started as typical New Orleans summer day. We were at work in "Casa Roca" when Phillip Geraci, III, made his entrance with a young friend. Geraci had been before at the store talking about the Cuban situation and has showed sympathy to our cause. In one occasion when he asked how he could help us I had given him some bonds of the DRE. We were selling those bonds to raise money to be sent to the main office in Miami. Recently, Geraci had informed me that the New Orleans police had stopped him from selling more bonds. Now Geraci was visiting with a friend.

After a few minutes of conversation another person came into the store and started browsing around, finally he approached us an introduced himself as Lee Harvey Oswald. I did not had the slightest idea that this new person was the same one that on April 10, 1963 had attempted to assassinate General Edwin A. Walker in Dallas, Texas. Oswald was very interested in our conversation and he asked me for some literature against Castro. He mentioned that he had military experience and offered his services to train Cuban in guerrilla/commando activities.

I explained to Oswald that I did not have anything to do with military activities and emphasized to him that my only activities were

---

[29] Spanish newspaper from Miami, Fl.

around press and propaganda alerting the American people about the dangers of Communism. Oswald looked at my eyes and introducing his hand in his pocket said that he wanted to contribute economically. I told him that I could not accept his contribution because the police did not allowed us to sell bonds because we were lacking a permit from the city.

We were engaged in a conversation among the four of us for about one hour and then I had to leave the store to visit a ship. I left in one direction, Oswald, Geraci and the other youngster went in the other direction.

Next day, while I was peddling in the ships by the Mississippi river, Oswald showed up again at "Casa Roca". He had come to see me and when he found out that I was not there, he gave my brother-in-law Rolando, his "Guidebook for Marines" as a present for me. When I returned to the store Rolando gave me the Oswald's book and told me that Oswald looked like a nice person. I told Rolando that I did not knew what it was but that there was something about Oswald that I didn't like him. One of my concerns was the possibility of Oswald been an infiltrator sent by the FBI, as previously threatened by agent De Brueys or an infiltrator sent by the "New Orleans Council for Peaceful Alternatives."

Three days later, on August 9, 1963, a Friday, I was returning to "Casa Roca" to replace my brother-in-law in daily co-management of the store because he had a medical appointment. I had just parked my 1953 Ford at the first parking meter in the block. I came out of the car and just when I was going inside I saw a friend of mine, Celso Hernández, who had just turned the corner of Canal and Decatur streets. Celso was very agitated and he called me before I could go inside the store. We went inside and Celso informed me that while coming out of a Jackson Street bus on Canal Street, in front of a Walgreen Drugstore he had seen a young man in the sidewalk with a sign saying "Hands off Cuba" and another sign in Spanish with the words "Viva Fidel".

Celso had reacted in the only way he could at that moment. He did not speak good English. He insulted the young man in Spanish and frustrated because of his poor English he came looking for me to go with him to confront this man. There was a Cuban that I had found a job for him at a restaurant located at the corner of Canal and Decatur streets and I went there looking for him to join us. I came back to "Casa Roca" and with Celso, we waited there until this young man, Miguel Cruz, obtained permission to leave. When Miguel appeared at the store, I grabbed the sign that I had over there showing the Statue of Liberty stabbed at her back, closed the store because Rolando had already left for his medical appointment and we went out looking for the Communist.

By Canal Street we were watching both sidewalks trying to find the pro-Castro person. Celso was going by one sidewalk, Miguel and I by the other. We asked several newspaper vendors if they had seen the person. After several blocks we decided to take a streetcar trying to spot him but to no avail. Some of the passengers were surprised when they saw us with our big sign. As I had closed the store I decided to return there disappointed that we had not been able to confront the young Communist. Celso and Miguel returned with me and we stayed, for a few minutes, chatting about the incident. They left and after a few minutes Miguel Cruz came back running and saying that Celso had spotted the Communist again on Canal Street and was keeping an eye on him in case that he goes to another location. We found the Communist in the seven hundredth block of Canal Street, almost in front of "Ward's Discount House" where I had worked as a salesman.

I cannot relate to you the sensation that came over me when I recognized the face of the Communist young man with the signs in favor of Fidel Castro. It is difficult to explain the feeling that you suffer when you discover a traitor, it was a revolting feeling that creeps up to your mouth when at the same time your mind get cloudy when anger is taking over you.

On one side, it is the contempt felt against the despicable human being that is able to betray those who are risking their lives because of their love for Freedom and Justice. On the other hand, the anger, the desire to do justice with your own hands, the desire to get physically even when a lot of times this move us to do something that we will have to repent for later.

The young American who had the two signs: "Hands off Cuba" and "Viva Fidel" was the same one who just four days before had come to "Casa Roca", shook hands with me and offered his services to train Cubans to fight against Castro, the same one who had tried to obtain information about our activities.

As soon as Oswald recognized me I could see, just for a second, a sign of disgust in his face, but he immediately produced a smile and extended his right hand with the intention of shaking hands with me. Undoubtedly that person had great cold blood.

After his act of treason he was now smiling and offering his hand looking for a handshake resembling the kiss of traitor Judas. Naturally I rejected the hypocrite handshake.

What I did was to vent my fury rebuking him in English asking him how much lower he could go. I told Lee Harvey Oswald that he was a traitor and a Castro's agent.

Immediately Oswald refused to argue with me and proceeded to continue giving away some yellow flyers of the "Fair Play for Cuba Committee, New Orleans Chapter" and a little book entitled "The Crime Against Cuba", by Corliss Lamont in which the author make a merciless attack against President John F. Kennedy.

Now it was around 1:00 p.m., being a Friday on Canal Street the principal commercial artery in New Orleans, many people stop their walk and surrounded us to watch what was going on, principally due to my yelling of "traitor", "Communist" and "Castro's agent". Noting that there were more than 20 people watching us, I stopped insulting Oswald and addressed the watchers in an effort to try to gain them to our cause.

I told them how Oswald had come to my store, how he had tried to infiltrate the DRE, how he had offered his services to train anti-Castro Cubans just to find him now with a sign saying "Viva Fidel" and spreading Communist propaganda. I explained to them that Oswald was nothing else than a Communist and an agent of Fidel Castro. I told them that Oswald wanted them to suffer in the same way that the Cubans were suffering in Cuba and to send them and their children to the execution wall.

That was the first time that I accused Lee Harvey Oswald, publicly, of been a Communist and at that moment he did not refute the accusation neither presented a demand against me when there were more than twenty witnesses that heard me calling him a Communist.

My words were heard and caused an effect. Immediately the surrounding Americans started to shout at him: "traitor", "Communist", "go to Cuba", "kill him", "son of a bitch" and even more violent expressions. The situation was getting hotter by the minute. One of the Americans grabbed Oswald by one arm and pushed him. In that moment a policeman arrived, he used to patrol that area, and approaching me asked me to leave and to let Oswald carry his demonstration or we were going to be arrested. Through my mind came the vision of how easily the Communists could operate in this country while in the countries occupied by them they did not permit any kind of opposition. I remembered that there had been thousands of Americans dead by Communism; that there are people been killed by Communism in Laos, Viet Nam, China, the Soviet Union, Korea and Cuba. I thought that if the young Americans were sent to far-away lands to fight Communism, it was not good, to allow here that the Communists operate freely stabbing Democracy by it back. I told the policeman that unfortunately I could not comply with his request because I was not going to tolerate this Communist to continue demonstrating in Castro's favor. The policeman did not answer me and left to call the Police precinct and inform them of what was going on.

Celso was desperate because his English was not good, then suddenly he grabbed Oswald's hand full of yellow pamphlets from the "Fair Play for Cuba Committee", tore them, and threw them up into the air. I approached Oswald, took my glasses off, and was ready to punch him when he reacted in an unexpected way by putting down his arms, like an X, and told me *"OK Carlos if you want to hit me, hit me"*, placing his face in the proper position to receive my punch. His cold blood paralyzed my arm. I realized that he was delighted that I would hit him, because in that way he could present himself to the public opinion as a victim of an irrational anti-Castro henchman. I managed to contain myself and limited to continue verbally insulting him.

In that moment two police cars put the brakes on the street very close to us. During the altercation I noticed somebody filming part of it and afterward I was, erroneously, told by a young Cuban lady who worked in the area that it was a Venezuelan tourist staying at the Sheraton Charles Hotel.

The police told the group of people gathered there to move on and they placed us, Celso, Miguel and Oswald in one patrol car, I was put in the other car driven by a policeman and riding with us was Lieutenant Gaillot who explained to me that we were being brought to the First District of Police located on Rampart Street in order to be questioned. As soon as we arrived to our destination the four of us were put in the same room at one side of the office. Some policemen started to question Oswald about his activities. According to the information that I was able to gather the police had been looking for Oswald that day when somebody had called to report what he was doing but Oswald was doing his demonstration like a guerrilla, a few minutes in one place, disappearing and then reappearing a few minutes later in another place. During the time he was been questioned in the same room that we were Oswald was showing his cold blood.

Knowing that he was in an inferior position to me because his previous attempt to infiltrate the DRE delegation in New Orleans Oswald stated that he did not have anything against me, his target or the culprit of everything according to him was Celso, whom he accused of destroying his fliers. In that small room and in my presence he stated that he was the representative in New Orleans of the "Fair Play for Cuba Committee" expressing that it was a well-known organization with branches all over the United States, he stated that it was an organization looking for a better understanding among the United States and Cuba mentioning that the Executive Secretary was Mr. Vincent Theodore Lee.

Asked by the police if he was a Communist he answered evasively and then one of the policemen questioning him asked how, if he was not a Communist he was disseminating propaganda defending Castro, a Communist who want to destroy non-Communist countries including the United States of America. Oswald kept silent refusing to answer the question.

I remember that one policeman asked Oswald if he had a job. When Oswald answered that he had been working at a coffee company but that now he was unemployed, the policeman recriminated him saying that instead of doing pro-Castro demonstrations he should find a job to take care of his family.

Some policemen asked Oswald where his office was located because in the yellow flyers only appeared the name A.J. Hidell and a P.O. Box number. Oswald explained that the office was not a fix place because the meetings of his Committee were held in rotation among the members. The police asked Oswald the name of the other members and Oswald refused to answer in front of me because he didn't like that I would know the names of the other members of his organization.

At that moment we were moved to another room leaving Oswald along with his interrogators. Lieutenant Gaillot called me aside and apologized explaining that according to the law he did not have any other choice than charge us with disturbing the peace and that we will have to put a bond of $25.00 to be able to go free until we go to trial. I asked permission to place a phone call to my wife and it was granted. I explained to Pochi what was going on asking her to get in touch with the relatives of Celso and Miguel and to have my brother-in-law Rolando to bring the $25.00 for my bond.

As soon as I returned to the room where Celso and Miguel were waiting for me I could see how Oswald was being transferred to another room for the interrogation to be continued. We were moved to a cell in the First District of Police and put together with common criminals who were awaiting to be moved to other prisons. We did not receive any special treatment. We had to turn everything in our possession including our belts and eye glasses. Once this was done we were put inside a police wagon to go to the Department of Identification.

I do not recommend that ride to anybody. Inside the wagon there were only two benches laterally on each side and you do not have anything to hold on to. In view that the drivers of these vehicles are always in a hurry you have to become an octopus in order to arrive harmless. When we arrived we were put in a cell until the moment they made us climb a staircase that ended at an office where we were booked as disturbers of the peace.

One by one they took our fingerprints and our photo. My number was 112-726. In reality I have to admit that at this office all the employees expressed their sympathies to us giving words of encouragement that made us feel better. When this activity was done we were brought, down the stairs, to the cell and await for the wagon that was going to bring us back to the First District of Police. This cell was the nearest one to the front door and we could hear the commentaries of the other detainees who believed that we were there for crimes like theirs. It is difficult to describe how the lack of light and the coolness of these cells are really depressing. Sitting on a bench and looking through the iron bars we talked about how cruel would have to be the suffering of those incarcerated in Cuba who were languishing without a ray of hope, of those who live dying a little bit everyday losing their liberties and with their lives chop down without betraying their dignity and their love for our fatherland.

We commented how impressive was to see ourselves behind bars knowing that we will be free in a few hours. In those moments we paid tribute to all those jailed in Cuba while the exiles enjoy their freedom. I thought about the sufferings of my brother Juan during the 20 months jailed in Cuba thanks to the betrayal of the Bay of Pigs. I also remembered the good times that I had expend with my good friend Tony Copado then suffering a sentence of twenty years in jail because he preferred to remain been a Cuban and not a Soviet-lover-Communist. Only those who had suffered prison could understand the amount of thoughts that could come to your mind in just a few seconds. Finally, the jail man appeared with a hard face and opened our door bringing us back to the police wagon.

The trip back was not that bad. When I looked out by one of the windows and felt the fresh air invading my lungs it came to my mind the suffering of the ill-fated members of the 2506 Brigade who were hoarded in the back of a truck to be brought to Havana. They could not feel the air that I was inhaling at that moment. They had been 160 brave Cubans without ventilation. When their truck arrived to Havana many of them had died asphyxiated. At that moment I realized that our ride in the police wagon was not that bad.

When we returned to the First District of Police, waiting for us there was Orestes Peña, owner of the Havana Bar, to whom Rolando had given $50.00 to pay for the bonds of Celso and me. Miguel Cruz' father paid for Miguel's bond and each of us received a summons to appear on August 12 for a trial at the Second Municipal Court.

As we were leaving the First District of Police I felt satisfied because I had taken a stand against a defender of Fidel Castro but I had felt impressed by the cold blood demonstrated by Lee Harvey Oswald. I was worry about the plans that the "Fair Play for Cuba Committee", the "New Orleans Council for Peaceful Alternatives" and Lee Harvey Oswald could have for New Orleans.

That night of August 9, I received a phone call from Francis Bartés, who at that moment was the New Orleans Delegate of the Cuban Revolutionary Council and he was asking me to attend a meeting at the house of Dr. Agustín Guitart. At the reunion, which was attended by around 10 more Cubans, among them Ramiro Montalvo who was a veteran of the 2506 Brigade. At the meeting it was approved a motion to give us all their support, they would be sending a delegation to the trial in solidarity with us, and in case that we would have to pay a fine they would be asking the Cubans in New Orleans to pay our fines. Once more the Cubans were united in a common cause: fighting Communism. I want to express my gratitude to all those present that night in special to Francis Bartés who representing another organization in New Orleans gave prove of his honesty and solidarity.

After the incident with Oswald, and after we recovered our freedom several Cubans and Americans offered their help. As we did not knew the legal proceedings to follow I thought it would be better to contact an American lawyer to represent us.

I called Mr. Kent Courtney, director of the "Independent American" who I had met some months before and was very sympathetic to our cause. Mr. Courtney promised to look for a lawyer and he would be concerting a meeting with him.

On Monday August 12, 1963, after I opened the store I went to the National American Bank to make a deposit for "Casa Roca". When I finished with the teller I recognized a person in line. It was the newsman Bill Stuckey. Stuckey had been working for some time at the "New Orleans States-Item" where he wrote a column about Latin American affairs. He had been one of the newsmen who I talked to before the DRE raid on Havana harbor and in more than one occasion I had furnished him material for his articles, now he was associated with WDSU-Radio where he had a weekly Saturday program. The title of his program was "Latin American Listening Post".

I went to talk to Stuckey, while he waited in line, and explained what had happened on Friday making him aware that the trial was set for 1:00 p.m., and suggested to him that it could be in his best interest to make public what would happen there. When I departed Stuckey thanked me for the information and told me that he would try to give publicity to the incident.

At my return to "Casa Roca" I talked over the phone to Kent Courtney who informed me that I had an appointment with the lawyer at 12:00 noon. Courtney told me not to worry about the honorary because he, Courtney, would take care of any expenses involved in the case.

At 11:30 a.m., Celso, Miguel and I were ready at "Casa Roca". Exactly at 12:00 noon we entered the Law office located at room 919 at the Maison Blanche building. After introducing ourselves we discussed the case with the lawyer and we agreed to meet in front of the courtroom at 1:00 p.m.

It was 12:45 p.m., when Celso, Miguel and I arrived at the building occupied by the Second Municipal Court. After a few minutes, starting arriving the Cubans in solidarity with us, among them, Francis Bartés (from CRC) and Dr. Agustín Guitart (from Rescate Revolucionario[30]). We took the elevator and the group of Cubans took their seats while I stayed at the door waiting for our lawyer. A few minutes before 1:00 p.m., the door of the elevator opened up and Lee Harvey Oswald walked to meet justice. Without paying attention to me, Oswald looked around and directed his steps to the section where the people of black color were sitting. Even in those moments Oswald was trying to give points to the "Fair Play for Cuba Committee" and to his idol Fidel Castro. He was trying to gain sympathy among the color people for his Committee and the Cuban dictator. Once again he impressed me not as a "crazy" type of person but as a cold calculating Marxist trying to obtain adepts to his cause.

I felt bad, not for me, but for the black people. Already in Cuba the black people was suffering the oppression of the Communists, the government did not allow black people to leave Cuba under normal terms because they did not wanted that publicity against them. The only way that the colored Cubans had to leave Cuba was by escaping in boats.

Exactly at 1:00 p.m., the public rose to their feet as the Judge, Edwin A. Babylon, entered the room. To this moment our lawyer had not showed up and I was preoccupied because Celso and Miguel did not speak English and mine was very limited. Once the Judge sat down, I opened the door, walked in and sat down next to Frank Bartés waiting for our trial to be called. After the first or second trial, a young man with a movie camera sat down in the front row.

As soon as the case been tried finished the Judge called the young man and reminded him that in New Orleans it was not allowed to film inside the courtroom while a case is being judged. As soon as the young cameraman returned to his seat the Secretary started calling the new case, which was ours. The first ones to be called were the policemen who had intervene in the case. Next, the Secretary pronounced four names: Lee Harvey Oswald, Carlos Bringuier, Celso Hernández and Miguel Cruz. In that same order we stood horizontally in front of the Judge.

We were asked if we plead guilty or not guilty. The first one to answer was Oswald who pleaded guilty. Immediately I studied the situation, I realized that Oswald was not afraid of been convicted because for the

---

[30]   Revolutionary Rescue

Communists is a badge of honor to receive guilty sentences. Also, by pleading guilty, Oswald was avoiding to be interrogated and he could not satisfactorily explain how we had originally met. When the Judge asked the same question to us, the three of us, one by one stated: *"Not guilty"*.

When Lieutenant Gaillot was called to depose he stated that he was called about the altercation and that when he arrived he detained all of us but that he was not able to determine how the incident occurred. Then I was called to testify.

I explained to the Judge that due to the lack of knowledge of English language by my two companions I wanted to explain that my defense also cover them. My heart was pounding on my chest; I was aware that the result of the trial would be how the Judge would take my words. In my mind I prayed to God to help us and at that moment I was sure I was *in God's hands.*

Looking directly at the Judge's eyes I stated: *"You honor, I am really sorry to have to appear in front of this court but I am satisfied that I am not guilty of doing anything against the Peace of the City of New Orleans as, by mistake, are the charges against us."*

Then I proceeded to explain what happened during Oswald's visit to "Casa Roca" on August 5th, showing the Judge Oswald's "Guidebook for Marines" that he had given as a present to me and opening the book I told him that there was no doubt about the previous ownership of the Guidebook because it showed Oswald's name at the top of the first page. I am sure that this was the decisive moment of the trial. I explained that the one who started the incident was Oswald when he tried to infiltrate the Delegation of the DRE in New Orleans and that what happened later on Canal Street was only a result of the original act of Oswald's attempt to infiltrate my organization, because it would not have been so serious of an incident on Canal Street without Oswald's original activities against me.

In my mind I had prepared a longer defense but looking at the Judge's eyes I realized that he understood my point. With that in mind I finished our defense repeating to the Judge that we felt not guilty in regard to the incident on Canal Street and that the only guilty person in front of him was Lee Harvey Oswald who had admitted so when he declared himself: "Guilty as charged".

Before sentencing, the Judge recriminated Oswald for his activities, stated that the charges against the three Cubans were dismissed and finally the Judge declared Oswald guilty of the charges against him, disturbing the peace of the City of New Orleans, and fined him $10.00. To my knowledge it was the only fine ever imposed on the assassin of President John F. Kennedy and I feel proud of my defense and the role I took in the incident.

While we were leaving the courtroom we were congratulated by the Cubans who came in our support and who had appeared in solidarity with us. We had struck a solid punch against the "Fair Play for Cuba Committee". Lee Harvey Oswald had been defeated in a Court of Justice in his native country, a country that he was betraying. For the first and only time Oswald had been convicted in a United States court of law. There at the Second Municipal Court of New Orleans, were kept the facts of the case, facts distorted by Communist propaganda using, in some cases, useful idiots attempting to distort historical facts.

Johann Rush, cameraman from channel 6 (WDSU-TV) filmed us leaving the courtroom together with the Cubans who had attended in solidarity with us. Johann Rush's camera also captured the figure of Lee Harvey Oswald. I still remember when Lee Harvey Oswald looked at the camera, as a well-trained Marxist-Leninist, thinking that at least he was giving good publicity to the "Fair Play for Cuba Committee". When we got out I saw our lawyer. He excused himself for not appearing in time and congratulated us in our victory. That night, August 12, 1963, WDSU-TV showed to the people of New Orleans, for the first time, the face of the person who three months later would assassinate President John F. Kennedy, promoter of the "Alliance for Progress" and target of vicious attacks from dictator Fidel Castro. I would like to mention that on that day when I met Johann Rush our encounter was not a friendly one. I was angered because Rush was interviewing Oswald and we didn't want any publicity for Oswald or the "Fair Play for Cuba Committee". With the years Johann Rush had been proved as a professional, decent and honest human being.

On Tuesday August 13, I went to "Casa Roca" to earn my daily bread. But God had some other plans for me. While at "Casa Roca" I received a phone call from newsman Bill Stuckey who expressed interest in knowing the address of Lee Harvey Oswald. I located the affidavit of our arrest by the New Orleans police and gave the information to Stuckey. In the affidavit Oswald address appeared at 4907 Magazine Street. Bill thanked me and I was ready to hang up when I asked him why he wanted to learn Oswald's address. Bill explained that after our incident on Canal Street it would be good to interview Oswald in his program "Latin Listening Post". Oswald real address was 4905 ½ Magazine Street.

I expressed to Stuckey my disagreement. I could not understand how he was going to give publicity to a Communist when in the Communist countries they don't allow any opposition or disagreement. I thought that the interview planned by Stuckey would help Oswald to gain followers among the listeners. I explained those points to Stuckey to no avail. Stuckey offered to do an interview to me the Saturday following Oswald's appearance in order for me to refute Oswald's position. I explained to Stuckey that the ones listening to Oswald on a given Saturday would not necessarily be the same ones listening to me the following Saturday therefore, my suggestion was to do a debate. I figured that in that way, both of us could be able to present our points of view at the same time and I was sure that the truth was in my side. Stuckey told me he would think about my idea.

On August 13, 1963, two Cubans showed up at "Casa Roca". They were Francisco González and Félix Sánchez, both had escaped from Cuba in a little boat, rescued at sea, and brought to the port of Progreso, Mexico. They were now in New Orleans in their way to Miami and were asking for help. Sánchez was Negro and González was White.

Following the directions of my brain, not CIA directions, I called a Press Conference at "Casa Roca". It was going to be good for the black people of New Orleans to hear what a black Cuban had to say. Sánchez told at the Press Conference how he had been imprisoned in Cuba and how the Castro's propaganda that the Negroes support his regime was untrue. The Press Conference was a success. It was in TV that day and in the "Times Picayune" next day. I repeat, contrary to what Fabián Escalante, Jefferson Morley, Harold Weisberg, Mark Lane and others could write it was my idea because I never had received any help, order or directions from any FBI or CIA agents. I was concerned about CIA agents and my intuition was telling me that the CIA had been highly infiltrated by the KGB and Cuban Intelligence services. I was going to be proved right when in August 20, 1978 "Granma" the Cuban Official newspaper, published statements of "our two men in Mexico" during Oswald's trip there, now former CIA agents, James Wilcott and Philip Agee orchestrating a show to implicate the CIA in the assassination of President Kennedy. What strange coincidence that these two renegade

CIA agents were the ones in charge of the CIA in Mexico during Lee Harvey Oswald contacts there with Cuban Intelligence Services and a "wet"[31] expert of the KGB.

On August 15, 1963 I received the visit on "Casa Roca" of Mr. Joseph W, Orlesh, Secretary to Director of Finance, City of New Orleans. Mr. Orlesh had received an anonymous telephone tip to the effect that the Cuban Student Directorate and Carlos Bringuier, whose place of business was at "Casa Roca", 107 Decatur Street, were selling bonds for the purpose of raising funds to help people in Cuba free themselves from the Castro regime and organize military commandos to that effect. Mr. Orlesh stated to me what he had been informed. Later on, Orlesh stated that I told him this was not correct. Mr. Orlesh also stated that he cautioned me about my solicitation or selling bonds without securing a permit from the City and that as he left "Casa Roca" he gave me an application for a permit to solicit funds. This incident was recorded in a FBI memo of December 3, 1963 prepared by Special Agent John Lester Quigley. Copy of this memo is in my archives. Lee Harvey Oswald and the "Fair Play for Cuba Committee" were trying to hurt me and Directorio Revolucionario Estudiantil (DRE).

Next day, August 16, 1963, I have not received any answer from Stuckey when Oswald did something again. I had been absent from the store for several hours and when I returned Rolando gave me a message from Carlos Quiroga. According to Quiroga, Oswald had done another demonstration this time in front of the International Trade Mart located at the corner of Camp and Common streets. This time Oswald was with two other subjects. I went to the International Trade Mart but Oswald was gone. I searched the surrounding areas but could not find him. Some of Castro's moles had tried to implicate me in this incident, even one of them, Mr. Robert Tanenbaum, Deputy Counsel for the HSCA stated that I was the one who had called the press about this demonstration. They lie and lie but they can't succeed because it is plainly not true.

There is a FBI memo written on December 13, 1963 by Special Agent Richard E. Logan[32] in regard to an interview with Mr. Bern Rotman and I copy the memo:

---

[31] Assassinations.
[32] Copy of this memo is also in my archives.

"Mr. Bern Rotman, Senior News Editor, WDSU-TV, Channel 6, New Orleans, advised that LEE HARVEY OSWALD was in the television station around August 16, 1963, at which time he was interviewed both on television and radio. He said the only contact he had with OSWALD at this time was when OSWALD was introduced to him, as OSWALD was been given a short tour of the news office of this station.

Mr. ROTMAN stated that a short time later OSWALD called him on the telephone and stated he was going to picket again. OSWALD then asked Mr. ROTMAN what date he would like OSWALD to picket. Mr. ROTMAN advised OSWALD that he did not want OSWALD to picket and had no interest as to what date he did picket, but he said if OSWALD was going to picket, the News Bureau of Channel 6 would like to be made aware of it.

Mr. ROTMAN said that the above was the only contact he had with OSWALD and he did not know OSWALD considered him friendly enough that he could put his name in his address book.

Mr. ROTMAN said that when he was contacted by OSWALD on the telephone, OSWALD did not say where or when or whom he was going to picket."

Lee Harvey Oswald did not have time to call again the TV station, he had done so before his picketing of August 16 when according to his wife Marina, he had placed an anonymous call to the TV station letting them know of the forthcoming event[33]. But the event that was going to make him leave the city of New Orleans was not going to happen until August 21, 1963 when we debated on WDSU-Radio.

Later that day of August 16, Quiroga came to "Casa Roca" and showed me a flyer almost similar to the one Oswald had been distributing on August 9, but this time there was a little difference. On August 9 the flyer had the name "A. J. Hidell" and as address a P.O. Box #. Now the new flyer had the name "L. H. Oswald" and as address 4907 Magazine Street. The flyer was inviting the reader to join the New Orleans Delegation of the "Fair Play for Cuba Committee" and was offering

---

[33] Marina and Lee, by Priscilla Johnson McMillan, page 351.

free literature. As the flyer also said "Everyone welcome" we decide to do so. Quiroga proposed to go himself to Oswald's house, posing as a non-refugee Cuban resident in the USA and sympathizer of Fidel Castro trying to find out what exactly was going on in Cuba in order to be able to defend Fidel Castro.

After discussing the risk that Quiroga was taking, due to the fact that he still had relatives in Cuba (I believe that at the time his father was in jail there), I accepted Quiroga's offer. That same evening Quiroga was paying back to Oswald and the "Fair Play for Cuba Committee" what Oswald had done before trying to infiltrate the Delegation of the DRE in New Orleans. During this time I was the only member of the Delegation of the DRE in New Orleans.

None of them: Carlos Quiroga, Celso Hernández or Miguel Cruz were, at the time, members of the DRE. My friend Celso was the only one that later became a member taking the position of "Secretary" of the Delegation.

When Quiroga arrived to the number 4907 Magazine Street he was surprised when he was told that Lee Harvey Oswald did not resided there. Quiroga showed to the lady who had opened the door the flyer showing that address. The lady, who appeared to be discomforted with the situation, told Quiroga that Oswald was living by the side of the house with the number 4905 ½.

Carlos Quiroga was received by Oswald who was distrustful because of the Latin aspect of Quiroga.

As follow was the conversation among Carlos Quiroga and Lee Harvey Oswald as told to me by Quiroga that night of August 16, 1963:

Oswald: We can talk but please don't hit me.
Quiroga: I am not here to hit you. I am interested in the "Fair Play for Cuba Committee" because I found this flyer on the street.

Quiroga proceeded to show Oswald the flyer, Oswald smiled and opened the door of the porch allowing Quiroga to enter the porch of the house.

Oswald: Are you Cuban?

Quiroga: Yes, I am Cuban. Some years ago, while a child, I came with my parents who now are deceased and I am married to an American lady.

Now sitting in the porch they continued the conversation but something happened that alerted Quiroga. Oswald's daughter, who had been playing and was dirty and without shoes, made her appearance and Oswald talked to her in a language that Quiroga did not understand. Oswald grabbed the child like a potato sack and put her inside the house.

Quiroga: Do you speak other languages?
Oswald: Yes.
Quiroga: Is that Russian?
Oswald: Yes, I speak Russian because I am learning it at Tulane University.

Quiroga: What do you think about those Cubans who had the problem with you? They did that because they do not know what they are doing and they are imperialists.
Oswald: Those Cubans are criminals. Imagine the type of laws that we have in this country that I was accused and fined in $10.00 and they were absolved at the trial.
Quiroga: What are your plans, the plans of the "Fair Play for Cuba Committee" in relation to the Cuban situation?
Oswald: Due to the imperialist propaganda, Fidel Castro is accused as a criminal. But in reality the vast majority of the population there is in favor of Fidel Castro and there is only a thin minority that do not adjust themselves to the new Socialist-Marxist system. Those who do not like the Cuban system should go out. Therefore that is why we have here a group of exiles, because they are criminals.
Quiroga: Right, I do not believe Fidel Castro is a dictator because all the population is with him.
Oswald: Clearly, Fidel Castro is not a dictator. What happen is that when there is a drastic change there have to be a little repression but as all Cubans are working voluntarily for the government Cuba soon will be reconstructed.
Quiroga: What do you think about the food and the standard of life in Cuba?

Oswald: Always when there is a change of system you will see rationing of food, clothing and other things.

Quiroga: What is your program with the "Fair Play for Cuba Committee"?

Oswald: What we are looking for is that the United States does not invade Cuba. In case that the invasion happens then I would defend Fidel Castro because no government has the right to invade another, no matter the fact if Fidel is or is not Communist. I am not against that Cubans, without the help of foreign governments with weapons, munitions and men invade Cuba.

Quiroga: How could the Cubans, without foreign aid, attack Fidel Castro?

Oswald kept silent.

Quiroga: Why is that the "Fair Play for Cuba Committee" is sometimes considered a Communist organization?

Oswald: The "Fair Play for Cuba Committee" is not a Communist movement and because we are a minority in the United States the press is against us, but one day we will be majority and the press will be ours.

Oswald proceeded to give Quiroga a green booklet entitled: "The Crime Against Cuba", by Corliss Lamont and a form to join the New Orleans Delegation of the "Fair Play for Cuba Committee" telling Quiroga he was proud of Quiroga joining the FPFCC and that as soon as everything required was met, Quiroga would be able to attend the meetings that the FPFCC regularly held in different houses of the other members of the organization.

Before they said good bye Oswald still had time to express his disappointment with some right wing governments in Latin America and he showed profound aversion against the Somoza family. They departed in a friendly way and Quiroga assured Oswald that he will be filling the application and he will return it to him as soon as possible.

Quiroga informed me of everything that transpired of his encounter with Lee Harvey Oswald. Immediately we tried to investigate who Lee Harvey Oswald was.

At "Casa Roca" the telephone rang and when I answered I recognized Bill Stuckey's voice. According to Bill, Oswald had accepted the radio debate and it had been scheduled for Wednesday August 21 at 6:00 p.m., at WDSU-Radio in the program "Conversation Carte Blanche". Stuckey also informed me that in the debate was going to be the moderator of that program, Bill Slatter.

GUIDEBOOK
for
MARINES

Fifth Revised Edition
First Printing
JANUARY 1, 1956

PUBLISHED BY THE LEATHERNECK ASSOCIATION, INC.
WASHINGTON, D. C.

129

AFFIDAVIT

PAUL DEGRA
DESK SERGEANT

State of Louisiana, City of New Orleans, Parish of Orleans

Second MUNICIPAL COURT, SECTION

THE CITY OF NEW ORLEANS, LA.
versus

1. Lee H. OSWALD, W., age 23
   4907 Magazine St., NO, La.

2. Carlos J. BRINGUIER, W., age 29
   501 Adele St., Apt. F, NO, La.

3. Celso A. HERNANDEZ, W., age 47
   519 Adele St., Apt. E, NO, La.

4. Miguel M. CRUZ, W., age 18
   3526 Magent St., Apt. C, NO, La.

Personally appeared before me, the undersigned

Judge of the Second Municipal Court of the City of New Orleans, duly commissioned and sworn.

Lt. Wm. Gaillot
Ptm. J. Wilson
Ptm. K. Heyward
1st Dist.

who having been duly sworn, doth depose and say:

That on Friday the 9th day of August 19 63 , at about 4:15 o'clock P M., on 700 Blk. Canal St. Street, between

and Streets, within the jurisdiction of this Court, one

Lee H. Oswald, Carlos J. Bringuier, Celso A. Hernandez and Miguel M. Cruz...

did then and there wilfully violate Ordinance No. 828 MCS Section 42-37 relative to

Disturbing the peace by creating a Scene...

All against the peace and dignity of the City of New Orleans.

Wherefore the deponent charges the accused with violating Ordinance No. 828 MCS Section No. 42-42

and prays that they be arrested and dealt with according to law.

Sworn to and subscribed before me, this
_____day of_____19____

_____
Judge.

Color	Age	Male	Female	Where Employed	Address of Employer

Time Paroled_____ By Whom Paroled_____For_____

NOTICE TO PRISONER:—You must appear in Second Municipal Court, 501 North Rampart St.,
1:00 P. M., Aug. 1 63 19____, without fail under penalty of fine and imprisonment.

FORM H. Q. No. 1

130

After a few minutes I received a call from Manuel Gil, Production Chief of INCA[34] who, to my surprise, told me that I would have another companion at the debate. According to Gil, Stuckey had invited Edward S. Butler, Executive Vice-President of INCA to also appear in the debate to refute Oswald's points of view. I concerted a meeting with Butler to coordinate our attack.

I was glad with the news because it solved two points: the language barrier and the nationality. I did not dominate the English language but now I would have the support of Butler in case of linguistic failures on my part. Also and the most worrisome to me was the fact that Oswald was American and I was Cuban and I was concern that Oswald could try to bring the debate to two points of views, the American and the Cuban. In that way he would gain support of people listening because he was American and I was a foreigner. Now, with Butler presence at the debate, that worry was put aside. Now there would be an American defending Dictator Fidel Castro and one American and one Cuban attacking Castro.

Getting close to the debate we held a meeting at INCA's office. With me was Carlos Quiroga who had informed me that Stuckey had interviewed Oswald in his radio program "Latin Listening Post", something that I was unaware of. There, at INCA's office Quiroga narrated to Butler his conversation with Oswald on August 16 and the fact that Oswald spoke in Russian to the daughter. When we left, Butler was in charge of obtaining more detailed information about Lee Harvey Oswald. On my part I wrote to the DRE in Miami asking for help with information about Lee Harvey Oswald and the "Fair Play for Cuba Committee".

On August 21, I had not receive an answer from the Miami office of the DRE and I decided to prepare my part attacking Communism in Cuba and not against Oswald or the FPFCC. Just in case I brought with me the "Guidebook for Marines" (Oswald's present to me). About 5:30 p.m., I arrived at WDSU-Radio located at 520 Royal Street in the New Orleans French Quarter.

At the lobby, waiting were Bill Stuckey and Lee Harvey Oswald. Stuckey rose from his seat and greeted me, afterward he signaled to

---

[34] Information Council of the Americas.

Oswald who also stood, and politely we shook hands. When Oswald sat down again I could notice that he was attired in a clean way with a suit and a tie. Unfortunately for him his suit was not the most convenient for the August weather in New Orleans. It was a very thick suit which later on I figured he had bought in the Soviet Union.

While we were sitting waiting for Butler I was chatting with Stuckey who, after a few minutes, excused himself going inside the studios to find out exactly in which one the debate was going to happen.

Taking advantage that Stuckey had left I decided to initiate a conversation with Oswald and told him: *"Listen Mr. Oswald, I would like to make clear to you that no matter the fact of our previous problems and our ideological differences I do not feel any personal rancor against you."*

Oswald nodded his head in agreement and with a smirk. My goal all of my adult life had been to convert a Communist and make him fight against that ideology, and looking at him I decided to try to do that and I said: *"I want you to remember that Communism is trying to destroy western nations and principally the United States, like they are doing against the institution of families. It could be that you, in good faith, are wrong, because as an American and as a father you should be opposing Communist ideas. If that is the case, and one day when you go to bed, when you rest your head over the pillow, you start to think that you could do something good for your Fatherland, for your family and for yourself, I would like you to know that you can come to me because, I repeat to you, I don't have nothing personal against you and I would receive you with open arms."*

Lee Harvey Oswald's response, with a smirk in his face, was: *"I am sure that I am in the right side and you in the wrong one and I know that what I am doing is right and what I would do will be the best."*

Immediately after that Oswald asked me about the 2 Cubans that I had presented on TV and in the newspapers on August 13 saying that it showed that we had a coordinated web and Oswald ended recommending me not to organize any invasion based on the "Guidebook for Marines" that he had gifted me, saying that it was obsolete and I could get killed.

After a few minutes Butler showed up and greeted both of us. It is possible that Bill Stuckey could have reappeared during our conversation because he mentioned it in his depositions. Stuckey brought us to the studio where the debate was going to start, a debate that many people had recommended me not to go but a debate that was going to destroy the figure of Lee Harvey Oswald and the "Fair Play for Cuba Committee" in New Orleans.

When we were introduced and the debate started I immediately realized that Stuckey and Butler had found damaging information against Oswald. Neither Stuckey nor Butler had given me any advance notice of what they had discovered. I realized that they had better weapons than me and I limited myself to two interventions during the debate. This is a lesson that many anti-Communists do not practice. When we have a common enemy we should not be blinded by our ego taking a personalized or individualized attitude. Our mission is to destroy our enemy, no matter who do it, and when we realize that somebody else has better weapons, we should let that person do the job.

Butler and Stuckey made public Lee Harvey Oswald's trip to the Soviet Union where he tried to become a citizen of that country. I was watching Oswald's face become redder and redder. He was devastated. I was surprised because, until that moment, I was unaware of the damaging information.

Almost at the end of the program I asked Oswald my second and last question:

Bringuier: *"Do you agree with Fidel Castro when in his last speech of July 26th of this year he qualified President John F. Kennedy, of the United States, as a ruffian and a thief? Do you agree with Mr. Castro?*

Oswald: *"I would not agree with that particular wording. However I and the er Fair Play for Cuba Committee does think that the United States government, through certain agencies mainly the State Department and the CIA has made monumental mistakes in its relations with Cuba. Mistakes which are pushing Cuba into the sphere of activity of let's say very dogmatic country such as China is."*

I do not have any doubts that I was *in God's hands* when I asked Oswald that question. It was the only time in Oswald's life, previous to the assassination of JFK, that Oswald had been asked a question about President John F. Kennedy. He used his Marxist rhetoric but he blasted Kennedy when he was attacking actions taken by the United

States government while President John F. Kennedy was the head of that government.

As soon as the debate ended I felt elated and I left the radio station in company of Ed Butler and his younger brother. As Butler showed to me a Press Release that he had prepared I thought that as Delegate of the DRE in New Orleans it would be good if I would do the same.

When I arrived to "Casa Roca", Quiroga was already there waiting for me. We exchanged views about the debate and Quiroga assured me that it has been a complete victory for us. From "Casa Roca" we went to my apartment where I wrote the Press Release in my limited English, hoping it would be well received by the New Orleans press. As it was night time we went to Quiroga's place of work where we made photocopies of the original document in order to give one copy to each of the news departments that we were going to visit. That night of August 21, 1963, we delivered them to United Press International, WDSU-Radio and TV, WWL Television, Times Picayune and the New Orleans States-Item. In the press release I related what transpired during the debate and at the end I wrote:

> ". . . we are proud as Cubans, that another time we discovered a Castro agent, an agent of those ideologies against which thousands of young Americans had been dying fighting in Korea, Laos, Viet-Nam and more recently in Korea another time, trying to preserve freedom and democracie (sic) in the world.
>
> We, Cubans who want to regain our freedom in Cuba, and at the same time protect your freedom, ask you Americans for four things:

1) *Help us destroy Communism in Cuba.*
2) *Write to your Congressmen asking for a full investigation on Lee Harvey Oswald a confessed<Marxist>.*
3) *Help those organizations like <INCA> directed by Mr. Edward Butler, whose lives are dedicated to fight Communism all over the world and especially in Latin America.*
4) *Be alert about the Communist infiltration in this Country, because Khrushchev (sic) said <I will bury you>.*

New Orleans, August 21, 1963
Carlos Bringuier
New Orleans Delegate
Cuban Student Directorate

The press ignored my Press Release but three months later they would be running after me to interview me.

On August 22, one day after the debate, I finally received an answer from the Miami office of the DRE. It was letter dated August 21st and signed by José Antonio Lanuza. It reads as follows:

Miami, August 21, 1963.

Dear Carlos:

> *I regret that I don't have enough information to help you in your debate with the people from the FPFCC. If you would have given me 72 hours you would have at your disposition all the information that you would like because we have very good relations with the Sub-Committee on Internal Security of the Senate which is who had been trying to obtain the proscription of the Fair Play.*

> *If at any other time an opportunity like this comes to you let me know ahead of time and above all never accept public debates without been prepared.*

> *The above mentioned Sub-Committee have a brochure entitled "Castr's (sic) network in the USA" (Fair Play for Cuba Committee) xxxxx part I dated February 14, 1963 in which appear the testimony of Vincent Theodore Lee, President of FPFCC.*

> *According to this brochure this person was in Cuba for the celebrations of the last January 1st. He spoke from the tribune and he even went to pick up rice with the "voluntary" workers.*

> *In his under oath deposition to the Sub-Committee this person invoked his rights under the % (sic) Ammendment (sic) almost two hundred times, including to some questions like if he was a member or if at any time he had been a member of the Communist Party.*

This person is in close contact with the Cuban Mission to the UN through the third secretary and he received orders and money from that embassy to promote demonstrations in favor of Presid. Dorticos when he visited the UN in October 1962.

The office of the FPFCC is located in the same building of the Communist Party (709 Broadway, NY).

At the Lee hearings in front of the Sub-Committee it was demonstrated that the Fair Play received money from the Castro government at least to start functioning and that the demonstrations and piquet carried on by this committee had been financed and directed from Cuba.

Lee was the leader of the Fair Play in Tampa until December, 1961. He participated in the disturbances of November 27, 1961 at the act convened by the DRE and Conte Agüero to honor the execution of students by Spain. At the trial of Lee it was proved that he offered money to several Cubans believing they were pro-Castro. In Bohemia magazine from Cuba dated January 2 of this year appear an interview of Lee with the renegade black American Robert Williams and his son. This person stated: Someday together we will win" regarding the FP and the Cuba regime.

On September 30, 1962 Lee went to Toronto, Canada where he got together with Julio Medina, ex-President of the July 26 (actually, in this country, it is considered as a Communist organization). This person, Medina, had to flight from NY to Toronto. There, at the meeting at the Walker House Hotel he received the first instructions for the demonstrations to be carried on at the UN. From this hotel they went to the house of Jose Nunez Tejero, Otelio Sanchez's uncle, who is the Attaché to the Cuban mission to the UN. Present at this meeting was Antonio Sueiro who had been captured in NY with orders, weapons and explosives to start a wave of sabotages in NY during last Christmas season. Sueiro at this moment is in Cuab (sic) for the exchange with "Pancho the Hook" and some others, among them him, for some prisoners in Cuban jails. This was in Dec/62. At that meeting orders were given by Gilberto Mediavilla, third secretary of the Cuban mission.

The demonstrations at the UN were on October 8 and the last meeting with Mediavilla was on October 4, 62.

OK Carlos this is it, good luck, and write me to inform how everything went. If you can, take pictures for Trinchera[35]. At another day contact me with more time.

An embrace,
Jose Antonio

The letter arrived on August 22, a day after the debate and too late for any useful information to be used on that date. On August 24, I answered José Antonio Lanuza with the following letter:

New Orleans, August 24, 1963
Mr. José Antonio Lanuza
Directorio Revolucionario Estudiantil
P.O. Box 805
Miami, Fla.

Dear José Antonio:

Unfortunately I received your letter the day after the debate, but we have to feel good because I can assure you that the Traitor Lee H. Oswald (the same one who tried to infiltrate the DRE here) left in such bad shape that most probably he would have to be transferred to another city by his organization.

The program was presented on WDSU-Radio which is the station with more audience here. We were there, the Traitor Lee H. Oswald for the Fair Play for Cuba Committee, Edward Butler for INCA (Information Council of the Americas) which is an organization that distributes in Latin America Truth Tapes against Communism. The radio moderator was Bill Stuckey who presented the program very well, and I was there as Delegate in New Orleans of DRE.

At the beginning of the program I asked Traitor Oswald to clarify the name of the organization he was representing there,

---

[35] Newspaper of the DRE.

*because I have misunderstood and was in doubt if it was "Fair
Play for Cuba Committee" or "Fair Play for Russia Committee",
hearing that he smiled and replied it was not necessary to
answer that because it was known that it was FPFCC, to that
I answered that I was suggesting him to change the name to
"Fair Play for Russia Committee", because before Fidel Castro,
Cuba had a standard of living above Russia and then I proceed
to compare, with statistics, both countries and that Fidel Castro
and Communism had destroyed everything. I spoke now, before
we were selling our sugar to the USA in the American market
showing the advantage it represented for the Cuban people and
how, now, Cuba sells sugar to Russia at the prices of the world
market, showing the difference in price, and that Russia was
paying 80% with weapons and machinery and only 20% in
dollars and the Cubans who were escaping daily from Cuba
would neither admit nor permit that he would claim to be there
as defender of the Cuban People and that the only thing that he
could defend there is a Russian colony.*

*After that, Ed Butler completely destroyed him showing proof
that Oswald had traveled to Russia in 1959 where he stayed until
1962 which was the year he returned here. How in 1959, Oswald
had brought his passport to the American Consulate in Moscow
resigning his American citizenship and obtaining the Russian
citizenship[36], his friendship with the Soviet Secretary of Foreign
Relations with whom he lived for two months in his own house[37]
This Oswald looked like a light bulb because his head became
completely red (like a typical Communist) and was not able to
defend himself. After a question from newsman Stuckey, Oswald
confessed to be a MARXIST. Later on he tried to explain that the
political view of the FPFCC is to obtain a better understanding
in the Cuban-American relations but I interrupted him asking
how that could be believed when so recently, Fidel Castro the
man who he represents, in his speech of July 26, 1963 qualified
President John F. Kennedy as a ruffian and as a thief and that
I was inquiring from him if he was in solidarity with that*

---

[36] In my faulty English I understood that but apparently it was not accurate.
[37] Another understanding due to my poor English.

qualification that Castro had made of Kennedy, and he answered that it was politics and that you could not believe those positions.

Oswald never was able to take the offensive because when we asked a question it was a question that answered itself and he didn't had a chance to do demagoguery politics. I repeat to you that is the opinion, inclusive of some Cubans and Americans that didn't like the idea of the debate with a Communist, that this guy had been totally destroyed.

Just in case, I am preparing a demonstration of Cubans together with another Cuban, Carlos Quiroga, who had shown very much interest in all of this and whom I know from Belen.

What I plant to do is invade the city with propaganda clarifying to the people who are the Fair Play and moving the public opinion in the city against the Fair Play, in that way the next time that they show up in the streets it would be the Americans the ones who will force them to retreat.

I have been promised a tape of the debate and as soon as I have it I will be sending one to you after I make a copy in that way you can enjoy it. I believe you should inform the Committee of Internal Security of the Senate of everything that happened here, of the attempt of espionage of Oswald in favor of Castro and his confession as a Marxist.

Ok Jose Antonio, don't worry that the DRE never looks bad, ah and if I accepted the debate was not because it was proposed to me but because I was the one who proposed it, because if not they were going only to interview Oswald, but realizing that WDSU wanted to do something I proposed the debate in order to be able to answer the lies of the Communists, as you see it came out well. Here the newspapers have not published anything about the incidents because according to them they don't want to give publicity to the FPFCC but I have the feeling that if the incidents would have been favorable to Fidel, those newspapers (it is a monopoly) would give them publicity.

My premonition became accurate. In a few days Lee Harvey Oswald left the city of New Orleans and went to Dallas for his final rendezvous with John Fitzgerald Kennedy. I learned about his departure because FBI Agent Warren C. De Brueys was passing by the sidewalk in front of "Casa Roca" and I asked him if he was investigating Oswald and he replied that Oswald had left the city.

In the meantime in the State of Florida, other things were happening related to our story. The Christian Democratic Movement had presented to the FBI in Miami, a Cuban named Fernando Fernández Bárcenas, accusing him of being a spy from Fidel Castro. This same person was the spy discovered at the training camp across Lake Pontchartrain.

On September 4, 1963, it was reported in the Miami press that the office of the Federal Bureau of Investigations was questioning a Cuban Communist "confessed spy". In those reports it was stated that Fernández affirmed that the espionage and subversive activities in all Latin America were been directed by the Cuban Ambassadors at the United Nations and Brazil.

According to published information, Fernando Fernández, a young exiled Cuban reporter, had made a "complete confession" of his espionage activities in a tape recording given to Christian Democratic Movement directed by Laureano Batista (no relationship to Fulgencio Batista).

In the taped statement, Fernández say that the organization that is active in Venezuela by the name of "National Forces of Liberation" are receiving weapons from Mexico and Cuba, these weapons been transferred at high seas. He continued stating that the web of subversion and espionage expand from the United States to the Bahamas until the far away south cone of South America. He pointed as leaders of the Web of Subversion and Espionage, Cuban Ambassador Carlos Lechuga who until recently was in Mexico and now is Chief of the Cuban Delegation to the United Nations; according to Fernández another of the leaders is Raúl Roa Kourí, Cuban Ambassador to Brazil and son of the Cuban Secretary of Foreign Relations. Fernández also stated that the person in charge of the south cone of South America is a reporter, José Rodríguez Méndez, Cultural Attaché to Brazil. In the recording, Fernández admitted that one of his duties is to investigate activities of Cuban exiles in Central America.

In the reports coming from Miami it is mentioned the letter intercepted in New Orleans addressed from spy Fernández Bárcenas to Lechuga, then Cuban Ambassador to Mexico. In one of the paragraphs the letter stated: *"I am circumstantially infiltrated in a commando group who is receiving training to carry a big operation against Cuba. I have more detailed information about the military plan. The attack is imminent and would be launched from Central America."*

In another paragraph the spy warns Lechuga: *". . . it is vital, from now, to August 8 you maintain alert."*

In the recording, Fernández named two associates of Lechuga in Mexico. One of them a Venezuelan, Hendel Cruzal, who he identifies as taking care of supplies of the terrorist organization <National Liberation Front>. The other is a Mexican, Osvaldo Anaya. He asserted that from Mexico weapons are delivered to the Venezuelan terrorists. According to him the weapons are brought in small Cuban fishing boats until they reach the high seas where they are transferred to Venezuelan boats.

Fernández assured that he arrived to the United States on January 11, 1961 but that he did not became involved with the web of espionage until last year when he was recruited in Kansas City, Missouri.

The Miami office of the FBI let Fernando Fernández Bárcenas free, alleging that it was not a crime that agents of Fidel Castro spy against Cuban exile groups because it is only illegal to spy against the United States and not against Cuban exiles that are violating neutrality laws of this country.

Fernández repudiated the recordings stating that they were taken under pressure, threats and torture stating that he is neither anti-American nor anti-Castro. He expressed that his most pressuring desire is to return to Cuba. He admitted writing the letter to Lechuga.

One thing that came to my mind with this incident is that, to my knowledge, in the New Orleans area never existed an anti-Castro training camp until the one established by the Christian Democratic Movement. At the same time that the spy is inside the training camp and in contact with Carlos Lechuga, Lee Harvey Oswald, a member of the "Fair Play for Cuba Committee" (which was founded with money given by Fidel Castro trough Carlos Lechuga and Raúl Roa Kourí), approached me offering his services as an ex-Marine and expert on guerrilla warfare to "train Cubans to fight against Fidel Castro"[38].

It is very hard to swallow this as a coincidence. I believe that in the middle of all of this was the Cuban Embassy in Mexico City. It was to that Embassy where the spy Fernando Fernández Bárcenas addressed his

---

[38] Diario Las Americas, Miami, Fl., December 4, 1963, front page.

letter. It was there the place where Lee Harvey Oswald went visiting after he left New Orleans, short time before the assassination in Dallas. This shows how Fidel Castro has spies in all countries, from Argentina to the United States, more recently here, the Wasp Web and the case of Ana Belen Montes.

A few days after the debate we held a meeting of Cubans at the home of Dr. Enriqueta Artze de Ibáñez, New Orleans Delegate of the Cuban Magisterial Directorate. I took the opportunity to propose launching a publicity campaign in the streets of New Orleans to unmask Lee Harvey Oswald and the "Fair Play for Cuba Committee". It was going to be made as an "Open Letter to the Citizens of New Orleans" and would be signed by all representatives of the different anti-Castro organizations in the City. I want to make clear, another time, that this was my own idea, I did not received any instructions, orders or any directions from the FBI, CIA or any other intelligence agency of the United States, contrary to what some distorters of the truth keeps spreading presenting me as an "agent", "operative" or whatever they want to call me.

At the meeting I was authorized to obtain quotes for the cost of impression of the flyers and it was estimated that the best day to do it would be from August 31 to September 7. Frank Bartés and I would be aboard a small airplane and we would drop the flyers over the city of New Orleans. This was feasible due to Bartés being a pilot. In the meantime different teams of Cubans would be stationed at the most centric streets in the downtown area passing out flyers to the people in the streets.

The first place that I visited was "Standard Printing Company" located at 424 Poydras Street. On August 27, I received the quotes from them. Then I went to "Pelican Printing Company", owned by my friend Kent Courtney, who after a few minutes gave me another quote.

But it was meant that this activity never would take place. Before I ordered the printing of the flyers I went to City Hall to see if there was any local regulation forbidden what we had in mind. After looking at the flyer, the person who took care of me informed that they were larger than the ones permitted: 3 ½" x 5 ½". That ruined our plans. I knew that the police was unwilling to act against us but we had to be careful with the Communists because if we do what we were planning they will raise hell against us. Another thing that influenced our decision to cancel the plan was that it involved a lot of papers. New Orleans was a city prone to fires and we did not want to put in jeopardy the citizens of New

Orleans. A few days after the assassination of President Kennedy, during a visit to Lieutenant Martello he told me that whoever gave me the original information at City Hall was wrong, that the size permitted was 8" x 11", like the one in our "Open Letter to the Citizens of New Orleans".

On August 29, 1963 the Cubans in New Orleans continued our work and in that day we send the following document to the President of the Human Rights Commission of the Organization of American States (OAS).

Honorable President of the Human Rights Commission
Organization of American States Washington D.C.
Your Excellency Mister President:

The Cubans in exile in the City of New Orleans, profoundly concerned because of the continuous and reiterated violations of the most elemental Human Rights, not against some groups but against a whole Country, been committed by the Communist Tyranny that usurp the power in Cuba, we ask this Human Rights Commission, with all due respect, to formulate our most strong protest in relation to the last public event that unmask, once again, the inhuman character of Fidel Castro dictatorship: The kidnapping, in the afternoon of August 13 of this year, at Anguila Key of 19 Cubans, who without committing any crime only were looking forward to escape from their Country, leaving all possessions behind them, only not to be massacred in the blood orgies with which International Communism is trying to drown the yearning of freedom of a People who do not resist themselves to become slaves.

This incident, without parallel, who bring us back to past centuries, it is even more transcendental when it is proved even with photos, that in order to do that the government of Fidel Castro had violated International Laws when his henchmen entered jurisdictional waters of another Nation and what is even worse, he disembarked soldiers and military equipment in the above mentioned Anguila Key, British possession, in order to commit this flagrant violation of the most elemental Human Rights.

143

The Civic-Revolutionary organizations of Cubans in exile in the City of New Orleans pray to Almighty God to enlighten this Human Rights Commission of the Organization of American States, in order for you to fulfill your obligation with the human and historical role for which it was created, and for you to publicly condemn the colonist government of Fidel Castro as a transgressor of each one and all the fundamental rights inherent to a human being, and cooperating to liberate not only these poor unfortunate Cubans illegally and criminally kidnapped by the Communist Tyranny but all SIX MILLIONS Cubans who are helpless suffering in the Martyr Island of the Caribbean under the despotic designs of Russian Imperialism.

New Orleans, August 29, 1963

Mrs. Enriqueta Artze de Ibáñez	*Frank Bartés*
Cuban Teachers Directorate	*Cuban Revolutionary Council*
Dr. Agustín Guitart	*Dr. Carlos Bringuier*
Revolutionary Rescue	*Cuban Student Directorate*

As it has been our sad history as exiles, the members of the Human Rights Commission of the Organization of American states continued drinking their whisky in Washington, D.C.; the British Government continued looking the other way avoiding a confrontation with Fidel Castro; Lyndon Johnson was more preoccupied with Viet Nam that with his own backyard and Jimmy Carter the future champion of Human Rights (?) continued planting peanuts in Georgia waiting for his time to go to Cuba to entertain Dictator Castro by playing baseball with him. In the meantime Fidel Castro was more encouraged to continue with his crimes and the Cuban people was ignored to continue their suffering while America slept. An America that didn't realized that was infected by Red termites who were working to destroy it from within.

We continued our daily life in New Orleans. On September 14, 1963 we wrote a letter to Gonzalo J. Facio, Chairman of the Council of the Organization of American States commending his stand "for democracy, justice and liberty in the American hemisphere". It was signed by Frank Bartés, Cuban Revolutionary Council; Dr. Enriqueta Artze de Ibáñez,

Cuban Teachers Directorate; Dr. Carlos Bringuier, Cuban Student Directorate and Dr. Agustín Guitart, Revolutionary Rescue. It was printed in the "Times Picayune" on September 15, 1963

On September 21, 1963 the "New Orleans States-Item" published a letter to the editor by a James Lewark, Jr., stating that he thinks students had the right to go to Cuba. The New Orleans States-Item of September 25, 1963 published a letter to the editor written by me as follow:

'6 Million Cubans"

Hold Another View Editor, States-Item:

On Sept. 21 in "Letters to the Editor" was published a view about the United States ban against travel to Cuba.

I never read any American attacking more unjustly his country and what it represents to the free world. Castro is the one who has built a wall of blood and murders depriving peaceful citizens of their right to freedom and democracy.

I think that to criticize the U.S. ban against the travel of Americans to Cuba is to take the wrong side in the cold war or to ignore the meaning of Castro, Khrushchev and imperialistic communism.

Finally, I am sure that Mr. James Lewark, Jr., has to ignore that 10,000 Cubans and Americans have been murdered by the Castro dictatorship that more than 80,000 Cubans and Americans have been suffering imprisonment in Cuba and that six million Cubans disagree with his opinion.

Dr. Carlos Bringuier
New Orleans Delegate, Cuban Student Directorate.

And, once more I repeat, neither the CIA nor any other Intelligence Agency of the USA government was ordering, directing, coaching or paying me to do these things.

On September 27, 1963 at 10:00 a.m., Lee Harvey Oswald arrived to Mexico City where he went to the Comercio Hotel located 4 blocks away from the bus station where he, using the false name O. H. Lee, took a room in the third floor.

There are different versions about what happened in Mexico City during Oswald's stay. According to the Cuban government Oswald went first to the Soviet Embassy to try to expedite his papers for traveling to the Soviet Union while obtaining a transit visa from Cuba. From the Soviet Embassy he went to the Cuban Embassy and was interviewed by Silvia Tirado de Durán who had been working at the Consular section for only three months. Mrs. Durán, Mexican born, was a fervent admirer of Fidel Castro and she was impressed with the interview writing in the application for visa: *"The applicant states he is a member of the USA Communist Party and Secretary of the Fair Play for Cuba Committee in New Orleans. He showed documents that proves his affiliations to the two before mentioned organizations"*. After visiting again the Soviet Embassy, in the afternoon Oswald returned to the Cuban Embassy with the pictures. He had a meeting with Cuban Consul Eusebio Azcue. According to a statement by Fidel Castro in July 1967, Oswald stated: *". . . that he wanted to work for us. He was asked to explain himself but he did not do it. After that Oswald returned and told the Cubans in Mexico that he wanted to liberate Cuba from Yankee imperialism stating that somebody should shoot President Kennedy . . . and that maybe he would do that"*.

The above is Castro's version of Oswald's visit to Mexico. But there are other versions more credible about Oswald's activities there.

For example German newsman Wilfried Huismann shows in his documentary *"Rendezvous with Death"* that Lee Harvey Oswald met in Mexico with Cuban Intelligence officer Oscar Marino who states that Cuban Intelligence used Oswald no because he was the best but because he was available. In his documentary Huismann also made public that while in Mexico City Oswald met with General Fabián Escalante, Chief of Cuban Secret Service. The "Castro version" also omitted the fact that Oswald was invited to a party of Communists and Communist sympathizers where he met the daughter of Octavio Paz, author and winner of a Nobel Prize and at which party Ms. Paz was told: *"Stay away from him. He is a dangerous man"*. The "Castro version" also fails to mention that the person contacted by Lee Harvey Oswald at the Soviet Embassy was none other than Valery V. Kostikov, a KGB agent who was operating under the cover of a Soviet diplomat. Kostikov was attached to the KGB department that handled kidnappings, assassinations and similar acts of political terror. Why Castro and the Cuban officials omitted these facts if they don't have anything to hide?

When Oswald returned to Dallas he rented a room at 1026 North Beckley Avenue using the false name of O. H. Lee the same false name he used when he rented the room at the Comercio Hotel in Mexico City. Why? Because since he left for Mexico City Lee Harvey Oswald had become a member of the Communist underground. Now he was on a mission.

In an important policy speech of September 28, 1963, the day after Oswald was in contact with General Fabián Escalante and other members of Castro's Intelligence Services, Fidel Castro made it clear that Cuba would continue its policy of revolutionary opposition to U.S. efforts to crush his government. He said that while Cuba welcomed the current easing of world tensions, he could not accept a situation where at the same time the U.S. was increasing its efforts to "tighten the noose" around Cuba.

"We will not accept a situation", Castro declared*", in which tensions decrease while they increase for us". We don't want tensions to increase in the world. No, we are happy to see tensions decrease. But we cannot consider ourselves at peace with the imperialists; we cannot consider ourselves at peace with an imperialism that is increasing its efforts to strangle us".*

"They are our enemies", he continued, *"and we will know how to deal with our enemies".*

If the above statements by Fidel Castro are not a declaration of War, I don't know how else they could be interpreted. If you are not at "peace" you are at "war". And he knew very well how to deal with his enemies and demonstrated how he deals with his enemies when on November 22, 1963, in Dallas, one of his agents Lee Harvey Oswald assassinated President John F. Kennedy.

The above mentioned speech by Fidel Castro was not a fabrication of Carlos J. Bringuier, the FBI, the CIA, the John Birch Society, or any other persons or groups affiliated with the Conservative anti-Communist side of American or international politics. The above mentioned speech was published on Monday, October 7, 1963 in "The Militant", one of the proCommunist publications subscribed to by Lee Harvey Oswald.

On October 8, 1963 I was feeling very sorry for the devastation in Cuba caused by Hurricane "Flora", while the Cubans were suffering,

"Che" Guevara, with his psycho mentality was blaming the United States accusing it of having directed the path of "Flora" to damage the Castro regime. That day I went to the Western Union and send a telegram to Cuba:

Prime Minister Fidel Castro
October 8, 1963
Havana, Cuba.

> *In your struggle to force communism in Cuba the population have suffered persecution, imprisonment and death. Today, nature more powerful than men devastate our island. In the name of Cuba I beg you don't increase the suffering of Cuban mothers. The devastation that is looming over six million Cubans could be alleviated with your resignation. Over corpses only vultures live.*

To my surprise, next day October 9, 1963 the Cuban government made the mistake of answering my telegram, their telegram read:

Carlos Bringuier
DRE Delegate
New Orleans
October 9, 1963

> *The workers of the cablegram industries more than ever united to our glorious Comandante Fidel Castro Ruz have, as final destination to your message sent if to the dumpster as it is coming from a filthy reptile as are all those who cowardly defame our glorious socialist evolution and as we understand only obey as miserable lackeys of imperialism, traitors to their fatherland, we have sent your message to the place that correspond the trash dumpster according its origin.*

Fatherland or Death

As you can imagine my answer to them was to thank them because if the children of "Fatherland or Death" sent my telegram to the trash dumpster it meant that it was received by its addressee, Fidel Castro. The DRE newspaper TRINCHERA of October 27, 1963 printed this incident on page 5.

On October 9, 1963, the "Times Picayune" published in page 3 of Section 1 the following article:

> "*Cubans in New Orleans protest Fidel*
>
> *The delegation of the Cuban Student Directorate in New Orleans Tuesday sent a telegram to Cuban Prime Minister Fidel Castro, protesting his prohibiting the City of Mayarí from soliciting aid in the Hurricane Flora disaster from the U. S. Naval Base at Guantanamo.*
>
> *Dr. Carlos Bringuier, local delegate of the group, said Castro's action proves once more the inhuman disregard of the Communist regime for the Cuban people*"

On October 10, 1963, the "Times Picayune" published a small article in regard to our Cuban festivity of October 10 which was going to be commemorated at 8:00 p.m., in the Auditorium of St. Rita School. The announcement had been made by Dr. Enriqueta Artze de Ibáñez, of the Cuban Teachers Directorate; Frank Bartés, of the Cuban Revolutionary Council; Dr. Agustín Guitart, of Revolutionary Rescue; Dr. Jorge Ledo, of Cruzada; and Dr. Carlos Bringuier, of the Cuban Student Directorate.

On November 15, 1963 a massive rally was held at Gallier Hall to receive and hear the words of Dr. Manuel Antonio (Tony) de Varona, President of the Cuban Revolutionary Council. When I spoke at the rally I spoke as Delegate of the Cuban Student Directorate (DRE) invited by the Cuban Revolutionary Council (CRC). Among the persons sitting at the main table were: 1) Dr. Manuel Antonio (Tony) de Varona; 2) Mrs. Elisa Cerniglia, Director of the Cuban Catholic Center; Mr. Frank Bartés, New Orleans Delegate of the CRC; Dr. Agustín Guitart, New Orleans Delegate of Rescate Revolucionario; Mr. Edward Butler, representing the Information Council of the Americas (INCA); and Father Teodoro de la Torre, spiritual father of all the Catholic Cubans in New Orleans.

On November 17, 1963, I wrote a letter to Luis Valentín Domínguez a young Cuban interested in the Cuban Student Directorate letting him know that I had already appointed Celso Hernández as Secretary of the Delegation and Miguel Aguado as Treasurer. Miguel Aguado was representing in New Orleans the former workers of the Cuban Telephone Company. Celso Hernández and Miguel Aguado proved, through the years, to be great Cubans and very good friends. In the letter I also mentioned that we had decided to open a bank account at the National American Bank and that at that moment we had $50.00 to be deposited.

On November 18, 1963, the "Times Picayune" announced that I was going to speak at the International House and they wrote in large bold lines: "Argentina to be Bringuier Topic". On November 20, 1963, the "Times Picayune" reported my speech with the title of the article showing in larger letters: "Speaker Tells of Red Tactics", and then in smaller letters "Propaganda Methods in Latin America Told". The "New Orleans States-Item" also published my participation at the International House. I would like to copy here the last paragraph of what was published on the "States-Item":

> Bringuier stated that what happened in Cuba could also happen in other Latin American countries as well as in the U.S. However, he said, "If you win the war of propaganda, you will not have to fight and will not see in your country what I have seen in mine".

On November 26, 1963 I received a letter from the National American Bank acknowledging the opening of the DRE account on November 19, 1963. In the way that the withdrawals were going to be was requiring two signatures, in all checks the signature of the Delegate should be present and then the signature of the Secretary or the Treasurer. The letter was signed by Anthony P. Chisesi, Assistant Cashier. I inherited a clean an honest name:
"Bringuier" I always have been very careful to keep it that way.

Undoubtedly we have lost the propaganda war. We have been able to make Coca-Cola available and liked all over the world, but we have lost the war showing the truth to the world. We have the example in Venezuela, Bolivia, Nicaragua, Ecuador and Argentina were populist demagogues who enrich themselves while attacking the United States had been able to fool the people and take over. We have the example with Oliver Stone and his "JFK" movie. We have the example with the hundreds of books published about the assassination of John F. Kennedy distorting the truth and infecting the mind of our youth with lies and more lies protecting the real culprits and smearing those who believe in Freedom and Democracy. We have not been good "community organizers".

And we have witnessed the example of a young charismatic community organizer who had become adored by a great majority of the American people been able to reach, served in a silver plate, the Presidency of the United States of America.

Seven decades ago the German people fell in love with another community organizer, Adolf Hitler. Five decades ago, the Cuban people fell in love with another community agitator, Fidel Castro. John F. Kennedy could not have foreseen in November of 1963 how another community agitator, Lee Harvey Oswald, with three shots will change the history of the world and of the United States bringing this country to the economic, political and social crisis that it is suffering today.

CHAPTER IX

———◦◉◦———

THE ASSASSINATION OF PRESIDENT JOHN F. KENNEDY

November 22, 1963 started as another normal day for me. Early in the morning I opened "Casa Roca" with my brother-in-law Rolando Peláez. A little after 12:30 p.m., I was at the back of the store when the telephone rang. Rolando answered and told me that his nephew Angel Pelayo Carreras wanted to talk to me. Angel Pelayo, who was working at "Howard, Weil, Labouisse, Friedrichs & Co." told me that they had just received a teletype that President Kennedy had been shot in Dallas. After a couple of minutes he called back stating that a new teletype said that Kennedy had been shot in the head where blood was seen.

I felt devastated. Kennedy had an obligation to us, the Cubans, to get rid of Castro. Less than a year before, he had made a formal promise to return the 2506 Brigade's flag to a Free Havana. If he die who could help us? When the news of President Kennedy death was announced I felt nervous. Who could have shot the President? With my experience as a former Secretary of a Criminal Court in Havana, different scenarios came to my brain, and all of them made me uneasy.

After a few minutes I received a phone call from Frank Bartés, delegate of the Cuban Revolutionary Council in New Orleans. Bartés was inviting me to send a telegram of condolence to Jackie Kennedy. I told Bartés that we should wait. In my opinion a telegram of that kind should be sent only after we know who was behind the assassination.

Through my mind had come different possibilities among them a stupid racist bigot, or a stupid right-wing extremist, and underworld vengeance, or a crazy lunatic and I believed that in order to use the proper words in the telegram, first we should know who had fired the shots. Bartés was disappointed with my negative. While all these thoughts were crossing my mind, hundreds of miles away, the new President of the United States, Lyndon B. Johnson was concerned with totally different thoughts. Johnson was concerned that the assassination "might be the work of Dallas zealots, yet it is almost as easy to conjure an international conspiracy aimed at decapitating the U.S. government before a devastating nuclear strike is launched".[39]

Rolando and I were glued to the television watching the news when I decided to go home and eat a late lunch.

When I arrived at my apartment in the St. Thomas Housing Project my wife prepared my lunch while I listened to the radio. While I was eating I heard that a person had been apprehended in relation to the assassinations in Dallas. When I heard the name Lee Harvey Oswald as the suspect I jumped from my seat, grabbed the phone and placed calls to the FBI and the "Times Picayune" to tell them who Lee Harvey Oswald was. That is something that Fidel Castro and the Communists will never forgive me for doing. The "Times Picayune" requested my presence at their offices.

When I arrived at the "Times Picayune", Butler and Stuckey were already there. Butler called me apart and told me to wait and not give any information until Stuckey finish dealing with the editor of the "Times Picayune" because Stuckey was trying to obtain a monetary deal. I was shocked. The President of the United States had been assassinated just a few hours ago and some Americans were trying to negotiate a monetary deal. To me it was grotesque. I told so to Butler and I informed the reporter who was trying to talk to me that I was not interested in receiving any economic gain that I would be willing to give all the information that I had without any economic deal. In one hand I was sorry for Stuckey but in the other hand I believed that it was my duty to cooperate without looking for monetary gains. And remember that at that moment I was living with my wife and four children in the St. Thomas Project one of the poorest sections of New Orleans.

---

[39] "The Kennedy assassination Tapes", by Max Holland, page 12.

The next day the "Times Picayune" printed an article with my photo and my recollection of my incidents with Lee Harvey Oswald. That same day of November 23, 1963 my name appeared in newspapers around the world including "The New York Times".

I was convinced that the sentence dictated by the Cuban tribunal had been accomplished. On April 3, 1962, the Cuban government had sentenced President John F. Kennedy when during the trial of the members of the 2506 Brigade, Cuban Attorney General Santiago Cubas stated:

> "As far as the other author, United States imperialism and its President, Kennedy, who admitted this great crime and took the responsibility for it, they will not be tried here. But President Kennedy and the U.S. Imperialists will have to answer for their crime before the court of the Peoples of the world which will punish them fully as their crimes merit".

There was no doubt in my mind, knowing the criminal idiosyncrasy of Fidel Castro, that President John F. Kennedy had answered for the crime committed against Castro and Castro had punished him as Kennedy's crimes merit according to Fidel Castro.

The night of November 22, 1963 was a night that I would never forget. I was interviewed on WDSU-TV Channel 6 and my interview was going to be eventually telecast nationally and internationally. After I related my encounters with Lee Harvey Oswald, and with my legal mind working, I said: *"I don't know if Lee Harvey Oswald is the assassin but if it is proved that he is the assassin then we will see that Fidel Castro's hand was behind the assassination".*

My statement brought Fidel Castro to the verge of collapse. He had counted as sure that Oswald was going to escape. According to the documentary "Rendezvous with Death" of laureate German newsman Wilfried Huismann, Castro's Chief of Intelligence General Fabián Escalante, had traveled in an small airplane on the day of the assassination from Mexico City to Dallas and was awaiting in the airport to pick up Oswald and when Oswald was apprehended Escalante flew back to Mexico City. Now Fidel Castro was very, very nervous thinking that Oswald could be linked to him and eventually talk and in the meantime there I was, in national and international television accusing him of the criminal deed. Fidel Castro called a meeting for next day to refute those "Machiavelically distorted lies".

On November 22, 1963 the FBI wrote the following memo:

ASSASSINATION OF JOHN F. KENNEDY

CARLOS BRINGUIER. 501 ADELE ST. APARTMENT "F", local delegate of the Directorio Revolucionario Estudiantil (Student Directorate) in Miami, called this office by phone approximately 10:25 PM, 11/22/63 and advised as follows:

He stated he had received a long distance call from the headquarters of the Student Directorate in Miami and they were aware of the fact that BRINGUIER had had an altercation with LEE H> OSWALD in New Orleans several months ago when BRINGUIER had objected to Oswald's distribution of Fair Play for Cuba literature in N.O. on Canal St. BRINGUIER stated that the Directorate in Miami had said they spoke to Secret Service Agent there name (DELETED IN MEMO) who had suggested that BRINGUIER contact the FBI for protection. BRINGUIER indicated that he felt that Castro was capable of being behind the President's assassination. He had no information in that regard but merely was of the opinion that Castro was capable of having Oswald perpetrate such an act.

BRINGUIER was advised that the FBI does not afford police protection and that if he felt in need of such protection he should contact the NOPD. He said he did not feel the need for such protection but that he sought his family should have such protection. He was advised he should call the N.O.P.D. He stated he did not think he would call the police and was critical of the fact that since this man Oswald was obviously pro-Communist that the Federal Investigations agencies could not avoid the President's assassination. Bringuier resides 501 Adele in the St. Thomas housing project.

The above date relative to Bringuier's statement he thought his family may need protection was furnished to Desk Sergeant (DELETED IN MEMO) Detective Bureau, NOPD by phone at approximately 10:45 PM (DELETED IN MEMO) took

Bringuier's name and address and said they would do nothing unless Bringuier requested protection.

Next day with a massive concentration in Havana Fidel Castro delivered his speech raising the following points:

1) *"Occasionally, in the middle of a Civil War, in the middle of a fear of repression, the revolutionaries are forced to defend themselves, are forced to kill to defend themselves".*
2) He portrayed Oswald as *"a madman, a mentally sick person".*
3) Castro labeled Oswald as a *"patsy"* charging that the accusation linking Oswald to the "Fair Play for Cuba Committee" was part of a plot to blame his regime for the assassination of President Kennedy.
4) Fidel Castro also portrayed Oswald as an *"instrument of the right wing"* and the *reactionaries"* of the United States trying to prove that Lee Harvey Oswald, the assassin, was not a member of the "Fair Play for Cuba Committee", declaring that not even in Dallas, nor in New Orleans, nor in the entire State of Texas, there is a chapter of the "Fair Play for Cuba Committee".
5) Castro alleged: *"Why Lee H. Oswald, a sympathizer of our Communist regime and a member of the "Fair Play for Cuba Committee" try to join the anti-Castro organization, the Cuban Student Directorate, as a military trainer?* And I quote him: *"why the devil a supposed sympathizer of the Cuban Revolution would want to join a piratical anti-Castro organization?"*

Fidel Castro's words apparently were directed to people lacking gray matter in their brains. It was simple: Oswald was trying to *infiltrate* the delegation of the Cuban Student Directorate in New Orleans in order to *inform the Castro government as a spy.*

6) Castro also stated that it was strange that the radio debate had occurred because it involved the "Fair Play for Cuba Committee" and he does not conceive the idea of such critics been allowed in the United States of America.
7) It was false that Oswald tried to infiltrate the New Orleans Delegation of the DRE.

8) He referred to my decision to not accept Oswald's help because *"Carlos Bringuier, delegate of the DRE in New Orleans, thought that Oswald could have been utilized by the CIA or the FBI".*

That night Fidel Castro was desperate. He was concerned that as Oswald could not rendezvous with General Fabián Escalante and had been apprehended. Oswald could talk. He had to gain time and move his moles inside the USA to slow down or stop any violent reaction from the government of the USA. He hated me because I had opened my mouth and used my brain to attack him in national and international television. He had to try to portrait me as a liar because he knew that I was not controlled by any intelligence service of the USA. If I would have been under the control of the CIA or any other intelligence service of the USA he could have, through his moles, forced me to stay quiet and not to attack him. Remember that I had never receive any payment, any money from any organization controlled by the CIA, FBI or any other agency of the United States government. That who pay you control you. As I was not paid by anyone, including the Cuban Student Directorate (Directorio Revolucionario Estudiantil) nobody could control me or make me shut my mouth. How many moles like Philip Agee, Ana Belen Montes, Edward Lee Howard or Mariano Faget were willing to help him survive?

On November 26, 1963, Zoila Díaz, who was the Secretary of the DRE office in Miami, wrote me the following handwritten letter:

"Mr. Carlos Bringuier New Orleans, LA.
Dear Carlos:

Just a few lines to give you a message from José Antonio[40].

From now on our goal is to move the public opinion of this country in every possible way that we could, but from now on we will work "behind the curtains", understand? We are going to provide all the information to others who are the ones who will bring it out publicly.

Because of the above, here they want you to remain silent, which means no interviews, etc. If this result in a big

---

[40] José Antonio Lanuza.

*investigation of if the DRE discovers anything then we will bring
you here.*

*José also told me to tell you that he received your letter with
the information and he is asking that if you have anything new
to report for you to communicate directly with him at his house at
any time. His phone is Canal-1-5701.*

*I only have to tell you to keep in touch about the activities of
the Delegation from now on I ask you to be careful and take care.*

Without anything else, receive my regards,

Zoila

The above letter surprised me. I was in New Orleans, my Delegation
was the one who Oswald tried to infiltrate, I debated Lee Harvey
Oswald, I had given out, three months before, the press release asking
for a Congressional investigation of Lee Harvey Oswald, and now the
Miami office was diplomatically telling me to shut up. As previously
had happened to me at the "Times Picayune" with the incident about
Bill Stuckey asking for money, I considered that it was more important
for the American People and for the world to know the truth. I was
an antiCastro Cuban; I was not receiving a salary from the DRE in
Miami, neither from the CIA or the FBI. I always had maintained my
independence, maybe that is why the CIA nor the FBI never tried to
enroll me. I was the person that had met Lee Harvey Oswald and now I
was been told to shut up.

After the assassination I tried to find out exactly who Lee Harvey
Oswald was, I knew that he was a Communist and a Castro admirer but
I wanted to know who he really was.

In my studies about him I have reached the conclusion that Lee
Harvey Oswald was a poor wrecked soul infatuated, first with Marxism
and later with Fidel Castro, who ended up double crossed by those he
admired. On October 3, 1956, at age 16, Oswald wrote a letter to the
Socialist Party of the United States asking information about their
Juvenile League. At one point the stated: *"I am a Marxist, and have been
studying Socialist principles for more than 15 months".*

The same type of Castro's moles who are now trying to portrait me
as a CIA agent are the ones who try to distort the truth about Oswald's
Marxism. Oswald admiration for Marxism was not fabricated at any

CIA center while he was in the Marines, but long time before that when, still a teenager, he was a romantic about Marxism who already had read Das Kapital at the New Orleans Public Library and had stated to an acquaintance, Palmer McBride, that he would like to kill President Eisenhower because he was exploiting the working class. Oswald praised Khrushchev and suggested to McBride that they join the Communist Party in order to *"to take advantage of their (Communist) social functions"*.[41]

Another friend of young Lee Harvey Oswald, William E. Wulf, testified to the Warren Commission about the following incident:

> *". . . started expounding the Communist doctrine and saying that he was highly interested in Communism, that Communism was the only way of life of the worker, et cetera, and then came out with the statement that he was looking for a Communist cell in town to join but he couldn't find any. He was a little dismayed at this and he said that he couldn't find any that would show any interest on him as a Communist, and subsequently, after this conversation, my father came in and we were kind of arguing back and forth about the situation and my father came in the room, heard what we were arguing on Communism, and that this boy was loudmouthed, boisterous and my father asked him to leave the house and then politely put him out of the house and that is the last time I have seen or spoken to Oswald."[42]*

When in 1959, Oswald left the United States and arrived to Moscow, his mother, Marguerite, was taken by surprise because she had been expecting Oswald destination would have been Cuba where Castro was already in power.[43]

On November 26, 1959, before almost four years to the date of JFK's assassination, Lee Harvey Oswald wrote from the Soviet Union the following letter to his brother Robert:

> *"Ask me and I will tell you I fight for Communism, I will not say your grandchildren will live under Communism. Look for yourself at history, look at a world map! America is a dying*

---

41 Warren Commission, page 165.
42 Warren Commission Hearings Vol. VIII page 18.
43 Warren Commission Hearings Vol. IV page 407.

country. I do not wish to be part of it, nor do I ever again wish to be used as a tool in its military aggressions . . . I have been a pro-Communist for years and yet I have never met a Communist, instead I kept silent and observed, and what I observed plus my Marxist leanings brought me here to the Soviet Union. I have always considered this country my own . . . In the event of war, I would kill any American who put his uniform on in defense of the American Government—any American."[44]

In less than four years Lee Harvey Oswald was able to fulfill his dream of killing an American President, not Eisenhower but Kennedy, and he fulfilled his threat when as doing so he killed the Commander in Chief. Still there are Communist moles who try to present him as a CIA agent and there are gullible people who believe them maybe they are part of the same 80% to which Donald Savery was referring to in our conversation at the Café Dumonde. Maybe they are part of the same ones who believe that we have never set a foot in the moon, the same ones who believe that Fidel Castro is a democratic President, the same ones who believe that Ernesto "Che" Guevara was a peace loving adorable romantic. There is a saying: *"There is a sucker born every minute,"* with the population explosion that is not true anymore. The truth is:

Lee Harvey Oswald was a Communist and as a Communist he assassinated President John F. Kennedy.

For those useful idiots who idolize "Che" Guevara I would like to quote him in an interview with the London Daily Worker on November 1962:

"If the missiles had remained, we would have used them against the very heart of the U.S., including New York. We must never establish peaceful coexistence. In this struggle to the death between two systems we must gain the ultimate victory. We must walk the path of liberation even if it costs millions of atomic victims."

---

[44] Warren Commission Hearings Vol. XVI, page 821.

Those were the words of the *peaceful loving* Che Guevara. Let the idiots idolize him.

They were willing to kill millions in New York. They were willing to assassinate President John F. Kennedy to obtain their ultimate victory. Maybe that is why on September 11, 2001 the Cuban leaders were celebrating with toasts at the news of the terrorist attack in New York. Ask the leader of the "Mothers of the Plaza de Mayo"[45] Hebe de Bonafini who that day was toasting with them in Havana.

Like if I was in my old courtroom in Havana I would like to synthesize the evidence to indict Lee Harvey Oswald for the assassination of President John Fitzgerald Kennedy":

1) *All three of the cartridge cases had been fired by Oswald's rifle. (WC—Vol. 3, page 415)*
2) *Both bullet fragments found in the front portion of Kennedy's car were fired by Oswald's rifle to the exclusion of all other weapons. (WC—Vol. 3, page 432)*
3) *Bullet found on Governor's Connally stretcher was fired by Oswald's rifle. (WC—Vol. 4, pages 32 & 38)*
4) *Oswald's palm print is found on Oswald's rifle. (WC—Vol. 4, page 24)*
5) *Oswald's fingerprints and palm prints were found in two boxes near the window of the sixth floor of the School Book Depository Building. (WC—Vol. 4, pages 32 & 38)*
6) *In the butt plate of Oswald's rifle were found some fibers that came from the same shirt that Lee Harvey Oswald was wearing the day of the assassination. (WC—Vol. 4, page 87) 7) Nitrates were present in the cast made of Oswald's hands. (WC—Vol. 4, page 276)*
8) *Oswald's fingerprints and palm prints were found on the brown homemade type paper sack found on the sixth floor of the Texas School Book Depository Building. (WC—Vol. 4, page 5)*
9) *Oswald's clipboard was found hidden among some boxes in the sixth floor of the Texas School Book Depository building.*
10) *Deposition of Oswald's widow, Marina Oswald, to the Warren Commission:*

---

[45] Communist-front organization in Argentina.

> *Mr. Rankin:* But from what you have learned since that time, you
> arrived at this conclusion, did you, that your husband
> killed the President?
> *Mrs. Oswald:* Yes, unfortunately, yes.
> *Mrs. Oswald:* He said that I should not worry, that everything would
> turn out well. But I could see by his eyes that he was
> guilty. Rather he tried to appear to be brave. However, by
> his eyes I could tell that he was afraid.[46]

This last statement of Marina Oswald make me rationalize that
Oswald was afraid because he was aware that he had botched the whole
affair when he had allowed himself to be arrested. Now, Oswald was
afraid that one way or the other he was going to be silenced in order to
spare the Castro's government of their involvement in the assassination.

On Sunday morning, November 24, 1963, I was at the office of the
Secret Service in New Orleans and already in the afternoon the agent
chatting with me was called aside. When he returned he informed me
that Lee Harvey Oswald had been shot. It is difficult to explain my
feelings at the moment, I felt like falling in an abysm. John F. Kennedy
was the President who had a debt of honor with us, he was killed by Lee
Harvey Oswald and now Oswald was shot and maybe killed before he
could be brought to a trial. It was a nightmare. I left the office of the
Secret Service in a state of shock.

With the years the pieces of the puzzle could be put together.

Piece 1) On June 6, 1959 Mafia boss Santos Trafficante and others
involved in gambling operations in Cuba were detained by the Castro
government. They were held in Triscornia where he received the visit
of Jack Ruby and he is released due to the intervention of Commander
Rolando Cubela Secades. Trafficante is allowed to leave Cuba, with his
money, and started to work as an informant for Castro's Intelligence
services.

Piece 2) On March 1961, Cuban Major Rolando Cubela Secades
establishes contact in Mexico City with the CIA. Contacts continued, on
and off, until 1965.

Piece 3) On June 1962, Lee Harvey Oswald leaves the Soviet Union
to return to the USA.

---

[46] Warren Commission Hearings, Volume 1, page 78.

Piece 4) On July 18, 1962 the KGB sends a secret telegram to Ramiro Valdés, Chief of the Cuban Secret Services informing him of Oswald's return to the USA and identifying Oswald as a sympathizer. This telegram was discovered at the Secret archives of the KGB after the disappearance of the Soviet Union. This telegram was written by Vladimir Aleksandrovich Kryuchkov to Ramiro Valdés (Chief of Cuban Secret Services) apprising the Cubans to contact Lee Harvey Oswald. Oswald had already returned, the previous month, from the Soviet Union to the USA. It should be noted that Vladimir Kryuchkov later became Chairman of the KGB, a member of the Politburo, and on May 21, 1991 visited Dictator Fidel Castro in Havana to inform him of the forthcoming coup d'etat in Moscow against Gorbachev.[47]

Piece 5) On November 1962, a month after the October Crisis, Cuban G2 establishes contact with Lee Harvey Oswald and assigned as his case officer Major Rolando Cubela Secades.[48]

Piece 6) On April 10, 1963, Lee Harvey Oswald carried out his first test as "sleeper" for the Communists by attempting to kill General Edwin Walker in Dallas, Texas.[49]

Piece 7) On August 5, 1963, Lee Harvey Oswald tried to infiltrate the delegation of the Cuban Student Directorate in New Orleans, Louisiana.

Piece 8) On August 9, 1963, Oswald is arrested on Canal Street, New Orleans, after a disturbance when he was passing out pro-Castro literature.

Piece 9) On August 12, 1963, at the Second Municipal Court in New Orleans, Lee Harvey Oswald is sentenced to a $10.00 fine for disturbing the peace.

Piece 10) On August 21, 1963, Lee Harvey Oswald is confronted in a radio debate at radio station WDSU in New Orleans where he defended the dictatorship of Fidel Castro and, when confronted with undeniable evidence, confessed that he was a Marxist.

Piece 11) On September 7, 1963, Fidel Castro, at the Brazilian Embassy in Havana, in an extemporaneous speech stated to the press: ***"Kennedy is the Batista of these times ... And the most opportunistic American President of all times. He is fighting a battle against us they cannot win. Kennedy is a hypocrite and a member of***

---

[47] "Brothers in Arms'" by Gus Russo and Stephen Molton, pages 184 & 185.
[48] "Rendezvous with Death", Documentary by Wilfried Huismann.
[49] "Warren Commission Report, page 175.

an oligarchic family that control several important post in the government. For instance, one brother is a Senator and another Attorney General . . . And there not more Kennedy officials because there are not more brothers." Later on in his speech he went so far as to threaten the leaders of the United States when he said: *"We are prepared to fight them an answer in kind, United States leaders should think that if they are aiding terrorist plans to eliminate Cuban leaders, they themselves will not be safe."[50]*

Piece 12) On September, Lee Harvey Oswald established contact with intelligence agents of the Cuban government in Mexico City, among them the Chief of a branch of Cuban Intelligence Services General Fabián Escalante. Oswald also established contact with Valery Kostikov who was an officer in the KGB's First Directorate assigned to "Department 13", the infamous KGB section in charge of terrorism, sabotage and assassinations. Oswald attended a party organized by the Cuban Embassy in Mexico and met the daughter of Octavio Paz, winner of a Nobel Prize. Ms. Paz was told at the party: *"Stay away from him, he's a dangerous man".[51]*

Piece 13) On September 1963, Néstor Sánchez became CIA case officer of Cuban Major Rolando Cubela and using an assumed name met with Cubela at the Pan American games in Porto Alegre, Brazil.[52]

Piece 14) On October 29, 1963, Desmond FitzGerald, who was in charge of CIA Special Affairs and close friend of Robert F. Kennedy, using an alias (James Clark), met with Cubela in Paris, France. During the meeting Cubela requested a "high powered rifle with a telescopic sight that could be used to kill Castro from a distance".[53]

Piece 15) On November 18, 1963, in a speech delivered at the Assembly of the InterAmerican Press Association in Miami, Florida, President Kennedy stated: *"It is important to restate what now divides Cuba from my country and from all the American countries: it is the fact that a small band of conspirators has stripped the Cuban people of their freedom and handed over the independence and sovereignty of the Cuban Nation to forces beyond this hemisphere. They have*

---

[50] "Red Friday", by Dr. Carlos J. Bringuier, page 6.
[51] Documentary "Rendezvous with Death", by Wilfried Huismann.
[52] "Live by the Sword", by Gus Russo, page 238.
[53] "Live by the Sword", by Gus Russo, page 239.

made Cuba a victim of foreign imperialism, an instrument of the policy of others, a weapon in an effort dictated by external powers to subvert the American Republics.

> *This and this alone divide us.*
> *As long as this is true nothing is possible.*
> *Without it everything is possible.*

Once this barrier is removed we will be ready and anxious to work with the Cuban people in pursuit of those progressive goals which, a few short years ago, stirred their hopes and the sympathy of many people throughout the entire hemisphere.

No Cuban need feel trapped between dependence on the broken promises of foreign Communism and the hostility of the rest of the hemisphere. For once Cuban sovereignty has been restored we will extend the hand of friendship and assistance to a Cuba whose political and economic institutions have been shaped by the will of the Cuban people".[54]

This speech, according to Desmond FitzGerald, was intended as a "message of support" from President Kennedy to the group headed by Major Rolando Cubela.[55]

Piece 16) On the morning of November 22, 1963, a small plane flying from Mexico City landed at the private Redbird airport in Dallas carrying as a passenger the Chief of a branch of Cuban Intelligence Services General Fabián Escalante[56]. Meanwhile in Paris, France a new meeting is going on by the CIA attended by, among others, Desmond FitzGerald and Cuban Major Rolando Cubela. The meeting is interrupted by the news that President Kennedy had been assassinated in Dallas, Texas. Lee Harvey Oswald is arrested after trying to escape and had killed Officer J. D. Tippit who had stopped him for questioning. Sometime later, after Oswald arrest had been made public, the small airplane left Redbird airport in Dallas, carrying General Fabián Escalante back to Mexico City as documented in a Secret memo written by Marty Underwood, assistant to President Lyndon B. Johnson.

---

[54]   Warren Commission Exhibit No.2695.
[55]   "Live by the Sword", by Gus Russo, page 276.
[56]   Memo by Marty Underwood to President Lyndon B. Johnson.

Piece 17) On November 1963, President Lyndon B. Johnson send FBI Supervisor Laurence Keenan to investigate Oswald's clandestine contacts in Mexico City. Less than 72 hours later, when everything was pointing to Castro as the culprit, Laurence Keenan was called back, ordered to stop the investigation, and to forget everything that he has learned. Keenan was told that everything related to his trip to Mexico City was "top secret". In the documentary "Rendezvous with Death" Keenan said: *"I had the chance to solve the case of our President's murder, and I screwed up. I'm still ashamed of that to this day".* General Alexander Haig, who in 1963 was Robert Kennedy's right hand man in carrying out military sabotage activities against Castro, stated: *"Bobby Kennedy is personally responsible for at least 8 assassinations attempts on Fidel Castro. Kennedy wanted to get rid of Castro, but Castro got him first".[57]*

Piece 18) On November 24, 1963, Lee Harvey Oswald is assassinated by Jack Ruby, longtime friend of Santos Trafficante. Oswald was not allowed to have his day in court or to give away his connections with the Castro government.

Piece 19) On December 10, 1964, Manuel Artime, ex-Chief of the Bay of Pigs 2506 Brigade and close friend of Robert F. Kennedy, had another meeting with Major Rolando Cubela who was again trying to infiltrate the CIA. At the meeting Cubela stated that a coup d'etat is been prepared in Cuba by a group of which he is the leader. According to Cubela the others involved were: Efigenio Almejeiras, Juan Almeida and Commander Guillermo García Frías. Artime reported to the CIA that Cubela could not be trusted and on June 23, 1965 in a cable to stations the CIA stated: *"Convincing prove that entire AMLASH (Cubela) group insecure and that further contact with key members of group constitute menace to CIA operations against Cuba as well as the security of CIA staff personnel in Western Europe."* The CIA ordered all contact broken and warned Artime, the first one that had warned them, that Cubela was not to be trusted. This attempt by Fidel Castro to fool the US government is very similar to the other one at the beginning of his revolution when he fooled President Trujillo of the Dominican Republic that cost my cousin Cucú Bringuier years in jail. Efigenio Almejeiras is still in Cuba, Juan Almeida died recently and the government honored his funeral,

---

[57] Documentary "Rendezvous with Death", by Wilfried Huismann.

Commander Guillermo García Frías is still in Cuba and all of them continued serving Fidel Castro.[58]

Piece 20) On March 1, 1966 the Castro government announced the arrest of Major Rolando Cubela Secades and Major Ramón Guin for counterrevolutionary activities involving the CIA. Major Cubela was found guilty and sentenced to thirty years in jail. Eventually, after a few short years, he was "released" and allowed to leave Cuba. Years later, Major Arnaldo Ochoa and Captain Antonio de la Guardia, were not awarded the same leniency and were executed at the "paredón" for crimes less grave than working with the CIA to assassinate Commander Fidel Castro. If Cubela would have been a true conspirator against Castro he would have been executed and not set free.

The forces trying to obscure the truth about the assassination of President Kennedy started moving their wheels almost coinciding with the shots fired in Dallas.

Earl Warren, Chief Justice of the Supreme Court, stated after the announcements of Kennedy's death and before the arrest of Lee Harvey Oswald: *"A great and good President has suffered martyrdom as a result of hatred and bitterness that has been injected into the life of our nation by bigots."*[59] Earl Warren was placing the blame on extreme right wingers who were considered by the leftists as "bigots". Two days later, when he delivered a eulogy in the Capitol Rotunda he blamed: *"forces of hatred and malevolence . . . eating their way into the blood stream of American life."*[60]

Author Max Holland in his book "The Kennedy Assassination Tapes" explains Lyndon B. Johnson feelings on that fatal "Red Friday", of November 22, 1963 when he quoted new President Johnson in this way: *"It may be the work of Dallas zealots, yet it is almost at easy to conjure up an international conspiracy aimed at decapitating the U.S. government before a devastating nuclear strike is launched."*[61]

Three possibilities surfaced in regard to who would conduct the investigation of the assassination: 1) A Texas Board of Inquiry; 2) The Senate Committee in Internal Security headed by Senator Eastland; and 3) The House Committee on Un-American Activities. The three had

---

[58] "Brothers in Arms", by Gus Russo and Stephen Molton, pages 425 & 426.
[59] "The Kennedy Assassination Tapes", by Max Holland, page 178.
[60] Same as above.
[61] "The Kennedy Assassination Tapes", by Max Holland, page 12.

legal reasons to carry on an investigation: A) The crime was committed in Texas; B) It was a crime that violated our Internal Security; and C) Definitively the assassination of the President of the United States was an Un-American activity.

The reader have to remember that at this time it has been already discovered that Lee Harvey Oswald had been in contact in Mexico with Valery Kostikov, officer of the KGB assigned to Department 13 in charge of terrorism, sabotage and assassinations; it had been made public that Oswald at one time deserted to the Soviet Union and his connections with the "Fair Play for Cuba Committee" in New Orleans; and besides that I had denounced in television that if Oswald was the assassin, Castro's hand would be discovered behind the assassination; and Castro had panicked and called a mass meeting in Havana to counter my charges.

On November 27, 1963, President Johnson had a telephone conversation with Senator James Eastland at 3:21 p.m. During the conversation Senator Eastland said to Johnson: *"Well, we plan to hold hearings and just make a record of what the proof is, that's all."* And then he continued: . . . *to show that this man was the assassin."*[62]

On November 29, 1963, Secretary of State Dean Rusk, one of the architects of the U.S. disasters in China during Chiang Kai-shek times, and in Cuba during the Bay of Pigs and the October Crisis, is now moving his wheels to stop the three approaching investigations in favor of a Great Presidential Commission, and in a conversation with Senator Mike Mansfield stated: *". . . possible implications of this, that if they were— the rumors were—to leak as of fact, and if there were anything in this that had not been fully substantiated, it could cause a tremendous storm. And it is very important that we work on the basis of the hardest possible information on the situation-".*[63]

Dean Rusk traitorous and bloody trail started when he was defending State Department employees of the attacks of anti-Communist Senator Joe McCarthy when McCarthy was exposing the Communist infiltration in the U.S. government; it continued when in May 1950 he wrote a memo entitled "U.S. Policy toward Formosa" in which he was instructing on how to overthrow General Chiang-Kai-shek, offering whatever

---

[62] "The Kennedy Assassination Tapes", by Max Holland, page 118.
[63] Same as above, page 123.

additional funds he could need and offering arms and munitions to Sun Li-jen an officer in the Chiang Kai-shek army.[64]

The above Rusk's memo was in reality a death sentence against U.S. ally General Chiang Kai-shek. A treasonous act by a man, portrayed by the liberal press as a peace loving person, against a firm anti-Communist leader and proved friend of the United States.

Dean Rusk was Secretary of State on November 22, 1963 and he also had been Secretary of State during the Bay of Pigs invasion. His hands were tainted with the blood of the brave members of the 2506 Brigade killed during the invasion. Dean Rusk was the mastermind of killing the "Trinidad Plan" which brought a sure victory to Fidel Castro.[65]

The wheels of whitewash and treason were moving to avoid a true investigation about the assassination of President John F. Kennedy.

From the beginning Johnson suspected that the assassination of Kennedy was the result of a Communist conspiracy. After been informed of Kennedy's death Johnson stated: *"We don't know whether this is a worldwide conspiracy. Whether they are after me as well as they were after President Kennedy . . . We just don't know."*[66]

On November 29, 1963, President Johnson is worried about the implications which could derive from the investigations and he called Senator Everett Dirksen at 11:40 a.m., and stated:

Johnson: *Two things. These investigations in the House and Senate on this Dallas affair . . . Hoover's is a little concerned about [them] reflecting on him. He's making a very full report on it. The [Texas] attorney's general getting an inquiry-a state inquiry [going on] he's a very young and able, and effective man. And we don't wanna. (sic)*

We got some international complications that could come out to us if we are not careful.

Dirksen: *Yes.*
Johnson: *So we've tryin' to figure out how we could best handle this thing, and seem to us we might ask a member of the [Supreme] Court,*

---

[64] "Blacklisted by History", by M. Stanton Evans, page 422.
[65] "Decision for Disaster", by Grayston L. Lynch, page 38.
[66] "The Kennedy Assassination Tapes", by Max Holland, page 14.

*might even ask Allen Dulles, might ask a couple of members of the
House, and a couple of the Senate, and wrap up three divisions
of government so we'd have a very high caliber, top flight, blue
ribbon group that the whole world would have absolute confidence
in.*[67]

Alas, the Warren Commission is born, and the Texas investigation,
the Senate Committee in Internal Security investigation, and the
investigation by the House Committee in Un-American Activities were
de facto aborted.

Many "authors", including Jim Garrison have constructed different
scenarios in regard to how many shots were fired at Dealey Plaza on
November 24, 1963, from where the shots were fired and who fired the
shots.

There are no serious disagreements in regard that the place from
where the shots were fired was the sixth floor window of the Texas School
Book Depository Building. There are various other locations from where
the scavengers had tried to position mysterious snipers firing fatal shots.
If we would believe them we would be confronting a situation where
nearly one hundred shots were fired. One of the most stupid versions
was launched by New Orleans District Attorney Jim Garrison when he
assured that the fatal shot had been fired from a "drain hole". But let us
see what the uncontroversial truth is.

Roy L Kellerman, assistant special agent of the Secret Service in
charge of the White House detail (Mr. Kellerman had been in the Secret
Service for twenty-two years before the assassination) was sitting in the
right front seat next to the driver in the car which carried President
Kennedy. These are parts of his testimony to the Warren Commission,
which for a strange coincidence was of no interest to Mark Lane who does
not even have Mr. Kellerman's name in the index of his book "Rush to
Judgment".

Mr. Kellerman: *As we turned off Houston onto Elm and made the short
little dip to the left going down grade, as I said, we were
away from buildings and were—there was a sign on the
side of the road which I don't recall what it was or what*

---
[67] "The Kennedy Assassination Tapes", by Max Holland, page 127.

> *it said, but we no more than passed that and you are out in the open, and there is a report like a firecracker, pop. I turned my head to the right because whatever this noise was I was sure that it came from the right and perhaps into the rear, and as I turned my head to the right to see whatever it was, I heard a voice from the back seat and I firmly believe it was the President's, <My God, I am hit> and I turned around and he has got his hands up here like this.*[68]

Senator Cooper: *Then it would be correct to say that it was your judgment at the time, at the time of the report . . .*

Mr. Kellerman: *It was my judgment, sir.*

Senator Cooper: *That it was to the right and to the rear?*

Mr. Kellerman: *That would be correct. It was my judgment, sir.*[69]

I would like to explain at this point, that at that moment the Texas School Book Depository building was to the right and to the rear of Special Agent Kellerman. Mr. Kellerman continued his testimony and said:

Mr. Kellerman: *Senator because all the matter that was—between all the matter that was blown off from an injured person, this stuff all came over.*

Senator Cooper: *What was that?*

Mr. Kellerman: *Body matter, flesh.*[70]

Mr. Specter: *When did you first notice the substance which you have described as body matter?*

Mr. Kellerman: *When I got to the hospital, sir, it was all over my coat.*

Mr. Specter: *Did you notice it flying past you at any time prior to your arrival at the hospital?*

Mr. Kellerman: *Yes, I know there was something in the air.*[71]

The above mentioned statements show without the slightest shadow of a doubt the direction of the shots. Mr. Kellerman was sitting on the

---

[68] Warren Commission Hearings Vol. II, page 73.
[69] Warren Commission Hearings Vol. II, page 101.
[70] Warren Commission Hearings Vol. II, page 77.
[71] Warren Commission Hearings Vol. II, page 78.

right front seat of the car. In between him and President Kennedy sat Governor Connally, and when the shot struck President Kennedy's head the "body matter" the "flesh" flew all over to the front seat of the car, which it could never had happened if the shots would have been fired from the front or from the side of the car as some "authors" claim. This is clear evidence that the shots that hit President Kennedy came from the direction of the Texas School Book Depository Building.

In his deposition Mr. Kellerman also explained that he observed an indentation in the framework of the windshield and directly to the right of the mirror holder inside of the car, and he also noticed some cracks on the inside of the windshield which were caused by parts of bullets, or by fragments of President Kennedy's skull.

No matter what any speculator, distorter of the truth, or publicity hungry person may say, this could not had happened if the killing shots had been fired from any other direction than from behind the President.

Mr. Kellerman:	*Oh, yes: very much. And I felt this windshield both inwardly and outwardly to determine first if there was something that was struck from the back of us or—and I was satisfied that it was.*
Mr. Specter:	*When you say struck from in back of you, do you mean on the inside or outside the windshield?*
Mr. Kellerman:	*Inside, sir.[72]*

Another witness who closely described the direction of the shots is a special agent of the Secret Service, Mr. William Robert Greer who was driving the car occupied by President Kennedy and who at that time had 18 years of experience in the Secret Service.

His testimony is intelligent and concise and as you will note he points out again that the shots were fired from the direction of the Texas School Book Depository Building. As you may suspect, his name is not mentioned in the index of Mark Lane's book "Rush to Judgment". Let's see what important testimony Mr. Lane omitted in his book:

Mr. Specter: *Going back to the shots themselves, Mr. Greer, do you have any reaction as to the direction from which the shots came?*

---

[72] Warren Commission Hearings, Vol. II, page 86.

Mr. Greer: *They sounded like they were behind me, to the right rear of me.*

Mr. Specter: *Would that be as to all three shots?*

Mr. Greer: *Yes, sir. They sounded, everything sounded, behind me, to me. That was my thought, train of thought that they were behind me.*

Mr. Specter: *Have you ever had any reaction or thought at any time since the assassination that the shots came from the front of the car?*

Mr. Greer: *No, sir. I had never even the least thought that they could come. There was no thought in my mind other than that they were behind me.*[73]

Another eyewitness to the assassination was Special Agent Clint J. Hill, who as member of the Secret Service was responsible for Mrs. Kennedy's protection. He was riding in the follow-up car, which was 5 or 8 feet behind the President's car. Special Agent Hill's recollection also located the shots as coming from the Texas School Book Depository Building.

Mr. Specter: *Now, as the motorcade proceeded at that point, tell us what happened.*

Mr. Hill: *Well, as we came out of the curve, and began to straighten up, I was viewing the area which looked to be a park. And I heard a noise from my right rear, which to me seemed as a firecracker, I immediately looked to my right and, in so doing, my eyes had to cross the Presidential limousine and I saw President Kennedy grab at himself and lurch forward and to the left.*[74]

Mr. Specter: *Now, do you know or had you ever had the impression or reaction that there was a shot which originated from the front of the Presidential car?*

Mr. Hill: *No.*[75]

The Presidential motorcade was composed of several cars. The first one was the lead car, the second one was the President's car, the third one was the Presidential follow-up car, and the fourth one was the Vice-President's car. In this fourth car was riding Special Agent Rufus Wayne

---

[73] Warren Commission Hearings, Vol. II, page 129.

[74] Warren Commission Hearings, Vol. II, page 138.

[75] Warren Commission Hearings, Vol. II, page 144.

Youngblood, from the Secret Service, who had been with the Secret Service for twelve years before the assassination and who was the Special Agent in charge of the VicePresidential detail. He explained his reaction to the shots in this way.

Mr. Specter: *Now, did you have any reaction or impression as to the source or point of origin of the first shot?*

Mr. Youngblood: *I didn't know where the source or the point of origin was, of course but the sounds all came from my right and rear.[76]*

At the time of the first shot Robert Hill Jackson, a photographer of the Dallas Times Herald, was traveling in the eighth car from the President. At that moment his car was almost half a block on Houston Street, that is, his car was directed toward the Texas School Book Depository building. I believe that I don't have to mention that his name does not appear on the index of Mark Lane's bestseller book "Rush to Judgment".

Mr. Specter: *Now, will you mark in a black "X" on 347 the spot where your car was at the time you heard the first shot?*

Mr. Jackson: *Right here approximately. And as we heard the first shot, I believe it was Tom Dillard from Dallas News who made some remarks as to the sounding like a firecracker, and it could have been somebody else who said that. But someone else did speak up and make the comment and before he actually finished the sentence we heard the other two shots. Then we realized or we thought that it was gunfire, and then we could not at that point see the President's car. We were still moving slowly, and after the third shot the second two shots seemed much closer together than the first shot, than they were to the first shot. Then after the last shot, I guess all of us were just looking all around and I just looked straight up ahead of me which would have been looking at the School Book Depository and I noticed two Negro men in a window straining to see directly above them, and my eyes followed*

---

[76] Warren Commission Hearings, Vol. II, page 150.

right on up to the window above them and I saw the rifle or what looked like a rifle approximately half of the weapon, I guess I saw, and just as I looked at it, it was drawn fairly slowly back into the building, and I saw no one in the window with it.[77]

The evidence clearly shows a rifle at the six floor window of the Texas School Book Depository Building contrary to the falsehoods spread by the "recyclers of lies" in their conspiracy books. The following statements should erase any doubts that may still be in your minds thanks to Oliver Stone, Jim Garrison, Joan Mellen or many others. These are excerpts from the testimony of James Richard Worrel, Jr., who was watching President Kennedy's motorcade:

Mr. Worrel: *Didn't get too good a view of the President either.—I missed out on there too. But as they went by; they got, oh, at least another 50, 75 feet on past me, and I heard the shots.*

Mr. Specter: *Did you observe anything at about that time?*

Mr. Worrel: *Yes, sir, I looked up and saw the rifle, but I would say about 6 inches of it.*

Mr. Specter: *What did you observe at the time?*

Mr. Worrel: *I saw about 6 inches of the gun, the rifle. It had—well it had a regular long barrel but it had a long stock and you could only see maybe 4 inches of the barrel, and I could see-*

Mr. Specter: *Where you able to observe any of the stock?*

Mr. Worrel: *Oh, yes.*

Mr. Specter: *How much of the stock were you able to observe?*

Mr. Worrel: *Just very little, just about 2 inches.*

Mr. Specter: *How many inches of the barrel then could you observe protruding beyond the stock?*

Mr. Worrel: *About 4 inches, I would say, not very much.*

Mr. Specter: *Now, at the time of the second shot were you able to observe anything at that precise instant?*

Mr. Worrel: *You mean as to firing it?*[80]

Mr. Specter: *As to anything at all. What did you see when the second shot went off?*

---

[77]   Warren Commission Hearings, Vol. II, pages 158-59.

Mr. Worrel: *Well, I looked to see where he was aiming and after the second shot and I have seen the President slumping down in the seat, and . . .*

Mr. Specter: *Did you see the President slump in his seat after the second shot?*

Mr. Worrel: *Uh, huh. And about that . . .*

Mr. Specter: *Did you look up and see the rifle between the first and second shots?*

Mr. Worrel: *Yes, sir. And saw the firing on the second and then before he could get a shot I was . . . I took in everything but specially the car, the President's car, and saw him slumping, and I looked up again and turned around and started running and saw it fire a third time . . .* [78]

Another important eyewitness to the assassination was young Amos Lee Euins who was just sixteen years old at the time when he was interviewed by the Warren Commission. He expressed what he witnessed in this way:

Mr. Euins: *I was standing here in the corner. And then the President come around the corner right here. And I was standing here. And I was waving, because there wasn't hardly no one in the corner right there but me. I was waving. He looked that way and he waved back at me. And then I had seen a pipe, you know, up there in the window, I thought it was a pipe, some kind of pipe.*

Mr. Specter: *When had you seen that thing you just described as a pipe?*

Mr. Euins: *Right as he turned the corner here.*

Mr. Euins: *Then I was standing here, and as the motorcade turned the corner, I was facing, looking dead at the building. And so I seen this pipe thing sticking out the window. I wasn't paying too much attention to it. Then when the first shot was fired, I started looking around, thinking it was a backfire. Everybody else started looking around. Then I looked up at the window, and he shot again. So you know this fountain bench here, right around here, well, anyway, there is a little fountain*

---

[78] Warren Commission Hearings, Vol. II, page 194.

right here. I got behind this little fountain, and then he shot again. So after he shot again, he just started looking down this, you know.

Mr. Specter: *Who started looking down that way?*

Mr. Euins: *The man in the window. I could see his hand, and I could see his other hand on the trigger, and one hand was on the barrel thing.*

Mr. Specter: *All right. Now, at the time the second shot was fired, where were you looking then?*

Mr. Euins: *I was still looking at the building, you know, behind this . . . I was looking at the building.*

Mr. Specter: *Looking at anything special in the building?*

Mr. Euins: *Yes, sir. I was looking where the barrel was sticking out.*[79]

Howard Leslie Brennan was another eyewitness to the assassination. Mr. Brennan, at the time, was working for a construction company. Let's see what he had to say in regard to the tragic events of "Red Friday", November 22, 1963.

Mr. Belin: *Mr. Brennan, could you please tell the Commission what happened from the time you sat on that retaining wall, what you saw?*

Mr. Brennan: *Well. I was more or less observing the crowd and the people in different building windows, including the fire escape across from the Texas Book Store on the east side of the Texas Book Store, and also the Texas Book Store Building windows. I observed quite a few people in different windows. In particular, I saw this one man on the sixth floor which left the window to my knowledge a couple of times.*

Mr. Belin: *Now, you say the window on the sixth floor, what building are you referring to there?*

Mr. Brennan: *That is the Texas Book Store.*

Mr. Belin: *Then what did you observe or hear?*

Mr. Brennan: *Well, then something, just after the explosion, made me think it was a firecracker being thrown from the Texas Book*

---

79 Warren Commission Hearings, Vol. II, pages 203 & 204.

Store. And I glanced up. And this man that I saw previous was aiming for his last shot.

Mr. Belin: *This man you saw previous? Which man are you talking about now?*

Mr. Brennan: *The man in the sixth story window.*

Mr. Belin: *Would you describe just exactly what you saw when you saw him this last time?*

Mr. Brennan: *Well, as it appeared to me he was standing up and resting against the window sill, the gun shouldered to his right shoulder, holding the gun with his left hand and taking positive aim and fired his last shot. As I calculate a couple of seconds. He drew the gun back from the window as though he was drawing it back to his side and maybe paused for another second as though to assure hisself (sic) that he hit his mark, and then he disappeared.*[80]

Mr. Brennan also clarified part of the chaos originated right after the shots were fired and how he tried to gain attention from police officers to tell them what he had seen.

Mr. Belin: *What did you do or what did you say to him?*

Mr. Brennan: *I asked him to get someone in charge, a Secret Service man or an F.B.I. That it appeared to me that they were searching in the wrong direction for the man who did the shooting. And he was definitely in the building on the sixth floor. I did not say in the sixth floor. Correction there. I believe I identified the window as one window from the top.*[81]

Another eyewitness was Special Agent of the Secret Service Winston G. Lawson, who was traveling in the lead car and when he was interviewed by the Commission he stated as follows:

Representative Ford: *Why did you look back? Is that the direction of sound?*

---

[80] Warren Commission Hearings, Vol. III, pages 143 & 144.
[81] Warren Commission Hearings, Vol. III, page 145.

Mr. Lawson:	*The direction of sound and the direction of the President.*
Representative Ford:	*Are you sure that the sound you heard came from the rear and not from the front?*
Mr. Lawson:	*I am positive that it came from the rear, and then I spun back that way to see what had occurred back there.*
Representative Ford:	*You are sure that the sound didn't come from the overpass?*
Mr. Lawson:	*I am in my own mind that it didn't. It came from behind me.[82]*

It is worthy to mention here that at that moment the lead car was located almost at the inlet of the sewerage system from which demented New Orleans District Attorney Jim Garrison said the fatal shot was fired.

Officer Marrion L. Baker from the Dallas Police Department was in his motorcycle almost parallel to the press car in which newsman Robert Hill Jackson rode. Officer Baker was facing the Texas School Book Depository building at the time of the shooting.

Mr. Baker:	*It hit me all at once that it was a rifle shot because I had just got back from deer hunting and I had heard them pop over there for about a week.*
Mr. Belin:	*What kind of a weapon did it sound like it was coming from?*
Mr. Baker:	*It sounded to me like it was a high-powered rifle.*
Mr. Belin:	*All right. When you heard the first shot or the first noise, what did you do and what did you see?*
Mr. Baker:	*Well, to me, it sounded high and I immediately kind of looked up, and I had a feeling that it came from the building, either right in front of me or of the one across to the right of it.*
Mr. Belin:	*What would that building in front of you be?*
Mr. Baker:	*It would be this Book Depository Building.*
Mr. Belin:	*How many shots did you hear?*
Mr. Baker:	*Three.[83]*

---

[82] Warren Commission Hearings, Vol. IV, page 353.
[83] Warren Commission Hearings, Vol. III, page 247.

Mr. Belin: *Officer Baker, did it appear to you that these sounds that you heard were from the same rifle or from possible more than one rifle?*

Mr. Baker: *I would say they was (sic) from the same rifle.*

Mr. Belin: *Did it appear that the sounds all came from the same source?*

Mr. Baker: *Yes, sir.*[84]

Meanwhile, on November 22, 1963 in the press car on Houston Street was riding James Robert Underwood, assistant news director of KRLD-TV and Radio in Dallas. He answered this question to the Commission.

Mr. Ball: *You realized they were coming from overhead and that would be from what source?*

Mr. Underwood: *That would be from the Texas School Book Depository Building.*[85]

Also traveling in the same press car on Houston Street was Malcolm O. Couch, television news cameraman with WFAA-TV in Dallas.

Mr. Belin: *Did you hear more than three shots?*

Mr. Couch: *No.*

Mr. Belin: *Now, between the first and second shots, is there anything else you remember doing or you remember hearing or seeing that you haven't related here at this time?*

Mr. Couch: *Nothing unusual between the shots. Uh—as I say the first shot, I had not particular impression; but the second shot, I remember turning—several of us turning—and looking ahead of us. It was unusual for a motorcycle to backfire that close together, it seemed like. And after the third shot, Bob Jackson, who was, as I recall, on my right, yelled something like, "Look up in the window! There is the rifle!" And I remember glancing up to a window on the far right, which at the time impressed me as the sixth or seventh floor and seeing about a foot of a rifle being . . . The barrel brought into the window.*

---

84 Warren Commission Hearings, Vol. III, page 269.
85 Warren Commission Hearings, Vol. VI, page 169.

Mr. Belin: *In what building was that?*
Mr. Cough: *This was the Texas Book Depository Building.*[86]

Traveling in the same press car was Tom C. Dillard, chief photographer of the Dallas Morning News and his report to the Commission was as follows:

Mr. Ball: *You have had experience with rifles?*
Mr. Dillard: *Yes, I have shot a great deal, so I am familiar with the noise that they made in the area. We were getting a sort of reverberation which made it difficult to pinpoint the actual direction but my feeling was that it was coming into my face and, in that I was facing north toward the School Depository . . . I might add that I very definitely smelled gun powder when the car moved up at the corner.*
Mr. Dillard: *There was never any question in my mind that there was more or less than three explosions which were all heavy rifle fire, in my opinion, of the same rifle. The same rifle fired three shots.*[87]

Governor John Connally was traveling in President Kennedy's car and sat just in front of him. Governor Connally was another victim, almost killed, by Lee Harvey Oswald. This is part of his testimony:

Gov. Connally: *I just sat there, and Mrs. Connally pulled me over to her lap. She was sitting, of course, on the jump seat, so I reclined my head on her lap, conscious all the time, and with my eyes open; and then, of course the third shot sounded, and I heard the shot very clearly.*

I heard it hit him. I heard the shot hit something, and I assumed again . . . It never entered my mind that it ever hit anybody but the President, I heard it hit. It was a very loud noise, just that audible, very clear.
Immediately I could see on my clothes, my clothing. I could see in the interior of the car which as I recall, was pale blue, grain tissue, which I immediately recognized, and I recall very well, on my trousers there was one

---

86 Warren Commission Hearings, Vol. VI, pages 156-157.
87 Warren Commission Hearings, Vol. VI, pages 165,166.

chunk of brain tissue as big as almost a thumb, thumbnail, and again I did not see the President at any time either after the first, second or third shots, but I assumed always that it was he who was hit and no one else.[91?]

Mr. Specter: *What was your impression then as the source of the shot?*
Gov. Connally: *From back over my right shoulder which, again, was where immediately when I heard the first shot I identified the sound as coming back over my right shoulder.*
Mr. Specter: *At an elevation?*
Gov. Connally: *At an elevation. I would have guessed at an elevation.*
Mr. Specter: *Did you have an impression as to the source of the third shot?*
Gov. Connally: *The same. I would say the same.*[88]

Jack Dougherty, who at the time of the assassination was on the fifth floor of the Texas School Book Depository building testified to the Commission:

Mr. Ball: *You told Mr. Johnson of the Federal Bureau of Investigation that when you were on the fifth floor, you heard a loud noise and it appeared to have come from within the building, but you couldn't tell where—you told him that on the 19th; did you tell him that?*
Mr. Dougherty: *Yes, sir.*
Mr. Ball: *Did it sounded like it came from the floor above you??*
Mr. Dougherty: *Well at the time it did-yes.*[89]

Another employee of the Texas School Book Depository building who testified to the Warren Commission was Eddie Piper, who stated:

Mr. Piper: *Yes; they seemed like they did come from the building, you know, by the vibration of that window-it seemed like nobody had shot in the window from the outside-it might have been coming from the building-is what I figured.*

---

[88] Warren Commission Hearings, Vol. IV, page 134.
[89] Warren Commission Hearings, Vol. VI, page 380

Mr. Ball: You told them that day that you thought it came from inside the building?

Mr. Piper: Yes.[90]

Another witness, Geneva L. Hine, who was in the second floor of the Texas School Book Depository building testified to the Commission as follows:

Mr. Ball: How many did you hear?
Miss Hine: Three.
Mr. Ball: Could you tell where the shots were coming from?
Miss Hine: Yes, sir; they came from inside the building.
Mr. Ball: How do you know that?
Miss Hine: Because the building vibrated from the result of the explosion coming in.
Mr. Ball: It appeared to you that the shots came from the building?
Miss Hine: Yes, sir.
Mr. Ball: Did you know they were shots at the time?
Miss Hine: Yes, sir; they sounded almost like cannon shots they were so terrific.[91]

Three co-workers of Lee Harvey Oswald were watching the motorcade from the window right below the sixth floor window of the Texas School Book Depository building. Bonnie Ray Williams, Harold Norman and James Jarman, Jr., testified to the Warren Commission as follow:

Mr. Ball: Did you notice—where did you think the shots came from?
Mr. Williams: Well the first shot—I really did not pay any attention to it, because I did not know what was happening. The second shot, it sounded like it was right in the building, the second and third shot. And it sounded—it even shook the building, the side we were on. Cement fell on my head.
Mr. Ball: You say cement fell in your head?

---

90 Warren Commission Hearings, Vol. VI, page 386.
91 Warren Commission Hearings, Vol. VI, pages 395, 396.

Mr. Williams:	*Cement, gravel, dirt or something from the old building, because it shook the windows and everything. Harold was sitting next to me, and he said it came right from over our head. If you want to know my exact words, I could tell you.*
Mr. Ball:	*Tell us.*
Mr. Williams:	*My exact words were, "No bull shit." And we jumped up.*
Mr. Ball:	*Norman said what?*
Mr. Williams:	*He said it came directly over our heads. "I can even hear the shell being ejected from the gun hitting the floor." But I did not hear the shell being ejected from the gun, probably because I wasn't paying any attention.*
Mr. Ball:	*Norman said he could hear it?*
Mr. Williams:	*He said he could hear it. He was directly under the window that Oswald shot from.[92]*
Mr. Ball:	*When the cement fell in your head, did either one of the men notice it and say anything about it?*
Mr. Williams:	*Yes, sir. I believe Harold was the first one.*
Mr. Ball:	*That is Hank Norman?*
Mr. Williams:	*I believe he was the first one. He said "Man, I know it came from there. It even shook the building." He said, "You got something in your head." And then James Jarman said, "Yes, man, don't you brush it out." By that time I just forgot about it. But after I got downstairs I think I brushed it out anyway.[93]*
Mr. McCloy:	*How many shots did you hear fired?*
Mr. Williams:	*I heard three shots. But at first I told the FBI I only heard two—they took me down—because I was excited, and I couldn't remember too well. But later on, as everything began to die down, I got my memory even a little better than on the 22nd, I remembered three shots, because there was a pause between the first two shots. There was two real quick. There was three shots.[94]*

Now let's see what another of Oswald's co-workers had to say. This is part of the testimony to the Warren Commission of Harold Norman:

[92] Warren Commission Hearings, Vol. III, page 175.
[93] Warren Commission Hearings,
[94] Warren Commission Hearings, Vol. III, page 179.

Mr. Norman: *I believe it was his right arm, and I can't remember what the exact time was but I know I heard a shot, and then after I heard the shot, well, it seems as though the President, you know, slumped or something and the another shot and I believe Jarman or someone else told me, he said. "I believe someone is shooting at the President," and think I made a statement "It is someone shooting at the President, and I believe it came from above us." Well, I couldn't see at all during the time but I know I heard a third shot fired, and I could also hear something sounded like the shell hulls hitting the floor and the ejecting of the rifle, it sounded as though it was to me.*

Mr. Ball: *How many shots did you hear?*

Mr. Norman: *Three.*

Mr. Ball: *Do you remember whether or not you said anything to the men as to whether or not you heard anything from above you?*

Mr. Norman: *Only I think I remember saying that I thought I could hear the shell hulls and the ejection of the rifle. I didn't tell I think I hear anybody moving, you know.*

Mr. Ball: *But you thought, do you remember you told the men that you thought you heard the ejection of the rifle?*

Mr. Norman: *Yes sir.*

Mr. Ball: *And shells on the floor?*

Mr. Norman: *Yes, sir.*

Mr. Ball: *Falling?*

Mr. Williams: *Yes.[95]*

Mr. Ball: *Did you see any dust or dirt falling?*

Mr. Williams: *I didn't see any falling but I saw some in Bonnie Ray Williams' hair.[96]*

Now, after 50 years of the assassination the recyclers of lies continue making money duping part of the American people and of the world population. On March 23, 1967 New Orleans District Attorney Jim Garrison stated that "it was becoming increasingly apparent that nobody

---

[95] Warren Commission Hearings, Vol. III, page 191.
[96] Warren Commission Hearings, Vol. III, page 192.

was shooting from the sixth floor window of the Book Depository building". The evidence clearly prove, to any sane person, without any doubt, that Garrison was lying on March 23, 1967.

The "useful idiots" can believe anything that their damaged brains would allow them to perceive as "truth" but the incontrovertible evidence prove that on November 22, 1963, Lee Harvey Oswald fired three shots from the sixth floor window of the Texas School Book Depository Building where the police found his rifle, the three shells and his prints.

Lee Harvey Oswald was not to be apprehended there. He escaped trying to get away out of the United States. He knew that he could not hang around his place of work, like the others employees did, because he was leaving behind his rifle. Oswald was confident that his "friends" were going to help him get out of the country. In his sick mind he considered that he was going to be received in Cuba as a "Hero of the Revolution" but his sick mind was not able to let him know that he was just a tool, a disposable tool.

In the meantime the KGB was working hard to influence American public opinion thru the liberal press and sympathetic individuals. One of these individuals was Mark Lane who received $1,500 from funds of the KGB[97]. As an example of disinformation trying to confuse American and World opinion is the following statement, under oath, to the Warren Commission by Mark Lane:

> *"From published accounts, and from my investigation, I can only find one person who thought that the shots came from the building, and that was the chief of police in Dallas, Jesse Curry, who said as soon as the shots were fired, he knew they came from the building. From the Book Depository Building."*[98]

We should find out how the CIA handled the investigation of the assassination of President John F. Kennedy. The three stooges could not have done better.

The following paragraphs have been copied from "The Investigation of the Assassination of President John F. Kennedy: performance of the Intelligence Agencies. Book V. Final Report of the Select Committee to

[97] "The Sword and the Shield" the Secret History of the KGB, by Christopher Andrew and Vasili Mitrohkin, page 228.
[98] Mark Lane's testimony to the Warren Commission, Vol. II, page 44.

study Governmental Operations with respect to Intelligence Activities. United States Senate. April 23, 1976".

"Following a June 1963 decision by a <Special Group> of the National Security Council to increase cover operations against Cuba, the CIA renewed contact with a high-level Cuban government official, code-named AMLASH[99]. At his first meeting with the CIA in over a years, AMLASH proposed Castro's overthrow through an <inside job>, with U.S. support. AMLASH considered the assassination of Castro a necessary part of his <inside job>. Shortly after this meeting with AMLASH, Castro issued a public warning reported prominently in the U.S. press about the United States meeting with terrorists who wished to eliminate Cuban leaders. He threatened that Cuba would answer in kind.

Five days after Castro issued this threat, the Coordinating Committee for Cuban affairs, an interagency planning committee subordinate to the National Security Council's Special Group met to endorse or modify then existing contingency plans for possible retaliation by the Cuban Government. Representatives of the CIA, and of the State, Defense and Justice Departments were on this Committee. The CIA representatives on this Committee were from its Special Affairs Staff (SAS), the staff responsible for Cuban matters generally and the AMLASH operation. Those attending the meeting on September 12 agreed unanimously that there was a strong likelihood Castro would retaliate in some way against the rash of cover activity in Cuba.

At this September 12 meeting this Committee concluded Castro would not risk major confrontation with the United States. It therefore rejected the possibility that Cuba would retaliate by attacking American officials within the United States; it assigned no agency the responsibility for consideration of this contingency.

Within weeks of this meeting the CIA escalated the level of its covert operations, informing AMLASH the United States supported this coup. Despite warnings from certain CIA staffers that the operation was poorly conceived and insecure, the head of SAS, Desmond Fitzgeral (sic), met AMLASH on October 29, 1963, told him he was the <personal representative> of Attorney General Robert Kennedy, and stated the United States would support a coup. On November 22, at a pre-arranged meeting, a CIA Case Officer told AMLASH he would provide rifles, with telescopic

---

[99]   Major Rolando Cubela Secades.

sights, and explosives with which to carry out his plan. He was also offered a poison pen device."[100]

It should be noted at this time that AMLASH was Castro's Major Rolando Cubela Secades. The report continues:

"Oswald visited Mexico City, where he visited both the Cuban and Soviet diplomatic establishments, and contacted a vice consul at the latter who was in fact a KGB agent. Despite receiving this information on Oswald's Mexico City activity, the FBI failed to intensify its investigative efforts. It failed to interview him before the assassination despite receiving a note from him warning the FBI to leave his wife alone.

Immediately after the assassination, FBI Director J. Edgar Hoover ordered a complete review of the FBI's handling of the Oswald security case. Within six days he was given a report which detailed serious investigative deficiencies. As a result of these deficiencies seventeen FBI personnel, including one Assistant Director, were disciplined. The fact that the FBI felt there were investigative deficiencies and the disciplinary actions it took were never publicly disclosed by the Bureau or communicated to the Warren Commission.[101]

Neither the CIA nor the FBI told the Warren Commission about the CIA attempts to assassinate Fidel Castro.

The individual who directed the CIA investigation for the first month after the assassination, testified that he felt knowledge of the AMLASH operation would have been a <vital factor> in shaping his investigation. His successor at the CIA also stated that knowledge of the AMLASH plot would have made a difference in his investigation.[102]

In 1965, the FBI and the CIA received information about the AMLASH operation, which indicated the entire operation was insecure, and caused the CIA to terminate it.

The assassination of President Kennedy again came to the attention of the intelligence agencies in 1967. President Johnson took a personal interest in allegations that Castro had retaliated. Although the FBI received such allegations, no investigation was conducted.

On the very day President Johnson received the FBI reports of these allegations, he met with CIA Director Richard Helms. The next day, Helms ordered the CIA Inspector General to prepare a report on Agency sponsored

---

[100] Page 3.
[101] Page 4.
[102] Page 5.

assassination plots. Although the report raised the question of a possible connection between the CIA plots against Castro and the assassination of President Kennedy, it was not furnished to CIA investigators who were to review the Kennedy assassination investigation. Once again, although these CIA investigators requested information that should have let them to discover the AMLASH operation, they apparently did not receive that information.[103]

On November 23, at 5:00 p.m. CIA Headquarters received a cable from Mexico station stating that the Mexican police were going to arrest Sylvia Duran, a Mexican national employed by the Cuban consulate who was believed to have talked to Oswald when he visited the consulate in September. Headquarter personnel telephoned the Mexico Station and asked them to stop the planned arrest. The Mexico Station said that the arrest could not be stopped.

After learning the arrest could not be prevented. Karamessines cabled the Mexico station that the arrest <could jeopardize the U.S. freedom of action on the whole question of Cuba responsibility>. The desk officer could not recall that cable or explain the reasons for transmitting such a message. Karamessines could not recall preparing the cable or his reasons for issuing such a message. He speculated that the CIA feared Cubans were responsible, and that Duran might reveal this during the interrogation. He further speculated that if Duran possess such information, the CIA and the U.S. Government would need time to react before it came to the attention of the public. (Author's note: I believe that 50 years is enough time to react).

Later that evening, the AMLASH case officer arrived in Washington. The case officer can't recall whether he reported to Headquarters that evening but he was in his office next morning, Sunday, November 24. Early this morning, the 24th the Mexico Station cable its response to a Headquarters request for the names of all known contacts of certain Soviet personnel in Mexico City. The purpose of obtaining these names was to determine the significance of Oswald's contacts with the Soviets and to assess their activities. AMLASH's real name was included in the list of names on the Mexico Station cable.[104] (Author's note: The real name of AMLASH <Major Rolando Cubela Secades> appearing at this moment as a contact of the KGB in Mexico and been the same who was manipulating the CIA to find out to what extent President Kennedy planned to go against Castro

---

[103] Page 6.
[104] Page 25.

should have started to turn the wheels of the investigation in the right direction, but the moles inside the U.S. government were already at work, this important fact was spiked and nobody would pay attention to it. After the receiving of the cable, Santos Trafficante's protégée, Jack Ruby, would solve the remaining problem and Lee Harvey Oswald would be assassinated to silence him, diverting and obscuring the investigation.

Thus early in the morning of November 24, the CIA officials investigating the assassination had come across AMLASH's name. Had routine procedure been followed, that name would have been checked in Agency files. Operational information, i.e., details of CIA plots with AMLASH to assassinate Castro, would not have been routinely provided. The decision to provide such information would have been made by Fitzgerald or Helms. The AMLASH Case Officer can recall no discussion about connections between AMLASH and the assassination of President Kennedy.

CIA files on its investigation of the President's assassination contains no evidence that such information was provided. The Desk Officer who coordinated the CIA investigation of the assassination testified he was not then aware of any assassinations plots and certainly was not then aware of the AMLASH plot.

Q. Did you know that on November 22, 1963, about the time Kennedy was assassinated a CIA case officer was passing a poison pen, offering a poison pen, to a high level Cuban to use to assassinate Castro? A. No, I did not.

Q. Would you have drawn a link in your mind between that and the Kennedy assassination?

A. I certainly think that that would have become an absolutely vital factor in analyzing the events surrounding the Kennedy assassination.[105]

(Author's note: How come the Desk Officer who was in charge of coordinating the CIA investigation of the assassination of President Kennedy was kept in the dark about the AMLASH operation? How deep had been the Communist penetration inside the CIA? Knowing about AMLASH undoubtedly would have brought an investigation about the possibility of retaliation by Fidel Castro.) Let's continue:

The Case Officer's <contact report> on the November 22 meeting with AMLASH bears the date November 25. He testified it was probably prepared on either November 24 or 25. The report does not note that the poison pen

---

[105] Page 27.

was offered to AMLASH also it does state that AMLASH was told he would receive explosives and rifles with telescopic sights. The Case Officer testified the contact report does not discuss the poison pen because Fitzgerald ordered him to omit that matter. He probably showed the report to Fitzgerald on the same day, but recalls no discussion with Fitzgerald about a possible connection between the AMLASH operation and President Kennedy's assassination. The Case Officer also stated that there was no reason to make such a connection and he certainly made no such connection in his mind. When asked why he did not associated President Kennedy's assassination by a pro-Castro activist with his own involvement in the AMLASH operation, the Case Officer stated that he does not know to this day that Oswald had any pro-Castro leanings.[106]

(Author's note: When the Case Officer states that "he does not know to this date that Oswald had any pro-Castro leanings was showing how are some of the agents working in the CIA. Was he just stupid or what? Oswald had become a deserter to the Soviet Union, he had written communication with the U.S. Communist Party and the "Fair Play for Cuba Committee" which letters had been intercepted by the U.S. Government, Oswald was a member of the "Fair Play for Cuba Committee", was a subscriber to Communist and Trotskyite publications, used the alias "Hidell" for "Fidel", while in New Orleans had been arrested and fined for passing out proCastro literature, his widow had testified under oath that he wanted to hijack a plane to Cuba, had visited the Soviet and Cuba Embassies in Mexico City, had tried to assassinated antiCommunist General Walker and in a radio debate on August 21, 1963 had confessed been a Marxist and defended Fidel Castro. And this Case Officer does not know to this date that Oswald had any pro-Castro leanings. Unbelievable but true.

But what it is even more intriguing is that the CIA had been aware that Fidel Castro was trying to assassinate President Kennedy. There is a CIA report dated March 15, 1962 in regard to Raul Jaime Diaz Arguelles y Garcia. In page 4 of the report the CIA states: *"Raul Diaz Arguelles is believed to be in complete charge of any activity as contemplated by Aldo Margolles Duenas involves a plot to assassinate the President of the United States." "Arguelles is presently the center of a zero lookout at all strategic points of entry, as well as Aldo Pedro Margolles."*

---

[106] Pages 27, 28.

There is another report from the CIA in which it is stated:

> <u>DFB 95904 dated 8 Dec 61:</u>
> *From the FBI to the Secret Service, requesting lookout for Aldo Pedro Margolles y Duenas, son of the Chief of Cuban National Police. MARGOLLES reportedly attempting to enter the U. S. to meet with Cuban agents and assassinate President Kennedy.*

> <u>Memo to Al Cox [03] dated 23 Jan 1962:</u>
> *MARGOLLES and ARAGONES are known to have fanatical tendencies. ARAGONES is one of CASTRO's right hand men and accompanies CASTRO in all public appearances. MARGOLLES and ARAGONES are known to have generated plot to assassinate President of U.S.*

> <u>WAVE 8793 (IN 13094) 18 Jan 1962:</u>
> *Re photos of MARGOLLES and ARAGONES involved in plot.*

> <u>DIRECTOR 38056 dated 27 Jan 1962:</u>
> *To most LAD Stations and Based. "Have received info, from Secret Service re plot assassinate President Kennedy generated by Aldo Pedro MARGOLLES y Duenas and Emilio ARAGONES y Navarro. Confidential source indicates plot in fact conceived and may be executed. Both considered fanatics. Advice whereabouts on continuing basis."*

There is another file from the CIA in regard to the subject Pedro MARGOLLES Duenas 201-315161 which reads:

> 13 Feb 62 <u>Ministry of Interior File Encl. 3 to UFCA 3302:</u>
> *13 Feb 62 Memo to secret Service from Wm. H. McClare. Raul DIAZ Arguelles, poorly regarded, was appointed Chief of Dept. of Technical Investigations Nov. 59. Feb 62 he reportedly was working with former U.S. gangsters who were deported from the U.S. Also reportedly affiliated with narcotics traffic. Believed is in complete charge of any activities contemplated*

*by MARGOLLES which involved plot to assassinate Pres. of
U.S. A known terrorist, DIAZ is capable in use of explosive
bombs and automatic weapons. Reportedly was responsible
for assassinations during Batista regime. Also believed to have
directed assassinations in past from somewhere in Mexico. Is good
friend of Rolando CUBELA.*

Now everything appears clearly, Fidel Castro was ready to kill
President John F. Kennedy, the question was when, where and by whom.

On January 17, 2010, I received the following email forwarded by
Ed Prida a former member of the Cuban Air Force and later member of
Fidel Castro's Intelligence Service: who now resides in Royal Palm Beach,
Florida.

From: *Ed Prida*
To: Three Frog

Points that Fabian Escalante denied in Bahamas Meeting.

1. *Gral. Fabian Escalante (role on JFK's Affair) there are two
    different source who claim he was in Texas on Nov 23, 1963.*
1.1. *The first information came from Magaly Gomez and she
    told it to me in 1983. "Mr. Escalante was in the USA
    in Nov 23, 1963". Magaly Gomez is the former wife of
    General Jose Chaviano, Castro's Security Guard. She
    worked as a radio operator for Fidel for a long time; she
    told me that she was working under direct orders from
    Fidel Castro. At the time I did not pay much attention to
    what Magaly said since she had sometimes exaggerated her
    role, but she really was Castro's Radio Operator.*
1.2. *The second source told me in 2009/2010 in West Palm
    Beach and Miami. The name of the source is Dr. Juan
    Antonio Blanco History Academy of FIU, former Senior
    Specialist America Department and Cuba's UN Diplomat;
    in Cuba he worked under the orders of the Cmdt. Manuel
    Pineiro Lozada. He received this information from own
    Fabian Escalante, in private conversation, who stated that
    he was flying in the Gulf of Mexico and due to bad weather*

his plane needed to land in Dallas in the days prior to JFK's assassination, this narrative was made to make some kind of justification as to why he was down in Texas; he was assigned by Fidel Castro to assist him with the JFK assassination.

2. *Two other high ranking Cuban Intelligence officers landed around Texas from August to November in 1963. According to the CIA, their names were Emilio Aragones Navarro (201274644 CIA file) and Aldo Pedro Margolles Duenas (207-315161 CIA file). Both had the intentions to assassinate JFK. around Texas from Aug to Nov 63 according CIA's Report were Emilio Aragones and Aldo Margolles both came to US for kill the President. The American Law Enforced got Alarm his troops from August 1963 to capture those peoples inside the US Territory. The leave evidence to be in USA in el Paso Texas and Dallas, they started the trip to US to Mexico in the Lazaro Cardenas Ranch in Mexico.*

3. *Air Transport*

3.1. *Cubana de Aviacion (Cubana Airline) Bristol Britannia 318 was waiting beside the taxiway in the Mexico DF Airport on Nov 20-23 1963 using a broken engine as a façade to pick up the Cuban Officer after he shot the US President John F. Kennedy, the plane took off without Air Traffic Control Authorization and kept Radio Silence until they landed at San Julian Air Force Base in Pinar del Rio. The names of the crew are Capt. Cesar Alarcon, copilot? Flight Engineer Mr. Rolando Barros Cubana de Aviacion Director, Hilario Hernandez AKA Yayo e Hipolito Villamil Forte AKA Polo both Engine Technicians.*

3.2. *Light plane landed close the Britannia that flew from Dallas to Mexico to leave Havana's Cuban Boys. Mexican Customs was avoided.*

3.3. *General Fabian Escalante gave the opposite version in his meeting in Bahamas Conversation*

3.4. *According the Rolando Barros source (My brother in Law): The passengers were: Emilio Aragones, Aldo Margolles, Caballo Loco, and Ramon Mercader?*

4. *Jaime Rubenstein in Cuba and Jack Ruby in US*

4.1. *Jaime Rubinstein/Jacob Leon Rubenstein in Cuba and Jack Ruby in US those names were used for the same person according Roberto Bergman his nephew. Mr. Ruby had Jewish Soviet ancestors were Heroes of the Brest Fortress, the first troop location attacked by German Army in August 1941. I scanned the pictures of his father in the soviet book named The Heroes of the Fortress Brest Mir Editorial URSS write by Sergei Smirnov; I remember that in the center of the book there are a bunch of pictures of Militaries Soviet who died fighting against the German Troops. I scanned this picture for Mr. Roberto Bergman in West Palm Beach some years ago because he keeps these pictures in a family photo album. The soviet ancestor and his nephew Roberto Bergman (US /Cuba Citizenship) Resident in Cuba gave two possible status;*

4.2. *Capri Hotel (Card Dealer)*

4.3. *Cafeteria's business owner.*

4.4. *Fabian Escalante said at the Bahaman Convention that the legal immigration documents of Jack Ruby and his trip and life in Cuba before 1959 because of the US threat to attack Cuba, papers needed to be moved to secure locations, and papers were lost to the environment, and to the disorganization of the people.*

5. *KGB/G-2*

5.1. *The Mayor Torres Menier, high rank Intelligence Cuban Officer stated that Harvey Lee Oswald and Jack Ruby met with the Cuban Intelligence founders of G-2 in the KGB Academy in Minsk, URSS in 1960-61, between them were Cmdt. Ramiro Valdes Menendez, Captain Jose Abrantes, Abelardo Colome Ibarra, and others. Harvey Oswald had very close relationship with those Cubans in the Intelligence Academy.*

5.2. *The KGB transferred Harvey Lee Oswald File to Cuba/ Cmdt. Ramiro Valdes, head of Ministry of Interior. 1962 according the Torres Menier Source Two days before and Fifteen days after the Cuban Air Force was in High Alert (Witness Ed Prida UM 1779 Interceptor Squadron Mig 19) Motor and Fuselage Technician at this time (1963)*

Exhibit 4. A sample of Communist propaganda written by Robert F. Williams, Communist fugitive, in Cuba. Cover page

Another thing that is important to mention here is the travel of Carlos Lechuga from Cuba to Mexico City during the same month of September of 1963 when Oswald got in contact with the Russian and Cuban Embassies. Remember that Carlos Lechuga was the person in contact with Fernando Fernández Bárcenas, the Cuban spy infiltrated inside the training camp of the Christian Democratic Movement in Louisiana. Carlos Manuel Lechuga Hevia, 45 years old at the time, traveled with diplomatic passport No. D/62/627 and his visa #833 was expedited by the Embassy of Mexico in Havana on August 30, 1963.

Since the time that Fidel Castro was in the Sierra Maestra he was obsessed with the idea of fighting the United States. When he rose to power he considered that he was strong enough to confront his enemy: The United States of America. He had two dreams: 1) Bomb New York and 2) Kill the President of the United States.

One year after the triumph of Castro's Revolution the FBI redacted a letter addressed to the Chief of the U. S. Secret Service and dated August 4, 1960:

> *This will confirm information orally furnished to Mr. Eugene P. Dagg of the Secret Service on the morning of August 2, 1960, by Special Agent A. J. Decker of this Bureau.*
>
> *On August 1. 1960, Dr. and Mrs. Warenskjolds of San Jose, California, volunteered the following information to our Honolulu Office. They advised that on July 29, 1960 they had met an <u>unidentified male</u> at the Canlis Broiler Cocktail Lounge, Honolulu. It is noted that the 1959 Honolulu Telephone Directory lists a Conlis' Charcoal Broiler Restaurant at 2100 Kalakaua Avenue, Honolulu. This individual, described as approximately thirty years of age, five feet ten inches tall, one hundred and sixty pounds, black hair, brown eyes, prominent teeth, well built, handsome and prosperous looking, identified himself as a <u>Cuban</u> in the sugar business. The Warenskjolds said that he referred to all United States citizens as "Al Capones" and asserted that "these people may find a bomb in their backyard, planted by Castro with outside help." Reportedly, he also declared that if Mrs. Warenskjolds knew where things were in San Jose, she could work on "their side."*

According to the Warenskjolds, this individual also asserted that the United States would find its President "with a bullet hole in his head" and further that Cuba would get even with the United States for what this country did to Cuba in the sugar field. The Warenskjolds said that, upon driving away from the cocktail lounge, this individual, who was alone, shouted "Hail Castro."

As you can see since 1960 what the Castro's followers wanted was to see the President of the United States "with a bullet hole in his head."

There is another report from the CIA dated 2 November 1964, which as many of these CIA memos were not released until 1998:

"On 23 November 1963 Professor fnu APIAGAS, a well-known Cuba's scientist and acquaintance of Subject at ICIDCA (Instituto Cubano de Investigaciones cana de azucar y sus derivados), told Subject that by chance he had been at the Havana airport on the afternoon of 22 November 1963. At 1700 hours an aircraft with Mexican markings landed and parked at the far side of the field and two men, whom he recognized as Cuban "gangsters" alighted, entered the rear entrance of the administration building, and disappeared without going through the normal customs procedure. APIAGAS' curiosity was aroused, and he was able to learn that the aircraft had just arrived from Dallas, Texas, via Tijuana and Mexico City. The plane had been forced to land at Tijuana due to engine trouble. By combining the date, the origin of the flight, and the known reputation of the two men, APIAGAS theorized that the two men must have been involved somehow in the assassination of President Kennedy. He speculated that Lee Oswald had acted in the pay of Castro, and that the two Cubans had been in Dallas to organize or oversee the operation. APIAGAS told Subject that he had been greatly disturbed by what he had seen and heard, and had to tell someone about it. He cautioned Subject not to tell anyone else about it, or they would be shot by the Cubans."

I am inclined to believe that this incident is referring to another airplane than the one described by Martin Underwood in which Fabián Escalante allegedly traveled from Dallas to Cuba, via Mexico City. These two Cubans "gangsters" had to have been members of the support teams to help Lee Harvey Oswald escape and bring him to the Red Bird airport.

There is another very interesting CIA memo kept secret and release only in 1998 which reads:

"MEMORANDUM FOR THE RECORD

SUBJECT: *Plots to Assassinate the President of the U.S.*
1. <u>*Description:*</u>
   Self-explanatory, Contains any traffic dealing with the subject.
2. <u>Findings:</u>
   a. <u>*Director 039064, 8 Dec 1962:*</u>
      Cable from Agency to Secret Service, FBI and State Dept. Security, text of a letter from Havana, dated 27 Nov 62, concerning plot to assassinate Pres. Kennedy. Letter was addressed to a Post office Box in Miami belonging to the Radio Libertad La Voz, Anti-Communists de America. Since the addressee was unknown to members of Radio Libertad, one of their Miami reps. passed the letter to a contact of JMWAVE Station. Addressee was Bernardo Adalberto MORALES-Rivero.

   b. <u>*DIRECTOR 4013, 8 Dec 1962:*</u>
      CIA Hqs. Provided Hqs. FBI and other addressees cited above traces on Bernardo Adalberto MORALES-Rivero who entered the U.S. in May 62 on fraudulent visa.

   c. <u>*UPGA 6884 10 Dec 1962:*</u>
      Dispatch from JMWAVE Station to TFK, Hqs. Stated that a similar letter, possibly written by same author, was in possession of Treasury Dept. Wash., D.C. by official who was in contact with CIA on the matter. JMWAVE forwarded the 29 Nov 62 letter from Jose MENENDEZ to Bernardo MORALES in Miami and suggested that HQS. Pass it to the Treasury Dept. for technical handling. JMWAVE was anxious to receive results of <u>both of the letters</u> on the

grounds that they may be part of a planned G-2 PW operation in the U.S. or against U.S. targets.

d. *DIRECTOR 04538 11 December 1962:*
   Hqs. CIA cabled traces to secret Service, FBI and State Security on Olga DUQUE deHeredia and Aida MAYO, Miami reps., of the org. Radio Libertad La Voz Anti-Communist de America, address to which letter to MORALES was addressed. DUQUE and MAYO turned the letter over to a contact of CIA, since MORALES was reportedly unknown to them. DUQUE was married to Humberto LOPEZ Perez, operator of Radio Libertad, Caracas, Venezuela; Aida MAYO was close friend of Fidel CASTRO and was believed to act occasionally on behalf of Cuban Government.

e. *DIRECTOR 04501, 11 December 1962:*
   Hqs. Cabled JMWAVE noting dissemination of information re letter, but fact that Cesar Augusto GAJATE Puig was not mentioned in dissem. as intermediary between JMWAVE Station and DUQUE and MAYO. Requested that protect GAJATE'S identity.

f. *WAVE 2266 (IN 33425) 11 Dec 1962:*
   Cabled WAVE traces on DUQUE, MAYO and Radio Libertad.

g. *Memo dated 12 December 1962 re info. From Secret Service:*
   Info from usual reliable source on Jose MENENDEZ Ramos, born in Cuba, was baker in Tampa, Fla., and member of exec committee of FPCC. After Oct 61 his wife defected to Cuba with children, and Jose left to join her shortly thereafter. Jose was later seen in Cuba by people who said he had a top job there. Jose also reported to be connected with INRA.

In another CIA filed also released in 1998 we read the following:

ZRNICK—24 Files
BOX 10, JOB # 75-752
SPACE 446-688

1. *"SEPIO" file contains a letter from one Mr. MENENDEZ, (mailed from: 12 Rue Du Chateau Du Roi, Cahors (LOT), France) to one Oliva LOPEZ at 5 de Febrero, NO 38—2, Mexico. The letter is of some interest as it was apparently written by a Mr. MENENDEZ, the same name used by the author of a previous letter mailed to Miami*

in November 1962 discussing plans for the assassination of President Kennedy (see the MENENDEZ soft files).

2. *The ZRKICK memo files, Vol I & II make reference to memos written on 22 and 29 November. They are not in the file.*

3. *The memo files contain no information from the period 19 thru 29 November 1963.*

4. *An intercepted message dated 27 October 1962 relates to question # 31 of the Inspector General memo: "Principal objective is the physical elimination of counterrevolutionary scum and the destruction of their centers."*

That the CIA and the Secret Service was investigating Castro's plots to assassinate President Kennedy there could be no doubt with all the above mentioned memos, but also it is good to read this memo from the CIA dated 12 December 1962, eleven months before JFK's assassination, and released in full not until 1998, which means the Warren Commission was never aware of it:

12 December 1962

Flynn called to pass on a couple of U.S. Secret Service reports which might fit into the possible plot Assassinate President Kennedy.

   1   From a usually reliable source:
      Jose MENENDEZ Ramos born 13 November 1921 in Cuba, 5'8" tall. 150 lbs, brown eyes, black hair, last address in U.S. was at 1211 ½ 17th Avenue, Tampa, Fla. He was a baker in a union bakery at 1506 9th Avenue, Tampa. He was a member of the executive committee of the FPCC. Shortly before October 1961 his wife Carrie Fernandez Menendez defected to Cuba with her children and subject left a short time later to join her in Cuba. He was later seen in Cuba by people who said that he had a top job in Cuba. Before he came to the U.S. it was reported that he had a position with the Communist Youth in Cuba.

   2   From another usually reliable source:
      Jose Menendez was connected with the Institute of National Agrarian Reform (INRA).

> *Source was of the opinion that this plot could be a harassment op conducted by the Cubans.*

Now, come on. With all this information how anyone with some common sense could not think of a possible Castro's involvement in JFK's assassination. The CIA had proven since 1960 that there was a Castro's plot to assassinate President Kennedy. It is not strange that Richard Helms, Director of the CIA would have been so inept that the thought did not cross his mind that Castro could have been behind the assassination as he declared to the Rockefeller Commission? I really don't know how come an ex-President of the United States, Jimmy Carter, could have become a friend of an assassin like Fidel Castro.

In regard to the "inefficiency" of the FBI let's continue:

> *Another official in the Nationalities Intelligence Section, reputed to be the leading Cuban expert within the Bureau, testified he was never informed of any CIA assassination attempts against Fidel Castro. This supervisor had no recollection of any Bureau investigation of Cuban involvement in the assassination.*
>
> *Q. Were there any meetings that you recall where there were discussions as to whether or not the Cubans were involved in the assassination of President Kennedy? A. No, I don't recall. I would say no.*
>
> *Q. Do you know if that possibility was investigated?*
>
> *A. Well, I can't even say that for sure, no, I can't.*
>
> *Q. Do you recall at any time ever seeing any memoranda or instructions that Cuban sources be contacted to see if there was any Cuban involvement in the assassination of President Kennedy?*
>
> *A. There were no such communications, to my knowledge, ever sent out from Headquarters.*
>
> *Q. If they were sent out, in all likelihood you would have known about it?*
>
> *A. Yes, I think I would have. It's[107]*

---

[107] Page 37.

The above paragraphs clearly show the "type" of investigation that Lyndon B. Johnson, the liberals and the "moles" wanted to conduct in order to exonerate Fidel Castro. Johnson was afraid, the liberals and the "Moles" were protecting their hero. Even more disturbing is the rest of the deposition of this supervisor.

This supervisor does not recall ever being informed of Castro's warning of retaliation. He did testify that he had been informed, he would have conducted his investigation differently.

Q. *We have here a copy of an article from the New Orleans Times-Picayune on September 9, 1963, which I think recently been in the press again, I will read a portion of it to you. It says "Prime Minister Fidel Castro turned up today at a reception at the Brazilian Embassy in Havana and submitted to an impromptu interview by Associated Press Correspondent Daniel Harker."*

Now, we have been told by CIA experts that Castro giving an interview at that time was something unusual.

Would you agree with that? **A.** *Yes.*

Q. *And it was also unusual that he would go to a reception at the Brazilian Embassy?*

A. *Uh huh.*

Q. *And the first paragraph of the article says, "Prime Minister Castro said Saturday night U.S. leaders would be in danger if they helped in any attempt to do away with leaders of Cuba." Then it goes on from there.*

Do you recall ever seeing that article or hearing that statement from Castro?

A. *No, I don't. In retrospect that certainly looks like a pointed signal . . . If it had come to our attention-you know, if this article had been routed to us, it would have been a typical reaction from headquarters, to instruct the key field offices handling Cuban matters to alert their sources and be aware, you know, be particularly aware of anything that might indicate an assassination attempt but there was no* *such communication, to my knowledge, ever sent out from headquarters.[108]*

It is very clear that the "investigation" was a whitewash intended to protect Fidel Castro. The United States Senate document continues: *On November 24, 1963 the Legat cabled FBI headquarters:*

> *Ambassador feels Soviets much too sophisticated to participate in direction of assassination of President by subject, but thinks Cubans stupid enough to have participated in such direction event to extent of hiring subject. If this should be case, it would appear likely that the contract would have been made with subject in U.S. and purpose of the trip to Mexico was to set up get away route. Bureau may desire to give consideration to polling all Cuban sources in U.S. in effort to confirm or refute this theory.*
>
> *The Committee found no indication that the Bureau ever attempted to confirm or refute this theory. Indeed, a FBI Headquarters supervisor's handwritten notation on the cablegram states: "Not desirable. Would serve to promote rumors."[109]*

Maybe that was the reason why FBI Supervisor Laurence Keenan after been sent to Mexico by FBI Director J. Edgar Hoover and after realizing that the evidence was pointing to Cuba was ordered to stop his investigation, return to the U.S. and keep his mouth shut.[110] It is clear that the role of the investigators was "not to investigate" but to let the liberal fascists continued their monumental attack against the conservative Americans and naming the City of Dallas "the City of Hate'.

Even more involving details in stopping a true investigation to confirm or refute the feelings of the U.S. Ambassador to Mexico could be clearly seen in this other page of the U.S. Senate document.

> *Richard Helms sentiments coincided with his Bureau supervisor's. In his November 28, 1963, cable to the CIA's Mexico station chief, Helms stated:*

---

[108] Pages 37, 38.
[109] Pages 40, 41.
[110] Documentary "Rendezvous with Death", by Wilfried Huismann.

> *For your private information there is a distinct feeling here in all three agencies [CIA, FBI, State] that Ambassador is pushing this case too hard . . . and that we could well create flap with Cubans which could have serious repercussions.[111]*

And here my question is, were we investigating the assassination of the President of the United States or were we protecting the role of Fidel Castro in it?

Let us see now the FBI's handling of the Oswald's Security case. What you are going to read is the same feeling that the author had, at that time, about the FBI handling of the investigation of Lee Harvey Oswald.

> *On December 10, 1963, Assistant Director J. H. Gale of the Inspection Division reported that there were a number of investigative and reporting delinquencies in the handling of the Oswald security case.*
>
> *Gale wrote:*
>
> *Oswald should have been on the Security Index; his wife should have been interviewed before the assassination, and investigation intensified-not held in abeyance-after Oswald contacted Soviet Embassy in Mexico.*
>
> *In the paragraph immediately preceding Gale's recommendation for disciplinary actions, he observes:*
>
> *Concerning the administrative action recommended hereinafter, there is the possibility that the Presidential Commission investigating instant matter will subpoena the investigative Agents. If this occurs, the possibility then exists that the Agents may be questioned concerning whether administrative action had been taken against them. However, it is felt these possibilities are sufficiently remote that the recommended action should go forward at this time. It appears unlikely at this time that the Commission's subpoenas would go down to the Agent level.[112]*

---

[111] Page 41.
[112] Page 50.

Director Hoover responded, "in any event such gross incompetency (sic) cannot be overlooked nor administrative action postponed."[113]

Assistant Director Cartha DeLoach responded to Gale's report as follows:

I recommended that the suggested disciplinary action be held in abeyance until the findings of the Presidential Commission have been made public. This action is recommended inasmuch as any "leak" to the general public, or particularly to the communications media, concerning the FBI taking disciplinary action against its personnel with respect to the captioned matter would be assumed as a direct admission that we are responsible for negligence which might have resulted in the assassination of the President. At the present time there are so many wild rumors, gossips, and speculation that even the slightest hint to outsiders considering disciplinary action of this nature would result in considerable adverse reaction against the FBI. I do not believe that any of our personnel would be subpoenaed. Chief Justice Warren has indicated he plans to issue no subpoenas. There is, however, the possibility that the public will learn of disciplinary action been taken against our personnel and, therefore, start a bad, unjustifiably reaction.[114]

The above paragraph remind me of an incident that I had, after the assassination, with FBI Agent Warren C. De Brueys when I told him that instead of him been losing his time investigating me he would have been investigating Oswald then maybe President Kennedy still would be alive.

Director Hoover, however, responded to DeLoach's recommendation, "I do not concur."[115]

On December 10, 1963, 17 Bureau employees (five field investigative agents, one field supervisor, three special agents in charge, four headquarters supervisors, two headquarters sections chiefs, one inspector, and one assistant director) were censured or placed on probation for "shortcomings in connection with the

[113] Page 50.
[114] Pages,50, 51.
[115] Page 51.

investigation of Oswald prior to the assassination." Although the transfers of some of these agents were discussed at that time, certain transfers were held in abeyance until the issuance of the Warren Commission's report on September 24, 1964.

One of the specific shortcomings identified by Assistant Director Gale was the failure to include Oswald's name on the Security Index. Indeed, of the seventeen agents, supervisors and senior officials who were disciplined, not a single one believed that Oswald met the criteria for the Security Index, [123]

When on August 21, 1963 I prepared the Press Release urging the people of New Orleans to write to their congressmen asking for a Congressional investigation of Lee Harvey Oswald, in my criteria he was a Security risk.

The document from the Senate continues:

> *In this regard Assistant to the Director Alan Belmont noted in an addendum to Mr. Gale's December 10, 1963 memorandum:*
>
> *It's is significant to note that all the supervisors and officials who came into contact with this case at the seat of the government, as well as agents in the field, are unanimous in the opinion that Oswald did not meet the criteria for the Security Index. If this is so, it would appear that the criteria are not sufficiently specific to include a case such as Oswald's and, rather than take a position that all of these employees were mistaken in their judgment, the criteria should be change. This is now been recommended by assistant Director Gale.*
>
> *Mr. Hoover made the following notations next to Mr. Belmont's addendum: "They were worse than mistaken. Certainly no one in full possession of all his faculties can claim Oswald didn't fall within this criteria."* [116]

> *On September 24, 1964, the same day the Warren Commission's report was officially released, Assistant Director William C. Sullivan wrote:*

---

[116] Page 51.

In answer to the question as to why Lee Harvey Oswald was not in the Security Index, based on facts concerning Oswald which were available prior to his assassination of the President, it was the judgment of the agents handling the case in Dallas and New Orleans, as well as supervisors at the Seat of Government, that such facts did not warrant the inclusion of Oswald in the Security Index. The matter has, of course, been re-examined in the Bureau and Mr. Gale by memorandum 12/10/63 expressed the opinion that Oswald should have been placed on the Security Index prior to 11/22/63. The Director concurred with Mr. Gale's opinion and administrative action had been taken.

Hoover wrote on this Sullivan memorandum that the Bureau personnel who failed to Include Oswald on the Security Index, "could not have been more stupid . . . And now that the Bureau has been debunked publicly I intend to take additional administrative action."[117]

Not surprisingly, Gale states in the "observations" section of the memorandum:

We previously took administrative action against those responsible for the investigative shortcomings in this case some of which were brought out by the Commission. It is felt that it is appropriate at this time to consider further administrative action against those primarily culpable for the dereliction in this case which have now had the effect or publicly embarrassing the Bureau.

After reviewing the Gale memorandum, Alan Belmont forwarded a one-page memorandum to Clyde Tolson on October 1, 1964. Belmont argued that:

I think we are making a tactical error by taking this disciplinary action in this case at this time. The Warren Commission report has been just released. It contains criticism of the FBI. We are currently taking aggressive steps to challenge the findings of the Warren Commission insofar as they pertain to the FBI. It is most important, therefore, that we do not provide a foothold for our critics or the general public to serve upon to say in effect, 'See, the Commission is right, Mr. Hoover has taken strong

---

[117] Pages 51, 52.

*action against personnel involved in this case and thus admits
that the Bureau was in error.'*

Mr. Hoover disagreed with Belmont's observation, writing:

*We were wrong. The administrative actions approved by me
will stand. I do not intend to palliate actions which have resulted
in forever destroying the Bureau as the top level investigative
organization.'*

Wise and strong words from J. Edgar Hoover. I am sure that when
Hoover took those steps he did so with a very heavy heart. The Bureau
was his life. He felt bad about the mistakes committed by his men but no
matter the fact of his declining health, due to his advanced age, Hoover
still was smart enough not to make the same mistake that Richard Nixon
would commit years later when in order to help his friends Nixon was
entrapped in a senseless cover-up.

Now we should move from the FBI to the CIA and study the
relationship between the CIA and the Warren Commission. We continue
obtaining information from the same U.S. Senate document.

*Indeed, AMLASH himself had access to high government
officials in Cuba. He was never asked about the assassination
of President Kennedy in meetings with the CIA in 1964 and
1965.[118]*

I believe that this is almost impossible to believe. You have a
high ranking Cuban Mayor and the CIA don't ask him about the
assassination? Unless the CIA didn't want to know what he could say
or those who were dealing with him were not interested in knowing for
whom AMLASH really worked.

*On December, 1, 1963, CIA received information that a
November 22, Cubana airline flight from Mexico City to Cuba
was delayed some five hours, from 6:00 p.m. to 11:00 p.m.
E.S.T., awaiting an unidentified passenger. This unidentified
passenger arrived at the airport in a twin-engine aircraft at
10:30 p.m. and boarded the Cubana airlines plane without*

---

[118] Page 59

passing through customs, where he would have needed to identify himself by displaying a passport. The individual traveled to Cuba in the cockpit of the Cubana airlines plane, thus again avoiding identification by the passengers.

In response to a Select Committee request of January 9, 1976, the CIA wrote it had no information indicating a follow-up investigation was conducted to determine the identity of the passenger and had no further information on the passenger, and no explanation for why a follow-up investigation was not conducted.[119]

The incident above referred match with the Marty Underwood memo to President Lyndon B. Johnson, identifying the passenger as Cuban General Fabián Escalante, as presented in Wilfried Huismann documentary "Rendezvous with Death".

The U.S. Senate Book V is full of interesting facts not published by the liberal press. Let's continue.

In early December 1963, even most intriguing information was received by the CIA, and passed almost immediately to the FBI. In the case of a Cuban-American, a follow up investigation was conducted. Although the information appeared to relate to the President's assassination and one source alleged the Cuban-American was "involved" in the assassination, the follow-up was not conducted as part of the FBI's work for the Warren Commission.

The CIA learned that this Cuban-American crossed the border from Texas into Mexico on November 23, and that the border had been closed by Mexican authorities immediately after the assassination and reopened on November 23. The Cuban-American arrived in Mexico City on November 25. He stayed in a hotel until the evening of November 27, when he departed in a late evening flight to Havana, using a Cuban "courtesy visa" and an expired U.S. passport. He was the only passenger in that flight, which had a crew of nine.

---

[119] Pages 60, 61.

In March 1964, the CIA received a report from a source which alleged the CubanAmerican had received a permit to enter Mexico on November 20 in Tampa, Florida. The same source also said the Cuban-American was somehow "involved in the assassination." There is no indication that CIA followed-up on this report, except to ask a Cuban defector about his knowledge of the Cuban-American's activities.[120] We are forced to mention here that the above dates connect the incident to the dates of President Kennedy's assassination and Lee Harvey Oswald's assassination. There is a Cubana airlines plane with a crew of 9 with a lone passenger, and the CIA did not conduct a follow-up investigation. Why? Let's continue with the U.S. Senate document.

The FBI did investigate this individual after receiving the CIA report of his unusual travel. However, by the time the Warren Report was published, the Cuban-American was still residing in Cuba and therefore outside FBI's jurisdiction. Before the FBI terminated the case, it had developed the following confusing and incomplete information.

The Cuban-American applied for a U.S. passport at the U.S. Consul in Havana in June 1960. In July 1960 he was issued a passport, but it was valid only until January 1963, when he would become 23 years old.

In May 1962 the Cuban-American requested that Cuban authorities permit his return to Cuba. The Cuban-American's cousin said the Cuban-American apparently did travel to Cuba sometime after May 1962, and spent several weeks there. In August 1962, the Cuban-American married an American woman. They lived in Key West until June 1963, when they moved to Tampa. In August 1963, his wife moved back to Key West because of marital problems. His wife and others characterized the Cuban-American as pro-Castro.

The Cuban-American allegedly told FBI sources that he had originally left Cuba to evade Cuban military service. Nevertheless, some sources told the FBI that the Cuban-American

---

[120] Page 61.

had returned to Cuba in 1963 because he feared been drafted in the United States, while others attributed his return to his worry about his parents or about his own health.

It was reported to the FBI that the Cuban-American had a brother in the Cuban military who was studying in the Soviet Union.

On November 17, 1963, according to several sources, the Cuban-American was at a gettogether at the home of a member of the Tampa Chapter of the "Fair Play for Cuba Committee", where color slides of Cuba were shown.

There was some talk about the Cuban-American having been at the residence for some time waiting for a telephone call from Cuba which was very important. It is understood that it all depended on his getting the "go ahead order" for him to leave the United States. He indicated he had been refused travel back to his native Cuba.[121]

This Cuban-American was at a meeting of the Tampa Chapter of the "Fair Play for Cuba Committee" five days prior to the assassination, being that the same Chapter that V. T. Lee had instructed, on May 29, 1963, Lee Harvey Oswald to contact. This Cuban-American was waiting for a call from Cuba giving him the "go ahead order" and this was happening five days prior to the assassination in Dallas. But neither the FBI nor the CIA told the Warren Commission about the Cuban-American strange travel to Mexico and Cuba, and the "Fair Play for Cuba" connection. Why? The U.S. Senate document continues.

On November 20, 1963, the Cuban-American obtained a Mexican tourist card at the Honorary Consulate of Mexico in Tampa and on November 23 crossed the border into Mexico at Nuevo Laredo. Since the Cuban-American was not listed as the driver of any vehicle crossing the border that day, the FBI concluded he crossed in a privately owned automobile owned by another person.

At a regular monthly meeting of the Tampa FPCC in December 1963, a woman told the group that she had telephoned

---

[121] Pages 61, 62.

*Cuba at 5:00 a.m. and was informed that the Cuban-American
had arrived there safely via Texas and Mexico. Another source
reported that as September 1964, the Cuban-American was
not working in Cuba but spent a great deal of time playing
dominoes.[122]*

I would like to mention that on page 60 of the U.S. Senate document
it is stated that the Cuban-American had left Mexico City at 10:30 p.m.
on November 22, 1963, but in the above paragraph [page 62] it is stated
that the Cuban-American crossed the border from the USA to Mexico on
November 23, which render impossibly that he could have left Mexico
City to Cuba the day before by crossing the border from the USA to
Mexico. Either there was a typographical error in one of those dates or
the investigators were wrong and were confusing two different individuals
and incidents. But let's continue with the US Senate document.

*The preceding was the extent of the FBI and the CIA
investigation. So far as can be determined, neither the
FBI nor the CIA told the Warren Commission about the
CubanAmerican's strange travel. Warren Commission files
contain an excerpt of the FBI check on the Cuban-American
at the Passport Office, but nothing else. In responding to the
Commission's request for information on the Miami chapter of
the FPCC, the FBI reported that the Tampa chapter had 16
members in 1961 and was active in May 1963.* (Author's note:
It is written that the Commission requested information
about the Miami chapter of the FPCC but the information
is provided for the Tampa chapter of the FPCC. It could be a
misprint.) *The FBI response did not discuss the Cuban-American
or the November and December 1963 meetings.*

*Moreover, a possible connection between Lee Harvey
Oswald and the Tampa chapter of FPCC had already been
indicated. Oswald applied to V.T. Lee, national president of
the FPCC, for a charter for a New Orleans chapter. Lee wrote
Oswald on May 29, 1963, suggesting Oswald get in touch with
the Tampa chapter, which Lee personally organized. Thus, the*

[122] Page 62.

*suspicious travel of this individual couple with the possibility that
Oswald had contacted the Tampa chapter certainly should have
prompted a far more through and timely investigation than the
FBI conducted and the results should have been volunteered to
the Warren Commission, regardless of its failure to request such
information.*

*In the two preceding cases the Warren Commission staff
was apparently not furnished with what seems to be significant
information relating to possible Cuban involvement.*[123]

The U.S. Senate document also point out about the knowledge of
plots to assassinate Castro. For example let's check this exchange in
between Senator Morgan and Richard Helms, Director of the CIA.

Senator Morgan: *. . . [in 1963] you were not . . . Just an employee of the
CIA. You were in the top echelon, the management level,
were you not?*

Mr. Helms: *Yes, I was Senator Morgan . . .*

Senator Morgan: *you had been part of an assassination plot against Castro?*

Mr. Helms: *I was aware that there had been efforts made to get rid of
him by these means.*

Senator Morgan: *. . . you were charged with furnishing the Warren
Commission information from the CIA, information
that you thought was relevant?*

Mr. Helms: *No sir, I was instructed to replay to inquiries from the
Warren Commission for information from the Agency. I
was not asked to initiate any particular thing.*

Senator Morgan: *. . . in other words, if you weren't asked for it, you didn't
give it.*

Mr. Helms: *That's right, sir.*[124]

Let's continue reading some unconceivable statements in the mouth
of the Director of the CIA.

---

[123] Pages 62, 63.
[124] Page 70.

In testimony before the Rockefeller Commission, Mr. Helms was directly asked whether he linked Oswald's pro-Cuban activity with the possibility that Castro had retaliated for CIA attempts against him.

Q. *Now, after President Kennedy was assassinated in November 1963, and after it became known to you that the individual, Lee Harvey Oswald, was believed very broadly to have done the shooting, that Oswald had done some activity in the Fair Play for Cuba Committee . . .*

Did you hold any conversations with anybody about the possibility that the assassination of President Kennedy was a retaliation by Oswald against the activity, the talks and plans to assassinate Castro?

A. *No. I don't recall discussing that with anybody. I don't recall the thought ever having occurred to me at the time. The first time I ever heard such a theory as that enunciated was in a very peculiar way by President Johnson . . .*

Q. *I am not asking you about a story, Ambassador, I am asking you whether or not there was a relationship between Oswald's contacts with the Cubans, and his support of the Castro government, his attempts in September 1963 to get a passport to Cuba, to travel to Cuba, his attempts to penetrate anti-Castro groups. Did this connection ever enter your mind?* **A.** *I don't recall its having done so.*[125]

This unbelievable way of thinking from former Director of the CIA Richard Helms tend to prove the low level mentality of Mr. Helms or how deep the enemies of the USA had reach inside our intelligence services. I don't believe that Mr. Richard Helms could have had so low degree of intelligence. But let's continue reading this important U.S. Senate document spiked by the liberal press.

Mr. Helms also testified he did not believe the AMLASH operation was relevant to the investigation of President Kennedy's assassination.

---

[125] Page 71.

The testimony of the AMLASH Case Officer is similar. He stated, "I find it very difficult to link the AMLASH operation to the assassination, I find no way to link it. I did not know of any other CIA assassination attempts against Fidel Castro, so I have nothing to link."[126]

But we have learned in 1998, when the CIA made public memos relating Fidel Castro's plots to assassinate President Kennedy, and later on, on the same U.S. Senate document Richard Helms and the AMLASH Case Officer are openly contradicted by the Desk Officer.

The Desk Officer who was in charge of the initial CIA investigation of President Kennedy's assassination, first learned of the AMLASH operation when he testified before the Select Committee:

Q. *Did you know that on November 22, 1963, about the time Kennedy was assassinated, a CIA case officer was passing a poison pen, offering a poison pen to a high level Cuban to use to assassinate Castro?*

A. *No. I did not.*

Q. *Would you have drawn a link in your mind between that and the Kennedy assassination?*

A. *I certainly think that that would have been-become an absolutely vital factor in analyzing the events surrounding the Kennedy assassination.*[127]

The Desk Officer clearly shows more investigative brains than former CIA Director Richard Helms and the Case Officer of the AMLASH operation. On the same U.S. Senate document the Chief of SAS Counterintelligence is also quoted:

The Chief of SAS Counterintelligence was asked whether it was reasonable to make a connection between AMLASH and President Kennedy's assassination:

---

[126] Page 71.
[127] Page 72.

Q. *In other words, you think knowledgeable officials, knowledgeable of both the Kennedy assassination investigation and of the AMLASH operation . . .*

A. *I think it would have been logical for them to consider that there could be a connection and to have explored it on their own.*[128]

The Chief SAS/Counterintelligence had similar observations. When questioned about the security of the AMLASH operations, he testified:

Q. *Did you know back in November 1963 that the CIA was meeting with AMLASH?*

A. *Yes, and I had expressed my reservations about such a meeting. I didn't consider him to be responsible.*

Q. *Did you know that Mr. Fitzgerald met with AMLASH in late October of 1963?*

A. *I believe I did. I have vague recollections of that now, yes.*

Q. *What was the purpose of the meeting?*

A. *I believe it was related to the assassination, an assassination plot against Castro, and as to this I had reference before. I couldn't recall the exact time frame, but I thought it was nonsense. I thought it would be counterproductive if it would have successful, so I opposed it.*

Q. *Did you know that Mr. Fitzgerald went ahead with it?*

A. *Yes, Mr. Fitzgerald and I did not always agree.*

Q *But he told you he was going ahead with the operation?*

A. *I expressed my reservations about it. He went ahead. He didn't ask my permission. He was my boss.*[129]

But if the CIA was playing, at least in 1963, a stupid game it shows that ignorance could be overcome but stupidity is forever. No withstanding all the above information about AMLASH/Cuban Major Rolando Cubela, and that Cubela could have been a double agent sent by Castro, the CIA again got involved with him in another coup d'etat against Castro. Stupidity or what?

---

[128] Page 73.
[129] Page 75.

Several months later, "A" a Cuban exile who had been involved in transporting explosives to New Orleans in 1963, contacted the Immigration and Naturalization Service with information about the AMLASH operation. This information was turned over the FBI which informed the CIA.

Representatives from both agencies interrogated "A" jointly in June 1965. The interrogation established that the Cuban exile knew that (1) AMLASH and others were planning a coup which involved the assassination of Castro, and (2) the CIA had been involved with AMLASH and others in the plotting.

Although "A" claimed that he and AMLASH were lifelong friends, the report of the interrogation do not indicate that he knew of the fall 1963 AMLASH-CIA meetings. The 1967 I. G. Report noted that information given by "A" suggested a link between the AMLASH operation and the 1960-62 CIA plots to assassinate Castro using underworld contacts. In other words, the information "A" provided raised the possibility that underworld figures who were aware of the assassination plots in which William Harvey participated, may have also been aware of the AMLASH operation.

On July 2, 1965, the FBI sent some of the details obtained from the interrogation to the White House, the Attorney General, and then DCI, Admiral Raborn. The CIA reaction to the information was to terminate the entire AMLASH operation. It cabled its stations:

"Convincing prove that entire AMLASH group insecure and that further contact with key members of group constitutes a menace to CIA operations . . . Under no circumstances are newly assigned staff personnel or newly recruited agents to be exposed to the operation." In an undated memorandum, the Chief of SAS Counterintelligence wrote:

"The AMLASH circle is wide and each new friend of whom we learn seems to have knowledge of the plan. I believe the problem is more serious and basic one. Fidel reportedly knew that this group was plotting against him and once

enlisted its support. Hence, we cannot rule out the possibility of provocation."

In the middle of 1965, the CIA interrogated AMWHIP one of the Cuban exiles who had been involved with the AMLASH operation from the beginning; a person who knew about the meetings between AMLASH and the CIA case officers in the fall of 1963. The report of the interrogation cautioned that analysis of the results was difficult since the examination was conducted in English and the subject had difficulty understanding the questions. The report recommended a second examination be conducted in Spanish. Nevertheless, the report tentatively concluded that the subject was deceptive during the interrogation and withheld pertinent information in one or more relevant areas.

The report noted that the subject apparently lied in response to certain questions dealing with AMLASH and with both the subject's and AMLASH ties to Cuban intelligence. During the examination, the subject told the interrogator that AMLASH had no plan to overthrow Castro and that the subject had never considered AMLASH's various activities as constituting a plan for such an objective. The subject said AMLASH never controlled a viable group inside Cuba which could attempt a coup against Castro. The subject said AMLASH had strong connections with Cuban intelligence and was probably cooperating with it in various ways. Although AMLASH had not mentioned these connections to his CIA case officers, the subject stated that AMLASH had mentioned them to him, and almost everyone else AMLASH met. There is no record of a second interrogation. The last documents in the file of this individual are dated only months after the interrogation, indicating that the CIA terminated all contact with him.

Although the CIA had received information that the AMLASH operation was insecure and the possibility that AMLASH was a "provocation," there is no evidence that the CIA investigated the possibility of a connection between its fall 1963 meetings with AMLASH, and the assassination of President Kennedy. Moreover, CIA files contained at least some FBI reports on "A" the Cuban exile who was involved in transporting explosives to New Orleans in 1963. These reports detail his involvement with anti-Castro exiles and underworld figures who were operating the guerrilla training camp in New Orleans in July 1963.[130]

The U.S. Senate Final Report also deals with allegations of Cuban involvement in the assassination of President Kennedy.

B. 1967: Allegations of Cuban Involvement in the Assassination.

In late January 1967, Washington Post columnist Drew Pearson met with Chief Justice Earl Warren. Pearson told the Chief Justice that a Washington lawyer had told him that one of his clients said the United States had attempted to assassinate Fidel Castro in the early 1960's and Castro had decided to retaliate. Pearson asked the Chief Justice to see the lawyer; however, he declined. The Chief Justice told Pearson that it would be necessary to inform Federal investigative authorities, and Pearson responded that he preferred that the Secret Service rather than the FBI be notified.

On January 31, 1967, the Chief Justice informed Secret Service Director James J. Rowley of the allegations.[131] (Author's note: Chief Justice Earl Warren, the same one who immediately after the assassination, even before Oswald had been arrested, had put the blame on "hate-mongers right wingers" never forced the investigative agencies to conduct an investigation that could lead them to find that Fidel Castro was behind the assassination. If the attorney's allegation would have involved right wingers or anti-Castro Cubans, Chief Justice Earl Warren would have contacted the FBI, CIA and the President of the United States to investigate that information.)

---

[130] Pages 78, 79.
[131] Page 80.

On March 21, 1967, the Washington Field Office sent FBI Headquarters ten copies of a blind memorandum reporting on the interview [with the lawyer]. This memorandum can be summarized as follows:

1) *The lawyer had information pertaining to the assassination, but it was necessary for him in his capacity as an attorney to invoke the attorney-client privilege since the information in his possession was derived as a result of that relationship.*

2) *His clients, who were on the fringe of the underworld were neither directly nor indirectly involved in the death of President Kennedy, but they faced possible prosecution in a crime not related to the assassination and through participation in such crime they learned information pertaining to the President's assassination.*

3) *His clients were called upon by a government agency to assist in a project which was said to have the highest government approval. The project had at its purpose the assassination of Fidel Castro. Elaborate plans were made; including the infiltration of the Cuban government and the placing of informants within key posts in Cuba.*

4) *The project almost reached fruition when Castro became aware of it; by pressuring captured subjects he was able to learn the full details of the plot against him and decided "if that was the way President Kennedy wanted it, he too could engage in the same tactics."*

5) *Castro thereafter employed teams of individuals who were dispatched to the United States for the purpose of assassinating President Kennedy. The lawyer stated that his clients obtained this information "from 'feedback' furnished by sources close to Castro," who had been initially placed there to carry out the original project.*

6) *His clients were aware of the identity of some of the individuals who came to the United States for this purpose and he understood that two such individuals were now in the State of New Jersey.*

7) *One client, upon hearing the statement that Lee Harvey Oswald was the lone assassin of President Kennedy "laughs with tears in his eyes and shakes his head in apparent disagreement."*

8) *The lawyer stated if he were free of the attorney-client privilege, the information that he would be able to supply would not directly identify the alleged conspirators to kill President Kennedy. However, because of the project to kill Fidel Castro, those participating in the project, whom he represents, developed through feedback information*

that would identify Fidel Castro's counter assassins in this country who could very well be considered suspects in such conspiracy.

The transmittal slip accompanying this memorandum noted, "No further investigation is being conducted by the Washington Field Office unless it is advised to the contrary by the Bureau." Had the interviewing agents known of the CIA-underworld plots against Castro, they would have been aware that the lawyer had clients who had been active in the assassination plots.

The Washington Field Office memorandum of the interview was rewritten at FBI Headquarters before it was sent to the White House, the Attorney General, and the Secret Service. The cover letter sent with this memorandum did not recommend any FBI investigation of the lawyer's allegations. As rewritten, this memorandum varies from the original field version in two significant respects. Three new paragraphs were added summarizing FBI file materials about CIA-underworld plots to assassinate Castro. In addition the rewritten version of the memorandum twice delete the words "in place" from the phrase "sources in place close to Castro." The supervisor who rewrote the memorandum could provide no explanation of the omission. (Author's note: Undoubtedly J. Edgar Hoover statement that the mishandling of the FBI's investigation on Lee Harvey Oswald *"have resulted in forever destroying the Bureau as the top level investigative organization"* was proved correct during the events investigating the alQaeda cell that carried on the massacre of September 11, 2001. When several blunders allowed the terrorists to carry on their plans as it is the example of the case of Zac Moussaoui when the Minneapolis agents of the FBI were stunned by headquarters refusal to even submit their request for a search warrant for consideration. In a memo written by Colleen Rowley, the Minneapolis office's general counsel where Rowley wrote that the Washington supervisor who presented the petition to the FBI's lawyers amended it to its detriment and omitted the additional intelligence supplied by the French.[132]

---

[132] "The Cell", by John Miller and Michael Stone with Chris Mitchell, page 299.

Neither the field agents who interviewed the lawyer nor the Headquarters supervisory agents assigned to the assassination case, could provide any explanation for the Bureau's failure to conduct any follow up investigation. When they were informed of the details of CIA assassination efforts against Castro, each of these agents stated that the allegations and specific leads provided should have been investigated to their logical conclusions.

Although the Select Committee had not been able to establish through direct evidence that President Johnson asked CIA officials about the lawyer's allegations, CIA Director Helms met with the President at the White House on the evening of March 22, 1967. Earlier that day, the President had been furnished the FBI memorandum which summarized CIA use of the underworld figures in plots against Castro and the lawyer's interview. On March 23, Director Helms ordered the CIA Inspector General to prepare a report on the CIA assassination plots.

On April 24. 1967, the I.G. began submitting portions of his report to Director Helms. The May 23 draft report which was the only draft retained by the CIA, refers to Drew Pearson columns and the lawyer's contacts with Chief Justice Warren, Rowley and the FBI, but does not analyze the retaliation allegations.

Sometime between April 24 and May 22, the Director met and orally briefed President Johnson on the I.G.'s findings. When questioned during the course of the Committee's investigation into CIA assassinations plots, Helms was not asked specifically whether he briefed the President about the fall 1963 AMLASH operations. Helms did testify that he did not brief President Johnson about the 1964 and 1965 phases because he did not regard AMLASH as an assassination agent. (Author's note: Once again, if Helms was not doing this in bad faith, what degree of intelligence did he had?). Although a note in Director Helm's handwriting, which apparently was prepared to use in briefing the President only refers to covert actions against Cuba through mid-1963, the I.G. report treated the AMLASH project from 1963 as an assassination operation.

Even before work began on the 1967 I.G. Report, the CIA analyst on the Counter intelligence staff who had been the "point *of record" for the CIA work with the Warren Commission was asked to analyze public allegations of conspiracy. This analyst was not furnished a copy of the 1967 I.G. Report and was not asked to determine whether there were any connections between CIA assassination operations and the assassination of President Kennedy. CIA records disclose that he did request a name check on "A," the individual who had been tangentially connected with an anti-Castro training camp in New Orleans. Although "A's" file at the CIA notes that he was aware of the AMLASH operation in 1965, the response to the name check did not disclose the fact. Indeed, it was not until 1975, during the Rockefeller Commission's study, that this analyst learned of the CIA assassination plots.[133]*

Now it would be good to present a list of potential witnesses involving Fidel Castro with the assassination of President John F. Kennedy.

1) **_Luisa Calderón._** A Member of the General Department of Investigation (DGI) of the Cuban government. Also Secretary at Cuban Embassy in Mexico City.

On November 22, 1963 the CIA's monitoring the Cuban Embassy recorded the following conversation reported on a blind Memo of May 1964.

Caller: "Luisa, Kennedy has been killed. Assassinated in Texas." *Luisa:* "No, really? When?
Caller: At one o'clock."
Luisa: "Fantastic! Wonderful! Luisa started to laugh. *Caller:* "Apparently his wife and brother were also wounded."

Both started to laugh.

Luisa: "Wonderful, what good news!"
Caller: "The consequences? Only good ones."

---

[133] Pages 85, 86.

Luisa: He was a family man, yes, but also a degenerated aggressor."
Caller: "Three shots in the face."
Luisa: "Perfect."[134]

Almost immediately after this conversation Luisa dialed a call out to someone called Nico. After commenting about the assassination and laughing about it the conversation went like this:

Nico: "Okay. At what time will the plane arrive?"
Luisa: "At four, and at four thirty they must be at the airport."[135]

A few minutes later, a woman caller contacted Luisa Calderón.

Caller: "Luisa, have you heard about Kennedy yet?"
Luisa: "Yes. I knew almost before Kennedy did.
Caller: "They have arrested the guy. He's president of the Fair Play for Cuba Committee."
Luisa: "I already know that. A gringo. Right?[145]

We have to remember that at the time Luisa Calderón was a member of the General Department of Investigation (DGI) of the government of Fidel Castro assigned to the Cuban Embassy in Mexico City and who had met Lee Harvey Oswald during his visit at the Embassy in September 1963.

2) ***Antulio Ramírez Ortiz:*** Was born in Puerto Rico but became involved in the revolution during the late fifties and after the triumph of the revolution was sent, as spy, to New York City. On May 1, 1961 he hijacked a National Airlines jet in Miami and flew to Havana where he was welcomed as a hero and started working for the Cuban Department of Intelligence under the orders of Ramiro Valdés, Interior Secretary.

During his work, around the fall of 1962 Ramírez Ortiz discovered a report from Alberto "Furry" Colomé Ibarra to his boss Ramiro Valdés

---

[134] "Brothers in Arms", by Gus Russo and Stephen Molton, page 14.
[135] "Brothers in Arms", by Gus Russo and Stephen Molton, pages 14, 15.

in reference to the information received from Vladimir Kryuchkov pertaining Lee Harvey Oswald. It read:

> *"The KGB has recommended this individual, Lee Harvey Oswald, to us, not pressing it much. He is North American, married to an agent of the Soviet Organism (Communist Party) who has orders to go and settle in the United States. Oswald is an emotional adventurer. Our Embassy in Mexico has been instructed to get in contact with him. Be very careful."*[136]

In 1961 Antulio Ramírez overheard many conversations at G2. He heard that the G2 had an agent with the cover name "The Professor" in direct vicinity of President Kennedy. After the Bay of Pigs "The Professor" reported that Kennedy was preparing another invasion of Cuba and Ramírez recalls that the G2 leadership got together and considered how one could eliminate Kennedy. Kennedy was much hated by the Cuban Secret Service.[137]

In November 1962 Antulio was having an affair with Olga Korchunova, wife of Dimitri Korchunov, an aide to the Soviet Ambassador to Cuba, but who appears on record as a "tourist".[138] And he learned different things. One Cuban mole close to Kennedy, called "The Professor", made Castro aware that the Kennedys-despite the agreement that ended the crisis were still considering a Cuban invasion. Antulio also learned that Castro had been given eighteen MIG's which Castro planned to use to bomb New York.[139]

Castro had assassinated thousands of Cubans, had tried to initiate a nuclear war bombing the USA with nuclear weapons during the missile crisis, he ordered the shooting down of a U-2, he obtained eighteen MIG's in order to bomb New York, he attempted to kill several Latin American presidents, but for the lefties and their idiotic liberal press, he was not going to be so crazy as to have killed John F. Kennedy.

Antulio, trying to avoid a catastrophe with the plans to assassinate President Kennedy, approached Alexis Kurth, Swiss Embassy official,

---

[136] "Brothers in Arms", Russo and Molton, page 188.
[137] "Brothers in Arms", Russo and Molton, page 140.
[138] CIA memo January 30, 1978.
[139] "Brothers in Arms", by Russo and Molton, page 222.

with a packet of material to be given to the U.S., but Kurth refused to accept it. Official U.S. records corroborate this.[140]

Antulio Ramírez Ortiz was born on November 20, 1926 at Santurce, Puerto Rico and was a supporter of Pedro Arbizu Campos, the extremist Puerto Rican nationalist and he went to Cuba in 1958 to support Fidel Castro. He was put in jail by the Batista government and he was release on January 1, 1959. Castro forces invited Ramírez to participate in an invasion to the Dominican Republic which failed. He went to New York and on May 1st, 1961 he hijacked to Havana a National Airlines plane which was in route from Marathon to Key West. While in Havana he started working with Ramiro Valdés and he had been credited to giving the Castro government advance information about the already defeated Bay of Pigs invasion.

While working with Ramiro Valdés, then head of the G2, he had the opportunity to see a file "Oswaldo-Kennedy" with pictures of the future Kennedy's assassin. According to him the file had originated with a memo from the KGB *"recommending this individual, Lee Harvey Oswald, but without much insistence. He is a North American, married to an agent of the Soviet Organization, who is under to establish herself in the U.S. Oswald is an emotional adventurer and our Embassy in Mexico has instructions about how to deal with him."*

Antulio Ramírez was finally apprehended in Miami on November 21, 1975 upon arrival from Kingston, Jamaica, subsequently pleaded guilty on March 4, 1976 to the 1961 hijacking of a plane to Cuba, and was sentenced to 20 years in jail at the Federal Penitentiary at Lavenworth, Kansas.

3) **_Juanita Castro:_** Fidel's sister, in her testimony of June 11, 1965 to the House UnAmerican Activities Committee stated:

> *"Fidel feeling hatred of this country cannot even been imagined by Americans. His intentions—his obsession—is to destroy the United States."*

4) **_Major Pedro Luis Díaz Lans_**: Former Chief of the Cuban Revolutionary Air Force, in 1959, after escaping from Cuba testified:

---

[140] "Brothers in Arms", by Russo and Molton, page 223.

Castro is always telling us we are going to have to fight the Americans—the Marines—and harping all the time of his theme. He wants war with the United States.

5) ***Philip Bonsal:*** United States Ambassador to Cuba sent a telegram to Washington quoting what he had overheard Raúl Castro saying in confidence during Raúl's visit to Moscow. According to Ambassador Bonsal what he heard Raúl saying was: *"My dream is to drop three atomic bombs in New York."*[141]

6) ***Oscar Marino***: He had been a senior Cuban spy, a founder of G2, an old weapons companion and colleague of Fabián Escalante. In 1962 he saw Lee Oswald's name on a foreign collaborators list.[142] (Marino is a pseudonym).

According to Marino, Oswald was recruited in the autumn of 1962, when he heard from the first time his name, and the first contact was made by Rolando Cubela, who encountered Oswald, at least twice, in Mexico City.

Marino had explained how Mexico was the center of activities of Cuban G2 in its war against the USA. Marino explained to German newsman Wilfried Huismann how Cubela had initiated the meetings with Oswald.[143]

7) ***Major Rolando Cubela Secades*** A member of Fidel Castro's elite Secret Service.

Friend and protector of Santos Trafficante. Assigned controller of Lee Harvey Oswald by Cuban Intelligence Service. Known as AMLASH by the CIA in plot to assassinate Fidel Castro. Arrested by Castro and let go free to live in Spain.

8) ***Pedro Gutiérrez.*** Mr. Gutiérrez was visiting the Cuban Embassy in Mexico City on September 30, 1963 or October 1, 1963 when he saw Lee Harvey Oswald with a Cuban National. He could only hear a few words of their conversation, among them: *"Cuba"*, *"Castro"* and *"Kennedy"*.

---

[141] "My Favorite Tyrant", by Humberto Fontova, page 3.
[142] Brothers in Arms", by Russo and Molton, pages 185, 186.
[143] "Rendezvous with Death", Documentary by Wilfried Huismann.

On December 2, 1963 he wrote a letter to President Lyndon B. Johnson and as result the FBI interviewed him four times and found the witness serious and credible. The CIA got interested in the witness and delivered him to the Mexican Secret Police. What this Mexican department did to him is not known but easy to imagine. Pedro Gutiérrez became another person who did not want to remember anything. In 1978 Mr. Gutiérrez in front of investigators of the House Select Committee on Assassinations retracted himself of his original declaration.

Mexican newsman Mauricio Laguna Berber working to help German newsman Wilfried Huismann managed to find the granddaughter of Pedro Gutiérrez to whom he asked why his grandfather had recanted his testimony. Gutiérrez granddaughter answered: *"He had problems"*. Mauricio inquired to which problems she was referring. Gutierrez's granddaughter answered: *"Shortly after mailing the letter to President Johnson, my grandfather received the visit of Cuban Secret agents. He was told to retract his statement or he would be killed."* It is good to mention here that Gutiérrez received the visit of the Cuban Secret agents, before he was contacted by the FBI. Who informed Cuba of his letter to President Johnson? After the CIA turned him over to the Mexican Secret Police he was coerced to retract his testimony and from then on Pedro Gutiérrez lived in constant terror until finally he opted to disappear, get an assumed name and cross the border to the United States where as far as it is known he was living during his 90's.[144]

9) ***Oscar Contreras.*** Contreras was a leader of a student group ("Revolutionary Block") at the Universidad Autónoma de Mexico[145] who at the end of September of 1963 met Lee Harvey Oswald at the coffee shop of the Faculty of Philosophy. After finding out that Oswald was trying to travel to Cuba, Contreras offered Oswald to spend the night at Contreras' apartment in the middle of Mexico City.

---

[144] "Cita con la Muerte", by Wilfried Huismann, pages 24-28.
[145] Mexico Autonomous University.

That night 4 of the members of the "Revolutionary Block" also expended the night at Contreras' apartment where Lee Harvey Oswald slept on a mattress. During their chatting Oswald expressed his love for "Fidel", "Che", "Cuba" and the Revolution.

Contreras contacted the Cuban Embassy thru a Peruvian revolutionary friend but was told to stop his relation with Lee Harvey Oswald because Oswald was a "CIA agent" and a very dangerous one. (The same misinformation later on used by Castro's Intelligence Service).

During those times Contreras used to attend parties organized by lefty's friends among them Silvia Durán and Elena Garro.[146]

10-11) ***Elena Garro de Paz*** and ***Helena Paz Garro.*** Mother and daughter very active during the 1960's leftist Mexico. Elena was married to Nobel Prize winner Octavio Paz. While "Che" Guevara was in Mexico preparing the revolution with Fidel Castro he, Guevara, was a visitor to their home.

Her daughter Helena, recounted to Wilfried Huismann how she had met Lee Harvey Oswald at a party, in Mexico City, attended also by Silvia Durán and Silvia's husband, Horacio. She said *"Lee Harvey Oswald attended the party with two other gringos. I was told he had been invited by Silvia. I invited him to dance but he rejected me".*

No matter the fact that mother and daughter had leftist ideology, on November 22, 1963, when they learned that Lee Harvey Oswald assassinated President John F. Kennedy, Elena Garro de Paz (the mother) convinced that Fidel Castro was behind the assassination went in front of the Cuban Embassy in Mexico and there, in Zamora Street, took her daughter by the hand and started yelling: *"Murderers, you killed President Kennedy!"* Cuban functionaries showed their faces through the windows to watch what was going on. Next day, Manolo Calvillo, a functionary of the Mexican government went to their house telling them that their house was under surveillance saying: *"The Communists have given orders to kill you."* He then took them in secrecy to the Vermont Hotel. After a week, when the Communists thought that everything was under control, they were allowed to return home.[147]

---

[146] "Cita con la Muerte". by Wilfried Huismann, pages 28-32.
[147] "Cita con la Muerte", by Wilfried Huismann, pages 34-37.

12) ***Fernando Gutiérrez Barrios.*** He was the Chief of the Mexican Secret Police and he was also a personal friend of Fidel Castro and Ernesto "Che" Guevara.[148]

13) ***César Morales Mesa.*** He was a black member of the Cuban G2. He had red hair and had been identified by witnesses as having been in contact with Oswald at the Cuban Embassy in Mexico City.

14) ***Rafael Núñez.*** Ex-member of the Cuban Diplomatic Service who served at the Cuban Embassy in Mexico City.

15) ***Antonio.*** An ex-employee of the Cuban Embassy in Mexico City.

16) ***General Fabián Escalante.*** Chief of Cuban Intelligence Services and identified by several sources as having been in touch with Lee Harvey Oswald during Oswald's visits to Mexico. Martin Underwood, Jr., former assistant to President John F. Kennedy and then assistant to President Lyndon B. Johnson wrote a memo "for your eyes only" to President Johnson stating:

> *"Early on the morning of November 22, 1963 a small Cuban airplane landed at the Mexico City airport. The single occupant transferred to another plane that was waiting at the far end of the airport. It immediately took off for Dallas, Texas. Later that evening the plane returned from Dallas and the occupant transferred back to the Cuban airplane. After many months of checking and rechecking we are confident that the occupant was Fabián Escalante.*
>
> *One of the top aides of Fidel Castro, Escalante definitely had been identified in a flight from Havana to Mexico City in September 1963.[149]*

17) ***Quintín Pino Machado.*** Known as the "hatchet man" for the Cuban Embassy in Washington during the first years of the Revolution who have been involved in acts of violence including beatings and abductions of defectors from Communist Cuba.[150]

Pino Machado was the alternate representative to the Organization of American States when Carlos M. Lechuga was the Ambassador to it.

---

[148] "Cita con la Muerte", by Wilfried Huismann, pages 36, 37.
[149] "Cita con la Muerte", by Wilfried Huismann, page 188.
[150] Secret Service Memo, page 406.

According to a Secret Service memo: *"The source cautions that Quintín Pino Machado should be considered a dangerous person. On November 29, 1963, 3-11-48 again contacted this office and revealed that while Quintin Pino Machado was in a drunken condition in Las Villas Province, Cuba (exact date not recalled) Machado boasted that he had almost succeeded in assassinating Dr. Enrique Huertas at Miami, Fla. (This office has no information regarding the latter assassination attempt of Dr. Enrique Huertas). It is noted however, that Dr. Enrique Huertas was among the invited guests at the dinner in honor of President John F. Kennedy held at the Americana Hotel on November 18, 1963 under the auspices of the Inter-American Press Association."*[151]

There were persistent rumors that Quintín Pino Machado was in Mexico during the stay of Lee Harvey Oswald there. There is another Secret Service Report regarding Quintin Pino Machado's possible involvement in conspiracy to assassinate JFK. It reads:

"SYNOPSIS"

Information has been received from 3-11-48 indicating that if the assassination of President Kennedy involved an international plot or conspiracy and that if it was established that Fidel Castro had anything to do with the plot or conspiracy, that the party responsible for carrying out any action on the part of Fidel Castro undoubtedly was Quintin Pino Machado, a Cuban terrorist used by Castro to carry out any Castro action.

(A) INTRODUCTION:

On November 27, 1963, 3-11-48 was interviewed in another matter and during this interview he furnished information we believe pertinent in connection with the assassination of President Kennedy.

(B) GENERAL INQUIRES:

During interview of 3-11-48 on November 27, 1963, he stated that if an international conspiracy or plot, or if Castro's intervention in the assassination of President Kennedy is in fact

---

[151] Secret Service Memo, page 362.

established, that Quintin Pino Machado would have been the intellectual director of the conspiracy or plot. Source related that Quintin Pino Machado belonged to the Communist Party but was better known as "belonging to Castro".

3-11-48 added that Quintin Pino Machado was a former Cuban delegate to the U.S. and subsequently the Cuban ambassador to Nicaragua. He stated that Machado is well known as a terrorist who also trained other youth in the manufacturing or placing of bombs and explosives and was the chief coordinator of sabotage for Castro against Batista.

18) *José Menéndez Ramos:*

In a report from the Secret Service it is stated:

On December 12, 1962, the records of the Immigration Service in Miami were checked for Jose Menendez y Ramos. He is of record under INS No. A6190210. He was born on November 11, 1921, at Guanabacoa, Cuba. He is five feet five inches (5'5") in height, 144 pounds in weight, has brown eyes and black hair, ruddy complexion. He lists his occupation as baker and mechanic. He is married to Caridad Hernandez de Menendez. He lists his father as Rufino Menendez, deceased, and his mother, Josefa Ramos.

The INS file reveals that Jose Menendez y Ramos first entered the United States on October 31, 1945, and remained until December 16, 1945.

He again entered the United States in February 3, 1946, with Cuban passport No. 2603, issued on June 29, 1943 which carried visa No. 1317 issued at Havana, Cuba, on January 24, 1946. His residence in the United States is listed as 1211 ½ 17th Avenue, Tampa, Florida.

He departed Tampa, Florida, on November 6, 1952 for a two-week pleasure trip to Cuba, and he was permitted re-enter the United States on December 23, 1952 with permission to remain until November 6, 1953.

The next notation in this file indicates that Menendez y Ramos submitted a request to return to Cuba and establish residence in that country, and he renounced all his rights and

privileges of a resident alien in the United States. He departed the United States on October 8, 1961, and returned to Cuba
   (Deleted.)
   (Deleted.)
   The report reflects that Menendez was elected an executive member of the FPCC. His wife, Caridad Menendez, is reported to be a U.S. citizen, having been born at Tampa, Florida. Menendez is reported to be "extremely" pro-Castro and defends the Castro regime.

   The report of 3-11-15 further reveals that Caridad Menendez was employed by Doctor Torretta at Tampa, Florida, but was dismissed because of a letter she wrote to a Tampa newspaper regarding the FPCC.
   Caridad Menendez was reported to be sympathetic to the Castro regime and as of September 6, 1961, she and her children returned to Cuba by way of Mexico.
   In report of 3-11-15 dated December 29, 1961, it reveals that as of October 23, 1961, Jose Menendez was known to have a "top job" in Cuba. He is also reported to have been a leader of Communist youth in Cuba before coming to the United States.

There is another memo of the CIA dated June 1977 and also released in full in 1998 which brings the possibility that "José Menéndez" is an alias of a Cuban named "Juan José Mulkay":

SUBJECT: Jose Menendez
  1. *Jose MENENDEZ in Havna (sic) wrote a letter to Bernardo MORALES in Miami, dated 27 November 1962, re a plot to assassinate President Kennedy.*
  2. *Believe he may be identifiable with Juan Jose Mulkay Gutierrez (201-86717) DGI. See memorandum on Mulkay.*

19. *Raúl Jaime Díaz Argüelles y García:*
The CIA kept a thick file (201-269882) on this individual in regard to the assassination of President Kennedy and other violent crimes committed by Raúl Díaz Argüelles. Let's read the following memo:

SUBJECT: *Raul Jaime DIAZ Arguelles y Garcia (201-269882)*
Known Terrorist

1. <u>UPGA 3302, Encl. 3, dated 13 February 1962 (Filed Ministry of Interior File Memo)</u> Att. Memo for secret Service:

    DIAZ has position of great influence in DTI (Department of Technical Investigation) of the DIER—Department of Investigation of the (Rebel) Revolutionary Army. He reportedly was working with former U. S. gangsters who were deported from the U.S. He also reportedly was affiliated with narcotics racket. He was believed to be in complete charge of any activity contemplated by Pedro MARGOLLES Duenas which involved a plot to assassinate President of the U. S.

    <u>WAS 50/7, dated 29 Jan 1962, Same File as above:</u>

    Stated that DIAZ was trained in Czech, to be head of political police of Cuba. Reportedly took refuge in Brazilian Embassy Havana as cover to get out of Cuba to carry on phase of secret activity. At this time DIAZ was head of DTI. Is known terrorist, was responsible for assassinations during Batista regime, capable in use of explosive bombs and automatic weapons. Also believed to have directed assassinations in past from somewhere in Mexico. Good friend of Rolando CUBELA.

    DIAZ died in an accident in Angola Dec. 75 when land mine exploded under jeep he was riding in.

    LAD/JFK Task Force

Now the CIA has established that Castro was intent on assassinate John F. Kennedy since 1960. He had several groups of people trying to achieve that end. Lee Harvey Oswald was just one of them, but it was the one who succeeded.

There is another CIA memo dated June 1977 and release "sanitized" in 1998 which reveals other signals pointing to Fidel Castro:

SUBJECT: *Lee Harvey OSWALD*
1. *Pertinent information from findings:*
    A. <u>*201-740221—Gilberto Nolasco ALVARADO Ugarte*</u>

ALVARADO walked-in to the U.S. Embassy Mexico City on 26 November 1963 and claimed that he had seen members of the Cuban Embassy, including CAPRICE-1, pass $6,500, to OSWALD on 18 September 1963 for the purpose of killing someone.

B. *WAVE 1465 (IN11710) dated 4 Feb 64 filed AMCOG Operation 19-6-63 (SW Message #30 dated Jan 64) AMCOG-3 reported: "According to what AMCOG-5 tells me, OSWALD was in Havana between 2 and 7 October 1963. A lady saw him in shirt sleeves, wearing good shoes and smoking American cigars accompanied by Clemente MORERA an employee of Terminales Mambisas who belongs to the DSE. He (OSWALD) was seen by the sister of Comandante Miranda."*

RIOD 2944 (IN 83322) dated 18 Dec 63 Filed VASLOUCH 19-6-56/3 Reported wide rumor of assassination on life of Fidel CASTRO after his T.V. appearance on 6 December 1963. Also a wide rumor that Cuban Jose "Pepe" LLANUZA met Lee OSWALD in Mexico before the Kennedy assassination.

LAD/JFK Task Force

20. *Captain Aldo Pedro Margolles Dueñas.*

A CIA Memo dated April 2, 1964 describes Margolles as follows:

1. NAME: *Aldo Pedro MARGOLLES Duenas (201-315-161)*

2. *OCCUPATION: Captain MARGOLLES Duenas is Vice Minister of the Ministry of Interior (EE 690, 28 Oct 1963, AIIDIAL/2)*

3. *SIGNIFICANCE OF TARGET:*

MARGOLLES is believed to be quite powerful in the Ministry of Interior, therefore leading us to believe that he would be in constant contact with the highest level personnel within the Cuban government. Since September 1963 he has been the Vice Minister of the Interior Ministry and previously was the Director of Police. He is a brother-in-law to Emilio ARAGONES Navarro and one source stated that he was ARAGONES protégé. MARGOLLES is a member of JUCEI for the Province of

Havana and a possible Communist leader. His brother, Carlos, was a secretary of ORI in Cienfuegos.

8. *CURRICULUM VITAE:*

On 3 December 1961 information of the Honolulu ODENVY Office reported that subject and Emilio ARAGONES Navarro were attempting to enter the U. S. in order to meet with CASTRO agents and assassinate President Kennedy. (DBF 95904, 8 December 1961)

K. On 9 January 1992, Secret Service was investigating a plot against Kennedy involving Subject and Emilio ARAGONES Navarro. (Memo for record 9 January 1962, filed WTL/4/CI "Liaison ODFOAN/JMWAVE")

21. *Policarpo López, Gilberto Gilberto López Rodriguez:*
In the exhaustive Mary Ferrell's database there is the following entry:
Record: POLICARPO LOPEZ, GILBERTO GILBERTO LOPEZ RODRIGUEZ

Sources CD 205, pp. 750-51; CIA 262; CIA 308-114; CIA 313-118; CIA 319-707; CIA 613262; Schweiker Report, pp.30, 61; CIA Box 6, Folder 8 (MMF 447); HSCA, Reel 14, Box 9, Folder E, F (AMKW 10)

Mary's Comments: DOB: 1/26/40. POB: Havana, Cuba. American citizen (son of American citizens); on Nov 20 1963, he secured a 15 day Mexican tourist card, No. M-8 24553, at Tampa, Florida. Entered Mexico by automobile at Nuevo Laredo on Nov. 23, 1963. Checked into Roosevelt Hotel, Room 203, on Nov. 25. Checked out on Nov 27 and departed for Havana via special airplane, Cubana Flight 465, and was only passenger allowed on plane. He had North American Passport # 310162 which expired 1/25/63. On 9/15/78, Seth Kantor said that in 1960 when Lopez obtained a passport, on the application he gave 2 references: Jorge Rodriguez Espinosa, 2518 Seidenberg Ave., Key West, Florida (Rodriguez crossed the border at Laredo 9/23/63), And Agapito Gonzalez, 2620 Williams St., Key West,

Florida. See also Miguel Casas Saez. HSCA asked CIA why there was no "P" file on him.

None of the above mentioned persons deposed to the Warren Commission. If Lee Harvey Oswald would have been brought to a trial, these people could have been questioned and there is no doubt in my mind that it would have been proved without the slightest shadow of a doubt that Fidel Castro was the mastermind behind the assassination. Fidel Castro used a mentally disturbed Communist, infatuated with Castro and his Revolution, to put an end to the danger that President John Fitzgerald Kennedy represented to Fidel Castro.

We have seen in this chapter:

A) The shots that killed President Kennedy were shot from the sixth floor window of the Texas School Book Depository building

B) There were three shots fired.

C) Lee Harvey Oswald was the only employee of the building who left without permission after the assassination.

D) Lee Harvey Oswald went to the room that he had rented using an alias (O. H. Lee), put a jacket on and grabbed his gun. Doing this Oswald proved that his intention was to escape, if not he would have remained either at the Texas School Book Depository building or at his room.

E) Oswald killed Officer J. D. Tippit when Tippit interfered in Oswald's escape.

F) Oswald's attempted escape was cut short after Tippit's assassination when he panicked and was arrested at the Texas Theatre.

G) The Chief of the Intelligence Services of Fidel Castro had arrived in a small plane from Mexico City to Dallas the day of the assassination and flew back, first to Mexico City then to Cuba, after Oswald's arrest.

H) Another member of the "Fair Play for Cuba Committee" crossed from Texas to Mexico after the assassination and flew to Cuba as the only passenger of a Cubana airlines plane.

I) Investigative agencies of the United States failed to properly investigate the assassination of President Kennedy and its connections with the attempts by President Kennedy to get rid of Fidel Castro, plans that Castro was aware of and plans that Castro publicly promised to retaliate.

J) List of witnesses involving Fidel Castro to the assassination of President John F. Kennedy.

All the above proves, without doubt, that Lee Harvey Oswald killed President John F. Kennedy firing three shots from the sixth floor window of the Texas School Book Depository Building. Oswald's actions after the shooting also prove that his intention was to escape. With the little money that he had in his pocket the distance for his escape was very limited unless he had an accomplice to take him out of the country. Lee Harvey Oswald didn't stay at his place of employment and went to the rooming house where he put a jacket and grabbed his revolver. By the "for your eyes only" memo of Marty Underwood Jr., we know that Fabián Escalante, Chief of Cuban Intelligence Service had arrived, in the morning, to Dallas from Mexico City. If the rendezvous with Oswald could have been accomplished his escape could have been secured.

It has been reported that a car painted with the colors of the Dallas Police Department honked its horn in front of Oswald's rooming house when Oswald was not yet there. When Oswald put his jacket on and his revolver at his waist he took to the street looking out for his escape.

Unfortunately for him and his mentors a veteran of 11 years in the Dallas police force, Officer J. D. Tippit was patrolling the area. At about 12:45 p.m. a description of the suspect in the shooting of President Kennedy was radioed by channel 1 for the first time. It was repeated at 12:48 and again at 12:55 p.m. The suspect was described as a "white male, approximately 30, slender build, height 5 foot 10 inches, weight 160 pounds". A similar description was given on channel 2 at 12:45 p.m.

About 100 feet past the intersection of 10th and Patton streets Officer Tippit called a man walking east along the south side of Patton Avenue. The man's general description was similar to the one broadcasted over the police radio. Tippit ordered the man to his patrol car. The man approached the car and was questioned by Tippit for a few seconds. Tippit got out of his car and started to walk around the front of his patrol car. As Officer Tippit reached the left front wheel the man pulled out a revolver and fired several shots. Four bullets hit Tippit killing him instantly.

Who was that man? Why, if he was not involved in anything did he kill Officer Tippit? On the day President Kennedy was assassinated several persons were arrested by Dallas Police on suspicion, but only one of them drew a gun and killed the arresting officer. Thanks to God, there were at least 12 persons who saw the man with the gun in the vicinity of Officer Tippit's murder. That man was identified as Lee Harvey Oswald.

After killing Officer Tippit, Oswald panicked, his cold blood disappeared. He had been identified by a police officer; he had missed his rendezvous with the person that was going to help him seek refuge in Cuba. Oswald's coolness disintegrated. Instead he had to seek refuge inside the Texas Theater without realizing that he was attracting unwanted attention. Finally police Officer M. N. McDonald attempted to arrest Oswald inside the theater only to receive a punch in the face from Oswald who tried to resist his arrest. Oswald was subdue after he tried to shoot Officer McDonald.[152]

This is the true history of the assassination, no science fiction creation like Oliver Stone's JFK. I am sure that I was *in God's hands* when He selected me to be in the heart of the crime of the Century, when He selected me to be able to expose Lee Harvey Oswald in New Orleans and also when He selected me to confront those distorting the truth trying to poison the mind of the American People, Humanity and History with their lies.

One thing that has been ignored by the liberal press is that Lee Harvey Oswald was an activist of the "Fair Play for Cuba Committee" before he came to infiltrate my organization in August 5, 1963. Prior to that, during the month of June 1963, Lee Harvey Oswald picketed a US Navy ship stationed in New Orleans. At that time Rafael Aznarez, a Cuban visiting the ship with his wife and some friends encountered Oswald who was carrying signs in favor of Castro and Aznarez verbally confronted him. On June 29, 1963 Rafael Aznarez wrote a letter to J. Edgar Hoover about the confrontation. Aznarez, who was a friend of mine and who frequently was visiting "Casa Roca" to chat with me, never mention that until after the assassination. This proves that Lee Harvey Oswald was already working for the "Fair Play for Cuba Committee" at least two months before he approached me trying to infiltrate my delegation of the Cuban Student Directorate in New Orleans. But the liberal press ignore that fact.

---

[152] "Red Friday", by Carlos J. Bringuier, pages 94-107.

CHAPTER X

NEW ORLEANS (1964-1967)

On January 10, 1964 the New Orleans States-Item referred to my communication to the Consul general of England in New Orleans:

Cuban Unit Here Blasts Bus Sale

> *The Cuban Student Directorate in New Orleans has protested to the British government the sale of buses to Fidel Castro's regime.*
>
> *Dr. Carlos Bringuier, New Orleans delegate to the directorate, told the Consul general of England that the money it will receive from Castro will be stained with the blood of Cubans assassinated in prison and on the execution wall.*
>
> *Dr. Bringuier asked the British government to reconsider the sale.*[153]

It was the beginning of 1964 when an unknown American entered into "Casa Roca" inquiring about Carlos Bringuier. He was unknown to me and his name was Rev. Billy James Hargis, Founder Director of Christian Crusade who was inviting me to appear and speak at their Convention to be celebrated on February 14, 1964 at Shreveport, Louisiana. I had never heard of Hargis but he was offering

---

153 New Orleans States-Item, January 10, 1964, Section 1, page 43.

me an opportunity to bring my side of the story about the Kennedy assassination. I was not receiving any salary from the DRE in Miami, therefore in my mind I was not an employee of the DRE and I was free to take my decisions without asking the Miami headquarters for permission to do so.

In Shreveport I delivered my full length speech about President John F. Kennedy's assassination. Rev. Billy James Hargis liked it and he offered me to join him in a tour to present my thesis that Fidel Castro was the mastermind behind the assassination. Again, as I was not working for the FBI or the CIA as some lefties have insinuated, I accepted without asking for permission from the Miami headquarters of the DRE.

On the issue of February, 1964, the New York Delegation of the DRE printed in its publication "D.R.E". Col. II No. 2 the following article:

Ruby was in Cuba in 1962-63

The Cuban Student Directorate, has announced, to have received information from its underground in Cuba according to which Jack Ruby, killer of the presumpt (sic) assassin of President Kennedy, Lee Harvey Oswald, was in Havana for a period of some days in late December 1962 and the beginning of 1963.

It had been told before, that Ruby only visited the Cuban capital in January 1959, during the first days of Fidel Castro's government and that this trip was for commercial purposes.

The Cuban Student Directorate (D. R. E.) assures Ruby was in Havana in late 1962 and early 1963, to which he arrived by plane from Mexico City. During his stay in Havana, he visited frequently a souvenir shop located at Prado St., in front of the Hotel Sevilla. This shop is owned by Salomon Pratkins.

On February 26, 1964, I left New Orleans on the first leg of a speaking tour that took me to the following cities:

San Diego, Riverside, Anaheim, Glendale, Mira Costa, Canoga Park, Long Beach, Santa Barbara, Bakersfield, Fresno, Hayward, San Jose, Los Gatos, San Francisco, Oakland and Sacramento in California. Boise, Idaho; Phoenix and Tucson in Arizona; Albuquerque, New Mexico and Tulsa, Oklahoma.

The tour was such a success that Hargis offered me to go in another tour which offer I accepted.

On Monday April 20, 1964 at 5: 30 p.m. we held a demonstration in front of the statue located at Canal and Claiborne, the Rough Rider statue to commemorate the 66th anniversary of the Joint Resolution of the U.S. Congress which plainly stated that THE CUBAN PEOPLE IS AND OUGHT TO BE FREE AND INDEPENDENT.

Our second leg of the tour with Christian Crusade started in May, 1964 and it covered:

Friday, May 8, Springfield, Illinois, Holiday Inn Motel.

Sunday, May 10, Minneapolis, Minnesota, meeting at YMCA, Benton Hall, 3:00 p.m.

Monday, May 11, Rapid City, South Dakota, Sheraton-Johnson Hotel.

Tuesday, May 12, Veterans of Foreign Wars, Scotts Bluff, Nebraska.

Friday, Saturday, Sunday May 15, 16 and 17, The First Evangelical Methodist Church of America, San Angelo, Texas.

Monday, May 18, Browntowner Motor Inn Roof Garden.

Tuesday, May 19, Liberty Hotel, Cleburne, Texas.

Wednesday, May 20, Angelina Hotel, Lufkin, Texas.

Thursday, May 21, Woodrow Wilson, Jr., High School Auditorium.

Friday, May 22, S. P. Martel Auditorium, Houston, Texas.

Saturday, May 23, Central Baptist Church, Plano, Texas.

An informant of the FBI rendered a report to the FBI about our speeches and I have copy of the memo written by the FBI.

Sunday, May 24, Central Baptist Church, Garland, Texas. (Three meetings, 11:00 a.m., 2:00 p.m., and 7:30 p.m.)

Monday, May 25, Community Hall, Dallas, Texas.

An informant of the FBI rendered a report to the FBI about our talk and I have a copy of the memo written by the FBI.

Tuesday, May 26, Oak Cliff Baptist Temple.

Wednesday, May 27, Corinth Baptist Church, Midland, Texas.

An informant of the FBI rendered a report to the FBI about our talk and I have copy of the memo written by the FBI.

Thursday, May 28, Robert E. Lee, Jr., High School Auditorium, Pampa, Texas.

Friday, May 29, Holiday Inn, Clovis, New Mexico.

Saturday, May 30, Maranatha Baptist Church, Odessa, Texas.

An informant of the FBI rendered a report to the FBI about our talk and I have copy of the memo written by the FBI.

Sunday, May 31, Calvary Baptist Church, Plainview, Texas.

Sunday, July 5, Continental Pueblo Motel, Pueblo, Colorado.

Tuesday, July 7, Boy Scout Hut, Riverside Park, Salida, Colorado.

Wednesday, July 8, Webster Hall, Gunnison, Colorado.

Thursday, July 9, Community Building, Greeley, Colorado.

Friday, July 10, Lesher Jr., High School Auditorium, Ft. Collins, Colorado.

On June 3, 1964, the New Orleans office of the FBI wrote the following report:

DIRECTORIO REVOLUCIONARIO
ESTUDIANTIL. (DRE)

Carlos Jose Bringuier advised on August 6, 1962, that at that time he had recently been named delegate at New Orleans, Louisiana, of the Directorio Revolucionario Estudiantil (DRE), which name is translated to English as Student Revolutionary Directorate. He also advised that he was the only member of the DRE in New Orleans. He advised that the headquarters of DRE are located in Miami, Florida. The records of Immigration and Naturalization Service at New Orleans reflect Bringuier's full name as used in Spanish-speaking countries as Carlos Jose del Sagrado Corazon Bringuier Exposito. He presently resides at 501 Adele Street, Apartment F, in New Orleans.

A source reported in 1963 that the only activity of the DRE at New Orleans was carried on by Carlos Bringuier, the delegate of DRE in New Orleans. This source stated that Bringuier's activities on behalf of the subject organization usually involved comments by Bringuier to further the anti-Castro cause, which comments usually find their way into some branch of the news media.

Another source who is a leader in anti-Castro activities in the New Orleans area advised on May 28, 1963, that the DRE has to his knowledge no members in New Orleans but is represented in New Orleans by a single delegate, namely Carlos Bringuier. This source describe subject organization in New

Orleans as a propaganda-type organization whose headquarters are located in Miami, Florida.

On June 2, 1964, both of the above sources, each of whom has a close contact with Carlos Bringuier, reiterated individually that to their knowledge subject organization is represented in New Orleans solely by Carlos Bringuier.

They added that the activities of subject organization in New Orleans in 1963 were limited to propaganda-type efforts of Carlos Bringuier, such as, making speeches, distributing bulletins regarding the situation in Cuba and, in general, publicizing anti-Castro information in any available channel in the news media.

The above memo clearly shows why the parrots of the Castro regime, like General Fabián Escalante, and the parrots of the left, writers like Weisberg, and Lane among others could not admit that yes, I was only involved in propaganda (and I was good at that). General Fabián Escalante is used to the Castro regime formula of imparting orders, like the ones that they gave to Roberto Santiesteban to destroy the New York Christmas of 1962 where the "Fair Play for Cuba Committee" was planning to massacre more people than Osama bin Laden on September 11, 2001. What I did in New Orleans was not ordered by the FBI, the CIA or any other intelligence service of the United States government, it was product of my own brain and my belief that I did not want the people of the United Sates to suffer what we were suffering in Cuba. The others, the leftists, the ones who want to distort the truth, the only thing that they can do is that: Distort the truth. But the facts are clear.

During the month of June of 1964, the DRE delegation in New Orleans created a "Feminine Section" and Miss Elsita Valdés Fonte was appointed to take over that section.

On May 22, 1964 it was published the statement by Capt. Carleton W. Voltz, 26, Frankfort, Mich., who recounted an incident, while he was in jail in North Korea, in a taped interview on May 22 in Seoul, Korea. Capt. Volz stated:

"I heard on Thanksgiving that he (Kennedy) had been assassinated. They were very proud of the fact. It was we a big smile that he said

President Kennedy had been shot by some loyal Communist Party member in the United States."[154]

On June 9, 1964, "The Times Picayune" published the following:

Cuban Delegate applauds Eshkol

Dr. Carlos Bringuier, Cuban Student Directorate delegate in New Orleans, has congratulated the Israeli prime minister for his actions in connection with Israel conflict with Egypt.

In a telegram to Prime Minister Levi Eshkol in Tel Aviv, Bringuier remarked:

"Congratulations for courageous actions (in the) preservation (of) your fatherland. Willing to give support (in) case you need it. Soviet imperialism should be stopped (in the) Far East, Middle East and Caribbean Sea. We pray God (that) our countrymen would learn (the) lesson (of) unity and sacrifice Israeli people are giving humanity."

On July 17, 1964 the Cuban Student Directorate in New Orleans in conjunction with the delegation of the Cuban Teachers in Exile conducted a picket in front of the Mexican Consulate in New Orleans. The New Orleans States-Item carry the story with also a picture of my wife and two of our daughters during the activity, it read:

Carlos Bringuier, a spokesman, said the demonstrators represented the Cuban Student Directorate.

One of the demonstrators, Miss Enrique Artze, was representing the delegate of teachers in exile, Bringuier said.

Bringuier said the demonstration was held against Mexico's failure to support a protest by Venezuela in the Organization of American states that Cuba is trying to overthrow the democratic government of Venezuela.

Placards carried by the demonstrators included such phrases as: "OAS Solidarity with Venezuela," "Vote No to

---

[154] The Houston Chronicle, May 22, 1964, Section 4, page 23.

*Castro", "Mexicans! Cubans! Unite Against Red Terror" and
"Red Cuba, No. Democracy, Yes."[155]*

On the issue of August 15, 1964 of "AZUL", the official newsletter of
the Delegation of the DRE in New Orleans I emphasized my thought,
brought out for the first time in June 1964, that the Communist were
trying to accomplish two goals: 1) Save Castro in Cuba; and 2) Avoid the
possibility of Barry Goldwater been elected in the November elections
as President of the United States. I had predicted that a crisis would be
created in the Far East in order to make the Johnson administration look
strong and with resolve and in the meantime taking away the lime lights
from Fidel Castro. Welcome Viet-Nam. Lyndon B. Johnson won the
elections, Fidel Castro had time to get his forces ready to invade Africa
and thousands of young Americans were killed in a war that was fought
not to win.

On September 27th, 1964 I gave to the press the following press
release:

From: DR. CARLOS BRINGUIER
New Orleans Delegate
Cuban Student Directorate

WARREN REPORT INCOMPLETE

*Today, September 27th 1964, has been made public the
Warren Commission report in regard to the assassination of
President John Fitzgerald Kennedy at the hands of Lee Harvey
Oswald, a Communist.*

*It is deplorable, deplorable indeed, that this report has
been made public incomplete. During the investigation that the
Warren Commission carried on in this City of New Orleans, they
questioned several persons including myself. But, unbelievable
they did not interrogated other persons who dealt with Lee
Harvey Oswald at the time he was here in New Orleans.*

*One of the persons who was not questioned by the
investigators of the Warren Commission was the Cuban (name*

---

[155] New Orleans States-Item, July 17, 1964, page 3.

withheld for security reasons) who tried to infiltrate, in August 16, 1963, the New Orleans Delegation of the Fair Play for Cuba Committee headed by Lee Harvey Oswald. This man talked to Oswald for about one hour in Oswald's house and Oswald assured him that "if the United States would try to invade Cuba, he (Oswald) would fight for Castro, against the United States". This conversation among the Cuban and Oswald was known by the Secret Service, the Federal Bureau of Investigations, and the investigators of the Warren Commission and I could not find a reason why, if they interrogated persons in this City that only knew Oswald from the time he was a child, they do not interrogate this man, that besides what Oswald told him, received from Oswald's own hands an application to become a member of the Fair Play for Cuba Committee and several pieces of literature defending the Communist Regime of Fidel Castro.

It is really strange the "whitewash" about the influence of Oswald's Communist ideology in the motivation of the assassination, but it is not the moment for us the Cubans, to try to prove the Communist plot which we believe moved Oswald to take the life of the President of the United States. This is the moment of the House Committee on Un-American Activities and the Senate Internal Security Sub-Committee to carry on an intensive, complete and PUBLIC investigation about Oswald's conections (sic) with Communist Cuba and the influence of the Communist ideology in his motivations to assassinate President Kennedy. This is the moment for the American People to wake up and ask why the Warren Commission hired a man, with a salary of $100.00 daily, as consultant, who have joined in several occasions Communist fronts organizations and who had sponsored the American students travel to Cuba in opposition to the State Department Regulations ("The Daily Oklahoman" May 15, page 30).

We the Cubans know, that assassination is one of the best weapons used by the International Communist Revolution. After Kennedy's assassination several plots were discovered in Latin America to kill the Presidents of different nations, all these plots inspired from Red Cuba, and just a few days ago, the Nicaraguan government discovered a Castro inspired plot to kill the President of that Nation, and we know that they will not stop until they will achieve their goal: COMMUNIST WORLD DOMINATION.

We Cubans, want to assure the American People that we will continue by ourselves the investigation of this plot and we are sure that if one day we would be back to a FREE CUBA we will find there the proofs that the Warren Commission did not find during the ten months of their investigation.

IN GOD WE TRUST

Before I wrote the above press release I had read in the New Orleans States-Item the information about the Warren Commission Report which disappointed me. While I was at the door of my own store "Casa Cuba", 115 ½ Decatur Street, I saw FBI agent Warren C. De Brueys walking by the sidewalk. We started talking and I was expressing my dissatisfaction with the Report. De Brueys did not like what I was saying and he expressed himself in that way, I was very angry and I told him: *"If the FBI instead of investigating us would have been investigating Oswald maybe your President would be alive today."*

De Brueys became angrier and told me that if I continue talking in that way *"I should remember that I was in this Country under the invitation of the United States and I could be expelled from the US."* If I was angry before, now I was fuming. I told De Brueys that he was talking not to a refugee but to a legal resident and that with my status, things were different. FBI Agent Warren C. De Brueys kept walking by the sidewalk.

It was not the first time that De Brueys and I have dissented. I remember that in another occasion we had a discussion about Communism in front of "Casa Roca" and he had stated that he worked for the government of the United States and that if one day the President declares himself a Communist he would have to obey the President. At that moment De Brueys was ignoring the teachings of Teddy Roosevelt when he said: *"Patriotism means to stand by the country. It does not mean to stand by the president."* De Brueys sounded like the 80% of American people referred by Donald Savery at our conversation at the Café Dumonde. On another occasion I had been approached by a couple of Latin Americans young men who had offered me some propaganda from Cuba including some Bohemia magazines and I had accepted to meet them at the YMCA building, by the Lee Circle. At their apartment they showed me several of the items and told me they can send them to me regularly from Ecuador. After I left their apartment I went to the office of the FBI to report the incident and the one who interviewed me was Agent De Brueys, maybe that was the first time that we met, I am not sure, but De Brueys was reluctant to investigate the ones offering me Communist propaganda. At another time, this time after the JFK's assassination, Agent De Brueys had walked into the store to ask questions about Celso Hernández. According to him they had information that Celso was a Communist who used to drive a bus in Cuba. I explained to De Brueys that Celso was not a Communist and that he had never been a bus driver in Cuba and that Celso learned to drive while in New Orleans. De Brueys had left disappointed with me. What he didn't know is that as he left the store he had done so leaving me with a disappointing opinion about his degree of intelligence. I was not thinking that he was a bad person just that he didn't have the ideal brain to be a FBI agent.

Maybe for those reasons there is a CIA report from February 20, 1967 in which CIA agent Lloyd A. Ray stated: *"that he had also learned from a local FBI agent and cleared source which keeps in touch with the Cuban situation that subject is the leader of a Cuban group; that he is dedicated anti-Communist and anti-Castro leader, but irresponsible and sensationalist and publicity seeker."*

Apparently the dislike in between FBI Agent Warren C. De Brueys and I was a two way street.

I had reasons to be angry with the Warren Commission. On December 3, 1963, "The Times Picayune" published that under study by a special court is a suit brought by the Southern Conference Educational Fund Inc., and Dr. James A. Dombrowsky, the organization executive director.

At the outset of Monday's hearing the court allowed Benjamin E. Smith, treasurer of the SCEF, and Bruce Waltzer, his law partner, to intervene as plaintiffs.

Leon D. Hubert, attorney for Smith and Waltzer, claimed that the state anti-subversion statutes are not justified in that an attack on the State of Louisiana could not possible be divorced from an attack on the United States. The paper noticed that "Plaintiffs Hold Red Laws Unconstitutional".

Who do you think that the Warren Commission appointed to help them in their investigation in Louisiana? None other than Leo D. Hubert. Another person that had been appointed to work with the

Warren Commission was Normand Redlich who had been a member of the "Emergency Civil Liberties Council", an organization that was not only against the House Un-American Activities Committee, but an organization that was considered a Communist Front by the House Un-American Activities Committee as well as by the Internal Security Committee of the Senate. As prove of the waste of time and money by some investigators of the FBI they even interviewed the obstetrician who delivered Mr. Redlich. Mr. Redlich ended up carrying on an important part in the work of the Warren Commission. The only thing missing it could have been for the Warren Commission to appoint Fidel Castro to investigate the assassination of President Kennedy.

And if you don't know who Benjamin E. Smith and Bruce Waltzer were let me bring forward and make part of this record a report of the Secret Service which appears as Commission Exhibit No. 3119, Volume 26, pages 762-767. Here are excerpts of that report pertaining to Oswald arrest with me in August 9, 1963:

> "Lt. Martello said at the time of Oswald's arrest, he had various pamphlets in his possession and these had been kept by Lt. Martello. He said that he would turn them over to this office if we so desired. He also stated that before been transferred to the First District, he had been assigned to the Intelligence Division, NOPD, for about two years and that during this time he became familiar with various Communist front organizations.
>
> He said that an address in the 1100 block of Pine Street, New Orleans, seemed to be the center of activity in New Orleans for various Communist-type front organizations. He said that a Dr. Reissman, a professor at Tulane University, lived at the Pine Street address where numerous meetings were held. He said that he had learned from one of his sources that Dr. James Dombrowsky was seen at several occasions at the home of Dr. Reissman and at the home of a neighbor of Dr. Reissman, name unknown, who is also supposed to be a professor at Tulane University . . .
>
> Mrs. Murrett said that this woman was very friendly but Oswald's wife appeared to be ill at ease. Further, that the woman had mentioned a Dr. Reissman, a professor at Tulane University,

New Orleans, as a friend and that Oswald had also mentioned that he knew, or was acquainted with Dr. Reissman.

She said that if she recalled correctly, either the Russian woman or Oswald made the remark to the effect that Dr. Reissman had visited with Oswald or Oswald had visited the Dr. at his home . . .

He (Lt. Martello) stated that while assigned to the Intelligence Division, he had learned that Dr. Leonard Reissman, home address 1221 Pine Street, New Orleans, a professor at Tulane University, was very active in an organization called NOCPA (New Orleans Council for Peaceful Alternatives) better known as "Ban the Bomb": Bruce Waltzer, previously mentioned, was very active in several organizations, including NOCPA. Lt. Martello said that it was his information that Waltzer made frequent trips to Mexico City, supposedly for the purpose of obtaining the finances from the Castro Government to keep the NOCPA and other organizations favorable to the Castro Government going.

Lt. Martello said that Dr. Reissman held meetings at his home in connection with the NOCPA as well as the Fair Play for Cuba organization. He related that in one occasion he had learned that a pamphlet pertaining to the Fair Play for Cuba organization had blown out of Dr. Reissman's car and apparently Dr. Reissman had not noticed this for the reason Lt. Martello had obtained possession from an informant.

I would like to mention that Dr. Bruce Waltzer was a partner in a law firm with Dr. Benjamin Smith. Dr. Benjamin Smith was registered in Washington, D.C. as an agent of Fidel Castro's government. Their attorney at the trial was Leon D. Hubert. Now, who can tell you that it was wise to appoint Leon D. Hubert as legal counsel of the Warren Commission in New Orleans a lawyer who represented a registered agent of the Castro's government? This situation reminds me the situation going on in the 1940's and 1950's when the State Department and other sections of our government were highly infiltrated by Communists and "friends" investigated and cleared "friends".

But don't hold your breath, the Warren Commission never called to testified Dr. Benjamin E. Smith, a registered agent of Fidel Castro's government, Dr. Bruce Waltzer, who according to Lt. Martello made frequents trips to Mexico to bring money from Castro's government to help pro-Castro organizations, and Dr. Leonard Reissman at whose house Lt. Martello had identified meetings of the "Fair Play for Cuba" been held. Their testimonies could "jeopardize" the work of the "architects" inside the Commission trying to exonerate Fidel Castro.

Another person that also was not called to testify to the Warren Commission was Carlos Quiroga, the anti-Castro man who received propaganda of the "Fair Play for Cuba Committee" from Oswald's hands and to whom Oswald told that if the United States would invade Cuba he (Oswald) would fight against the United States. Here come the same question. Why?

When, during my investigation, I read the 26 Volumes of the Warren Commission I discovered some other things, for example a couple of interesting statements to the Commission by Marina Oswald:

"Mrs. Oswald: Of course he tried to console me that I should not worry that everything would turn out well. He asked about how the children were. He spoke of some friends who supposedly would help him. I don't know who he had in mind. That he had written to someone in New York before that.*

This bring to mind a couple of things. First, he had written to someone in New York "before" the assassination. We know that in New York were the offices of the "Fair Play for Cuba Committee" located in the same building where the office of the USA Communist Party was located. Also in New York was the office of the United Nations Delegation of the Castro's government.

The second statement from Marina who caught my interest had to do with the attempt by her husband to assassinate anti-Communist General Edwin Walker and his relationship with a leftist man who had befriended him, George De Mohrenschildts.

Mrs. Oswald: By the way, several days after that, De Mohrenschildts came to us and as soon as he opened the door he (De Mohrenschildts) said: 'Lee how is it possible that you missed?'*

This clearly shows that George De Mohrenschildts was aware that Oswald had tried to kill General Walker. This is the same George De Mohrenschildts who once greeted Soviet Deputy Anastas Mikoyan as "comrade" and invited him to dinner. The same George De Mohrenschildts who was a known admirer of the Chinese Communist Regime.[156]

---

[156] Warren Commission Hearings, Vol. VIII, page 463, and Vol. IX, page 215.

CHRISTIAN CRUSADE

presents to

Carlos Bringuier

CHRISTIAN CRUSADE GUARDIAN OF
FREEDOM AWARD

FOR COURAGE, DEDICATION AND LOVE OF FREEDOM--
THE MAN WHO EXPOSED THE ASSASSIN OF THE AMERICAN
PRESIDENT, AND WITH HIS TESTIMONY, AWAKENED
MILLIONS TO THE THREAT OF COMMUNISM INTERNALLY
IN THE UNITED STATES

(Date) Aug. 9, 1964 (Signed) Billy James Hargis
Founder-Director

The AMLASH penetration of the CIA and some exile groups continued and on December 30, 1964 there was a meeting between Manuel Artime (former Chief of the 2506 Brigade) and AMLASH (Rolando Cubela). The CIA reported about it in a memo dated January 6, 1965 in which it is stated:

> *"During a six-hour meeting, Cubela stated that three groups are involved in a coup against Fidel Castro and plan to use troops to seize power. The three groups are: One from the Directorio Revolucionario (DR), led by Cubela himself; one from the 26th July Movement led by Efigenio Almejeiras Delgado, Vice-Minister of the Armed Forces for Special Affairs; and another separate 26th of July Movement group headed by Commander Guillermo García Frías, Commander of the Western Army."*

Here I want to clearly bring out the difference in between two organizations: The "Directorio Revolucionario" (DR), founded in the 1950's during the struggle against the Batista government and the "Directorio Revolucionario Estudiantil" (DRE) founded in Cuba in 1959 during the struggle against the Communist government of Fidel Castro. Many so-called writers confuse both organizations that were entirely different. I never belonged to the "Directorio Revolucionario" (DR). I was delegate in New Orleans of the "Directorio Revolucionario Estudiantil" (Cuban Student Directorate) (DRE).

The other amazing thing is the naiveté of Artime in his trust of Cubela. I can't say the same about the CIA because, as I never trusted the CIA (my main reason to not have any contact with them), I believe that the moles inside the CIA were playing Castro's game. Rolando Cubela is alive living in Spain; Efigenio Almejeiras never lost his position in the Castro government; and Commander Guillermo García Frías is considered one of the richest man in Cuba (as you will read in the next paragraphs) and Manuel Artime, the former Chief of the 2506 Brigade is dead.

In an email distributed by "La Voz de Cuba Libre" dated June 16, 2007, there is a list of the richest persons in Castro's Cuba and in it it is stated:

"Guillermo García Frías, Commandant of the Revolution. Responsible of flora and fauna in Cuba. For many years he had managed in an individual and private way the exportation of animals in special that of fighting roosters. Also he owns several boats and stores specialized in western items. He also has the government concession for rental of game preserves to international tourists."

If Rolando Cubela (AMLASH), Efigenio Almejeiras and Commander Guillermo García Frías would have conspiring to depose Castro they would have been executed decades ago in Cuba. But the three of them are alive today. They were the architects of another April fool joke against the American People. Sadly, the CIA believed them for some time.

On March 27, 1966 a group of around 40 anti-Viet Nam protesters carried a demonstration around the neutral ground of Loyola Avenue in front of the Federal Building in New Orleans. The group was formed by members of several leftist organizations including:

"Tulane University Liberals Club", "New Orleans Federation of Anarchists", "New Orleans Viet Nam Committee", "Southern Coordinating Committee" and the "Spartacists". "The Times Picayune" reported the demonstration and wrote:

> *Three members of the Cuban student Directorate, an anti-Castro organization, also counter picketed in the area, carrying signs reading, "Draft all Peace Creeps," and "Viet Cong Go Home." They were joined by an American who carried a similar sign.*

Cubans Assail Reds

> *Carlos Bringuier, a Cuban refugee, and one of the counter pickets, said that they were participating in the activity because "We have seen that the Communists don't make love, but rather death. These people (the anti-war pickets) are mistaken. They haven't seen those 20,000 Cubans murdered like we have. And I*

am sure that if Lee Harvey Oswald were alive, he'd be right out there with that group."[157]

The newspaper also published a picture showing the leftists and showing me with my sign.

On November 12, 1966 we obtained another nice victory with our confrontation with the leftists in New Orleans. At the Jung Hotel, on Canal Street, there was a Regional Foreign Policy Conference sponsored by the Foreign Relations Association of New Orleans, International House and Tulane University. The Times Picayune reported the incidents as follow:

> *A group protesting U.S. involvement in Viet Nam was first on the scene about 8 a.m. About 10 persons made up the group, which was identified as the New Orleans Committee to End the War in Viet Nam.*
>
> *They were later joined by the Cuban group made up of members of the New Orleans Delegation of the Cuban Student Directorate and the Coordinating Committee of Exile Cubans in New Orleans.*
>
> *The anti-Viet Nam group carried hand-painted signs reading: "War is Good Business. Get Out of Viet Nam," "American Aggressor, Viet Nam Victim," and "U.S. Corporations Profit from Viet Nam War."*
>
> ### Large Cuban Group
>
> *In contrast, the Cubans' neatly lettered signs in red and black ink read: "Down with Communism," "Help Cuban Freedom Fighters," "Win, Don't Withdraw," "What about Cuba?" and "Don't Betray America."*
>
> *Swallowed up by the larger Cuban picket group, the anti-Viet Nam War group left about 9:10 am. The Cubans, though, stayed on most of the morning.[158]*

---

[157] The Times Picayune, March 27, 1966, Section 1, page 10.
[158] The Times Picayune, November 13, 1966, Section 1, pages 1 and 22.

On November 21, 1966, I sent a telegram to President Johnson which reads:

> *On third anniversary of President Kennedy's assassination at the hands of a Castro agent American people should know about Fidel Castro participation in it. America should also be told that Lee Harvey Oswald was executed—before public opinion could focus against Fidel Castro as the man responsible for the Kennedy killing.*
>
> *If your government by its silence permit the distortions of facts now been carrying out by the Communists then your government will become an accomplice in the brainwashing of the American people.*
>
> *John F. Kennedy promised five years ago to liberate our country. Castro is still in Cuba and Kennedy was assassinated. If the truth is not told, Kennedy will not rest in peace.*

On November 26, 1966 a meeting was held in New Orleans, at the Notre Dame Seminary, to commemorate the execution of students in Cuba while Spain was ruling Cuba in November 27, 1871. Six hundred Cubans gathered and we had visitors from other areas among them Jorge Más Canosa (who later on would become President of the Cuban-American National Foundation), Dr. Orlando Bosch (Director of MIRR), Antonio Calatayud (From RECE) and Bob Angers (From the Daily Advertiser of Lafayette, Louisiana). The event was prepared in order to raise money for RECE to carry on armed attacks against the Castro dictatorship.

My speech that night was as follows:

> *Mr. Jorge Más Canosa, representing RECE*
> *Mr. Antonio Calatayud, representing RECE*
> *Dr. Orlando Bosch, Director of MIRR Mr. Bob Angers, from the Daily Advertiser.*
> *Compatriots:*
> *Tonight we are gathered here to civically commemorate our sad date of November 27, 1871.*
> *Tomorrow there will be 95 years of that sad day in our history, in which eight students from the Medical School were*

executed by militiamen at the service of a foreign government that then occupied our land like another Colony more.

That barbaric deed of eight youngsters assassinated by those militiamen moved world public opinion in favor of our cause.

Today, 95 years after that, we find that there are not eight, not 800, not even less than 8,000 Cubans who had been assassinated by the Communist tyranny that oppress our Fatherland.

In 1871, public opinion was mobilized against such crime.

Today we watch as countries united by blood to our cause like it is the case of Spain, who even in 1871 saved his honor with the valiant defense and noble attitude of Captain Capdevila, who courageously defended those medical students, now stain themselves and provoke our nauseas when they maintain diplomatic and commercial relations with the Castroite satrapy helping the Communist regime to function.

Which means, the fact that we have to lament the assassination of tens of thousands of Cubans by the Communist dictatorship, have not moved world public opinion against Castro's government in a decisive and overwhelming way. In the other hand we found ourselves in the sad and regrettable position in which, day by day, we are been abandoned by those called to help us according to logic and geopolitical dictates.

This criminal abandon toward our cause, and our necessity of been united, to unite efforts to obtain our goals, is what had moved this Coordinating Committee who had invited all of us tonight.

I would like to clarify that this Committee as indicated by its name is not another organization of exiles, but an agglutination of forces to consolidate our sacrifices and be able to offer a little more in our struggle against Communism.

We, ourselves have to make this effort. We can't wait for those who abandoned General Chiang Kai-shek, we can't wait for those who impassible watched how the Hungarian people was massacred by the tanks of Russian Imperialism, we can't wait for those who betrayed us in that tragic April 17, and we can't wait for those who today persecute all those who want to confront, with weapons in their hands, the murderers of our fellow brothers, we can't wait for them to change their policies and dignify themselves honoring their obligations.

I would not like to be accused as a pessimist, because it would be an injustice that I, whom am convinced that we will return to a free and democratic Cuba could be accused of pessimism. No, I am not a pessimistic, I am realistic, and it is this realism who make me foresee that if is only a few those who are willing to sacrifice and work hard, our horizon of freedom and democracy in Cuba will not come closer as are our desires.

A few days ago I visited the City of Miami, and I can assure you that if the ones who are working, in one way or another, for the liberation of Cuba are not able to move those who with different excuses keep themselves without supporting the organizations that already are in existence, our situation would become even more critical and the only one who would benefit for that would be Fidel Castro.

It is not my intention tonight to express harmonious and full of hope words to raise your optimism, making you to go to bed happy of what you have heard.

I know that many of you here tonight already are supporting different organizations and I congratulate you for your patriotic attitude, but that is not enough, It is inconceivable that after a deep analysis of our situation there could be a Cuban willing to go to a dance at a night club who is not economically supporting the struggle for liberation of our Fatherland.

Our crisis, and it is sad to say so and I am not excluding myself from this, our crisis is lack of sacrifice.

We believe that by living out of Cuba we are already sacrificing enough and therefore we can dedicate ourselves to enjoy the beauty of life as it is offered so openly and so abundantly in this country.

In Cuba we suffered persecution and the Communist terror, and when we arrive to exile yelling that Communism is the system most contrary to Christianity, we forget the first and most principal Christian belief, converting ourselves in potentially Communists when we forget "love your neighbor as yourself".

Where is our Christian charity when we have dare to go dancing while Alberto Muller, Antonio Copado and hundreds of thousands of Cuban rot in denigrated captivity? And I repeat, that I do not excuse myself of this criticism, and it is for that same reason, because I do not exclude myself and because I believe that my main obligation in this exile, is not for the Cubans that are out of Cuba but toward those unlucky ones who had the misfortune and the courage to sacrifice their lives for a Cuba where would reign a real Christian spirit, it is why I am speaking to you tonight, and I am doing so with total frankness.

Our situation today, November 26, 1966 is incredible sad, lamentable, incomprehensible, and tragic.

Our families have become divided, sometimes because of the geographical distance and other times by another distance more thorny, more painful and difficult to overcome, which is that created by ideological differences.

We have been dispossessed of the land that saw us been born and they have tried to humiliate, insult and degraded us as if we were worms unable to produce anything good.

But there is something that we have to be grateful of, and it is that we have had the opportunity to demonstrate to ourselves the falsehood of those accusations.

Wherever we Cubans have arrived, we have triumphed, either as professionals, businessmen or workers.

We have surged from below, without anything, struggling many times against the disadvantage of the language and we have accomplished that when they talk about the Cubans they do so with respect and sympathy.

Even so, we have committed the error of take care of our problems in a selfish and antiChristian way when we forget those who are suffering in Cuba.

Today, we have among us, two Cubans who fight to return us the Fatherland that was stolen from us. This two gentleman are not super humans neither they have come from outer space, they are Cubans born in our Fatherland, they were brightened by the same sun that brightened us and educated in the same principles that we were educated.

They are aware of our limitations and our efforts, but they refuse to turn their back to the anguished cries of those inside Communist dungeons, they tremble of indignation at their impotence of not been able to help even more to the downfall of the Castro regime. People who had suffered what our people had suffered, and who still do not resign themselves to call an end to the struggle, is honorable people who honor those brave Cubans who fought in 1868 and 1895 but who were not able to see their sacrifices consecrated until the instauration of our Republic on May 20, 1902.

I would like to tell Mr. Jorge Más Canosa and Dr. Orlando Bosch, that in the name of the Cuban Student Directorate in the City of New Orleans, and in the name of this Coordinating Committee, you can count with our most enthusiastic and firm support.

This moment is not a moment for divisions or personalizations.

Cuba today is in a higher position than the Directorate, MIRR, RECE, ALPHA or any other organization.

Our order had to be: return to Cuba, and to achieve that we have to be ready to help all those who are fighting against the Communist tyranny.

Our wish of today is to obtain the necessary equipment for RECE to move forward and confront the henchmen of the regime.

But when we are able to obtain that equipment we could not sit down, relax and say: We already did our part.

No. We have to ask ourselves: What else can I do?

To answer that question is one of the purposes of this Coordinating Committee, and I believe that our only patriotic answer is promising ourselves that after we find the equipment for RECE, and we can do that with our effort, we have to offer also our cooperation to those brave commandos of MIRR.

Instead to sitting to rest we have to promise ourselves to try to find the necessary equipment to carry on a military action to destroy a center vital to the Castro's economy. And then, when that operation is completed, which should be known as "Operation New Orleans", and after that we should not stop.

We will cooperate to punch again the Communist dictatorship until the name of New Orleans become a four letter word at the lips of the militiamen who had sold our Country.

We will not stop in our struggle, until we manage to open with our own hands the locks of the jails where our brothers are.

We will not stop until the Cuba regain their freedoms, because we were not born slaves and we don't have flesh of slaves.

And then, when our effort is known and become contagious to other cities, those who have betrayed us and abandon us would not be able to stop the final march for the liberation of our Fatherland.

We have in our hands our own destiny. We only have two paths: One will bring us to Cuba, to the liberation of our beloved Fatherland and to the peace of mind of our conscience.

The other, will convert us in pariahs without Country, in infrahuman persons, able to turn our backs to those who had sacrificed themselves for us. And confronted with the alternative that could convert us into a Country of heroes or a Country of parasites, we have to go into the thoughts of our Apostle when in his great vision said:

"If a People do not dare its hard chains
To break with his hands
That People could change Tyrants
But never free they could be."
Independence or Death! . . . We shall return!

That meeting was a success but Castro's moles were working hard trying to bring divisions among us.

On December 1, 1966 former Cuban Ambassador to the United Nations, before Castro, Emilio Núñez Portuondo wrote a nice article in the newspaper "Diario Las Americas" highly recommending my new pamphlet "Cuba Betrayed".[159]

On December 12, 1966 Dr. Ernesto Freyre, from "Representación Cubana del Exilio" (RECE) wrote me the following letter:

---

[159] Diario Las Americas, December 1, 1966, page 5.

501 Adele
New Orleans, La.

Dear Dr. Bringuier:

Our Delegate in that city as well as our representatives, Jorge Más and Antonio Calatayud, have spoken to my highly enthusiastically of your valuable and patriotic cooperation to the meeting of November 26.

They also inform us of your words full of patriotism, wisdom and sensibility.

That is why it is my satisfaction, in the name of this organization, and in the name of our representatives and Delegate, express to you our recognition and congratulate you for your participation and words.

Very truly yours,
Dr. Ernesto Freyre

On December 25, 1966, I sent the following telegram to Jack Ruby at Parkland Hospital, Dallas, Texas:

As I am of the opinion that President Kennedy's assassination was instigated by Fidel Castro I am asking the opportunity to visit you at the hospital and ask some questions to you. If you don't have something to hide I am sure that you will let me question you.

Dr. Carlos J. Bringuier
New Orleans Delegate
Cuban Student Directorate

Apparently Jack Ruby had something to hide because he never gave me the opportunity to question him.

CHAPTER XI

———◦◍◦———

THE GARRISON "INVESTIGATION"

In late December 1966, David W. Ferrie walked into my store "Casa Cuba", located at 111 Decatur Street, asking me to talk to Dr. Carlos Bringuier. When I told him that he was talking to Dr. Carlos Bringuier he looked a little confused because it seems he was expecting a different type of person. I am certain that at that moment he did not recall we had met in late September or beginning of October 1961, at his house, for a period of approximately 5 to 10 minutes when I had gone there accompanying Sergio Arcacha Smith (at the time Delegate in New Orleans of the Cuban Revolutionary Council) and Mr. Carlos Quiroga.

Since I never had a good impression of David Ferrie, I asked him what he wanted. He told me that he was interested in finding out the whereabouts of Mr. Arcacha because, he said: Arcacha could verify some points in regard to him.

Ferrie told me that the New Orleans District Attorney had been conducting an investigation into the assassination of President Kennedy and that Garrison was going to frame him (Ferrie), because Garrison was going to run for a higher office and he needed some publicity.

I recall that I answered Ferrie that he should not be nervous because this is a free country and here nobody could be framed without evidence. Immediately Ferrie stated that in this country a man could be ruined just with a bad publicity campaign against him. We kind of enter into an argument when he told me that there was no justice in this country and that all Judges should be hanged. To my mind came the figure of my father, a former Cuban judge and I told him he was wrong.

When Ferrie realized that I did not sympathize with him he left the store. For the first time I had the hope that maybe someone was really interested in investigating the assassination of President Kennedy. New Orleans District Attorney Jim Garrison could be that person.

During the last few days of 1966 a group of Cuban refugees came to New Orleans through Mexico. They landed at the Moisant International Airport in New Orleans and at the airport was congregated a group of Cubans waiting for their arrival and with us were several newsmen from the local TV stations and newspapers. I was there not only as a Cuban but also as News correspondent for Radio Station WFAB from Miami, Florida and I talked to one of the newsmen present, Sam DePino, a newsman from Channel 12 TV. In our conversation, and in the presence of Carlos Quiroga who was also there, I mentioned to DePino that it would be good for him to look around the New Orleans District Attorney's office because, as I explained to him, there was an investigation going on in regard to the assassination of President Kennedy.

I would like to point out that on that particular day I was under the impression that the investigation of Mr. Garrison was going in the right direction and that the New Orleans District Attorney was trying to find links of Oswald and the Communists. I was surprised when Sam DePino told me that he already knew about the investigation, and even more, that he had been supplying some information to the District Attorney's office.

During the following weeks I learned that some Cuban refugees had been interrogated by Garrison. One of them, who even was not in the United States at the time of the assassination, was so nervous about the possibility of been publicly involved in this affair, that according to a mutual friend, the poor man took a whole bottle of tranquilizers the same day of the interrogation and the family had to call a physician to save his life.

Around the end of January, Assistant District Attorney John Volz visited me at "Casa Cuba" asking questions in regard to my testimony to the Warren Commission. He was particularly interested in what I could know about Sergio Arcacha Smith, former Delegate in New Orleans of the Cuban Revolutionary Council (CRC).

A few days later, Assistant District Attorney Volz returned to "Casa Cuba" and asked me if I could go with him to the District Attorney's office because they wanted to question me. I remember that it was a Saturday in the afternoon. When we arrived at the office they took me into a small room with a mirror in the wall. Immediately I realized that somebody else would be watching from the other side of the mirror.

Several investigators were there among them was First Assistant District Attorney James Alcock. The questioning commenced in a nice and polite way but a few minutes later I found out that instead of been questioned as a witness with desire to cooperate I was treated like an accused person. I requested them to stop for a minute because they were all wrong. They had particular interest in Sergio Arcacha Smith and in Ricardo Davis. They were trying to implicate me in a training camp that Ricardo Davis and the "Christian Democratic Movement" had across Lake Pontchartrain during the summer of 1963. They assured me that Lee Harvey Oswald was seen in that training camp. At one point they asked me if I had been there and when I denied having done so they told me: *"How could I tell them that when there are witnesses who say that they had seen me there."* My reply was simple and to the point: *"If any person testifies that, then that person has to be either a liar or a sob."*

On one of the following days I met on the sidewalk of "Casa Cuba" two Americans who I had previously met at the bar "New World" on the night of September 1st, 1966. That night there was a propaganda film for the Viet Cong been shown there. I had ask Carlos Quiroga to go with me that night in order to debate and destroy their point of view. When Quiroga arrived at the bar he recognized a friend of him working for the Intelligence Division of the New Orleans Police Department who was there and Quiroga reported to him our presence and our motive to be there. I debated the organizers of this Communist group at that meeting. In fact, one of them publicly stated that he was a Communist and this was a young man I only knew by the name of Fred but whose real name was Frederick Bernard Lacey, Jr . . . The other one that I knew was Bob Head, who was the organizer of the demonstration against the Viet Nam war in front of the Jung Hotel on Canal Street during the seminary of the State Department about the foreign policy of the United States which was held on November 1966 and Bob Head was also the publisher of the pro-Communist newspaper NOLA Express. When we met now, on the sidewalk of "Casa Cuba" we started chatting and after a while Bob Head left but Fred came inside my store. We started discussing Communism, which discussion lasted for hours when suddenly the conversation changed subject to the assassination of President Kennedy. To my astonishment Fred's thesis about the assassination was exactly the same thesis that Mr. Garrison himself had told Carlos Quiroga in two previous occasions and Quiroga had already advised me of it. The assassination of President Kennedy was the result of an anti-Castro plot. If I am not wrong Fred Lacey was one of the victims of Jim Jones at his People's Temple in Jonestown, Guyana where in November 18, 1978, 908 members perished.

On January 21, 1967 Quiroga was called to Garrison's office and subjected to a long interrogatory by Garrison himself. Quiroga asked that the interrogatory remain secret fearing harm to his parents who were still in Cuba but unknown to Quiroga, Garrison proceeded to tape record the meeting. Later on, Quiroga became aware of the existence of a transcript of the interrogation when a copy was given to him by newsman Sam DePino. According to DePino the transcript had been given to him by Garrison's office. I have to mention here that when Quiroga read the transcript he found out that Garrison's office had changed some of his answers which meant the District Attorney of New Orleans was falsifying their own fraudulent obtained documents.

On Monday, January 23, 1967 at about 7:45 p.m., Quiroga's wife, Maria Schiro, answered the phone at her house. A man's voice told her that he was going to kill Quiroga because Quiroga had gone to the District Attorney's office several times, adding that he had killed fifty people in one day and one more was not going to make a difference. As soon as Quiroga got home he called the FBI and the New Orleans Police Department reporting the death threat. The police immediately contacted the District Attorney's office. Next day the District Attorney's office contacted Quiroga and told him to go with his wife to see if she could identify the voice of the man who had called their house. They played a tape with Jack Martin's voice.

Here I want to explain that Jack Martin was a private investigator and a drunk who had been supplying erroneous information to Garrison. Garrison using this erroneous information to build his case. At the end of Garrison's investigation, when Clay Shaw was declared "Not Guilty", Jack Martin called me to congratulate me for my stand against Garrison.

A few minutes after Quiroga's wife recognized Jack Martin's voice they were brought to Garrison's office, where Garrison received them in a very polite way and apologized to Quiroga stating to him that he believed everything that Quiroga had told him and that it was not necessary for Quiroga to take a lie detector test.

On Saturday, January 28, 1967, while Quiroga was at the District Attorney's office to bring some information that he had previously promised he saw that in a small room Jack Martin was been questioned. Quiroga waited outside and when District Attorney Investigator Louis Ivon came out, Ivon told him that Jack Martin had confessed that he was the one who threatened to kill him on January 23, 1967. Quiroga requested permission from Ivon to talk to Martin and find out why he had threatened to kill him. Ivon hesitated but told him it was OK.

Quiroga walked into the room and Jack Martin told him that the reason why he had called Quiroga's house was because he was drunk and did not know what he was saying. Quiroga proceeded to ask questions to Martin and realized that all the wrong information that Garrison had about Quiroga had been furnished by the drunk in front of him. Suddenly, Ivon stopped Quiroga from continuing the interrogation but it was too late. Martin has told Quiroga that Arcacha had left New Orleans just prior to the assassination. When Quiroga had asked him in what year that had happened, Martin answered that the assassination had been in 1962. Quiroga was ordered by Ivon to leave the room and after a few minutes Ivon joined Quiroga, and with his hand on his gun told him: *"If this sob changes his mind about what he had told us I am going to break his head open."* Quiroga was chock to see that Ivon was going to take Martin home instead of putting him in jail.

On February 13th, 1967, I decided that it would be a good idea if I would have the opportunity to talk in person with Jim Garrison. I had been in New Orleans for six years and I could help him to clarify any doubt or misinformation that he could have received in regard to any person or persons that I could have known. I thought it was necessary to put to rest rumors about the involvement of anti-Castro Cubans in the assassination, rumors that could hurt, not only the Cuban refugees in this Country, but rumors that also could hurt Americans and even the United States itself. On that date I called Assistant District Attorney John Volz and I asked him to arrange a meeting with Garrison. A few minutes later Volz returned my call and told me that New Orleans District Attorney Jim Garrison would be delighted to talk to me next day.

Next day, February 14th, I arrived at Garrison's office and the one who received me was First Assistant District Attorney James Alcock who was with other investigators. I started explaining about the rumors and the statement that have been reported to me about a Judge at a party announcing that soon the investigation about the assassination of President Kennedy will be publicized in an exclusive article on Life Magazine. I explained to them how the Communists were going to use this investigation to discredit the image of the United States all over the world. Minutes later Jim Garrison arrived at his office and finally I was introduced to him.

I was completely sure that as soon as I talk to Garrison everything would be clarified. But apparently, at this time, was when everything started to go wrong. Minutes later Garrison outlined his case to me. Jim Garrison, the New Orleans District Attorney, stated plain and simple that Lee Harvey Oswald was not a Communist, but instead Oswald was really an antiCommunist. Garrison continued explaining his thesis and stated that Oswald had been brought to New Orleans by Conservatives. I recall Garrison referring to the Conservatives as "Patriots" using an ironic accent like discrediting the words "Patriots" and "Conservatives". Then Garrison told me that the person who had brought Oswald to New Orleans was William Riley a person who I had never met. Then Garrison showed to me pictures of different people who I have never met, among them a picture of Clay Shaw asking me if I knew him. My answer was the truth, I had never met Clay Shaw, and I even did not know who he was. Another picture shown to me was that of a person they identified as Guy Bannister, a person who also I have never met but that I have heard about him that he had been with the FBI and later on head of the New Orleans Police Department, and positively a Conservative anti-Communist. Another person mentioned was Carlos Marquez a former Cuban Consul in New Orleans who had died some years before.

Garrison was surprised when I told him that his thesis was the most ridiculous thing that I had ever heard in my life. I also told him that I knew that his investigation not only was going to finish in zero, because I had met Oswald and I was sure that Oswald was a Communist, but that in the meantime the Communists were going to use all the rumors around his investigation to smear the Cuban refugees and hurt the image of the United States around the world. I also explained to him that when his investigation finishes in zero, then the Communist will tell the world that the Federal Government had put pressure on him (Garrison) not to discover the truth. At one point I turn to his investigators who were present and told them that they had to be stupid or they were working for the Communists.

As you can imagine the situation was becoming very tense between Garrison and me. At one point he told me that maybe somebody had been fooling me. My reply was: *"Maybe somebody had been fooling me but maybe somebody is fooling you and I do not know who the fool is, you or I."* I suggested him that it would be better if he would start investigating those who had been furnishing him that type of information.

New Orleans District Attorney Jim Garrison rose to his feet and told me that he would not discuss anything else with me unless I would volunteer to take a lie detector test. My answer was that he was either a Communist or a "sob" and that he could put me three lie detectors including one in, and then I made a sign to my genitals to him.

In my opinion this was the turning point in my relationship with the New Orleans District Attorney. Garrison was used to intimidate people with his height and his melodramatic attitude. He never expected my reaction. He realized that it was not easy to intimidate me.

Immediately, Garrison rose up and order one of his men to take me to another location to undergo the lie detector test. We arrived at the Southern Marine and Aviation Building located at 610 Poydras Street. There I was introduced in room 309 in which were located two companies: 1) N.O. Private Patrol Service; and 2) "Gurvich Systems". Gurvich was the last name of one of his investigators, who by coincidence, I had been told, lost a daughter at Jim Jones People's Temple in Guyana. There, for the first time in my life I undertook a lie detector test.

Some of the questions asked were: 1) If I knew if Arcacha and Oswald had met; 2) If I knew if Davis and Oswald had met; 3) If I knew if Carlos Quiroga and Oswald had met. At that moment I asked this particular question to be changed because I knew Carlos Quiroga had met Oswald on August 16, 1963 when Quiroga tried to infiltrate Oswald's organization. Therefore I requested that the question be changed to the following: "If I knew if Carlos Quiroga had met Lee Harvey Oswald on another occasion than the one I had stated"; 4) If I had met with Lee Harvey Oswald in any other occasions that those stated by me to the Warren Commission. Other questions asked were in regard to Clay Shaw, Guy Bannister and others that I do not recall. When they finished I demanded that one more question should be included in this test: "If I believe that the investigation of Mr. Garrison was the most ridiculous thing I had ever heard in my life". They refused to include that question.

When I left the Gurvich's office I could not believe that it was true everything that was happening. For a moment I thought it was a nightmare but when I realized it was real I decided to write a letter to John Edgar Hoover, Director of the FBI. To me, the CIA was not an Agency of the government to be trusted. I had heard and read how that Agency, with many honest people in it, had been infiltrated by the Communists and I could not deposit my trust in it. On the other hand I have had always faith in the FBI as a serious organism and in Hoover as an antiCommunist. This was my letter to Hoover:

Mr. John Edgar Hoover
Director of the Federal Bureau of Investigations.
Washington, D.C.

Sir:

As you have to know I am the same person who was arrested in New Orleans on August 9, 1963 with Lee Harvey Oswald and the same who debated him on a radio debate.

The reason of this letter is to let you know of an amazing thing that is going on in this city. The District Attorney Mr. Jim Garrison is carrying on an investigation in regard to the connections of Lee Harvey Oswald in the city as if Oswald were in contact with some anticommunists people in New Orleans.

When I am writing you this letter I have just returned from a lie detector test which was offered to me by Mr. Garrison. Some of the general ideas of Mr. Garrison are that:

1) Oswald was brought to New Orleans by Mr. Riley from the Riley coffee co. and according to Mr. Garrison this man, Mr. Riley is an anti-Communist Conservative.

2) *Oswald was not a communist but an anticommunist and as that he carried out the assassination.*

3) *They are trying to tie facts and issues that are impossible to be tied, showing contacts of Oswald with Cuban refugees.*

As I understand that this whole thing will finish in zero in regard to try to find any possible Cuban refugees participation in the assassination I don't have any fear as a single person or as part of the group of Cuban refugees in the city, but as anticommunist I am convinced (already I received the information that Life Magazine will carry an article on the investigation) that the ones who are going to use this thing are the communists. They first put the blame on the CIA, the FBI and even on you. Later they put the blame, as Radio Havana Cuba implied on November 22, 1966, on President Lyndon B. Johnson. Now, they are ready to put the blame on us "Cuban refugees". We don't have the power that the CIA or the FBI or the President of the United States have to oppose the smear that they will use against us. For that reason I am asking that you direct a complete investigation on those who are spreading these false rumors.

Very truly yours,
Carlos Bringuier

The following Saturday morning I visited voluntarily Mr. Garrison's office. There I met the New Orleans District Attorney who apologized for the way he had treated me at our previous meeting. Garrison also told me that I had passed the lie detector test superbly. In fact, according to Garrison, the lie detector test given to me, assured him that I was telling the truth.

I told Garrison that my main interest was in the truth, that I was not willing to frame neither the Communists nor the anti-Communists and that I was willing to help him, without need of receiving any salary. I also stated to him that I was glad, that at least in the newspapers, have not been mentioned any involvement of Cuban refugees up to that moment. Then Garrison answered: *"So far"*.

On February 17, 1967 a big headline in the "New Orleans States-Item" read:

DA HERE LAUNCHES BROAD JFK DEATH "PLOT" PROBE

The New Orleans newspapers started to print information provided by the District Attorney's office trying to implicate anti-Castro Cubans. They were saying that Sergio Arcacha Smith was living in Dallas, Texas.

I try to place a call to Arcacha asking the operator for his phone number but I was told that it was a private number and it could not be disclosed to me. I had not talked to Arcacha in years and when he departed from New Orleans, in 1962, we were not talking to each other. I did not like Arcacha but I was sure that he was going to be framed by Garrison for something Arcacha was not part of. In my desperation I told the operator that it was a matter of life and death and gave her my name and telephone number to forward it to Arcacha. A few minutes later my telephone was ringing and I heard Arcacha's voice. It was good that at that time I was able to speak with a human operator and not to a computerized system.

I explained to Arcacha the situation in New Orleans and mentioned to him that someone had told the New Orleans District Attorney that he, Arcacha, had meetings with Oswald in New Orleans during 1963. Arcacha told me that there were investigators from New Orleans in Dallas trying to obtain information about him questioning Cubans in that city.

Arcacha also stated that one day when he opened the door of his house he saw two of Garrison's investigators standing on the sidewalk, one of them appearing to be Russian. Later on I figured that this one should have been Gurvich.

On February 19, 1967, the "Times Picayune" published a long article saying in part:

> Garrison's office is seeking a "physically powerful and dangerous" Cuban who is "believed to be one of a group of Cubans who reportedly hid behind a billboard on the parade route in Dallas on Nov, 22, 1963."
>
> Supposedly, the Cuban was photographed in New Orleans handing out "Fair Play for Cuba" pamphlets.
>
> Garrison and some aides are supposed to have covered the Miami waterfront extensively looking for the Cuban. But he is now thought to have left the country.

The stupidity was so clear that I could not comprehend how it was possible that the New Orleans newspapers were so blind. But as it happened in Cuba with Castro, stupidity became rampant in New Orleans. I started referring to Garrison as a Fidel Castro without the beard.

I believe that it was on Monday February 20, 1967 that David Ferrie showed up again at my store. He claimed to be not feeling well and I decided to invite him to drink some coffee at a restaurant located one block away from "Casa Cuba" on Decatur Street. While we sat down drinking coffee Ferrie was telling me that he had to clear his name and that Garrison was persecuting him. I was feeling piety for the poor guy but nevertheless we had some disagreements when Ferrie told me that whoever think that Oswald was a Communist had to be a nut. As I was, and I am, convinced that Oswald was a Communist I took his words as an insult but I let it pass because he was feeling a painful headache when he departed. Immediately, to cover my back, I called the District Attorney's office and talked to Louis Ivon informing him of my meeting with Ferrie I was surprised when Ivon told me that they were already aware of it. I was glad that I called because I was trying to avoid any kind of entrapment from Garrison's office, because he became famous for that, charging persons with unrelated charges in order to smear them. My impression at the moment was that David Ferrie was becoming crazy.

Next day, on February 21, Alberto Fowler came to "Casa Cuba". I knew Fowler as a Brigade 2506 veteran and as Director of International Relations for the City of New Orleans.

Fowler was expressing his doubts about the investigation and he said that the representative in New Orleans of Life Magazine had been working with Garrison in the investigation since the beginning. According to Fowler, the wife of the Life Magazine representative is of French origin and 100% for Castro. Fowler also said that this lady had known some information that he (Fowler) had only mentioned to Garrison and she had been asking about Arcacha's whereabouts and also for information about the Christian Democratic Movement long before the investigation came out publicly in the press. Fowler stated that he had arguments with this lady which arguments had ended by him telling her that he didn't want to talk to her anymore because she was a Communist. According to Fowler this lady also was representing two Communist magazines from Europe. I took Fowler's information but I could not trust him, he was, according to him, working with Garrison and Garrison was helping the Communists. It would not be the first time that Alberto Fowler made a mistake, he had done that when been a member of rich and aristocrat family in January 1, 1959 when Batista fled he put in his arm a bracelet of the July 26 Movement.[160]

It is good to bring out here my believe of how Garrison investigation started. The representative in New Orleans of Life Magazine to whom Alberto Fowler was referring was David Chandler. Chandler was the one who originated the whole investigation. Chandler wanted to tie up the assassination of President Kennedy to the Mafia and to Carlos Marcello. He brought the idea to Garrison who became captivated with the possibility of being in the spotlight of all the publicity surrounding such investigation. The only problem for both of them, besides the truth, was that Jim Garrison in reality was a drunk, corrupt and abusive District Attorney with strong ties with the Mafia.

Jim Garrison used Chandler to obtain enough information to start his so called investigation and then "divorced" Chandler and joined forces with pro-Communist individuals like Mark Lane and Harold Weisberg. One incident that shows the real Jim Garrison was the confrontation that he had with Aaron Kohn, Executive Managing Director of the New Orleans Metropolitan Crime Commission. When Mr. Kohn started investigating corruption in the New Orleans area Jim Garrison reacted by placing Mr. Kohn in jail. Nobody reacted in New Orleans against this dereliction of duty by the District Attorney because the District Attorney had dirt in the majority of the corrupt political establishment in Louisiana. Remember that in Louisiana every time that elections for Commissioner of Insurance came, the opposing candidate against the incumbent was promising to end corruption. When he wins, the old incumbent was sent to prison for corruption and in the next election it would repeat the same history. In the meantime the Attorney General for the State of Louisiana was Jack P. F. Gremillon who ended himself in jail.

How come Jim Garrison was going to implicate the mafia to satisfy David Chandler leftist attack when he, Garrison, was part of the Mafia? That is how everything started in New Orleans for the "investigation" conducted by the idol of Oliver Stone.

---

[160] "Tocayo", by Antonio Navarro, page 58.

I continued going to the District Attorney's office, appearing as a bona fide helper, but trying to clarify wrong allegations. I was surprised to see how the New Orleans District Attorney's office was run by such incompetent people. I recall that one day they were asking me about the whereabouts of a Cuban because they were ready to order his arrest in order to be able to interview him. The one approaching me with the request for help was First Assistant District Attorney James Alcock who later on was named Judge in the City of New Orleans. I asked Alcock: *"Have you checked the telephone book?"* I wish you could be able to see the face of Alcock at that moment. He went to get the white pages of the telephone directory and voilà to his surprise my brilliant idea had paid results, because right there, in front of his eyes, was the name, address and telephone number of the person that they had been unable to locate. The person was called and the situation resolved. To me it was like a movie of the "Three Stooges" working in the New Orleans District Attorney's office.

On another occasion while I was in "Casa Cuba" I saw a Cuban coming into the store to use the public phone that I had at the front of the store. I knew him, his name was Emilio Santana. I knew that Santana had a criminal record and I did not pay too much attention to him.

Next day I was called by the District Attorney's office to act as an interpreter. I went there and I was surprised when I saw Santana in the office. First Assistant District Attorney James Alcock told me that I was going to be the interpreter for Santana. Alcock instructed me to tell Santana not to get nervous because the questioning did not have anything to do with robberies or drugs. The whole idea was that Santana was a reliable witness who was providing them the "evidence" that they needed in order to implicate Sergio Arcacha with Oswald. I accurately translated Santana's words. Santana was saying that he had seen Arcacha in a meeting of "Alpha 66" in Magazine Street at a time when Oswald was in New Orleans but that I knew Arcacha wasn't. When Santana finished his deposition, Alcock's face was exulting, he was showing his happiness; finally, in their minds, they had nailed Arcacha lying. Perjury charges would be forthcoming according to Alcock's imagination. I decided to ask Alcock that as I had literally translated Santana words if it was possible that I could ask him a couple of questions which may help clarify the situation. Alcock consented, and then I asked Santana if the "Alpha 66" meeting that he was referring to had been held at the service station of the Suarez brothers at the corner of Magazine Street and Washington Avenue. Santana responded that it was correct, that the meeting had been at Suarez' service station. I had asked the question because I knew that the Suarez brothers were sympathizers of "Alpha 66". Then, I asked my second question which was based on the fact that I knew the Delegate in New Orleans of "Alpha 66" who at that time was a Cuban named Luis Bretos, and I also knew that Bretos physical complexion had kind of resemblance to Arcacha's. I knew that Arcacha was not in New Orleans at that time and Arcacha had never been involved with "Alpha 66". My question to Santana was: *"Do you remember if the person that you said it was Arcacha could have been Luis Bretos?"* Emilio Santana responded: *"That is, that is the name of that man, Bretos, Luis Bretos."* I am sure that you can visualize the stupid face of Alcock when I translated Santana's answer and Alcock realized that the stage that he had been building crumbled in front of him.

When the meeting was over I was surprised when I saw a man that had been sitting with us while I was translating Santana's deposition, rose and told Alcock: *"For the record, I want to say that the translation provided by Carlos Bringuier has been totally accurate."* At that moment I realized that the invitation from Garrison's office for me to serve as translator for Emilio Santana had a dual purpose, been one of them try to entrap me. If I would have made any changes during Santana's deposition I would have been charged with obstruction of justice.

When we left the District Attorney's office I was chatting with Santana about how come he had become involved in this situation. He said that he was in Miami when he was contacted by Garrison's investigators and that he was offered a plane ticket, a hotel room, meals and some drugs in order to come and testify in New Orleans. This was the office of the New Orleans District Attorney Jim Garrison, who years later Castro's propagandist Oliver Stone was going to portray as champion of law enforcement.

On February 20, 1967 I prepared a memo to the District Attorney's office recounting my involvement up to that moment and giving my ideas in regard to his investigation.

During the morning of February 22 it was discovered the body of David W. Ferrie, only two days after our last meeting drinking coffee. He was found dead in his apartment at 3330 Louisiana Avenue Parkway. The coroner stated that Ferrie died of natural causes. Jim Garrison categorized the dead as suicide. Up to this date I believe that he could have been murdered by one of Garrison's henchmen.

On March 9, 1967, an investigator from Garrison's office showed Carlos Quiroga a picture of Ferrie with another person which person Quiroga identified as Julián Buznedo, a Cuban who had been in New Orleans in 1962 and who is a veteran of the 2506 Brigade. Up to that moment, Garrison's star witness Perry Raymond Russo had not mentioned any name of Cubans been at the "party" in which the allegedly plot occurred at Ferrie's apartment. After that, at the time of Clay Shaw's hearing, Russo identified two Cubans been in the "party", one of them was supposedly this man Julián Buznedo. Later on, during the week of March 18/19 Russo was introduced in Baton Rouge, Louisiana, to my friend Miguel Cruz and Russo stated to Cruz that Julián Buznedo was at the "party".

In the meantime during the weekend of March 25/26 Julián Buznedo was brought to New Orleans by the District Attorney's office. Buznedo occupied room 937 at the Roosevelt Hotel and was questioned at the Garrison's office. Buznedo denied been in New Orleans in 1963 in which year Perry Russo sword the "party" had been held. After a while Buznedo was introduced to Russo and he, Buznedo, denied ever having met Russo before and the District Attorney allowed Buznedo to go back to Denver, Colorado, where Buznedo was living. Unfortunately for Buznedo he had become a good suspect for two reasons: 1) Buznedo was Cuban; and 2) Buznedo was a veteran of the 2506 Brigade.

I would like to enter, for future historians my opinion about Perry Raymond Russo, who was a cab driver in New Orleans and was criminally used by Jim Garrison. I graduated as a Doctor of Law and I am not a psychologist but I firmly believe that Russo did not have all his marbles in the right place of his brain. Jim Garrison subjected Russo to hypnosis and triggered Russo's ambition for fame. Like in some other instances in this truculent affair, after one of these characters open their mouth they have to maintain what they have invented or are subject to being charged with perjury. In my opinion Perry Raymond Russo was another victim of Jim Garrison.

On April 2, 1967. The Times Picayune reported that the District Attorney had formulated charges accusing Gordon Novel and Sergio Arcacha of conspiring with the late David W. Ferrie to commit simple burglary of a Schlumberger Wells Service munitions dump 40 miles southwest of New Orleans. At the end of the article appeared the following:

Cuban Student Group Blasts DA's Tactics

The New Orleans delegation of the Cuban Student Directorate said it is "surprised by the low level tactics used by the district attorney's office" in its accusations against Sergio Arcacha Smith.

A press release issued Saturday by Carlos Bringuier, New Orleans delegate of the directorate stated:

The New Orleans delegation of the Cuban Student Directorate wants to make public the following statements:

We don't know, if the charges against Mr. Sergio Arcacha Smith—burglarizing a Houma munitions bunker in 1961—are true or false.

"We are surprised by the low level tactics used by the DA's office bringing out these accusations against Arcacha Smith at a time that they are investigating a supposed plot to kill the late President Kennedy that could lead the public opinion to judge Arcacha Smith guilty by association.

We do know that, at the proper time, those responsible for these Communist-inspired smears against anti-Castro Cubans and conservative Americans will be charged with much more important charges than this filed against Arcacha Smith. Even if would be proved true these charges against Arcacha Smith, the result would be that Arcacha Smith had been charge for his efforts to liberate his country from the Communist tyranny defended by Mark Lane. On the other hand, Arcacha Smith would feel glad that at least he had not been charged for activities tended to betray his own country, undermine the credibility of its institutions and deliver it into the hands of international Communism, which look like are the activities in which had been engaged some people in New Orleans from some time ago to this moment.

*"We are asking again to the responsible citizens
of New Orleans to respect their institutions, to respect
the government of the United States and don't allow
themselves to be fooled by these smears which already
involve, according to Mark Lane, those, and some in very
high places who would do all in their power to prevent that
day from coming. We witnessed in Cuba how Communists
took over the country, smearing and discrediting our
institutions and we are witnessing here how they and their
fellow travelers are paving the way to do the same traitor
job in this wonderful country."*

Sometimes it is hard to comprehend how I escaped unscathed my almost daily public confrontations with the District Attorney of New Orleans. But I was confident that I was better prepared than him, I had the truth on my side and what it was more important I was *in God's hands.*

By the end of April, I had a meeting with Walter Sheridan who was preparing a program for NBC regarding Garrison's investigation. I learned that Walter Sheridan, a very close friend of Robert F. Kennedy was like a special envoy of Bobby Kennedy who was very disappointed with Garrison's activities. After we interchanged information I told Sheridan about Carlos Quiroga and the persecution that he had been subjected by Garrison and his subordinates. Sheridan asked me to participate in the forthcoming program but I declined the invitation explaining to him that I would be more helpful by not coming to the forefront in his program. I informed him about everything that I had witnessed at the District Attorney's office. During our conversation I was well aware that Walter Sheridan had been sent to New Orleans by Bobby Kennedy in order to derail Garrison's activities.

On April 28, 1967 I wrote a letter to Ricardo Pardo who at the moment was President of the Cuban Lyceum José Martí in New Orleans. We have had a meeting at the Lyceum to discuss the attack of Garrison against the anti-Castro Cubans and I had been sadly surprised to see some of them taking side with Garrison ideas. To my mind it had come back the beginning of Fidel Castro in Cuba when all the idiots were for Castro. Now some of the Cuban idiots in New Orleans were telling me that the District Attorney had to have some evidence and that he could be right. Yes, and Castro celebrated free elections in eighteen months as he has promised. I always believe that ignorance can be overcome but idiotism is forever. In my letter I notify Ricardo Pardo that I was voluntarily resigning from that organization.

On April 30, 1967, I received a telephone call from Alberto Fowler, Director of International Relations for the City of New Orleans and Investigator for DA Jim Garrison. Fowler was a colorful man. According to the book "Tocayo" written by Antonio Navarro, Fowler had been a collaborator of Fidel Castro during the struggle against Batista and had belong to the 26th of July Movement, in the other hand Fowler was one of the members of the 2506 Brigade and suffered jail in Cuba after their defeat. During our conversation Fowler stated that Garrison was planning to prove that it was Gordon Novel the person who pulled the trigger in Dallas and not Oswald.

On May 6, 1967 the Times Picayune published a report about a suit that I filed against Gambi Publications Inc., publishers of the magazine "Saga" and Harold Weisberg, Hyattstown, Md., author of the book "Whitewash-The Report on the Warren Commission Report", and the magazine article "Kennedy's murder-Buried Proof of a Conspiracy". My attorney in this suit was Néstor Márquez Díaz who I was using at different times because he never charged me any fees. I knew that Márquez Díaz was not in good judicial standing went I heard that Federal Judge Christemberry had prohibited him to set another foot in his court and that if he, Márquez Díaz, disregard that threat the Judge would file a motion to disbar Márquez Díaz.

I was surprised when one morning I read in the Times Picayune that I had withdrawn my suit. I went to see Néstor Márquez Díaz who told me that if I did not like what he has done, to suit him and his malpractice insurance will pay me. For a moment I was disoriented. I was fighting the District Attorney and powerful leftist forces and now it would appear as that I could not get along even with my own lawyer. I knew that what Márquez Díaz has done was despicable, but I would look bad by suing him. I never talked to him again. I do not know what kind of favor he could have received from Jim Garrison. An idea flourished in my brain at that moment that he could have made a deal with Garrison. Jim Garrison was using collateral charges against different people. If I would have agreed with Márquez Díaz to sue him and collect from his insurance company, Garrison could have turn against me and entrap me accusing me of fraud against my lawyer's Insurance Company. Eventually, Néstor Márquez Díaz left New Orleans and moved to his native Puerto Rico. Years later I read in the New Orleans newspaper that he had been stabbed to death there. Who else he could have damaged while practicing law there? I don't know.

On May 8, 1967, the office of the FBI in New Orleans wrote a report, of which I have a copy, stating:

Harold Weisberg and a Garrison investigator
taking picture of Dr. Carlos J. Bringuier.

Dr. Carlos J. Bringuier in Casa Roca

Dr. Jorge Ramos, Brazilian Ambassador Vasco Leitao da Cunha,
Dr. Carlos J. Bringuier, Ricardo Pardo and Carlos de la Vega.

ASSASSINATION OF PRESIDENT JOHN FITZGERALD KENNEDY DALLAS, TEXAS, NOVEMBER 22, 1963

At 10:37 a.m. on April 6, 1967, Carlos Quiroga, 3134 Derby Place, New Orleans Louisiana, appeared at the office of the Federal Bureau of Investigation (FBI) and furnished the following information:

Carlos Bringuier, an active anti-Castro Cuban, has been told by Alberto Fowler, investigator for District Attorney James Garrison that Garrison plans to serve a subpoena on the Central Intelligence Agency (CIA), in order to make that organization produce a photograph which was supposedly taken by them of Lee Harvey Oswald and a companion entering the Cuban Embassy in Mexico City. Fowler states that the individual accompanying Oswald is an agent of the CIA.

On April 22, 1967, Quiroga was interviewed by Hugh Aynesworth, correspondent of Newsweek Magazine. Quiroga told Aynesworth everything he knew concerning the Garrison investigation and in turn Aynesworth advised him that the attorney of Alvin Beaubouef, former associate of David W. Ferrie who is one of the figures in the Garrison investigation, has a tape recording of an investigator of Garrison's office offering $3,000 bribe to Beaubouef to change his testimony regarding Garrison's investigation. Garrison is supposedly aware that this tape recording exists and is now blackmailing Beaubouef with a photograph which shows he and David Ferrie engaged in sexual activities. Aynesworth indicated that an article critical of Garrison's inquiry will shortly appear in Newsweek.

On April 29, Quiroga met with Walter J. Sheridan, correspondent for the National Broadcasting Company (NBC). Sheridan indicated to Quiroga that he was aware of the existence of the aforementioned tape recording and they had attempted to acquire it from Beauboeuf's attorney but the price wanted for it was too high. Sheridan stated that NBC plans a television program regarding the Garrison investigation.

Quiroga indicated that both of the above correspondent were directed to him by Sergio Arcacha Smith, a key figure in the

Garrison probe and former Cuban exile leader in New Orleans. Quiroga advised them, as he had advised District Attorney Garrison's office when given a lie detector test, that he, in the past, has in no way been affiliated with the CIA or the FBI.

Quiroga advised that when the investigation by District Attorney Garrison first began he thought that Garrison might actually have something, but it is now his belief that Garrison's investigation is a witch hunt. Initially in the investigation, Quiroga made available to Garrison an album which he, Quiroga, and his wife had compiled regarding the, "Crusade to Free Cuba," in the New Orleans area. Since that time, names appearing in this album have continually appeared in the Garrison investigation.

Quiroga indicated that the, "Crusade to Free Cuba," was organized in New Orleans to raise funds among Cuban exiles and American citizens to fight against the Castro Government.

Bringuier advised Quiroga that Alberto Fowler had told him that Garrison wanted to have lunch with him in the coming week, but this may now be called off because Bringuier has filed a law suit against Garrison and author Jack Wiesberg. Bringuier reportedly has photographs which he recently took of Jack Wiesberg and a Garrison investigator taking photographs of Bringuier's bar, "La Habana", on Decatur Street in New Orleans.

Jack Wiesberg: is the author of Whitewash Quiroga stated that he and his wife will travel to Texas in the next week, during which he will visit Arcacha Smith. Quiroga plans to question Arcacha Smith concerning his knowledge of munitions thefts from bunkers in the New Orleans area.

What you have read above is the actual memo from the FBI and I want to clarify a couple of errors in it. First, I have never owned or been associated with the ownership, management or employment with any Bar in my life. The owner of the Bar "Habana" was Orestes Peña, this bar had rooms upstairs where Mark Lane used to stay for some time and on the night of May 31, 1979 it was raided by local and Federal lawmen for hang out of alleged prostitutes[161] and in November 7, 1979 Orestes Peña was

---

[161] The Times Picayune, June 1, 1979, Section 1, page 1.

sentenced to serve six months in jail and pay a fine of $5,000.[162]Second, the author referred to in the memo as Jack Wiesberg was in reality Harold Weisberg. I want this clarified because this is the way how errors, falsehoods and mistakes are recycled and presented as "facts" by distorters of the truth, and the above errors are part of an official FBI memo.

On May 9, 1967 Carlos Quiroga was informed by Salvadore Panzeca, attorney for Clay Shaw, that Orleans Parish District Attorney James Garrison planned to indict Quiroga on perjury charges when Quiroga would appear before an Orleans Parish Grand Jury. Panzeca stated to Quiroga that Garrison will attempt to show that Quiroga and Bringuier were at an anti-Castro training camp on the shores of Lake Pontchartrain with Lee Harvey Oswald.

On that same day of May 9 the New Orleans States-Item published an article in which it stated:

> *Garrison contends that Oswald was not a Communist, as he was pictured in the Warren Report, but a U.S. intelligence operative who was working closely with anti-Castro Cubans here and in Dallas.*
>
> *The Garrison contention about Oswald was disputed yesterday by Dr. Carlos Bringuier, head of the New Orleans delegation of the Cuban Student Directorate.*
>
> *He said his organization sent a letter to the House Committee on Un-American Activities several months ago asking it to <investigate Mr. Garrison's investigation.>*
>
> *<This delegation had four encounters with Lee Harvey Oswald in the summer of 1963,> Bringuier declared, <and even on Aug. 21 of that year we were asking for a congressional investigation of Oswald as a confessed Marxist.>*
>
> *He challenged the CIA and the FBI to <answer charges made against them> by Garrison.*

That was the afternoon newspaper. Already in the morning The Times Picayune had also published an article with the title: *"Subpoena goes to exile here".* It was referring to Carlos Quiroga. Later on the article stated:

---

[162] The Times Picayune, November 8, 1979, Section 1, page 1.

Garrison termed a recent *New Orleans States-Item* story concerning Oswald and the CIA in New Orleans "essentially correct".

"Oswald's Fair Play for Cuba actions in New Orleans constituted a transparent sham. These actions were designed as a cover, while he was engaged in no Communist activity whatsoever."

"His associations here were exclusively—not merely frequently, but exclusively—with persons whose orientation was anti-Castro, all of whom were plainly connected with federal agencies here."

Oswald's associates, Garrison said, were involved in a variety of revolutionary activities which were carried out with the full knowledge and consent of the CIA and the FBI.

These activities ranged from planning guerrilla strikes to procuring ammunition for smuggling into Cuba, he said.

"Federal agents were in close proximity to and well aware of these activities," said Garrison.

"They would positively—not just probably—know of Oswald's total involvement with the individuals engaged in anti-Castro planning and operations."

Exile Leader denies Garrison's Charges

A Cuban exile leader here Monday denied charges by District Attorney Jim Garrison that his people had any connection with United States federal agencies conspiring against Fidel Castro and declared John F. Kennedy was killed in a Communist plot.

Dr. Carlos Bringuier, head of the New Orleans Delegation of the Cuban Student Directorate, said his organization sent a letter, months ago to the House Committee on UnAmerican Activities asking it "to investigate Me. Garrison's investigation."

The Cuban leader said it is up to the Central Intelligence Agency and the Federal Bureau of Investigations to "answer charges made against them" by Garrison that Lee Harvey Oswald, lone Kennedy assassin named by the Warren Commission, was working with them in anti-Castro activities.

"This delegation had four encounters with Lee Harvey Oswald in the summer of 1963," said Dr. Bringuier, "and even on Aug. 21 of that year we were asking for a congregational investigation of Oswald as a confessed Marxist."

"When a conspiracy is made to put the blame of that infamous crime on us" he added, "then we have to tell all the new Quislings infiltrated in this country that we prefer to die than to allow all our prestige cut to pieces."

He added, "Oswald was a Communist, he was a Castro agent in this country, and as that he took the life of the President of the United States."

Asked about the Cuban leader's statements, Garrison said he had no comment.

In this public confrontation, when we looked at each other, Garrison blinked first. He was lying and he knew that. I was better prepared than him to debate about the assassination and what it is more important he knew that he was a liar and that I was telling the truth. In my heart I believe that it was his fear of confronting me what stopped him to move against me. He never subpoenaed me, he never brought me to a Grand Jury, never put me in the stand at Clay Shaw's trial, never charged me with anything. Jim Garrison limited himself to lie to the press. Maybe in the back of his mind he remembered our first personal confrontation on February 14, 1967.

On May 10, 1967, I was contacted over the phone by René Carballo. Carballo was a Cuban who had been helping the CRC in New Orleans and with whom I have had differences in the past. Carballo line of questioning over the phone immediately lighted a red light in my brain. He let me know that he was carrying his own investigation into the assassination of President Kennedy and was currently furnishing the results to a reporter for the New Orleans States-Item. Carballo claimed that Richard Davis, reportedly the head of an anti-Castro training camp on the shores of Lake Pontchartrain was, in actuality, not the leader of the camp, which camp in fact was run by an individual known as "The Mexican". Carballo stated that he had received this information from a Cuban refugee in Miami. It was Carballo's contention that it was "The Mexican" who accompanied Lee Harvey Oswald on his visit to the Cuban Embassy in Mexico City. Carballo inquired about my past contacts with the FBI and requested the names of any Special Agent whom I had contacted. I told him that I didn't have any dealings with the Federal Bureau of Investigations and that I was not familiar with any agents of the FBI. To me this phone call could have been originated even from the office of District Attorney Jim Garrison. If it was a fishing expedition from the DA he left without any fish because there was none to be caught.

That same day at 10:30 a.m. Carlos Quiroga answered the subpoena to the Grand Jury but instead to be brought there he was lead into the office of Assistant District Attorney Andrew (Moo-Moo) Schambria. In my opinion Moo-Moo have to have been previously a boxer, according to the features of his face. At his office Moo-Moo accused Quiroga of lying in a polygraph examination he had been previously given by the Orleans Parish District Attorney's office. Schambria advised Quiroga that he better change his testimony before the Grand Jury and admit that he knew about the firearm used to kill President Kennedy, and the fact that the "Fair Play for Cuba Committee" was, in actuality, a front organization for Lee Harvey Oswald in his anti-Castro activities. Schambria stated that if Quiroga did not change his testimony, he would be indicted for perjury by the Orleans Parish Grand Jury on Friday, May 12, 1967.

Quiroga denied that he lied on the polygraph examination and refused to change his testimony.

I want to mention something about Carlos Quiroga. Quiroga and I had attended the same school in Cuba but when I arrived to New Orleans and started to get acquainted with Sergio Arcacha, Quiroga and I were almost in opposite sides of the field in regard to Arcacha, but I want it to be known my recognition that Quiroga always acted as a man and as a gentleman. He did not allowed the henchmen from the District Attorney to intimidate him. Quiroga and his wife suffered a lot during the prostitution of justice carried on by Garrison and the cohort of Communists that dominated Garrison's brain. At one time, when Quiroga had been called to the District Attorney's office he was brought to a room by one of Garrison's investigators (if my memory doesn't fail me it was Louis Ivon). After been told to sit close to a table, they brought a rifle with a telescopic sight and rested it on the table. The investigators left the room leaving Quiroga alone with the rifle on top of the table. Quiroga sensed that something was wrong and he never dare to touch the rifle. He decided to take a nap. Quiroga was smart and lucky, knowing Garrison and his illegal means to achieve publicity I do not have the slightest doubt that if Carlos Quiroga would have made the mistake of touching the rifle, that rifle would have appear later on, discovered by the New Orleans District attorney, at a convenient place, with Quiroga's fingerprints on it.

Those were the type of criminals who were in possession of the District Attorney's office in New Orleans. We suffered through that and Carlos Quiroga was man enough to survive the ordeal.

On May 23, 1967, I mailed the following letter to the DRE in Miami:

> *Mr. Juan Manuel Salvat.*
> *2465 S.W 8th St. Miami, Fla. 33135*
>
> *Dear Salvat:*
>
> *First of all, I wish to God that when you receive this you will be in good health with your family and that everything would be going well.*
>
> *I am enclosing a copy of the telegram that we sent today to President Johnson in relation to the case of Felipe Rivero Díaz. I would like that you will send a copy to his organization because I don't have their address.*
>
> *In regard to here I would tell you that Mr. Garrison continues with his craziness. The last that he had done is to directly accuse the anti-Castro Cubans for the assassination of Kennedy and that the CIA knows the names of the ones who carried it out because they were CIA agents that organization, the CIA, covered up the act. He said Oswald didn't pull the trigger and apparently he is going to put the Laureano Batista's training camp in the spotlight of the plot. Almost a month ago I was at the office of the District Attorney as a translator for a Cuban that they were questioning and one of the pictures that they were showing to him was of a . . . Batista Falla, but his first name was not Laureano which means it could a be a brother of him if he has one.*

293

Today they just subpoena a close friend of mine, who attended Belen and who is the one I sent to Oswald's house to talk to him, posing as a pro-Castro, in order to find out what Oswald was planning to do in New Orleans. Already, last week, this boy Carlos Quiroga had been subpoena to the Grand Jury but when he arrived, an assistant to the District Attorney brought him to his office where he was threatened that if he didn't change his testimony he would be charged with perjury. Now he is under subpoena for tomorrow and there is a theory that after that I would be subpoenaed, but in an interview published in today newspaper Garrison said that in the assassination not a legitimate Cuban organization was involved which apparently exonerate the DRE and the MDC. You have to be here to know what is going on, in the early morning hours of Sunday May 14, somebody took a shot at the window glass of my store, in my opinion to terrorize me, but I don't believe that it would be right to feel fear here in exile and allow us to get fear, don't you believe the same? What the Mullers and the others imprisoned in Cuba would think?

OK, Juan Manuel you would know if anything happens to me because I have given instructions to immediately call you. I don't know until when the American government is going to allow this to continue, but sometimes I think, have not them allow what is happening in Cuba?

Greetings to your family and you receive an embrace of your brother,

Carlos Bringuier

On May 29. 1967, the New Orleans States-Item published an article with the headline *Garrison Reiterates call for probe of CIA* where he stated: *"there will be other arrests and they will probably be before the trial"* of retired businessman Clay L. Shaw. He also said: *"Kennedy was not killed by Lee Harvey Oswald who the Warren Commission concluded was the lone assassin. The President was killed by a group of conspirators made up of Latin Americans opposed to Fidel Castro and of former CIA employees. Oswald himself was not a CIA agent but had <obviously> been an intelligence employee of the government."*

At the beginning of June I took a trip to Miami where I met José Antonio Lanusa, of the DRE in Miami, I learned from him that Alberto Fowler had contacted Lanuza by phone and stated that Garrison will prove President Kennedy was assassinated by Cuban exiles and that I was aware of Oswald's affiliation with the CIA. Lanuza also stated that he had been personally contacted by Mr. Alcock, Assistant District Attorney for Garrison, who accused Lanuza of knowing about Oswald prior to the assassination. Alcock indicated that this information had been furnished by Claire Booth Luce.

I want to bring out how when you have an important event like the assassination of President Kennedy there are people whose adrenaline fluid so rapidly that they want to become part of history and in the process alter the facts, most of the time unintentionally. I don't doubt that "after" the assassination Lanuza had mentioned to Claire Booth Luce the encounters that I had with Oswald in August 1963. Lanuza had to know about Oswald "before" the assassination because I had requested from him information about Oswald "before" the radio debate.

On June 16. 1967, I met unexpectedly Alberto Fowler on Canal Street in New Orleans. Fowler told me that the investigation had become complicated because Garrison had information that an identical double for Lee Harvey Oswald exists and this individual is a "double agent" of the FBI. Fowler also indicated that Garrison will drag out the trial for over a year in order to develop and present new evidence. In my mind Garrison had become even more mentally perturbed.

On June 17, 1967. The New Republic published an article by Fred Powledge about the Garrison investigation and referred to me in the following terms:

> Carlos Bringuier, who is the New Orleans delegate of the Cuban Student Directorate, an anti-Castro organization, was visited by Lee Harvey Oswald in the summer of 1963. Oswald said he wanted to help fight Castro, but he looked fishy to Bringuier. A few days later, Bringuier saw Oswald handing out Fair Play for Cuba leaflets and he got into a fight with him. When I first saw Carlos Bringuier, it was a few days after the assassination. We were drinking Cuba libres. Bringuier, who was a criminal court secretary in Havana before his exile, was making a little money managing Casa Roca, a dry goods store,

and coordinating anti-Castro efforts at the same time. He was, and still is, one of the few people involved in any of this mess who sound honest when they say they are not employed by any spy agency.

Now he runs his own store, Casa Cuba, two doors away from Casa Roca. He started his business with $300. He has a fine home in Gretna, across the Mississippi, a beautiful wife, a flock of children, and two cars. On one of the cars is a bumper sticker supporting the war in Viet Nam and on the other is a decal depicting a caterpillar holding a Cuban flag in one hand and a shotgun in the other, with the proclamation, Volveremos ("we shall return"). Bringuier also has a complete set of the Warren Commission reports and he is writing a book that argues that Lee Oswald was, indeed the assassin.

"Oswald did it, and he did it in the way the Warren Commission said," he argued one night. "But I differ with the Warren Commission on the motivation. The motivation was that he was at least influenced by his commitment to communism, or he was ordered to do so by the Castro government."

As for Jim Garrison he said: "I think he needs psychiatric treatment."

"As a matter of fact, there is more basis for the idea that Garrison knew Oswald before the assassination than there is any connection between Oswald and the CIA or anti-Castro Cubans or with David Ferrie." He plucked Vol. XVI of the Warren report from the shelf, turned to exhibit 93, and quoted from a memorandum Oswald had written about his own background: "I infiltrated the Cuban Student Directorate and then harassed them with information I gained including having the N.O. city attorney general call them in an put a restraining order pending a hearing on some so-called bonds for invasion they were selling in the New Orleans area." (Sic)

Bringuier said this meant that Oswald had somehow got in touch with Garrison who would be the "N.O. city attorney general," and gotten Garrison to put an end to the bond drive. New Orleans authorities, he said did stop the sale of the invasion bonds. "There is more solid information to link Oswald with

Garrison right here, "said Bringuier, snapping his thumb against the book, "than there is to link him with anyone else."

There is an FBI memo (of which I also have a copy) dated June 18, 1967 which stated:

> *Carlos Quiroga and Carlos Bringuier are two anti-Castro Cuban refugees, who knew Oswald in summer of 1963. We have received information in the past that Garrison is attempting to blame anti-Castro Cubans for the assassination. Data in attached wherein Garrison alleges that a double for Lee Harvey Oswald is an FBI double agent is completely false and giver further indication that Garrison is mentally unbalanced.*

On June 19, 1967, NBC telecasted Walter Sheridan program entitled "The JFK Conspiracy-The Case of Jim Garrison". Garrison, like Fidel Castro, didn't like critics and had tried to stop NBC from telecasting Sheridan's investigation but NBC stood firm. Garrison described Sheridan as a "former investigator of the federal government" ignoring that Sheridan was a close associate of Robert Kennedy.

Around this time I received a phone call from Aaron Kohn, Managing Director of the New Orleans Metropolitan Crime Commission who wanted to interview me, I went to the MCC office and Mr. Cohn produced a tape recorder to keep a record of the interview. When the interview ended, after a couple of hours, Mr. Cohn told me: *"I am very glad that a brain like yours is involved in this event."*

On June 20, 1967, shortly after my interview with Aaron Cohn, The Times Picayune published the following

Probe of DA's Conduct Urged:

> *The Metropolitan Crime Commission urged Monday night that Dist. Atty. Jim Garrison's procedures in his presidential assassination probe be investigated.*
>
> *Following an emergency session held in connection with the National Broadcasting Company's hour-long program dealing with the controversial investigation, the MCC said it was*

"appalled by the accumulation of accusations against Dist. Atty. Garrison and members of his staff."

The privately financed anti-crime group added: "We belief official action is required to thoroughly probe the conduct of affairs in the district attorney's office. Within several days, we will inform the public of the action we believe must be taken."

The statement was issued by E. C. Upton, Jr., MCC president, who said the commission thinks "these accusations can destroy faith in justice."

The Metropolitan Crime Commission was, like me, expecting the Secretary of Justice, Ramsey Clark, to stop Garrison's prostitution of Justice but we were ignorant of the fact that Attorney General Ramsey Clark was very much inclined to the leftist ideas that were behind Jim Garrison.

On June 20, 1967, sport personality Hap Glaudi during his newscast on Channel 4 (WWLTV) delivered a little speech defending Jim Garrison, something out of the sport features of the newscast. Next day I wrote the following letter to Mr. Glaudi:

New Orleans, June 21st, 1967
Mr. Hap Glaudi
Sports Director
WWL-TV
New Orleans, La.

Dear Mr. Glaudi:

Last night I was really surprised with your "impromptu" defense of Mr. Jim Garrison who you usually calls as the Jolly Green Giant.

My surprise was originated in my opinion about your person. I have been always sympathetic about you, more when I hear you telling "God bless you."

I attended a Jesuit school in Havana, Cuba, for eleven years and for my deep religious convictions I feel sympathy for anyone who close his programs telling "God bless you."

I don't know Mr. Clay Shaw but I happen to know a little bit about this whole fraud. When Mr. Garrison try to put the blame on us Cuban refugees I know that he is lying and what is worst: He knows it also.

We have suffered more than any other country in this hemisphere and now we have to see, here in this City, which according to its Mayor "is moving ahead", how a District Attorney invites irresponsible propagandists as Mark Lane and Harold Weisberg to attend sessions of the Orleans Parish Grand Jury. You said something that is really true: "Mr. Garrison is the New Orleans District Attorney, your District Attorney and the District Attorney of all New Orleaneans." It is a shame but it is true!

History will prove that your District Attorney has done one of the best services that those who don't believe in any God could have wished to ever receive.

History will prove that your District Attorney has been involved in what I believe are plain and clear un-American activities. History will also prove that we, Cuban refugees, didn't have nothing to do with the infamous assassination of John F. Kennedy.

But how many reputations had been destroyed by your District Attorney? I personally know of one case of one person who did not appear in the NBC documentary who has been threatened twice by the office of your District Attorney and who, at one moment, received a death threat from one of the witnesses of Mr. Jim Garrison.

It is your right to think as you like. But it is also my duty as Catholic and as antiCommunist to let you know that I also saw in Cuba newsmen assuming the defense of Fidel Castro, just to later become disillusioned when they saw that they have been defending the wrong side. For some of my fellow countrymen it was already too late, many of them have been sentenced to prison for crimes that they had not committed or were executed. For some of those newsmen their awakening came also too late and they were suffering starvation in a Castro's prison. I hope that God will open your eyes and the eyes of your Countrymen before it is too late here.

You reacted against the NBC documentary but I did not see you react against the Channel 4 documentary entitled: "The

Garrison investigation. The first 90 days", in which Mr. Garrison accused the Cuban refugees of being the real murderers of Mr. Kennedy. That day I had to suffer seeing my wife crying upset for the smear against us. After that program I did not see you asking that the trials and the charges should not be aired in Television but in the Courts of Justice. I believe that Justice should be equal for both sides. Not just for the side of Mr. Garrison. We also have a right to be respected and if your District Attorney have any charge to file against any Cuban let him go to the Courts and charge that particular Cuban and not go to a Television program and make those accusations in such irresponsible way.

There has been already too much talk about "The Shame of Dallas". I believe it is already time that someday we start talking about "The Shame of New Orleans."

I love this City. Personally I have received many proves of friendship from Citizens of this City, and I am linked to this City by strong emotional feelings: my grandmother was born in New Orleans in the last century. But as I see what is happening in New Orleans I have to disagree with Mayor Schiro. I believe that Mr. Garrison and some of his supporters are moving New Orleans backward, and when I see so many people duped by these propagandistic I have decided to move out of this City and out of this State as soon as Garrison's case is finished.

I am sure that one day you will understand my feelings and look at this letter with sympathy because, I repeat, I don't have nothing against you personally.

And I am sure that someday you will recognize the tremendous damage that Mr. Garrison has done not only to us, Cuban refugees, but to your City and your Country. Until that day come: "God bless you."

Very truly yours,
Dr. Carlos J. Bringuier
New Orleans Delegate
Cuban Student Directorate

Next day, Hap Glaudi announced during his sport cast the receiving of my letter.

By the end of June I received a telephone call from Sam DePino, who in my opinion was "fishing" for Garrison. DePino told me that he had received information that Garrison would try to connect an ex-Nazi, whose name I do not recall, with the assassination of President Kennedy.

According to my recollection that ex-Nazi was big in propaganda, and was portrayed to me by DePino as living in Mexico City and as the head of the Central Intelligence Agency (CIA) in Mexico.

If my memory doesn't fail me it was either at the end of May or the beginning of June that things were turning for the worst for me. One day Mr. Wilson, a former FBI agent and then investigator for Clay Shaw, came to Casa Cuba and we went for a walk on Canal Street. Mr. Wilson advised me that they had information that I could be charged in relation to the assassination of President Kennedy and arrested, at any time, by orders of the District Attorney. He was inquiring from me what my plans were if I was arrested. I told Mr. Wilson that I had worked very hard to have the little money that I had and I would not allow Garrison to ruin me with legal expenses. I made Mr. Wilson aware that if the United States government allows Garrison to carry on his prostitution of Justice by arresting me, then I would declare myself in hunger strike and die in prison. I believe that Mr. Wilson was impressed by my attitude.

Then one evening, I saw some cameramen bringing cameras to the sidewalk in front of Casa Cuba. I found out that they were from United Press International (UPI) and they told me that they have been informed by their New York office to come to my store because Garrison had ordered my arrest. I told them: *"Well, you will be seen the first anti-Castro Cuban arrested in the United States by a Communist District Attorney."* After one hour they left and told me Garrison has rescinded the order for my arrest.

For months, night after night, my wife had suffered the attacks from Garrison to the Cuban exiles, on TV. It was discomforting to me see her crying every night in our bedroom. Now she was also pregnant with our 5th child. I decided that she needed a rest and I did not want to let my children watch on TV that I have been arrested in relation to the assassination of President Kennedy. I opted for getting airplane tickets for them and send my wife and the children in a vacation to Buenos Aires, Argentina.

I took them in my car, a 1960 Pontiac Bonneville to Miami. On June 11, 1967 they arrived to Buenos Aires. It was the last time that I saw my brother Julio alive. On June 12, I was back in New Orleans ready to continue defending the name of the Cubans and confronting a demented District Attorney. While my family was in Argentina, Julito, in Miami was watching the baseball All Star game when suddenly he lost consciousness. Julito was brought to the hospital where he apparently recovered after been diagnosed with nervous tension. We were able to talk long distance over the phone and I noticed that his words were slurred, not as normal as before. He was brought again to the hospital for a follow-up checkup and while there he lost consciousness again. This time the diagnostic was correct but bad. He had suffered a brain aneurism. Julito underwent three brain surgeries but never recovered dying months later weighing around 60 pounds. During that period of time I flew five times from New Orleans to Miami.

On July 11, 1967 the Diario Las Americas, of Miami, Florida published a large article about me. It was an interview with Benjamín de la Vega. In the interview I expressed that Garrison investigation was against the Cubans in exile. I ended the interview forecasting that all of those in the wagon of Garrison's investigation would end up asking for political asylum in Castro's Cuba. Undoubtedly I was young and naïve. I didn't realize how deep was the Communist infiltration in the United States of America.

On that same day of July 11, 1967 I wrote the following letter:

Editor
WDSU-TV
New Orleans, La.

Sirs:
I am one of the thousands of human beings who had the opportunity to escape from my Country.
I came to the United States looking for Freedom and Justice and I chose these City to live in with my family because of the emotional idea that my grandmother was born here in the last century.
For me it was impossible to believe that the same thing that happened in my Country, Cuba, could ever happen in this

wonderful Country. We had in Cuba a big liar who undermined the credibility of our institutions and accused and imprisoned anyone who tried to tell the truth in regard to what was going on.

Today I am astonished to see how a District Attorney can lie and lie without been legally and morally punished for his un-American activities that are undermining the credibility of your institutions, the image of your nation, and even worst, who is filing charges against anyone who try to tell the truth in regard to what is going on in this City.

I have seen many individuals and officials talking many times about "patriotism" and "Americanism", but if they are really "patriots" and truly "Americans", now they have the opportunity to defend the integrity, image and honor of the United States of America, and this apply from Governor McKeithen and Mayor Schiro, down to the single individuals in the street, the rich and the poor, the black and the white.

John Edgar Hoover testifying under oath to the Warren Commission stated: **. . . the man (Oswald) was not doubt a dedicated Communist. He prefers to call himself a Marxist, but there you get into the field of semantics. He was a Communist, he sympathized thoroughly with the Communist cause.**[163]

At least you in WDSU could feel proud that you are not betraying your boys in Viet Nam who are dying so many miles away to protect the Justice that Mr. Garrison is trying to destroy in this very City of New Orleans.

I would like to finish by quoting a statement of the Cuban Hero, José Martí, which maybe would be good for some officials and all of us to think about:

"To watch commit a crime in silence is to become an accomplice."

Respectfully yours,
Dr. Carlos Bringuier
New Orleans Delegate
Cuban Student Directorate P.O. Box 2506, N.O. La.

---

[163] Warren Commission Hearings, Vol. V, page 104.

While Pochi was with the kids in Buenos Aires I contacted her and as apparently the District Attorney had desisted in his idea of arresting me I told her to return which she did and they arrived back to Miami on August 3, 1967.

Unfortunately the baby girl that we were bringing to this world had suffered too much during the pregnancy and when my wife was approximately seven months pregnant we had to take her to the hospital where after being examined by the physician he said to us that the little girl had die. That little girl who never had a chance because of the demagoguery of the Communists converging in New Orleans to help the DA was another victim of the shameful tactics of Jim Garrison and his henchmen.

On December 7, 1967, Mark Lane spoke at Tulane University in regard to the assassination of President Kennedy. As in his usual lectures on this subject, Lane used halftruths, innuendos and distortions of the truth in order to misguide his audience. At that time I didn't know what later I read in the book "The Sword and the Shield" by Christopher Andrew with Vasili Mitrokhin who had been exfiltrated from Russia in 1992 after 30 years of work at the KGB archives where it is mentioned in page 228 that the New York residency of the KGB had sent Lane $1,500.00 to help finance his research. Also, in the same page, it is written that through the same intermediary the KGB provided another $500.00 to Mark Lane for a trip to Europe in 1964 and one of the KGB agents in contact with Lane was Genrikh Borovik who later maintained regular contact with Lane. The "liberal" press had fallen in love with Lane and now this individual was disseminating his falsehoods at Tulane University.

When Mark Lane finished his dissertation he allowed a period of time for questions and I raised my hand like many others. Lane was calling all the others and ignoring me. I rose to my feet and with my white handkerchief in my right hand I was waving it calling his attention. I was lucky, I not only called his attention but the attention of the public and what it was even more important the attention of Iris Kelso, a reporter for WDSU-TV Channel 6. I would like to mention here that among the public that had been applauding Lane remarks I recognized the face of Perry Raymond Russo, star witness of Jim Garrison, and I was told that another applauding was Mr. Albarado, who was the Chairman of the New Orleans Grand Jury that indicted Clay Shaw.

Mark Lane realized that he had to allow me to speak and he asked what I wanted to say, referring to me as Dr. Bringuier. My answer was to tell the audience how surprised I was that an institution, like Tulane University, where our youngsters were attending to learn, they would allow a person like Mark Lane to spread so many lies and half-truths, that I was requesting from Tulane University equal time to refute what Mark Lane had said and if he wanted to debate me I would be delighted to do so at that time. Then, Mark Lane made a mistake by misjudgment, he invited me to the podium to address those present. I was not intimidated, it is true that it was his crowd, but I had the truth on my side. I went to the podium and started speaking. Lane was at one side behind some curtains. At one time I looked at him and I could see his face become red and redder and it reminded me of Lee Harvey Oswald during the WDSU radio debate. Tulane University granted me equal time and I was scheduled to speak in the Cram Room, University center, on Thursday, January 4, 1968 at 8:00 p.m. The television stations in New Orleans showed the confrontation.

I would like to mention that for the New Orleans press Jim Garrison was a hero, but there were two women reporters that read him perfect: 1) Iris Kelso, from WDSU-TV and 2) Rosemary James, from WWL-TV.

Next day, on December 8, 1967 the New Orleans States-Item reported the incident under the headline:

Exile Rips Lane's Warren Assault

On January 4, 1968, I went to Tulane University and talked for about a couple of hours.

Mark Lane never showed up. In attendance there were more than 200 persons. Next day The Times Picayune covered my lecture with the headline: *"Cuban Criticizes Writer on Kennedy Assassination"*:

Exile speaks on Lane's book at Tulane

A Cuban exile leader strongly suggested Thursday night that author Mark Lane cited only witnesses who reinforced his theory on the Kennedy assassination when writing his book and neglected to cite others who might have refuted his findings.

Dr. Carlos Bringuier, head of the New Orleans Delegation of the Cuban Student Directorate, spoke at University center at Tulane University. Dr. Bringuier had demanded equal time to refute statements made by Lane who spoke at McAllister Auditorium on the Tulane campus on Dec. 7.

The 33-year-old Havana native, who fled Cuba in 1960, charged that the Warren Commission report "shows that 99 per cent of what Lane said is inaccurate and a distortion of the facts"

Lane the author of "Rush to Judgment," a book critical of the Warren Report, maintained in his speech Dec. 7 and in his book that President Kennedy was killed in a conspiracy and that federal agencies are ignoring or concealing the truth.

Relying heavily on extracts from the Warren Commission report during his almost two hours talk, Dr. Bringuier said that he believed the former president was shot and killed by Lee Harvey Oswald from the Texas School Book Depository Building in Dallas, Tex.

"If, as Lane claims, a shot from the front knocked flesh and brain tissue forward in the automobile, this is a new law of physics," the Cuban said.

He said that Texas Gov. John B. Connally told the Commission that the shots came from the back, over his right shoulder.

Dr. Bringuier charged that the driver of the death car was not quoted in Lane's book or mentioned in the index.

The driver, Dr. Bringuier said, told the Warren Commission that the shots came from behind him, to the right rear of him. The driver also stated, the Cuban leader said, that he did not believe the shots came from the front.

Dr. Bringuier also read testimony of a 16-year-old Negro youth who was standing at Houston and Elm in Dallas at the time of the assassination.

The Negro, Dr. Bringuier said, told the Commission that he had seen what appeared to be some sort of pipe in an upper story window of the book depository.

The Cuban leader warned that "forces are trying to bring about a revolution in this country. They are saying that anti-Castro Cubans were involved in the assassination."

"They know as long as the people of the United States believe in the institutions of the nation, such as the FBI, they cannot take over. When you begin to doubt your institutions-that is when they will try to take over."

He termed charges that right-wing extremists killed President Kennedy as "ridiculous." He reaffirmed that Oswald did the deed and that he was a Trotskyite extremist and former Chairman of the Fair Play for Cuba Committee in New Orleans.

Dr. Bringuier received a long ovation following his talk.

The talk was also reported in Lafayette, Louisiana by a great American friend, Bob Angers, who in his column "Anecdotes and antidotes" in the Advertiser reflected about my words.

On January 18, 1968, one of the most honest, dedicated and intelligent leader of the Cuban exiles, Luis V. Manrara, President of "The Truth about Cuba Committee, Inc." wrote me the following letter:

Dr. Carlos Bringuier
Carlos Enterprises
111 Decatur Street New Orleans, La. 70130

Distinguished Compatriot:
I don't have to tell you that I am very well aware of your valiant attitude in New Orleans in defense of our Fatherland and our freedom.

Our mutual American great friend, the magnificent newsman Bob Angers, had just sent me his article published on the 14 of this month in THE ADVERTISER and I want to congratulate you for you courageous denounce of this strange person Jim Garrison.

As a token of my appreciation and admiration that I feel toward you, in another package I have the pleasure to send you an autographed copy of my last book "Betrayal Opened the Door to Russian Missiles in Red Cuba", which I am sure will be of your interest.

Please know that you have in me a friend and that you can count on me and my Committee in everything within our reach in defense of God and freedom.

Very cordially,
Luis V. Manrara
President

On February 22, 1968 I spoke in Lafayette, Louisiana to the Rotary Club invited by Bob Angers. My speech was reported in The Advertiser by Joan Treadway. She ended the article in this way:

Logic Debated

"Garrison trying to build his point to me by saying 'anything is possible' but with this logic you could say Oswald is from Mars."

Others hit in Bringuier's speech were: Jack S. Martin, a star witness of Garrison, whom he said, had threatened a Cuban friend of his in New Orleans; Mark Lane, author of the anti-Warren Commission, "Rush to Judgment" whose pieces, he said were published in communist newspapers; Harold Weisberg, author of three books, one of whom Bringuier contested in a libel suit and Ben Smith, head of Eugene McCarthy's campaign, who, he said is registered as a proCastroite.

Bringuier stated: "When I say these things, I may lose many things, but I would prefer to die fighting than to become a coward in the U.S. If I have to fight Communism in this country too, I will. I love this land."

There have been different individuals some of them, in my opinion, agents of Fidel Castro who had tried to confuse the people of the United States alleging Oswald's presence in Miami, Fla. We know that Oswald by sure had been in Louisiana, California and Texas in the U.S. We know that he had been in Russia, Mexico and there are witnesses that situate him in Cuba.

But there are no credible evidence that he ever was in Miami or with the CIA. There is a Cuban, Antonio Veciana, who had brought speculation in this regard, only favoring conspiracy theories advocated by Fidel Castro and leftists Americans. Castro's intelligence agents I am sure played a role in disseminating these falsehoods. There is a memo from the Miami Office of the FBI to Director and SACS Dallas, New Orleans and Washington. This memo explains how people get confused and facts are changed. As I had said before several times we can find people well intentioned without the desire to fabricate falsehoods but for some reason or the other they get confused or they want to show that they are in the "inside" of what is going on and say things that are inaccurate. Let's read:

> *SECRET*
>
> *RE WASHINGTON FIELD TELETYPE TO DIRECTOR AND SACS, DALLAS, MIAMI AND NEW ORLEANS, NOVEMBER 26, 1963. ALLEGING SUBJECT APPEARED IN MIAMI TWO OR THREE MONTHS AGO AND ATTEMPTED TO INFILTRATE STUDENTS REVOLUTIONARY DIRECTORATE (DRE).*
>
> *JOSE ANTONIO LANUSA, AGE 24, INTELLIGENCE OFFICER FOR DRE AT MIAMI, ADVISED ON NOVEMBER 27, 1963, THAT HE IS RECEIVING ALL HIS INFORMATION RE SUBJECT'S ATTEMPTED INFILTRATION OF DRE FROM CARLOS BRINGUIER, DRE DELEGATE AT NEW ORLEANS, AND THAT THIS ATTEMPTED INFILTRATION OCCURRED IN NEW ORLEANS AND NOT MIAMI. LANUSA SAID HE HANDLE PROPAGANDA FOR DRE.*
>
> *LANUSA SAID HE TELEPHONED DR. GUILLERMO BELT IN WASHINGTON, D.C. ON NOVEMBER 25, 1963 TO DISCUSS THE PRESIDENT'S ASSASSINATION. HE EXPLAINED TO BELT THE ATTEMPTED INFILTRATION OF OSWALD INTO DRE OCCURRED, NOT AT MIAMI AS INDICATED BY BELT, BUT AT NEW ORLEANS, BUT THAT BELT MUST HAVE MISUNDERSTOOD.*

LANUSA REITERATED THAT TO KNOWLEDGE OF DRE, OSWALD HAS NEVER BEEN IN MIAMI.

The above memo clearly shows how sometimes a rumor could start. Lanuza knew that the attempted infiltration had happened in New Orleans, and he discuss this event with Dr. Guillermo Belt who is in Washington D.C. Dr. Belt was a very decent and honest Cuban exdiplomat and he misunderstood Lanuza and thinks that the attempt of infiltration of Oswald had happened in Miami, and Dr. Belt talk with other persons about the incident. The word spread around that Oswald had tried to infiltrate the DRE in Miami. Meanwhile the scavengers and conflict managers working for Fidel Castro exploits this human and honest mistake and create the legend of Oswald in Miami.

In the afternoon of October 9, 1968 while I was in Casa Cuba I received the visit of a lady who identified herself as Dione Turner who gave me her address as Post office Box 1282, Louisiana State University in New Orleans, Louisiana 70122. Ms. Turner informed me that approximately two weeks ago she had received a letter from Philip Geraci III, According to her Geraci was now a member of the United States military stationed in Viet Nam. Geraci requested in his letter that Ms. Turner transmit a message to me. In his message Geraci wanted me to know that he had been contacted by Harold Weisberg, author of the book "Whitewash" who had been assisting Garrison in his investigation. Geraci was not telling Ms. Turner of the method used by Weisberg to contact him. Geraci claimed that Weisberg had told him that he, Geraci, would be subpoenaed by the New Orleans District Attorney's office to appear in front of the Grand Jury in order to say that he had been previously hired by Carlos Bringuier, and that he, Bringuier, and some other Cubans had gone to a training camp in the New Orleans area. Geraci asserted that Weisberg had added that if Geraci did not comply with this request he would be indicted for perjury by the Orleans Parish Grad Jury.

Turner further informed that Geraci's mother had been cooperating with Garrison and had made some kind of deal with him. She did not indicated what kind of deal had been made. Turner commented that an agency, which she did not identified, was building a case against Weisberg because he was spreading KGB propaganda in the United States.

Turner stated that Geraci was due to arrive in New Orleans shortly as one of the members of his family is very ill. She added that she does not know what Geraci plans to do regarding the situation. I told Ms. Turner to write to Geraci and tell him to go ahead and testify to the Grand Jury and tell them the truth.

I did not know at the time that the Juvenile Division of Jefferson Parish, Louisiana had a record on Geraci. On April, 20, 1965 Geraci had ran away from his house and under psychiatric treatment at Tulane University Medical School in New Orleans. On May 29, 1965 Geraci was arrested at Jackson, Mississippi and released to his parents in Metairie, Louisiana in order to be committed privately to an insane asylum. On July 30, 1965, Philip Geraci III's parents had him privately committed for treatment to the State Hospital at Mandeville, Louisiana. He was diagnosed with schizophrenia reaction with obsessive compulsive features and with the recommendation for further evaluation and treatment. I found this information on the papers obtained by me under the Freedom of Information Act from the FBI. I also found out that later that year of 1968, Philip Geraci III died of accidental electrocution.[164] In my opinion, this poor kid, Philip Geraci III was another victim of Jim Garrison, at his young age Geraci should not had been submitted to Garrison terror and persecution.

What I told Ms. Turner that Geraci should do was to appear in the Grand Jury and tell the truth and it was the only recommendation that I could have made. I always said the same to everybody involved: tell the truth. At that time, and now, I don't know who Ms. Turner was. I did not know if a trap was been putting in place for me. I knew that Garrison was at a dead end with me but if I was not very careful and do or say something wrong he always could have charged me with obstruction of justice.

One thing that should have brought Garrison closer to insanity was one of those coincidences that occurs when you are *in God's hands*. When I started working as co-manager of Casa Roca, around October 1962, I went to the Post office across the street and rented a Post Office box. When they gave me the key to it I was gladly surprised when I found out that I had been assigned the #2506, the same # of the Cuban

---

[164] "Case Closed", by Gerald Posner, page 496.

Brigade who fought at Bay of Pigs. One day, at the start of the Garrison investigation I went to pick up my mail when one of the employees, who was very friendly with me, told me: *"Carlos, investigators from the District Attorney came yesterday asking how come you got that number and they are under the impression that we gave that number to you because the CIA has ordered us to do so"*. He was almost laughing saying how stupid the Garrison's investigators were.

Years later, after the Garrison investigation had ended, I had to move out of the building where I had my own store, Casa Cuba, because I lost my lease, and I had to move my business to 2048 Magazine Street and I closed the P.O. Box at the Custom House Postal Office on Decatur Street. Eventually that office was terminated and I decided to rent another box at another Post Office located across Lafayette Square. To my surprise when I picked up my key it was for number 2506. If that is not to be *in God's hands* I don't know any other explanation, but I am sure that Jim Garrison was going berserk about that.

In 1970 Jim Garrison published his book "A Heritage of Stone" explaining in detail his new version about the assassination. In page 140 he wrote:

> *"The contrive nature of Oswald's activity is readily apparent in his encounter with Carlos Bringuier, a dedicated anti-Castro Cuban exile. At the confrontation, hot words developed. Oswald then said, 'Hit me, Carlos,' Bringuier obliged and struck him. In municipal court, Oswald rather than Bringuier, pleaded guilty and paid a fine, another scene for the drama."*

Those are the words of the New Orleans District Attorney Jim Garrison. At least he did not insulted me, ha called me a "dedicated anti-Castro Cuban exile", but he insulted History when he wrote that I obliged and hit Oswald, attesting that something that never happened had happened. I never hit Oswald, that was part of the public and judicial record, but this was the same District Attorney who had said that Oswald did not shoot anyone on November 22, 1963. This is the same District Attorney who gave more than ten versions about the assassination and some gullible people believed him and the leftist press love him, even Fidel Castro became one of his admirers. Oliver Stone would try to make him and idol and a victim. But in reality Jim Garrison was only a drunk, a corrupt politician used by the Communists to try to destabilize the government of the United States of America.

Jim Garrison died on Wednesday October 21, 1992. For some time I had known that he was sick and when he died I was convinced that he had died of aids but apparently I was wrong. A physician friend of mine told me after Garrison's death that he had the opportunity to review Garrison's medical record and he was convinced that Garrison had died of cirrhosis of the liver.

Finally his abuse of alcohol had caught up with him. Garrison could not harm anymore innocent people. Now he was *in God's hands* and I hope that he is paying eternally for all the crimes that he committed, for all the lives that he ruined, and for all the lies that he spread.

CHAPTER XII

---◆◉◆---

NEW ORLEANS (1968-1995)

Life continued during and after the Garrison's investigation. Bills had to be paid and children had to be raised and our struggle to make the people aware of the crime been committed against Cuba never stopped.

On March 14, 1968 the New Orleans States-Item carried the following note on page 2:

Cuba Regime Complicity in Hijack Seen

Complicity of the Cuban government in the hijacking of a National Air Lines plane, has been charged by Dr. Carlos Bringuier, a delegate of the Cuban Student Directorate.

He said the lives of 59 plane passengers were endangered in the hijacking this week.

This new act of piracy, he said, shows once again, the criminal activities of Castro's agents, not only in Cuba, but right here in the United States.

The officer who received the hijackers, Bringuier said, is well known to this delegation. "He is the chief of the Department of Internal security in Cuba, and is also the director of some of Castro's infiltration groups in the United States. At one time he was chief of Castro's bodyguards."

"The fact that the Cuban government knew beforehand of their arrival shows the complicity of the Castro government in this

criminal act that has only parallel with the tactics of the Gestapo in Nazi Germany, said Bringuier."

Meanwhile I was trying to bring Senator Robert F. Kennedy to New Orleans and I had sent an invitation for him to address us on April 5, 1968. On March 18, 1968, Robert Kennedy wrote the following letter to me:

Dr. Carlos Bringuier
Delegate
Cuban Student Directorate
New Orleans Delegation
Post Office Box 2506
New Orleans, Louisiana 70116

Dear Dr. Bringuier:
Thank you for your kind invitation to address the Cuban community in New Orleans on April 5ᵗʰ.
Although I would very much like to be with you for this event, my schedule is such that I would be unable to attend. I appreciate your thoughtfulness in inviting me, and perhaps I will be able to join you another time.

With best wishes,
Sincerely
Robert F. Kennedy.

Unfortunately Bobby Kennedy was unable to join us another time because on the night of June 5, 1968 he was assassinated by Sirhan Bishara Sirhan another Castro sympathizer.

By the end of April 1968 there was a big reunion in New Orleans, It was the First Regional Reunion of the O.A.S (Organization of American States) and the Ambassadors were confronted with the inconvenient problem that to enter into City Hall they have to walk in between two Cuban ladies with a big Cuban flag and a group of Cuban exiles. Around 4:00 p.m. they converged in front of the International Trade Mart and the Rivergate Complex they again had to enter in between two files of around one hundred Cuban exiles, who with flags and handmade signs were asking them to obey the treaties signed ordering the eradication of Communism from this hemisphere. To the surprise of many liberal newsmen, some of the Ambassadors applauded the attitude of the Cuban exiles. The Cubans formed a large group around the Cuban flag and sang the Cuban National Hymn. The Ambassadors applauded again our attitude and Mayor Victor Schiro joined them in their applauses. Later on Mayor Schiro invited some of us to attend a reception of May 1 with him and the Ambassadors. That night I met several of them including Vasco Leitao Da Cuna and Eduardo Ritter Aislán. That same night, for the first time I saw Clay L. Shaw in person, he was one of the persons invited by Mayor Schiro.

On May 26, 1968 our good friend and great American patriot, Bob Angers managed to propose a Republican Party Resolution calling for Cuba's liberation. The elections of 1968 were approaching and in one side was Richard Nixon and in the other was Eugene McCarthy, whose campaign manager in Louisiana was a registered agent of Fidel Castro, therefore our choice was simple: we had to back the campaign of Richard Nixon. The text of the Resolution, which I believe clearly explain what have happened to the United States was as follows:

A REPUBLICAN RESOLUTION

Calling for Cuba's Liberation
To be proposed to Third Louisiana
Congressional District Convention
Of the Republican Party, Lafayette,
Louisiana, May 26, 1968 by
Bob Angers, Jr. (Box 52247, OCS,
Lafayette, La. 70501
Phone: (318) 233-1663

WHEREAS, it is the sense of this convention that the time has arrived for the United States of America to assume the initiative against the worldwide Communist Conspiracy;
WHEREAS, aggressive subversion, terrorism, sabotage and guerrilla warfare have been mounted against the countries of the Western Hemisphere by the Castro Communist Regime in Cuba, with military and other assistance from extra-continental powers;

316

namely, the Soviet Union, Red China and certain Communist elements from Vietnam and Eastern Europe;

WHEREAS, the anatomy of this assault has been documented and exposed singly and/or collectively by public, quasi-public and private agencies, organizations and committees such as the United States Senate Internal Security Subcommittee; Permanent Subcommittee On Investigations Of The Committee on Government Operations; United States Senate; The Committee On Un-American Activities, House of Representatives; The Federal Bureau Of Investigations; The Organization of American States (OAS); The Tri-Continental (Communist) Conference established in Havana, Cuba in January, 1966, and its offspring, The Latin American Solidarity Organization (LASO); The Joint Legislative Committee On Un-American Activities, State of Louisiana; The Senate of the State of Florida; The Truth About Cuba Committee, Inc., Miami, Florida; the U. S. Citizens Committee For A Free Cuba, Inc. of Miami, and Washington; The American Security Council, Chicago; Cuban Exile organizations and news media in the United States and Latin America; and others;

WHEREAS, the "Communist Threat To The United States Through The Caribbean" reflects sworn testimony by knowledgeable United States and Latin American leaders before the U. S. Internal Security Subcommittee that bares the International Communist Conspiracy to subvert the Western Hemisphere, dating back to 1959;

Whereas, the fact that Cuba still bristles with Russian missiles established by photographs and eyewitness accounts is set down in the book, "Betrayal Opened The Door To Russian Missiles In Red Cuba," written by the reliable Luis V. Manrara, President of the Truth About Cuba Committee, Inc. in January, 1968.

Whereas, Paul D. Bethel, one of the leading U. S. authorities on Latin American affairs, a former State Department official, and editor of a special bulletin for the U. S.

Citizens Committee For a Free Cuba, Inc., has warned that Soviet Russia and Red China and the Viet Cong cooperate in the operation of communist training bases in Cuba;

Whereas, the interlock of Communist-action and Communist-front organizations operating in Louisiana and the rest of the United States with Red Cuba has been shown by the U. S. House Committee on Un-American Activities, the F. B. I. and other agencies;

Whereas, Louisianans H. Rap Brown, Chairman of the Student Non-Violent Coordinating Committee; and the late Lee Harvey Oswald, communist assassin of the president of the United States and a member of the Fair Play For Cuba Committee, have helped to reaffirm the link of radical U. S. groups with Fidel Castro's Cuba;

Whereas, the Louisiana Joint Legislative Committee, in its series of hearings entitled "Activities of the Southern Conference Educational Fund, Inc. in Louisiana" as well as its exposé on "The Spartacist League and Certain Other Communist Activities in South Louisiana," has helped to bring the proximity of the communist threat into sharper focus for Louisianans;

Whereas, these and other sources have shown the American people that radical hate groups like the Revolutionary Action Movement (R. A. M.) and the W. E. B. Dubois Clubs have received much of their impetus and guidance in street rioting, racial disorders, campus rebellions and anti-Vietnam activity from Cuba;

Whereas, the distinguished Negro journalist, Carl T. Rowan, writing in the May, 1968 edition of Reader's Digest, documents how Spain, Canada, France, Great Britain and other friends of the United States are helping to finance Castro-Communist existence;

Whereas, numerous United States and hemispheric organizations, by resolutions, treaties, doctrines, and other acts, underscored a Joint Resolution of the U. S. Congress, adopted April 20, 1898, that proclaimed that "Cuba is, and of right, ought to be, free and independent;

AND WHEREAS, this Convention recognizes that no American is free as long as Cuba is enslaved;

NOW, THEREFORE, BE IT RESOLVED, that the Convention of the Third Louisiana Congressional District of the Republican Party, meeting this 26th day of May, 1968,

318

in Lafayette, Louisiana, does reaffirm the "Cuba and Latin America" plank, incorporated in the Declaration of Principles and Platform of the Republican Party of Louisiana; as well as the various tenets of the Republican National Platform, presented to the Republican National Convention July 14th, 1964, in San Francisco, California, and more particularly, "The Geography of Freedom" section, as it relates to a free and independent Cuba.

BE IT FURTHER RESOLVED that this Convention more specifically recommends that a plank be written into the platform of the Republican Party at the National Convention in Miami, Florida, calling for the immediate liberation of Cuba from her communist yoke, the freeing of thousands of political prisoners held captive in the jails of Cuba, and the economic and social rehabilitation of the island Republic;

BE IT FURTHER RESOLVED, that the United States formulate its plan and submit it to the member nations of the Organization of American States, calling for the elimination of the Castro communist regime in Cuba, but that it act alone, if necessary; that it declare a state of national emergency; that it advise all nations to cease and desist in transporting supplies to Cuba; that it direct all acts of subversive intervention by the Castro regime be terminated immediately; that a Cuban Government in Exile be recognized and Cuban exiles prepared for the re-occupation of their native country; that the subjugated people of Cuba, including the Castro armed forces, be called upon to revolt against their dictator; and that an ultimatum be served on Fidel Castro to surrender the reins of government, and permit the constitutional processes of Cuba to be restored, and liberty and freedom made a reality in Cuba once again;

AND BE IT FURTHER RESOLVED, that the members of the Platform Committee of the Republican Party of the State of Louisiana are hereby petitioned and directed to take whatever steps are necessary to incorporate in the National Platform of the Republican Party at the August Convention in Miami, Florida, the sense of the delegates of this Convention calling for the immediate liberation of Cuba.

THUS DONE AND SIGNED this 26th day of May, 1968 at Lafayette, Louisiana.

Unfortunately the Republican Party was unable to deliver what Bob Angers, Jr., and the Louisiana Republican Party was asking for in order to not only save Cuba but also to save the United States. At this writing the Communist had footholds in Venezuela, Ecuador, Nicaragua, Chile, Argentina, Paraguay, Uruguay and Brazil. And we have Barack Hussein Obama as President of the United States with comrades Hilary Clinton, Nancy Pelosi, etc., etc. etc.

On June 5, 1968 The New Orleans States-Item published some of my comments after the death of Senator Robert F. Kennedy:

> Bringuier said as he watched the election returns come in from the California presidential primary he was "thinking the only one who could have helped us (the Cubans) was Se. Kennedy."
>
> He said he has sent a telegram to Mrs. Ethel Kennedy which reads:
>
> "In this tragic moment, in the name of all Cuban refugees, I want to express our condolences for this stupid attack and we pray God for the life and recovery of your husband." He said "this is a tragedy for this country. Violence from one side or from the other is not good." He said he is deeply sorry for all Americans.[165]

On August 23rd 1968 I continued my activities in defense of freedom without any contact with the CIA or any other agency of the United States government. On that day I wrote a letter to Clarence Henry, Chief of the International Longshoremen Association in New Orleans in order to show our support for the people of Poland and their leader Lech Walesa.

With the presidential elections approaching we were moved against the wall by the two candidates fighting for the nomination of the Democratic Party. Sen. Humphrey and Eugene McCarthy represented the peaceful left and the violent left. On the other party Richard M. Nixon was becoming the apparent front runner. We decided that we had to support Richard M. Nixon, therefore the "Cuban Americans for Nixon" committee in New Orleans was founded. Its members were: Salvador Acosta, Luis Balart, Luis Balart, Jr., Carlos Bringuier, Carlos

---

[165] The New Orleans States-Item, June 5, 1968, page 4.

de la Vega, Adelaida de la Torre, Alberto Fowler, Luis Guevara, Agustin Guitart, Celso Hernández, Felipe Medina, Ramiro Montalvo, Alton Ochsner, Jr., Ricardo Pardo, Luis Pérez, Carlos Quiroga, Raúl Rodríguez, Luis Rabel and Louise Smith.

On the night of October 11, 1968 we conducted a very important political reunion in favor of Richard Nixon, several hundred Cubans, close to a thousand, were present to hear the speakers. I was honored by been assigned as the Master of Ceremonies. Among those present that night were: Joe Sheldon, Chairman of the Republican Party in New Orleans and also Chairmen of Nixon's campaign in New Orleans; Dr. Alton Ochsner, Sr., Campaign Chairman for Dave Treen; Jeanne Boese, National Committee Women of the Republican Party in Louisiana; Joe Lipiparo, 8th Ward leader; Anne Ogden, Co-Chairman of Ward & Precinct Organization in New Orleans; Bill Keck, Chairman of Commissioners in New Orleans; Dr. Alton Ochsner, Jr.; Bob Angers, Jr., Nixon-Agnew Presidential Elector, 3rd Louisiana District; Dave Treen, Candidate to the House of Representatives and later on Governor of Louisiana; and Dr. Emilio Núñez Portuondo, former Cuban Ambassador to the United Nations.

Our participation in the "Cuban Americans for Nixon Committee" was an arduous one.

We worked hard to obtain Nixon's victory in Louisiana, besides the members of the Committee I would like to mention some Cubans who gave everything in them in this cause: Mrs. Isabel Barreto, Mrs. Isabel Balart, Mrs. Judith Cuscó, Mrs. Lidia Ledo, Mrs. Rosa Maspons, Mrs. Juana Pequeño, Raúl Díaz, José Luis Díaz, Raúl Valdés Fonte, Pablo Rodríguez, Israel Corral, Julián Tablada, Enrique Bascuas, Javier Baños, Mrs. Norma Torres, Del Valle, Antonio Gómez, José Cortizas, Mrs. Nancy Cortizas and Mrs. Dolores Maspons.

We worked hard, we collected money for the Republican Party and we opened a bank account # 05-1672-4 at Bank of New Orleans.

Later on there was a Republican Party gathering to hear the Speak to Nixon-Agnew Program in New Orleans.

On October 23, 1968, Richard M. Nixon wrote the following letter to me:

Dear Mr., Bringuier:

Governor Agnew and I want to thank you for taking time to attend the Speak to NixonAgnew Program in your city. We were sorry to hear that you did not participate in recording a message to us. We hope that in the future you will share your thoughts with us on the issues confronting this nation whenever you can.

We feel that every citizen should express his opinion on the issue so that government for the people and by the people can have real meaning.

We hope that your voice will be strong and clear on November 5, Election Day.

Sincerely,
Richard Nixon

My reason not to participate in sending a message was that I still was not an American citizen. I limited myself to help the one that I considered was the lesser bad of both candidates. The one that I considered that presented a better opportunity to obtain Cuba's freedom.

On November 5, 1968 I was at the Republican Party gathering in New Orleans celebrating with Joe Sheldon and Dave Treen the victory of Richard M. Nixon.

On Tuesday November 19, 1968 CBS presented a program that was a piece of Castro's propaganda and moved me, without any orders from the CIA or any other government agency, to write the following letter:

November 23, 1968
Network Director CBS-Television Network 51 West 52nd. New
York, N. Y. 10016

Sir:

    Last Tuesday from 9:00 p.m. to 9:30 p.m. your network
presented a program entitled "Cuba: 10 years of Castro" which
has originated a great commotion among the Cuban colony in
this country.
    In that program, following a clear pattern of Castro's
inspired propaganda the seed was planted among the T.V
watchers of the invulnerability and inevitability of the Castro's
government in Cuba. Using what we could call distortion
of the truth, CBS gave the impression to the American People
that Castro is not executing any more those who don't accept his
dictatorship and that instead Castro gives them the opportunity to
be reeducated and return to freedom; it is stated in that "show"
that before Castro there were many Cubans starving and many
Cubans having more than what it was necessary for them, and
that now, under Castro, everybody have enough to eat; among the
numerous distortions of the truth your program spread one that is
absolutely unacceptable to all Cubans in exile, that is that before
Castro Cuba was a place of corruption, and that now corruption
don't exist in Cuba any more.
    Just a few weeks ago, the world press learned of another
series of executions in Cuba and even Castro himself appeared
in Cuba's television announcing that "many heads will roll". Let
me ask you, WHY CBS didn't showed that part in the program?
    Until January 1st 1959 Cuba was the Latin American
country with less mortality and anyone who visited our Nation
before Castro's revolution has to admit that Cuba was the most
prosperous Nation south of the border of your great Nation. Let
me ask you, WHY CBS didn't quoted these statistics or didn't
bring out the contradiction of a Country with the lowest percent
of mortality in Latin America and the smear of having been a
country in which many were starving?

I don't know to what corruption your speaker was referring last Tuesday when he repeated at least twice that before Castro Cuba was a place of corruption. Because what is most amazing is that corruption has not disappeared from Cuba, but by the contrary your own program showed how the minds of thousands of children are been corrupted by the most immoral system that humanity had ever known. WHY CBS didn't show how small girls are separated from their parents and are send to agricultural works from where they come back most of the time already corrupted and sometimes even pregnant? WHY CBS didn't showed last Tuesday that Cuba after Castro has become the biggest bordello in the whole world where all the "invited Communists", "fellow travelers" and "useful idiots" could enjoy all what the Cuban people, the one who really suffer, could not reach.

Finally I want to remind you that we the Cubans failed to the Communist tactics and propaganda. There were in my country many honest newsmen that spread Communist propaganda without realizing the danger of that job. Today, the lucky ones are in exile, others are starving to death in Castro's dungeons, and some others have given their lives for something that many have and don't appreciate: FREEDOM.

In the name of the Cubans in exile, in the name of those who are suffering in my Country, I am asking you for the pertinent equal time to set the record straight pertaining your last Tuesday special.

Very truly yours,
Dr. Carlos Bringuier
Delegate

As you can imagine there was no response from CBS. For years I have believe that CBS stand for "Castro Broadcasting System". We had sent another letter to WWL-TV, CBS affiliated in New Orleans, with the same result.

On February 24, 1969 another prominent Cuban in exile visited the City of New Orleans, this time was a former Cuban businessman and now Cuban leader against Castro, José Elías de la Torriente who came to New Orleans to explain his plan to overthrow Fidel Castro. We had a gathering at the Cuban Lyceum José Martí. Hundreds of Cubans attended and I had the opportunity to meet José Elías de la Torriente and chat with him about his plan.

Unfortunately the "Plan Torriente" did not materialize and five years later on April 12, 1974, Good Friday, at 9:00 p.m. José Elías de la Torriente was assassinated while sitting at his house, 709 Cremona Avenue, Coral Gables, Florida, watching T.V. with his wife when a sniper fired a shot that went through his head.

At the time of his dead Torriente was 70 years old, but he had enraged Fidel Castro when in October 1971 commandos of his organization attacked the town of Boca de Sama, Oriente province, causing several deaths among Castro's troops. Dictator Castro took to the airwaves and pronounced a vicious attack against Torriente.

On April 15, three days after the assassination, Radio Havana broadcasted some words about Torriente depicting him as *"the counter-revolutionary leader and self-appointed head of a group of enemies of our revolution who among other crimes took credit for the criminal attack against the fishing town of Boca de Sama, Oriente province."*

On November 1974, Felipe Rivero, one of the leaders of the anti-Castro movement denounced the assassination as Castro inspired fingering Carlos Rivero Collado, who from his Miami exile had fled to Cuba to join the Revolution, as the material author of the murder. In his statement he said:

> *Radio Havana broadcasted: Rivero Collado understood that reason was on the side of the Cuban revolution and he started to carry on important revolutionary work in the exterior in favor of the revolution. Because of his work and proves of his solidarity toward the revolutionary Government he was authorized to return to the country."*[166]

Fidel Castro felt invincible, he had carried on the assassination of President John F. Kennedy and got away with it. Now the time has come to start eliminating those leaders in exile that could jeopardize his reign in Cuba. He had done it before. He would kill and place the

---

[166] Replica Magazine #216, November 20, 1974.

blame in others like he had done in November 1958 when my cousin Ruskin Medrano had been assassinated by his terrorists of the 26th of July Movement in the hijack of the Cubana Airlines and they had put the blame on the Batista's forces until after the triumph of the Revolution they had admitted that they were the culprits. Now was the time to spread the rumors, easily endorsed by the liberal press and the naïve Cubans in exile that those assassinations in Miami were the result of in-fight among the Cuban leaders in exile. No wonder John Edgar Hoover called the Communists "Masters of Deceit".

On April 9. 2007 Carlos Rivero Collado, after having returned from Cuba to Miami, denounced as false the accusations of the, at the time already defunct, Felipe Rivero. The author of the Torriente's assassination had left a note identifying himself with the Code name; "Zero". Years later when the Communist guerrillas en Nicaragua, with the help of the Jimmy Carter's administration were waving war against President Anastasio Somoza (remember that Lee Harvey Oswald also hated Somoza) a new star caught the imagination of the liberal press, that new star of the Communists was using the name of "Comandante Zero".

Another Cuban leader in exile that was "problem" to Fidel Castro was the former Cuban Senator Rolando Masferrer. Masferrer was the descendant of Luis Masferrer Grave de Peralta a Colonel of the Cuban army during the Independence war. He had studied at the University of Havana where he graduated at the top of his class. Had become a Communist (like Eusebio Mujal), fought in the Spaniard Civil War on the side of the Communist and finally was expelled from the Cuban Communist Party in 1945. Together with my cousin Manolo Castro had been a founder of the Cuban revolutionary group MSR[167]. Manolo Castro had been assassinated by Fidel Castro in 1948 and after Batista coup in 1952 Masferrer became an ardent anti-Communist. When Batista left on December 31st 1958 Masferrer left Cuba and arrived to Miami to avoid execution from Castro. On April 24, 1959, Frank Kappel, Supervisor, Criminal Intelligence, Miami Police, received information that the Castro government was going to kidnap Rolando Masferrer and bring him to Cuba. During a joint investigation with the FBI it was discovered that Masferrer was going to be detained by two Agents of the Immigration Service who will produce "phony credentials" telling

---

[167] Movimiento Socialista Revolucionario - Socialist Revolutionary Movement.

Masferrer that he was wanted at a special Immigration hearing. Masferrer was going to be brought to an airport and would be put in an airplane bound for Cuba. Fortunately for Masferrer the Miami police put an end to the kidnap

I never met Rolando Masferrer but around December of 1966 I took a trip to Miami to visit my brother Julio and while there I paid also a visit to the parents of my friend Villito Sánchez Ocejo. When I arrived at their residence I was surprised to see that over the dining table there were several military uniforms that Mrs. María Antonieta Sánchez Ocejo was sewing. They explained to me that those were the uniforms that the troops of Rolando Masferrer was going to use in their forthcoming invasion of Haiti. Masferrer have made a connection with some Haitian revolutionaries to overthrow the dictatorship of Duvalier, when they would succeed Masferrer would have free use of Haiti to prepare an invasion to liberate Cuba. If all the plans were successful, they explained to me, Dr. Virgilio Sánchez Ocejo, Sr., would become President of Cuba.

On January 1967, Dr. Rolando Masferrer and 75 of his followers were arrested at Marathon, Florida while preparing to invade Cuba.

Masferrer continued his struggle to liberate Cuba and coincidentally he was a friend of José Elías de la Torriente. On October 31, 1975 Rolando Masferrer was leaving his house and when he started his car the explosion killed him. Once more Fidel Castro knew how to deal with his enemies. John F. Kennedy, José Elías de la Torriente y Rolando Masferrer would not endanger his dictatorship any longer. Cuban leader Dr. José Miró Cardona escaped death when his car also exploded in Miami. Dr. Enrique Huertas, President of the Cuban Physicians in exile also escaped another Castro's plot to assassinate him. That is why I feel so glad that I was able to save Eusebio Mujal's life in Buenos Aires when Castro ordered his assassination. On March 3, 1969 The Times Picayune published my statements in regard to Jim Garrison:

Delegation aim is impeachment
Garrison is denounced by Cuban Group

The New Orleans Delegation of the Cuban Student Directorate Sunday called for the impeachment of District Attorney Jim Garrison "for the prostitution of his office." It added

that Clay L. Shaw should receive public and official apologies from the City of New Orleans and the State of Louisiana.

In a statement issued in behalf of the CSD delegation, its president, Dr. Carlos Bringuier, said that only when these things are accomplished will justice be done.

He added: "Since the beginning of Jim Garrison's so called investigation we have denounced it as un-American activities directed at undermining the credibility of the American people in the foundation of this nation."

"Even at one time we asked for an investigation of Garrison, (author Mark Lane and others by the House Un-American Activities Committee)."

Dr. Bringuier added that since his group has had knowledge of Garrison's investigation at its inception, "we were absolutely sure that the only verdict that could have been rendered was 'not guilty,' simply because Clay L. Shaw was innocent and we have faith in the honest people of this nation."

He said that during the two years of the investigation, Cuban exiles have been smeared by Garrison, "his lackeys and his gurus."

"But our sufferings," he added, "could not be compared to those of an innocent man who was smeared and brought into an open circus . . ."

He said that Louisiana is "in a crisis that only Louisianans can solve."[168]

But the forces of evil kept working against the American people. On March 5, 1969, it was reported that a new President and Vice-President of the United States had taken the oath of office in Washington D. C. They took the oath of office as President-in-exile and VicePresident-in-exile. The President-in-exile was Negro activist and comedian Dick Gregory and the Vice-President-in-exile was none other than the leftist who had received money from the KGB, attorney Mark Lane. Let me quote here some of the statements expressed by Dick Gregory after he took the oath:

---

[168] The Times Picayune, March 3, 1969, Section one, page three.

"You do something about the crime syndicates and we'll quit snatching' pocketbooks," Gregory said in addressing the white folks who comprised about half of the crowd of 100. "And let me tell you why we hate you. You must understand this. It's the system we hate, not you, really, but we hold you responsible."

"You're victims of the same trick, the stinking', white, corrupt, racist, filthy system."

To the blacks: "We've got to reform the capitalistic system. If you have to destroy it to reform it, then destroy it. No one in his right mind could be on the side of criminals and law violators, but . . ." the words were lost in applause.

"You want to know why 15,000 black kids came to Chicago? To change the system. For 10 years white kids have been going to Ft. Lauderdale, Fla., every spring and getting drunk and tearing up the town but nobody cared because they were no trying to change the system.

"If you whites really freak out on violence, get out on that Indian reservation and cut my Indian brothers loose."[169]

Now we see 44 years later that the same message had been spread through misguided Pastors like Jeremiah Wright and others who try to influence the worshippers who attend church every Sunday. With their insidious work they keep asking for "Change" and "Hope" and the listener don't realize that the "change" that they want is to destroy the United States of America and create a new country where the white people would become second class citizens; and the "Hope" that they want to impose on us is the hope to survive in a racist revolution.

On April 23, 1969 the following was published in New Orleans:

The Cuban Exile

Discussion Topic

"The Cuban Exile" will be the topic of a discussion by refugees from the Caribbean island at 7 p.m. Friday at Louisiana State University in New Orleans.

---

[169] Memphis Press-Scimitar, March 5, 1969, Section three, page 33.

Presented by the Pan American Student Organization at LSUNO, the discussion will be held in the University Center and is open to all interested parties.

Panelists include Dr. Carlos Bringuier, Jose Vilasuso, Dr. Carlos M. Estevez, Dr. Agustin C. Guitart, and Dr. Otto Oliveras. All of the panelists, along with their families, now make their home in New Orleans.[170]

At the end of 1969, my book "Red Friday" was published. The Times Picayune reviewed it in this way:

Tragic Day in Review

That "it was the Castro's 'line' inside the Communist movement that pulled the trigger of Oswald's rifle, is the conclusion of Carlos Bringuier, in his newly published "Red Friday," a paperback symbolically bound in red (Hallberg and Co., Chicago.)

This work about the assassination of President Kennedy is an account of the activities of Oswald and an indictment of those who do not accept the findings of the Warren Report, among them Jim Garrison and Mark Lane.

Bringuier is the exiled Cuban who is said in the book's preface to have been the man who "put a stop to Lee Harvey Oswald's Fair Play for Cuba activities in New Orleans," and who tells he believes Oswald's was Communism's planned instrument against the United States and its government.

Pretty fair review but as usual, The Times Picayune was misrepresenting the information to the public. "Red Friday" was a hardcover book, not a "paperback" one.

On Friday December 5, 1969 the Republican Southern Conference was held in the City of New Orleans. A dinner attended by Vice-President Spiro Agnew was held at a cost per ticket of $500.00 per person, I received one free from the Louisiana Republican Party. That date I had

---

[170] New Orleans States Item, April 23, 1969, page 30.

the honor of meeting personally with the Vice President of the United States aboard the S.S. President on the Mississippi river.

On the same day Howard H. Callaway, National Committeeman from Georgia wrote me the following letter:

> *November 5, 1969*
> *Mr. Carlos Bringuier*
> *The Jung Hotel New Orleans, Louisiana*
>
> *Dear Mr. Bringuier:*
>
> *Welcome to New Orleans!*
> *I hope that you will join Congressman Jim Collins and me for breakfast on Saturday morning at 8:30 a.m. in meeting room # 9.*
> *This will give us a chance to get together for a while before the day's business begins. Jim and I look forward to seeing you then.*
>
> *Sincerely,*
> *HOWARD H. CALLAWAY*
> *National Committeeman from Georgia.*

On Friday January 9, 1970 I had the honor to assist at the installation ceremony for Gerald J. Gallinhouse as United States Attorney for the Eastern District of Louisiana, and also to the following reception at Brennan's Restaurant. Gerald J. Gallinhouse was the typical honest, sincere and nice politician. I would never forget that walking on Decatur Street with my son Carlos Jr., Gallinhouse was walking on the opposite sidewalk and when he saw us he crossed the street and with a smile in his face shook hands with me saying *"Glad to see you Doc."*

On January 19, 1970, The New Orleans States-Item published very interesting statements by Warren Commission member Senator Richard B. Russell. After saying that he is convinced that someone else worked with Lee Harvey Oswald in planning the assassination of John F. Kennedy, Senator Russell stated:

331

"I think that any other Commission you might appoint today would arrive at that conclusion."

"There were too many things—the fact that he was at Minsk (in the Soviet Union), and that was the principal center for educating Cuban students . . . Some of the trips he made to Mexico City and a number of discrepancies in the evidence, or as his means of transportation, the luggage he had and whether or not anyone was with him—that caused me to doubt that he planned it all by himself."[171]

By this time there were not only Lyndon B. Johnson, General Alexander Haig and many others who were now convinced that Fidel Castro was behind the assassination.

By the end of January, precisely on January 22nd, 1970 the Republican Party of Louisiana presented a Certificate of Appreciation to three Cubans in Louisiana: Carlos Bringuier, Carlos Quiroga and Carlos de la Vega. My certificate states:

"for his tireless efforts on behalf of the Republican Candidates for President, VicePresident and Congressman from the Second Congressional District of Louisiana in 1968, and for exemplifying true dedication to political freedom and human dignity.

The aforesaid person has demonstrated the strengths of his convictions by performing this service to the Republican Party, the State of Louisiana and to the United States of America.

He has furthered the cause of the Two Party System and brought to the attention of the citizens of New Orleans the principles of the Republican Party of Louisiana.

IN TESTIMONY WHEREOF, I have hereunto set my hand on this 22nd day of January of 1970

SIGNED
Joe S. Sheldon, Jr.
Chairman, Orleans Parish Political Action Council

---

[171] The New Orleans States-Item, January 19, 1970, front page.

One thing that I can assure the reader is that neither Carlos Quiroga nor I, had any political ambitions. Both Quiroga and I never tried to ask for political gains for ourselves and never requested or occupied political jobs. Our goal, our hearts were set on try to help the freedom of Cuba and the poor Cubans that were suffering there. We were not political prostitutes trying to use the name of Cuba to obtain personal benefits for us.

Coincidentally on the same day, January 22, 1970 the New Orleans Community Chapter of the Young Americans for Freedom also awarded me their Certificate of Merit for substantial sacrifice in the cause of Liberty Under Law.

On January 29, 1970, I prepared a picketing at the International House in New Orleans.

The Times Picayune editor, George Healy, had invited a group of "newsmen" from the Soviet Union to visit the City of New Orleans. That night we went there with a group of around 40 Cubans and I was surprised when I discover that there was another group demonstrating, it was a group of Jewish people also protesting the visit of the Communist "newsmen". As expected, next day The Times Picayune didn't publish anything in regard to the picketing, but the wire services took care of that. Following is the article published, on January 30, 1970, in The Morning Advocate of Baton Rouge, Louisiana:

Cubans, Jews Demonstrate Against Visiting Russians

NEW ORLEANS (UPI)—A Cuban exile leader who once scuffled with Lee Harvey Oswald led a demonstration Thursday night against 11 visiting Russian journalists.

About 35 Cubans exiles and 15 Jews participated in a joint protest against high-ranking Soviet editors and broadcasters. The Russians ignored the demonstrators and refused to accept any anti-communist leaflets as they walked into International House, where a dinner was planned in their honor.

Carlos Bringuier, leader of the New Orleans delegation of the Cuban Student Directorate, led the demonstrators in reading off the names of President John F. Kennedy and 483 Cubans allegedly assassinated by Fidel Castro and the communists.

Bringuier had a down town fist fight with Oswald four months before the 1963 assassination of President Kennedy after Oswald tried to distribute pro-Castro leaflets here.

Shouted "Presente"

As they did after the reading of each name, the Cuban demonstrators shouted "presente" to signify that the dead were still with them in spirit.

It was the third time that Jewish had demonstrated against the Russians since the journalists began their 17-day tour of the United States.

Upon their arrival in New Orleans Thursday, the Russians denied that their country discriminates against Jews.

L. N. Tolkunov, editor in chief of Izvestia, told newsmen that the discrimination charges were "concocted" and are "greatly damaging the relations between our countries."

"The position of Soviet Jewery is on a par with other citizens of our country," he added.

The Cuban demonstrators carried signs saying "Down with Communism", "Reds go Home" and "Peace Yes, Slavery No." They stretched out a huge Cuban flag and dropped the names of Kennedy and the 483 Cubans dead into the unfurled banner.

Meantime, Label Katz, a New Orleanian who formerly was international president of B'nai B'rith, said Jews would demonstrate against the Russians at all their public appearances here Friday and Saturday.

Katz criticized Russia for supporting Egypt against Israel and Bringuier said "we are demonstrating in support of the people in slavery in Cuban under Russian imperialism."

There were no serious incidents reported in connection with the demonstration, which faded away as a pelting rain came down after the Russians entered.

But, unreported in the press there was a serious incident during the demonstration. As George Healy, The Times Picayune editor was coming out of his car he had to cross the line of persons picketing and assuming that the one in front of him was "a poor Cuban exile", Healy pushed the person who fell into the ground, and Healy continue his steps and made his entrance to the International House. After a few moments George Healy was informed that it was not "a poor Cuban exile" who he had just pushed to the ground but a rich blind leader of the Jewish community in New Orleans. Healy came back to the street and apologized to the Jews group. As you have to expect, Mr. George Healy dislike of me increased like a rocket.

That demonstration was one of the best that I organized and, once more, I have to remind the reader that it was my sole idea, not an idea of the CIA or any other intelligence agency of the United States.

On May 1970 Richard E. Warren became the National Mobilizer of a group called "AMERICANS FOR PEACE NOT SURRENDER" the group directing the activities was formed by:

Dr. Carlos Bringuier—Producer
Alan Bock—Los Angeles Coordinator
Joel Weiner—Chicago Coordinator
Lee Edwards—Washington Coordinator
Paul Bethel—Miami Coordinator
Ron Docksai—New York Coordinator

He then addressed the population in this way in an open letter:

Citizens:

Radicals and Tyrannist Revolutionaries are attempting to create confrontations between students and police by using every American's desire for PEACE as a means of securing SURRENDER in Vietnam, which would insure a communist victory in Asia, and lead to worse wars and more bloodshed in Asia, Europe, Latin America, and here.

Let's show President Nixon, and the World, that Americans are for PEACE. But NOT SURRENDER. To pull out of Vietnam without having the communist pull-out would mean the assassination of over two million Christians in Vietnam. Moreover, our own security is in jeopardy. Surrender would certainly invite more attacks, greater bloodshed, and further violence.

Therefore, we are planning to have a nation-wide "Memorial Day Parade and Rally" on Saturday, May 30, 1970, in New Orleans, Washington, Miami, Los Angeles, New York, and other major cities.

You, your family and friends are needed to make the Memorial Day Parade the convincing rally for Peace NOT SURRENDER that it must be.

On Sunday May 31st, 1970 The Times Picayune wrote the following article:

Patriotism March is Held Downtown
Estimated 1,500 Are in Memorial Day Event
By Betsy Halstead

Downtown New Orleans experienced an unusual display of patriotism Saturday as an estimated 1,500 persons marched from Jackson Square to City Hall as part of ceremonies throughout the city marking Memorial Day.

Later the American Legion First District, sponsored a memorial ceremony at Duncan Plaza in front of City Hall. Gerald J. Gallinhouse, U.S. Attorney for the Eastern District of Louisiana, was the principal speaker.

People of all ages gathered in Jackson Square before noon Saturday to begin a march up Decatur St. to City Hall.

Organized by the New Orleans chapter of Americans for Peace, Not Surrender, the march drew representatives from a variety of patriotic groups such as the American Legion, the Veterans of Foreign Wars, and Young Americans for Freedom. Cuban refugees, now living in New Orleans, also took part in the march.

Ten year old Shelly Landry of New Orleans, an American Legion "Little Miss Poppy" led the parade. With her was John E. Dakin, Jr., of American Legion Post 307, dressed as Uncle Sam.

TWENTY CARRY FLAG

Twenty people followed them carrying a large American flag. Behind them men and women marched carrying a huge blue sign which read "Peace not Surrender."

The paraders began to move from Jackson Square as the clock struck noon at St. Louis Cathedral across from the square.[172] I was honored to have been the Producer of this event maybe the best Memorial Day Parade in the history of New Orleans. Among the speakers were Mayor Moon Landrieu who proclaimed the day Memorial Day and U.S. Attorney Gerald J. Gallinhouse. During the demonstration we burned an effigy of Dictator Fidel Castro and representatives of the Vietnamese colony burned a Viet Cong flag. Canal Street pedestrians reacted to the parade in different ways. A group of men and women in front of Holmes Department Store applauded as we marched by, waving our American flags. Some men took off their hats and placed them over their hearts as the American flag passed by. Other people waved or took photographs of the parade. A police motorcycle escort stopped traffic along the route to let the parade pass.

It was a beautiful day in New Orleans and for New Orleans and I was proud to be the Producer of such a parade. Again, I was not receiving orders of the CIA, FBI or any other intelligence agency of the government.

In the meantime the "reds" continued their efforts to destroy the United States, they were following the shots fired by Lee Harvey Oswald on November 22, 1963, the shots that initiated the Revolution in the United States. On August 8, 1970, Jane Fonda and Mark Lane held a press conference in Washington D.C. when they opened a "GI Office" in the nation's capital to hear the cases of servicemen with complaints against the armed services. Jane Fonda didn't want to hear complaints of servicemen tortured by the Vietnamese with the aid of Cuban Special Forces sent by Fidel Castro to Vietnam to torture our soldiers.[173]

Once again at the end of September 1970 the New Orleans States-Item published an editorial that attracted my attention. I sent the following letter to them, which they published:

[172] The Times Picayune, May 31, 1970, pages 1 & 2.
[173] The Times Picayune, August 10, 1970 Section four, page eight.

Dr. Carlos J. Bringuier

Chilean Marxists

I would like to express my disagreement with your editorial entitled "Communism in Chile."

I don't believe that "refusal of the Chilean Congress to endorse the election of Dr. Salvador Allende, a Marxist, would be counter-productive to the United States, in spite of the political ideologies involved," as stated in your editorial.

I do believe that in the Chilean Democratic system the Congress has the right to choose when none of the contenders reaches a majority. As you pointed out, "Dr. Allende already has made clear the consequences of such a refusal. For openers, he would call a general strike." This proves, once more, the extremist determination of Dr. Allende, Castro's arm in Chile.

I have to admit your ignorance about Communism when you stated: "if the prospect of another Communist stronghold in Latin America is unsettling, the alternative—division and chaos—is worse."

Mr. Editor, do you know what Communism has brought to all countries today under red slavery? Yes, division and chaos, besides terror, mass assassinations and hundreds of thousands of political prisoners. And believe me I had to make a tremendous effort to admit that what really moves you is just ignorance, because the above mentioned statement in itself appears to me unbelievable to come from a literate person.

If we follow your logic, we should turn the United States government over to the Students for a Democratic Society, the Fair Play for Cuba Committee or directly to the Communist Party to avoid the "division and chaos" that international communism has brought into this nation.

I hope the Chilean people will stand for freedom and democracy and they will refute the communism of Dr. Allende. If they fail to act, and communism is established in Chile that will mean the beginning of the end of their freedom, and maybe to yours.

Carlos Bringuier
New Orleans Delegate,
Cuban Student Directorate[174]

---

[174] The New Orleans States-Item, September 24, 1970, Page 8.

History has proved me right. The Chilean Congress was intimidated and named Dr. Salvador Allende President of Chile. Immediately Dr. Allende started a plan to convert Chile in a new Cuba. When the masses woke up and General Augusto Pinochet was forced to revolt against the Communists Fidel Castro wanted to convert the figure of Allende in another Che Guevara, but when Allende, like Che Guevara, decided to surrender, the only way for Castro to stop it was by ordering the assassination of Salvador Allende at the Chilean Presidential Palace. Dr. Salvador Allende was another "useful idiot" assassinated by orders of Fidel Castro.

On October 16, 1970 The Driftwood of LSUNO published the following article about "Operation Unification,"

O U Stresses Common Goal
By Nancy Sarrat

"I would like to say here today, rather than harping on our differences, let us work together on our common goals," said John Casanova, founder of "Operation Unification."

This was the main theme of last Friday's program which included such speakers as: Dr. Carlos Bringuier, Dr. Alton Ochsner, Richard Warren and Juanita Castro, refugee sister of Cuban dictator Fidel Castro.

Dr. Carlos Bringuier, a Cuban refugee, spoke to the small audience on "Cuban Subversion toward the United States." He said, "this country is slowly being taken over by the Communists. We had better ban together now because tomorrow might be too late."

He outlined the steps for the Communist takeover of America. "It begins with infiltration of local, state and federal government. The youths are turned against law and order, the government and their families. The next step is to infiltrate the church, the news media, civil movements, labor unions, the schools and the military. The final step starts with peaceful marches, then peaceful disobedience, followed by sabotage of public institutions, rioting, assassinations, open revolution and finally establishment of a Communist dictatorship."

339

Situation 100% worse

Dr. Bringuier said, *"Today I have to recognize that the situation in many American universities is 100% worse than that of the Cuban universities at the time of the takeover."*

"I consider that the US has the best system in the world today. Many people take for granted what they have here, even the little things. There is no Coca-Cola in Cuba."

He was followed by the celebrated surgeon and member of the Information Council of the Americas (INCA), Dr. Alton Ochsner, who spoke on "Marxism-A Killing Cancer." "If Communism is so good why do they need walls to keep the people in? They should have walls to keep others out," said Ochsner.

"As a Doctor, I try to prevent cancer, we as people refuse to see our nation overtaken by this killing cancer, we'll soon see our nation totally destroyed."

Then The Driftwood referred to the words pronounced by Juanita Castro, Fidel Castro's sister:

"Juanita Castro, who denounced her brother Fidel for his open tyranny and oppression, told the audience, "Fidel has thousands of agents in this country who are here to overtake the government of the United States of America."

The Driftwood showed my picture with Juanita Castro as I was acting as her translator.

On April 20, 1971, I sent the following telegram to President Richard M. Nixon:

CASTRO'S INSULTS AND THREATS SHOULD BE ANSWERED WITH COURAGEOUS AMERICAN TRADITION. EITHER AMERICAN LEADERS WAKE UP AND REALIZE THAT ONLY A FREE CUBA COULD RESTORE PEACE TO CONTINENT AND SECURITY TO AMERICA OR WE ARE LIVING LAST YEARS OF FREEDOM IN WORLD. WE WANT YOUR HELP

TO LIBERATE CUBA AND SAVE AMERICA, NO POLITICAL JOBS.

Carlos Bringuier

Unfortunately all those words were in vain. Cuba is still in slavery and the United States and the world are living very close to see the end of freedom.

On May 8, 1971 The Times Picayune published my following letter:

What's in a Name

Gretna
Editor, The Times Picayune:

The recent riots and demonstrations in Washington, D.C., and several other cities of the United States have proved once more that the American press is actually committing suicide and in this way is helping the Communist cause.

For us Cubans, this is not a surprise because we saw it happening in Cuba. We saw the Cuban press portraying Fidel, Raul and their cohort of assassins as new Robin Hoods.

Here we see how the Communists raise their clinched fist, how they parade the Viet Cong flag and how they speak loud and clear about overthrowing the U.S. government, but for the American Press they are only "anti-war protesters."

When a Communist sympathizer of Fidel Castro is involved in bombings of public buildings the American press portrays this person as a "peace worker. "But let me ask you, what kind of "peace" do these Communists want? Do they want the murderous "peace" that oppresses the people of Czechoslovakia, Hungary, Russia, Cuba, etc.?

I just want to remind the American people, newsmen and readers alike, that your main duty should be to defend your democracy, to save your country, and not to sell it for 30 silver coins.

You still have time. Call the Communists, anarchists or "useful idiots," but please don't call them "peace workers."

CARLOS BRINGUIER

On Tuesday October 26, 1971 an incident occurred at the New Orleans International Airport that grabbed national and international attention and provided me with what I consider my most important demonstration in the history of New Orleans besides my incidents with Lee Harvey Oswald.

That date the New Orleans States-Item in his final edition reported:

Plane held; Entry Refused
'MYSTERY' CUBANS FLY IN
By WILLIAM H. ADLER

A Cuban plane with 22 persons aboard landed at New Orleans International Airport this morning, apparently against the orders of the U.S. State Department.

The State Department said the Cubans have no visas and would leave here later today.

Several hours after the plane landed, the 19 passengers and three crewmen remained locked in U.S. Immigration Service offices at the airport and the plane was under guard.

The State Department in Washington said that about 7 a.m. today and "without advance word of any kind," a flight plan was filed with Houston Air Traffic Control for a Cuban turbo-prop aircraft to leave Havana at 8 a.m. for New Orleans.

THE PLANE landed here at 10:17 a.m. and passengers told U.S. authorities they have come to New Orleans for a meeting of the International Association of Sugar Cane Technologists now under way here.

The State Department said it advised Cuba on Sept. 24 that visas would not be approved for members of a Cuban delegation to the sugar cane meeting.

State Department communications with Cuba were conducted through the Swiss Embassy in Havana and the Czechoslovakian Embassy in Washington. The United States and Cuba maintain no direct diplomatic relations.

THE STATE Department said the plane would be refueled here and would return to Cuba this afternoon but a spokesman for the firm that handles refueling operations at New Orleans International indicated that plan might hit a snag.

Greg Desselle, a supervisor for the refueling firm, General Aviation Corporation said:

"The plane hasn't been refueled and if they don't have American money, they're not going to get any of my fuel." He said the State Department has told his firm it will not stand good for the cost of fuel for the plane.

THE LANDING of the red, white and blue plane obviously caught local officials of federal agencies by complete surprise.

The U.S. Customs Services here said it had not advance notice the plane was en route to New Orleans. The local office of the U.S. Immigration Service referred all questions to Washington.

The State Department said that after it got word that flight plan had been filed it did not have time to notify the Federal Aviation Administration to turn the plane back.

THE PLANE was being held at the east end of the airport. Unarmed Customs Service guards were standing next to the plane. The U.S. Public Health Service placed the plane under quarantine.

While federal officials would not release the names of any of those aboard the plane, an airport official released the names of the plane's crew.

Gordon W. Stout, superintendent of the New Orleans Aviation Board, said the pilot is Ray Morina. The other crewmen were identified by Stout only as Cuillen and Valdes.

THE ARRIVAL of the Cubans spurred a one-man protest by Cuban refugee Carlos Bringuier, who said he is a member of the Cuban Student Directorate.

Bringuier carried a hand-lettered sign that read: "Reds Go Home." The word red was painted in red letters, the rest in black.

"Demonstrations of Cubans in New Orleans"

United States Senate

COMMITTEE ON
AGRICULTURE AND FORESTRY
WASHINGTON, D.C. 20510

April 11, 1977

Dr. Carlos Bringuier
111 Decatur Street
New Orleans, Louisiana 70130

Dear Dr. Bringuier:

Thank you for an excellent letter. You certainly have a far sharper perception of the forces at loose against freedom in the world than do most of my colleagues in government.

In the past few years, I have had many talks with representatives of South American governments, and last year I spent some time in Argentina, Chile and Uruguay. I have seen myself the reasons why these countries have had to take stern measures to preserve their stability, independence and freedom.

I am afraid that what the President's double standard preachments about "human rights" are going to do in Latin America is to create a solid bloc of countries that are anti-communist but just as fiercely anti-American. It is unrealistic to think that we will keep any allies in this world when we are so solicitous for the welfare of terrorists, anarchists and revolutionaries and disregard the rights of the majority.

I have made many speeches and statements pointing to these dangers, and to the great folly of surrendering our sovereignty over the Panama Canal. Given the tremendous majorities which the liberals have in the Congress, and their domination of the newspapers and television, it is difficult to get the truth across, but I shall continue to do my best for world freedom and the security of our own homeland.

Sincerely,

Jesse Helms

JESSE HELMS:of

Enclosures

Letter from Senator Jesse Helms to Dr. Carlos Bringuier.

345

CAPTIVE NATIONS WEEK
RALLY
SATURDAY JULY 26,1986 2:00 PM
ST. LOUIS CATHEDRAL/JACKSON SQUARE (MALL) area

B
O
R
N
i
n

H
A
V
A
N
A

C
U
B
A

D
O
C
T
O
R

o
f

L
A
W

CARLOS J. BRINGUIER

NATIONALLY KNOWN SPEAKER and
LECTURER AGAINST COMMUNISM

Author of "RED FRIDAY"

About the assassination of John F. Kennedy

OTHER
ACTIVITIES

WNOE 1060 am Radio
"Let's Talk It Over"
with Joe Culotta
Sunday July 20, 9:30 am

WSMB 1350 am Radio
with Charles Travis
Friday July 25, 2:00 pm

Estoril, Feb, 9/970

Dr. Carlos Bringuier
P.O. Box 2506
New Orleans, La. 70116

Querido amigo:

    Le agradezco su libro "Red Friday" y le dedicaré tiempo para terminarlo. Por lo que llevo leído hasta ahora, me parece muy bien documentado, y no obstante lo difícil del tema, espero y le deseo los éxitos que Vd. merece.

    Tengo en mucho aprecio su ilustre apellido, tanto como estimo a su querida familia.

    Le saluda afectuosamente,

Fulgencio Batista.

Letter from ex-President Fulgencio Batista to Dr. Carlos Bringuier.

Certificate of Appreciation

WTIX

presents this certificate of appreciation on _7/20/80_ to

Dr. Carlos Bringuier

for increasing community awareness by sharing his views on the subject of

Captive Nations Week

on the WTIX Public Affairs Program,

"Let's Talk It Over"

JOE CULOTTA, Moderator
Let's Talk It Over

WILLIAM E. ENGEL, General Manager
WTIX Radio

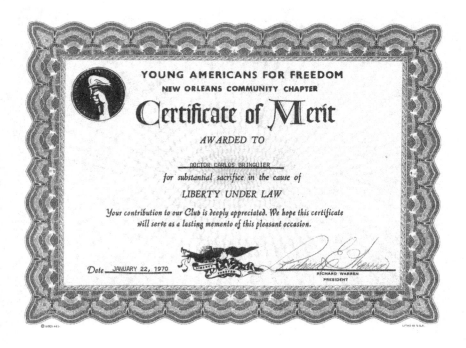

YOUNG AMERICANS FOR FREEDOM
NEW ORLEANS COMMUNITY CHAPTER

Certificate of Merit

AWARDED TO

DOCTOR CARLOS BRINGUIER

for substantial sacrifice in the cause of

LIBERTY UNDER LAW

Your contribution to our Club is deeply appreciated. We hope this certificate
will serve as a lasting memento of this pleasant occasion.

Date JANUARY 22, 1970

RICHARD WARREN
PRESIDENT

UNITED STATES OF AMERICA

State of Louisiana

The Republican Party of Louisiana

ORLEANS PARISH POLITICAL ACTION COUNCIL

KNOW YE, that the Chairman of the Orleans Parish Political Action Council in the name of the Republican Party of Louisiana, does hereby express the highest esteem and appreciation to

Carlos Bringuier

for his tireless efforts on behalf of the Republican Candidates for President, Vice-President and Congressman from the Second Congressional District of Louisiana in 1968, and for exemplifying true dedication to political freedom and human dignity.

The aforesaid person has demonstrated the strength of his convictions by performing this service to the Republican Party, the State of Louisiana and to the United States of America.

He has furthered the cause of the Two Party System and brought to the attention of the citizens of New Orleans the principles of the Republican Party of Louisiana.

IN TESTIMONY WHEREOF, I have hereunto set my hand on this 22nd *day of* January, 1970

SIGNED

Chairman, Orleans Parish Political Action Council

350

94TH CONGRESS	SENATE	REPORT
2d Session		No. 94-755

THE INVESTIGATION OF THE ASSASSINATION OF PRESIDENT JOHN F. KENNEDY: PERFORMANCE OF THE INTELLIGENCE AGENCIES

BOOK V

FINAL REPORT

OF THE

SELECT COMMITTEE TO STUDY GOVERNMENTAL OPERATIONS

WITH RESPECT TO

INTELLIGENCE ACTIVITIES

UNITED STATES SENATE

April 23 (under authority of the order of April 14), 1976

El Ecuador ha sido, es y ~~CI~ 825.904~~
será País Amazónico

CERTIFICADO INTERNACIONAL DE VACUNACION O REVACUNACION
INTERNATIONAL CERTIFICATE OF VACCINATION OR REVACCINATION
AGAINST SMALLPOX
CERTIFICAT INTERNATIONAL DE VACCINATION OU LE REVACCINATION
CONTRE LA VARIOLE

Certificase que
This is to certify that _Maria del Carmen Bringuier_ nacido(a) el / date of birth / né(e) le : 4/IX/1923 Ecuador
je soussiné(e) certifie que
cuya firma aparece a continuación _Maria del Carmen Bringuier_ sexo / sex / sexe : F
whose signature follows
dont la signature suit

ha sido vacunado(a) o revacunado(a) contra la viruela en la fecha indicada.
has on the date indicated been vaccinated or revaccinated against smallpox.
a été vacciné(e) ou revacciné(e) contre la variole á la date indiquée.

Fecha / Date	Indique con "X" si se trata de: / Show by "X" whether: / Indiquer par "X" s'il s' agit de:	Firma y calidad profesional del vacunador. / Signature and professional status of vaccinator. / Signature et qualité professionnelle du vaccinateur.	Sello autorizado. / Approved stamp. / Cachet d'authentification.	
1a	Primovacunación efectuada. / Primary vaccination performed. / Primovaccination effectuée.		1a	1b
1b	Leído como positivo / Read as successful / Prise — Leído como negativo / Unsuccessful / Pas de prise			
2 5 IX 1962	Revacunación ...	Dr Luis Pya... EPIDEMIOLOGO	3	
3	Revacunación ...			
4	Revacunación ...		4	5
5	Revacunación ...			
6	Revacunación ...		6	7
7	Revacunación ...			

International Vaccination Form showing
Maria del Carmen Bringuier as born in Ecuador.

Bringuier said that in addition to coming to the airport to protest the presence of Cubans, he came to see if he knew any of the passengers or crew aboard the plane.[175]

This incident became the best demonstration held by me in New Orleans. That day I was at my store "Casa Cuba" when I received a phone call from a friend of mine. His name was Miguel J. González and he worked for Delta Airlines at the New Orleans International Airport.

Miguel informed me of what was going on at the airport with the arrival of the plane from Cuba, immediately I prepared a sign and drove to the airport. I am sorry to contradict once again my detractors: No involvement of CIA agents or FBI agents.

Before I left the airport that day another friend of mine joined me in the demonstration, his name is Reinaldo González my former neighbor and friend from El Vedado, Cuba, and now my friend and neighbor in Terrytown, Louisiana. Reinaldo was also a relative of Miguel J. González.

Next day I returned to the airport and a larger group of Cubans joined me in the protest. By the third day an unbelievable amount of 1,000 Cubans were demonstrating in front of the airport. The tension was growing, I remember that one of my good friends José Cortizas was very angry with the situation. Rumors started to run, one among them was that a bomb would be thrown against the airplane. At that moment I discussed the situation with some agents of the FBI. Eventually the government option was to move the plane and the Castroites to the Naval Air Station located in Belle Chasse, Louisiana about 20 miles south of downtown New Orleans.

Finally, Fidel Castro trust failed. In my opinion there were two possible reasons for his irrational move to send the airplane and his agents "without visa" to the United States. First, there could be some maneuvers with his agents within the government of the United States to force the administration to dialogue with him. Second, it could be an irrational trust by Castro to show the administration that he can put a plane in the heart of the United States when he decides so. Either way he failed, as I had made him previously fail in Buenos Aires when he had tried to assassinate Cuban Unions leader Eusebio Mujal.

---

175 The New Orleans States-Item, October 26, 1971, Front page.

During that incident I saw the largest demonstration ever, of Cubans in the City of New Orleans, against Fidel Castro.

On June 17, 1972 a very strange incident occurred that changed the history of the United States. The leftists who had used Lyndon B. Johnson had tried to bring down his government during the Jim Garrison investigation but the must that they achieved was Johnson not running again. That night of the 17, a group of men broke in into the offices of the Democratic Party in the Watergate building. According to some reports they were looking for proofs that Fidel Castro was helping in the campaign of George McGovern. One of them was a Judas with his own agenda.

On May 24, 1973, The Times Picayune reporting about the Watergate scandal wrote the following:

> Alch[176] said Fensterwald first came to his attention during attempts to raise $100,000 bail for McCord following McCord's conviction.
>
> Alch said he contacted Fensterwald at McCord's direction with $40,000 of the bail money. The rest came from McCord's family and its contacts.

BAIL MONEY

> Alch said he could not understand why Fensterwald was so willing to work at raising the bail money since Fensterwald told him at one point he had never met McCord.
>
> But at a later meeting involving the two attorneys and McCord, Alch said Fensterwald mentioned that in the past years McCord had submitted checks to Fensterwald for the Committee for the Investigation of the Assassination of the President. Alch said McCord responded, "Yeah, that's right."
>
> Fensterwald had run an organization looking into the 1963 assassination of President John F. Kennedy. There was no elaboration on this point.

---

[176] Gerald Alch, former lawyer for convicted Watergate burglar James McCord.

In the period when McCord was talking with senate investigators—testimony that was widely reported—Alch said Fensterwald called him several times in Chicago.

PHONE CONVERSATIONS

"in one telephone conversation he said to me 'what do you think of all that is going on'? Alch said. "I replied, 'whatever is right for Jim McCord is all right with me.'

"Mr. Fensterwald replied: "We are going after the President of the United States.' I replied that I was not interested in vendettas against the President but only in the best interest of my client-to which Mr. Fensterwald replied: 'Well, you'll see, that's who we're going after, the President'."

In regard to Bernard Fensterwald you can read more about it in Chapter XVI. James McCord was the conflict manager infiltrated inside the group that broke in into Watergate.

McCord was the one who kept silent while the others perjured themselves and then, all of the sudden, felt that he had to tell the truth and spilled out everything, after Richard M. Nixon had committed the mistake of trying to save some of his friends. It was a brilliant trap. Nixon and the others fell for it and Fensterwald and the left was happy to make Nixon resign. Even today there are some who condemn Nixon and pray for the "Hope" of Obama.

On March 19, 1976, a dispatch from the Associated Press stated that a spy for the Cuban government allegedly was involved with a San Francisco area terrorist group plotting the assassination of President Ford and presidential challenger Ronald Reagan at the Republican National Convention at Kansas City, in August, according to a report of the Chicago Tribune.[177]

A member of the Emiliano Zapata Unit, a terrorist band active at the moment having received credit for a dozen bombings, turned informer for the FBI told federal agents that a Cuban adviser using the code name "Andres Gomez," a person identified by federal agents and Latin

---

[177] New Orleans States-Item, March 19, page A6.

American intelligence experts as a member of the Cuban spy organization known as Directorate of General Intelligence.[178]

I have not seen any report about the conclusion of these assassination plots but we have to remember that in reality the two persons threatened with assassination, Ford and Reagan, eventually were subjects of that type of aggression.

On March 31, 1976 The Times Picayune published my following letter to the Editor:

Disagrees on Cuba

> *I strongly disagree with your March 26 editorial "U.S.-Cuba: Dangerous Game."*
>
> *That type of journalism is the one that has been brainwashing and softening American public opinion, paving the way for the time when maybe you or another "capitalistic" Newspaper will reason that it will be better to surrender to communism than to fight for our ideals, liberties and properties.*
>
> *The United States is not looking for a major military confrontation with Cuba, but if the United States wants to remain as a free nation we cannot allow Castro to take over nation after nation as the United States didn't allow Hitler to keep conquering the world in the name of National Socialism.*
>
> *Fidel Castro, with his doctrine of "international solidarity," is making a mockery of our position as leader of the free world. In his achievement he has been greatly helped by the worst Congress in U. S. history, by a masochist press that in the name of "freedom of the press" is digging its own grave, by a weakened executive power still drugged by Mr. Kissinger's "détente," and by a chorus of useful idiots who will be the first ones assassinated if Fidel Castro's dream come true.*
>
> *I particularly disagree with your judgment about the American people. I believe the great majority of Americans are not ready to risk the known consequences of allowing Fidel Castro's intervention in the internal affairs of other countries.*

---

[178] Same as above.

We all know that if we allow that, we are not only betraying the Spirit of '.'76 but sentencing our children to live under the slavery of communism.

Dr. CARLOS BRINGUIER

At the beginning of April 1977 I wrote a letter to all the U.S. Senators apprising them of the danger of the Fidel Castro's dictatorship 90 miles away from our shores and the possibility of the United States surrendering the sovereignty of the Panama Canal to a foreign government.

The response was great but the letter that most impressed me was the one signed by Jesse Helms, Senator from North Carolina, it reads:

April 11, 1977
Dr. Carlos Bringuier
111 Decatur Street
New Orleans, Louisiana, 70130

Dear Dr. Bringuier:

Thank you for your excellent letter. You certainly have a far sharper perception of the forces at loose against freedom in the world than most of my colleagues in government.

In the past few years, I have had many talks with representatives of South American governments, and last year I spent some time in Argentina, Chile and Uruguay. I have seen myself the reasons why these countries have had to take stern measures to preserve their stability, independence and freedom.

I am afraid that what the President's double standard preachment about "human rights" are going to do in Latin America is to create a solid bloc of countries that are anti-communist but just as fiercely anti-American. It is unrealistic to think that we will keep any allies in this world when we are so solicitous for the welfare of terrorists, anarchists and revolutionaries and disregard the rights of the majority.

I have made many speeches and statements pointing to these dangers, and to the great folly of surrendering our sovereignty over the Panama Canal. Given the tremendous majorities which the liberals have in Congress, and their domination of the newspapers and television, it is difficult to get the truth across, but I shall continue to do my best for world freedom and the security of our own homeland.

Sincerely,
Jesse Helms

In September 18, 1978 a great Cuban, historian Herminio Portell-Vilá wrote a letter, from Washington D.C., to me that I quote:

My friend Bringuier:

I just received your letter with the copy of "Bohemia" article and the photocopies of the stamps. Keep the originals because they are of great value.

Here, the abjection is to the maximum. Yesterday, the famous investigators proclaimed their gratitude because they went to Cuba to interview Castro, they asked him if he had anything to do with the assassination of Kennedy, he responded "no" and they accepted it remaining very freshly. After that, Castro sent a Cuban Communist mulatto, Azcuy, who had talked to Oswald at the Communist Cuba Embassy in 1963, and tried to cover up the situation. Oswald had stop in Havana in 1959, from New Orleans to Moscow, in a ship of Lykes Bros., and these people continue ignoring it. Ruby had been co-owner of Prado 88, in La Habana, next door to the flower shop "Milagros" and made frequent trips to La Habana. They also have decided to ignore this.

Castro, while drunk, sitting at the stairs of the Brazilian Embassy in La Habana, on September 7, Day of Independence, had uttered threats against Kennedy weeks before his death. When the news arrived to La Habana it was organized a great march of jubilation with a jack ass representing Kennedy, but somebody advised Castro that it could bring difficulties and urgently the march was suspended.

358

Clearly there are a lot of more things, but the order now is to get an understanding with Castro, who again will deceive the United States. What are painful are those queer fishes who allowed themselves to go to La Habana and become his toys. OK! In the last century there were also people like them but Cuba managed to become free.

I am writing to Mr. Guichard, I am invoking your name and I am offering him "tapes", free and in a regular way. I would like he accept.

If one day you come here do not forget to let me know. Receive a cordial greeting from your old friend.

Herminio Portell-Vilá

For years Herminio Portell-Vilá had been a well-known respected intellectual in Cuba and for a long time he was the President of the Cuban-American Cultural Institute in Cuba until the Communists government dissolved it. Now he was working with the American Security Council in Washington, D.C., and he was living in Arlington, Virginia.

At the beginning of April 1980 some incidents occurred in Havana that brought happiness and sadness to the Cubans and to the Americans. A passenger bus was reaching Embassy Row in the Miramar subdivision when the bus driver stop the bus and asked everybody to get out because it was broken. There were only four passengers who remained in the bus beside the driver. They were together in a plot to gain entrance to the Peruvian Embassy.

They smashed the fence around the Embassy and when they were already inside land of the Embassy they asked for political asylum. They did not have any weapons but the policemen surrounding the Embassy were well armed and when the truck accelerated to smash the fence, those Communist policemen opened fire against the bus. In the crossfire between the Communists policemen a policeman got killed.

An angered Fidel Castro opened his mouth accusing the refugees of killing the policeman and stating that those who wanted to leave the island could do so. In a few days 10,000 Cubans were inside the Peruvian Embassy. Some people thought that it was a Castro's mistake. I think otherwise.

At those moments the dissatisfaction of the population with the Communist regime was increasing in Cuba as in a pressure cooker. It was time to release the pressure and use the opportunity to invade the U. S. with his spies. An accomplice to the crime committed against the Cuban and American people was the worst President, up to that moment, in the history of the United States of America: Jimmy Carter.

A lot of incidents could be narrated about the criminals and the spies sent by Castro during the Mariel Exodus, but the case of José Vigoa is a clear cut example. Vigoa had been recruited by the Soviet Union and sent to study at Sulokov Military School and the Frunze Academy. In 1979 Vigoa spent six months in Angola, Africa, as a special operations officer with the Russian-Castro troops. In 1980 he also spent three months in Afghanistan in a special operations force with the Russians. In 1980 he reached the coast of the United States during the Mariel exodus. In June 28, 1999 he started a crime spree in Las Vegas, Nevada, that lasted more than 24 months where he, and his gang, hit six hotels using Russian AK-47's causing at least the death of two Armored Transport Services employees: Gary Dean Prestidge and Ricardo Sosa, two innocent hard working Americans who paid with their lives for the ineptitude and complicity of Jimmy Carter. Vigoa was finally apprehended and while he was in jail it was discovered an attempt for his escape. The jailers discovered in his cell documents related to *"biological warfare, chemical poisons and plots to blow up a Florida nuclear power plant during a hurricane."*[179] If Fidel Castro and Vigoa would have succeeded hundreds of thousands of innocent persons would have died in Florida alone, thanks to Jimmy Carter.

In total 125,000 Cubans came in the exodus. Only in the month of May came 86,488 Cubans. The irony and the crime was that the great majority of the arrivals were not ordinary Cubans but criminals and mentally sick Cubans. Hundreds were agents of the Castro regime easily infiltrated in the United States. Many of the ships came carrying not only "Marielitos" but large amount of drugs as explained to me by some of them.

It has been estimated by some that 25,000 of the "Marielitos" were honest, hardworking Cubans looking for freedom, the rest, 100,000 were scum. The exodus lasted until October 31, 1980 just enough to save the

---

[179] "Storming Las Vegas", by John Huddy.

United States of a disaster when the reaction of the American people was to defeat Jimmy Carter in the upcoming presidential elections.

In New Orleans it was pandemonium. The Leo Frade to whom I had written a letter from Buenos Aires in 1960 was now Episcopal Pastor in New Orleans and was raising money to contract a ship to go to Cuba and bring relatives of the desperate Cubans in the city. When I had met him in New Orleans at the Cuban Lyceum José Martí and reminded him of his letter he had looked at me and said: "Coño[180] what a memory you have." I attended one of those meetings were a delegation of the Group of 75 that had gone to Cuba to shake hands with Castro was present. One of them invited me to go to Cuba and assured me that I would not confront any problems there. Besides been *in God's hands* I consider myself to be in good mental health and decline the invitation.

Reverend Leo Frade stated at the meeting:

1) The meeting was a response to the call coming from the Group of 75.
2) He had brought already 6 flights of Cubans to the United States.
3) He already had one ship to bring people from Cuba.
4) He said that the Cuban flag was loved by the Cubans here in the United States and by the Cubans who remain in Cuba, even if we don't like to believe it.
5) The ship that he had is worth 5 million dollars, it was built in 1979 and could bring 300 persons.
6) The wait would have to be about a month long.
7) Those who want to bring relatives would have to pay $300.00 per person, and if there was any money left at the end it would be distributed equally among the participants.
8) This could be achieved thanks to the channels of communications established by the Chief of State of Cuba and the Cuban community in the exterior.
9) Leo Frade ended stating that he was a "pacifist."

Recently Leo Frade was again in the news. Now he is a Bishop of the Episcopal Diocese of South East Florida since May 6, 2000, and he gained notoriety when the renegade Catholic priest Alberto Cutié was discovered with his girl-friend by a paparazzi in South Beach.

---

[180] A four letters word in Spanish.

Monsignor Leo Frade brought Alberto Cutié to his Church and finally married Cutié and the girlfriend.

Several people in New Orleans went in their own boats to bring relatives and were forced to bring also criminals and mentally disturbed persons with them. Several of those Cubans from New Orleans told me that while waiting for their passengers they had been questioned by members of the Intelligence Department asking several questions about Cubans in New Orleans, and my name had been mentioned by Castro's henchmen.

When the "Marielitos" started to arrive to New Orleans we felt sadness for them and tried to help them. After a few days I realized what kind of people were them as they were visiting my grocery store at 2048 Magazine Street. I told them that now they had a great opportunity ahead of them, that this is a great Country and that they would have to forget what they have been in Cuba. That yes, this is a great Country, but that this Country also have great jails, great hospitals and great cemeteries. I remember in particular one of them who had a bicycle and used to come to my grocery to buy cigars and one day he told me that he did not came to the U.S. to work, that when he needed money he was going, during the night, to St. Charles Avenue and rob old ladies. I mentioned that to the policeman that was doing private patrol in our neighborhood. Eventually this criminal had left the Country for Costa Rica. Enrique had also told me that he was in jail in Cuba serving a sentence of 20 years for having killed his brother-in-law when he was given the opportunity to leave the jail and come in the exodus sponsored by Fidel Castro and accepted by Jimmy Carter. Many of these Marielitos who visited my grocery ended in jails and cemeteries like thousands others throughout the United States. Many Americans died victims of these criminals thanks to Fidel Castro and Jimmy Carter.

After the Mariel exodus I realized that Che Guevara and Fidel Castro had fulfilled their dream of creating a "New Man" in Cuba. Sadness invaded me because I realized that, after years of indoctrination, an important segment of Cubans was not anymore the same type of Cubans that I had left there, it was almost a different race, almost subhuman. I felt very sad for Cuba.

One of the great honors that I received in my life was when the Daughters of the American Revolution invited me to be the main speaker at their Convention in New Orleans. It was held on January 11, 1978 at the Marriott Hotel on Canal Street. As my wife was working at the store I brought with me my daughter María Elena. My speech was as follows:

> *I am delighted to have the opportunity to address you today, a fine group like you "Daughters of the American Revolution," and I would like to dedicate my words to the memory of two native New Orleaneans, two American ladies that were born in this city during the last century. One of them was Mrs. Irene Lapeyre, the other Mrs. Maria Laredo. One was my great grandmother, the other my grandmother.*
>
> *During their times there were also moments of struggle, moments of testing, moments of challenges.*
>
> *What America is today is the result of a continuing chain of challenges, struggles and sacrifices that have made us the greatest country on earth. Through history, generation after generation of Americans had to overcome the challenges of their times, and today it is our generation the one that have to overcome the challenges ahead of us. But as always happens there are not two situations alike.*
>
> *For example, during World War II, the main challenge, the main threat was from outside. Our soldiers went to far-away beaches, to far-away lands, to far-away seas to battle the enemy.*
>
> *Today our challenge not only comes from the outside but also from within. I want to make it clear that no matter the fact that there are some people who claim that we are at peace, that we are enjoying a period of peaceful coexistence, that "détente" is working . . . The truth is that we are at war, in some regions it could be called "cold war" in other regions it is not so cold.*
>
> *Today we are confronted with a situation where at the same time that we are being encircled from the outside, we have been subverted from within; we have been undermined from inside, the red termites are at work.*
>
> *At the time of the Second World War, America was a strong filled nation: our family ties were strong, our morals were high, our will to survive was second to none.*
>
> *Today we are witnessing the result of the tremendous attack against our youth: drugs, permissiveness and lower education has taken its toll. Our family ties are disappearing at a fantastic pace;*

our morals are at its lowest heights and as a result of these, our will to survive as a free Republic is weakening day after day. And what it is worst is when we see the infiltrators, the useful idiots reaching different segments of our society and our government.

I would like to know what would have been the reaction of the American press if in the late 30's United States Senators would have traveled to Nazi Germany shaking hands with Adolf Hitler and returning to America to propagandize the Nazi regime?

The reaction of the American press and of the American people would had been strong against them and at least they would had been ran out of office.

But today, what are we seeing?

We are seeing Senators like George McGovern who was repudiated in 1972 by the overwhelming majority of the American people, going to Red Cuba and propagandizing in favor of the Castro bloodthirsty dictatorship.

We are seeing Senators like Frank Church, traveling to Communist Cuba and stating at his return that he had found a friend in butcher Castro. And at this very moment, Senators of the United States can be seen ready to surrender part of our territory, because that is what the Panama Canal is, part of the territory of the United States.

And I believe that if we at least have a minimum of dignity, each one of the Senators who votes in favor of surrendering the Canal should be run out of office in the next elections.

I hope that the new treaties will be defeated. I hope that we will save the Canal, and we have to work to save it.

There are two Senators in Louisiana: Senator J. Bennett Johnston I believe he has made clear his position against surrendering the Canal, but as I understand it that is not the case with Senator Russell Long, and each one of us should write a letter to him stating our position and making very clear that we will not vote for anyone who cast his vote for the new treaties.

And this is one of the hypocrisies of some so-called Liberals. They attack Pinochet in Chile, Videla in Argentina and anyone who opposes the Communist terrorists, but at the same time they want to improve relations with Dictator Castro and they want to surrender the Panama Canal to a Marxists dictator like Torrijos.

And then it comes the moment when you don't know if they are working consciously for the advantage of International Communism or if they simply are useful idiots.

It would have been beautiful if today we could count with a new Teddy Roosevelt. He would have kicked them where they deserve.

In February 1898 after the battleship "Maine" was sunk at Havana harbor, Teddy Roosevelt, then Under-Secretary of the Navy, said to Senator Henry Cabot Lodge: "If I would be the President I would invade Cuba tomorrow."

And I tell you today, if the President of our Nation, or if the Congress of our Nation would have the most elemental degree of common sense, or if they would like to spare our Country of darker days, we should be invading Cuba tomorrow to kick Dictator Castro where he deserves.

Then, those 40,000 Cuban troops that are trying to make a Red continent out of the Black continent, those 40,000 Cuban troops will revolt against their leaders, and the red aggression in Africa will come to an end. And then, the Latin American countries will dedicate their efforts to improve the standard of living of their people, because then the terrorists will not have a sanctuary in Cuba, they will not have a sanctuary to be trained right in the middle of the Americas and only 90 miles from our shores, and then the assassinations, the kidnappings, the terrorism and the guerrillas will come to an end.

But for that, we have to take a stand and tell our President and tell our Congress: "WE ARE FED UP" we don't accept this anymore.

When we do this, everything will change.

There are some who says that America is a dying Country. Dictator Castro says it. Dictator Torrijos believes it. This is nothing new, there have been others who had said the same thing. For example there was another person who on November 26, 1959, wrote a letter that in part said, and I quote: "Ask me and I will tell you I fight for Communism. I will not say your grandchildren will live under Communism. Look for yourself at History, look at a world map! America is a dying Country."

The person who wrote that, almost 20 years ago was Lee Harvey Oswald. Oswald the Castro agent who assassinated President John F. Kennedy.

Today we have to say to them, we have to say to Dictators Castro and Torrijos, we have to say to Oswald and to all those useful idiots who are trying to sell us out: "YOU ARE WRONG." America is not a dying Country. America is a Country of brave men and a Country of brave women like you, Daughters of the American Revolution, because you will stand up and keep America as the land of the free.

And when Castro, Torrijos and all the others had joined Hitler, Mussolini, Lenin, and Stalin in Hell, then our flag will still be there because with your courage America will never die.

I was very impressed when I realized that my words had reached home, and those fine women gave me a standing ovation. I still keep the plaque that they presented to me as a token of their appreciation.

In 1980 also the prediction by President Miguel Ydígoras of Guatemala was proved to be correct. Fidel Castro extended his long hand to Paraguay and his henchmen assassinated exPresident Anastasio Somoza, Jr. Once more Castro proved his power to assassinate Presidents. On September 23, 1980 the New Orleans States-Item published a letter sent by me in regard to the assassination of Anastasio Somoza, Jr., it read as follows:

The assassination of Anastasio Somoza at the hands of the fanatical members of international communism could serve to open the eyes of those who still don't understand the threat of Dictator Castro only 90 miles away.

To a certain degree a parallel could be drawn between the lives of Somoza and John F. Kennedy. Both were the architects of the Bay of Pigs invasion. Both promised to visit a Cuba free of communism. Both in their own and separate ways opposed the threat of communism in this hemisphere. Both failed to fully comprehend that our confrontation with communism in general and with Castro in particular is a very dangerous one, failing to realize that they were not dealing with a leader of different political or social views but with a gangster who is willing to resort to political assassinations without any hesitation.

If John F. Kennedy had taken the decision of having Castro deposed, not just playing high society games but with a serious decision and recognition of his danger, Castro would not be in power today and Kennedy would still be alive.

The same could be said of Anastasio Somoza, who even at the last minute didn't resort to an open declaration of war against the communist dictator from Cuba, training, aiding and arming international mercenaries to establish a communist dictatorship in that Central American country. This dictatorship we are aiding today with $75 million that will serve to indoctrinate agents who one day will come here to disrupt our order and our system.

Today Anastasio Somoza and John F. Kennedy are part of history. Both were assassinated and Castro is enjoying a healthy life. Lee Harvey Oswald fulfilled the dream of dictator Castro in the same way that the Latin American "Lee Harvey Oswalds" carried out in Asuncion the orders from Havana to eliminate Somoza.

The political leaders of this country, so involved in playing the game of inner politics, should put a minute aside to consider the priorities and wonder what is more important. To keep playing the political games and one day wake up in front of a communist execution squad, or stand up and make peace and stability return to our hemisphere and our country?

And history proved me right when it was learned that the mastermind of the assassination was Fidel Castro using one of his disciples. His name was Enrique Haroldo Gorriarán Merlo born October 19, 1941 in Argentina. After studying Economics Gorriarán joined the Revolutionary Worker's Party (PRT). In 1970 he joined the Revolutionary People's Army (ERP), the military branch of the PRT.

Gorriarán traveled to Cuba where he received training in assassinations and terrorism. At his return to Argentina he was incarcerated but he managed to escape, first to Chile, and then to Cuba. In 1973 he became the Commander in chief of the ERP. From Cuba,

Castro sent him to Nicaragua to join the Sandinistas and following Castro's orders he went to Asunción, Paraguay, where on September 17, 1980 he directed the commando group of terrorists that assassinated Anastasio Somoza.

In 1983 Gorriarán returned to Argentina and following Castro's steps on January 20, 1989 he commanded an attack similar to Castro's against the Moncada barracks in Cuba, but this time was against the La Tablada barracks in Argentina. In the attack 39 persons died and like Castro did before, Gorriarán escaped. Eventually he had to leave Argentina.

With the Montoneros in power in Argentina, Gorriarán returned there where he organized the Worker's Party. On September 22, 2006, at 64 years of age, this Argentinean Lee Harvey Oswald died in Argentina when the hate that he carried in his inside exploded his arteries.

On October 10, 1980 I took a fly to Tampa, Florida. I went to the first meeting of the Delegates to the Permanent assembly of the Junta Patriótica Cubana (Cuban Patriotic Junta). The DRE had passed away and was not longer functioning. The Cuban Patriotic Junta had been organized and I was selected as its Delegate in Louisiana. President of the Junta was a very honest Cuban and old fighter for democracy Dr. Manuel Antonio (Tony) De Varona. Dr. De Varona had been Prime Minister during the government of Dr. Carlos Prío and also was one of the leaders of the Cuban Revolutionary Front (CRF) who was used by the U.S. Government to launch the betrayed Bay of Pigs invasion.

During October 11 and 12, all Delegations presented their report of the work done in their different geographical areas and the meeting adjourned on the 12 with a great speech delivered by Julio Estorino in representation of the Cuban Municipalities in Exile. It was a moving speech that made me realize that I was in the same City, Tampa, where José Martí also had spoken to other previous Cuban exiles.

For the presidential elections of 1980 we formed in New Orleans a group called "Hispanic Group pro-Ronald Reagan." This group was totally separated from the Louisiana Republican Party. We contributed to Ronald Reagan victory by making announcements on KGLA Radio at $8.50 each spot and in November 1, 1980 I paid KGLA Radio the amount of $297.50.

After the November 4th elections of 1980, the Junta Patriótica Cubana (Cuban Patriotic Junta) of which I was the Delegate in Louisiana called for a Thanksgiving Mass to be held on Thursday, November 27 at Annunciation Church, 1221 Mandeville Street.

The purpose of this Mass was to thank God for the victory of Ronald Reagan, ask God to guide President Reagan and to help him restore peace in Central America. God heard our prayers and granted us much more: we witnessed the implosion of the evil Soviet Empire. The Mass was celebrated by Father Pedro Núñez and was a success.

By 1981, a very active leftist group was CISPES (Committee in Solidarity with the People of El Salvador) located at 2714 Banks St., New Orleans, LA., 70119. It is of particular interest the address above-mentioned, which happened to be the same as the new address of People's Bookstore (Librería del Pueblo) a very active pro-Castro organization in New Orleans. I managed to get listed in their mailing list and in that way I kept informed of their activities. Their newsletter was coming with forwarding address at: Hope House, Inc., 916 St. Andrews St., New Orleans, LA 70130, and they were asking to send contributions to CISPES c/o Sister Gay Redmond. Also mentioned in their newsletter was Sister Cynthia Sabatier.

On March 21, 1981, CISPES convoked a Memorial Mass for the occasion of the first anniversary of the assassination of Bishop Oscar Romero, of El Salvador. The Mass took place on Saturday March 21, 1981 at the Sisters of St. Joseph Provincialate, 1200 Mirabeau Avenue (off St. Bernard Ave.) The Major celebrant was Bishop Nicholas D'Antonio.

I want the reader to understand my situation, after 11 years of education at the Catholic School Belén in Cuba, I was a fervent Catholic, but in Buenos Aires I had seen how the Communist were infiltrating the churches, including the Catholic Church not only with Communist agents but also with useful idiots that paved the way for the split of their followers. In Argentina I even had met a couple that when talking politics they assured me that they considered themselves "Catholic-Communists".

At the beginning of January 1981 I had an encounter with Bishop D'Antonio, I had been approached by several Cubans and Latin American parishioners of Christ the King Church in Terrytown, Louisiana who were appalled by a sermon delivered at a Sunday Mass by visiting Bishop D'Antonio. According to them Bishop D'Antonio was openly praising the guerrillas of the Farabundo Martí National Front and at the same time launching a virulent attack against the armed forces of El Salvador. We called for a meeting of some anti-Castro activists in the area with Father Pedro Núñez of Christ the King Church, Padre Núñez obliged setting a meeting with Bishop D'Antonio and us.

The meeting was held at Christ the King Church and several women expressed their disagreement with Bishop D'Antonio's message and told him that if he wanted to do politics he should create his own political party but not do it from the pulpit. Bishop D'Antonio was sitting, looking at his watch with a dull face, listening to their words. When my turn to speak came up I told Bishop D'Antonio:

> *"You are a Bishop of the Catholic Church who follows the principles of Jesus Christ who preached love, not hate, and you come here, to this Church to preach hate. I don't blame you if you want to praise the Communist guerrillas, I acknowledge your right 'as a person' to do so, but what I find very disappointing is your message 'as a Bishop', full of hate, against the Armed Forces of El Salvador. Those soldiers are also sons of God and they deserve your love and not your hate. I cannot believe that a Bishop of the Catholic Church, a Church so persecuted by the Communists could be closer to Satan than to God".*

A few minutes later Bishop D'Antonio looked at his watch and adjourned the meeting. When I confronted Bishop D'Antonio, I already knew about his feelings and ideology. I had been informed that while he was doing the same preaching in Honduras, one day the military authorities had taken him from his Church to the airport and expelled him from Honduras due to his pro-Communist activities. At the airport Bishop D'Antonio confronted the military officer who was expelling him and inquired about his clothes and other personal items. The military officer had answered: *"Your personal items will be sent to you in the next plane but you leave in this one."*

Eventually the Catholic Church transferred him to Florida where he became Vicar for Latin America. In 1987 Monsignor Nicholas D'Antonio moved the 300 members National Conference of Catholic Bishops to adopt a blunt statement criticizing U.S. support of the contra rebels in Nicaragua. Monsignor D'Antonio was confronted by New Orleans Bishop Philip Hannan and Cardinal Bernard Law of Boston, unfortunately for the Catholic Church Monsignor Nicholas D'Antonio convinced the majority of Catholic Bishops in support of the statement in favor of the Communist Nicaraguan forces of Daniel Ortega.[191] The damage that proCommunists like Nicholas D'Antonio have done to the Catholic Church will eventually be recorded by History during future generations.

But this was one of a few incidents that I encountered with members of my Church who were betraying Jesus' ideas. One day, passing in front of my store on Magazine Street was the Hispanic priest in charge of a nearby Catholic Church. We started to chat and I asked him why his Church was renting his grounds to the "Librería del Pueblo" a pro-Communist bookstore, then located one block away from my store. I was feeling bad that the Communist could organize dances there, on Church grounds, and collect money for their lefties activities. The Catholic priest response shocked me: *"We need the money."* I could not believe what I was hearing, young Cubans were being assassinated in Cuba yelling to the Communist assassins *"Viva Cristo Rey"* (*"Long live Christ the King"*) and this priest was giving this cynical answer to me. I remember that I looked him in the eyes and responded: *"if what you need is money you better open a brothel in your Church and I am sure that you can make a lot more money."*

On another occasion I was at the store on Decatur Street and my wife at the store on Magazine Street when each one of us did something unaware that the other was doing the same thing. There was a Catholic nun that was always visiting us and portraying the people with money as exploiters. Her name was Sister Leonila who was always spreading hate against the rich people. She had forgotten the tenth commandment. Well, that day she came first to the store on Decatur Street and started her conversation in her usual way but that day I couldn't take it anymore, I took her by her shoulders and put her out of the store telling her that I didn't want to see her anymore. At night time, while eating dinner at our house, I found out that after our confrontation in Decatur Street, Sister Leonila had gone to the store in Magazine Street preaching the same hate against the people with money and my wife had reacted in the same way putting her on the sidewalk out of the store.

To me was very heartbreaking to watch the infiltration inside the Catholic Church. I had known very nice Catholic priests. I had attended school at Belén School, a Jesuit School, for eleven years. I had seen how Castro had put inside the "Covadonga" ship many of the good priests that I had met in Cuba, sending them into exile to Spain. I also was concern because of the big division among the ranks of the Catholic Church in between real Catholics and proCommunist dissenters. The Communist infiltration did not stop with the Catholic Church they were doing the same thing with the Baptists, Episcopalians, etc.

One of those great Cuban Catholic priest visited New Orleans to speak to the Cuban community. I had the opportunity to introduce him at the meeting attended by hundreds of Cubans and to deliver a speech at the gathering. His name was Father Ismael Testé. Father Testé was an exemplary Catholic priest who was the founder in Cuba of "Ciudad de los Niños"("Boy's Town") where he educated thousands of Cuban children who also received training to work in different areas. He had done a great job until Fidel Castro put his eyes in "Boy's Town". Castro had his own ideas about children, he did not want them, educated at "Boy's Town" learning the teachings of Jesus Christ, he wanted the children to become "Pioneros"[181] and murderers like Che Guevara. Castro wanted to indoctrinate the children in the teachings of Karl Marx, Lenin and Stalin. Castro tried to entrap Father Testé utilizing a Communist woman who was going to try to frame him. Father Testé was appraised of Castro's plans and managed to escape from Cuba. Now he had come to speak in New Orleans.

After the meeting we went to eat doughnuts and coffee at the Café Dumonde. While there Father Testé told me: *"Bringuier, as a priest I have to pardon the Communists but it is better to pardon them after they are dead."* He told me how much he had suffered thinking in the poor boys at "Boy's Town" who now were indoctrinated with hate and not with the love of Jesus Christ and how Jesus had spoken about those who victimize children. Father Testé wanted children growing up with love to Jesus, Fidel Castro wanted children to grow up to become new Lee Harvey Oswalds.

On December 27, 1981, The Times Picayune published the following:

Anti-communists protesters greet cruise ship passengers.
Passengers embarking on a Christmas holiday cruise
Saturday afternoon aboard the Russian cruise ship M.V Odessa
got a little more than they had bargained for.

---

[181] Pioneers, atheist youth groups of the Communist government.

As they drove up to the riverfront area in cabs, tour buses or cars to board the vessel, they were greeted at the corner of Julia and South Front Streets by a small but vocal group staging an anti-communist rally in support of Poland's Solidarity faction.

The group predominantly Hispanic people called itself "Junta de Exilados de Louisiana."

The protesters carried placards stating "Solidarity with Solidarity," "Freedom for Poland" and various pleas criticizing Fidel Castro and alleged communist movements throughout Latin America.

Carlos Bringuier, a long-time anti-Castro figure in New Orleans, told the assemblage, "We are a free people who prefer to live in a free land other that our own rather than be slaves under communism."

During the protest, some participants heckled passengers en route to the wharf area, shouting toward open car windows. "Don't help the Russians" or "Stop supporting the Russians." There were no incidents.

Two Russian flags were burned.

On January 1, 1982 it was announce that the M.V. Odessa, a Russian cruise ship based in the port of New Orleans had cancelled his schedule 19-day cruise to Los Angeles. The "Odessa" was allowed to dock in New Orleans and discharge its U.S. passengers but when it leaves New Orleans it will not be allowed to return to the United States because President Reagan's sanctions against the Soviet Union.[182]

Undoubtedly I was *in God's hands* when I organized the demonstration against the "Odessa" and in support of Poland's Solidarity faction. It was my idea. No CIA or FBI agents told us, moved us or influenced us to go ahead with that demonstration just "before" Reagan's actions which I was unaware of. It was another great victory.

In 1959 The United States Congress passed a Joint Resolution providing for the designation of the third week of July as "Captive Nations Week." In 1959 there were 28 captive nations by 1986 there were 49. Luckily and thanks to millions of freedom fighters, today (2013) there are only a handful. When I am finishing this book, dark clouds show the

---

[182] The Times Picayune, January 1, 1982, Section 1, page 14.

increasing peril that the world is confronting now to become a "Captive World."

July 26, 1986 was not a day of exception in our struggle. Alton Ochsner, Jr., M.D. was a giant of a civic leader in New Orleans and every year he organized the "Captive Nations Week" with different activities. I was honored to have met Alton Ochsner, Jr., who I considered my good friend, and who, like his father, always supported the anti-Castro position. During several years he invited me to appear with him, during "Captive Nations Week" in different local radio stations to deliver our message of solidarity and hope to those oppressed by Communism. A newsman that was always happy to see us was Joseph Culotta, from WTIX-Radio.

On Saturday July 26, 1986 we held a massive rally sponsored by the Caribbean Commission and the John Birch Society. The program was announced as follow:

Master of Ceremony	*Mr. Jorge Maspons*
The Star Spangled Banner	*Mr. Gerald E. Marshall*
Invocation	*Rev. Peter Newman*
	"Our Lady Queen of Vietnam"
What is Captive Nations Week all about?	*Mr. Rolland A. Neve*
And year of capture	*Mrs. Bethsy Pizarro*
	"Club de Profesionales Cubanos"
Eulogy to the Nicaraguan Freedom Fighters .	*Dr. Alton Ochsner, Jr.*
	Chairman Caribbean Commission
Speaker for/from Vietnam	*Mr. Kang Dangi*
The National United Front For the Liberation of Vietnam	
Let there be peace on earth	*Mr. Gerald E. Marshall*
Speaker for/from Nicaragua	*Carlos Sampson*
Introduction of Principal Speaker	*Mr. Jorge Maspons*
Principal Speaker	*Dr. Carlos Bringuier*
Closing Remarks	*Mr. Leo P. Champagne, Sr.*
God Bless America	*Mr. Gerald E. Marshall*

Benediction ....Re. David Mai
Westbank Vietnamese
Baptist Church

When Oliver Stone was filming his movie JFK he went to New Orleans to do part of his job. He contacted me because he wanted an interview. I agreed and went to his hotel early one morning.

At my arrival the one who opened the door of the hotel room was movie actor Kevin Costner and I waited for a few minutes sitting in a chair. Apparently Costner and Stone had finished taking a shower. I didn't have any predisposition against them but I felt some wrong electricity going on between them. Stone explained his movie to me and when he finished I was disturbed by what I had heard and told him that his movie was going to be based on lies and not in the truth. Stone responded that I would have to consider that what he was filming was a "movie" not a "documentary", and that gave him the license to "fictionalize."

I told Oliver Stone that with that type of movie he was going to do a disservice to history and to this country, that he will be inflicting serious mental damage to mainly young people who will grow up thinking that those "fictionalized" parts were "true history." At that time I could not foresee that this same Oliver Stone talking to me at that moment, years later was going to go to Cuba to film a "documentary": "Comandante" in which he deposited all his love for a sadistic criminal like Dictator Fidel Castro. I told Kevin Costner that it was pitiful that he would be trying to portrait a drunkard, corrupt and demented Jim Garrison as a decent man because that was an impossible mission. I left disappointed because these two persons, Stone and Costner, were ready to ambush the truth and present a science fiction B movie as something real. When I was leaving Kevin Costner came running after me and followed me to the elevator asking me for things that I could do to help them. My elevator went down and that was the last time that I saw Kevin Costner in person.

After some months I was contacted by an oriental person working in the movie and we were discussing what amount of money I would be willing to receive to cooperate with the movie. I told him: *"If you want me to cooperate I would have to be paid the same amount that you are paying Jim Garrison and it would be a great deal for you, because he is lying and I would be telling the truth." The oriental never answered me. My names is in the credits of "JFK" but I never received one penny.*

Eventually the movie proved to be a bomb but without any questions, damaged a lot of young people's minds. Only the faithful liberal press and "useful idiots" pseudo intellectuals gave praise to such fraudulent movie. Since that day the artistic and personal lives of Oliver Stone and Kevin Costner had gone down the tube. On August 2005 it was published in a dispatch from the associated press how low Oliver Stone had descended:

> *"**Los Angeles**—Oscar winning director **Oliver Stone** has pleaded no contest to a misdemeanor possession of marijuana while driving charge stemming from a police checkpoint stop.*
>
> *Stone's attorney entered the plea for his client Wednesday in Beverly Hill Superior Court, according to a spokeswoman for the Los Angeles County District Attorney's office.*
>
> *The director, who won Academy Awards for Platoon and Born on the Fourth of July, was not in court.*
>
> *Stone, 58, was arrested at a drunk driving checkpoint on May 27. He paid a $100.00 fine and court assessments, a court representative said.*
>
> *In 1999, Stone pleaded guilty to a misdemeanor marijuana possession charge and driving under the influence.*[183]

Eventually Oliver Stone became an unofficial spokesman for Dictator Fidel Castro and more recently he had been associated with "the lost link between the humans and the monkeys" Dictator Hugo Chávez from Venezuela. It is unfortunately that we don't have a House Committee on Un-American Activities.

On August 1989 the ex-Secretary of the Interior Ministry, José Abrahantes, the same one who had the argument with me in 1959 when his parents occupied my parents' house in Alta Habana, was going through difficult times. The corrupt Dictatorship of Fidel Castro had been involved in trafficking rugs and laundering money for the Mafia, now they were confronted with reality and reality had caught up with them. The United States government had proof of their involvement and

---

[183] Houston Chronicle, Friday August 12, 2005, Page A2.

there was a sealed indictment in Florida against Raúl Castro. As they did with the assassination of President Kennedy when they carried on the assassination of Oswald to divert the attention, now they had decided to divert the attention of the international authorities and put the blame in different figures of the government. Among them were General Arnaldo Ochoa, the brothers De la Guardia and José Abrahantes. On August 28, 1989 the official paper of the Revolutionary government announced that the Cuban Attorney General was asking 20 years in jail for Abrahantes. General Ochoa and one of the De la Guardia brothers were assassinated by a Castro's execution squad. José Abrahantes, former Castro's right hand man, was sentenced to 20 years in jail but he didn't serve his whole sentence, suddenly he suffered a "heart attack". I had been told that José Abrahantes was assassinated by Castro's orders while Abrahantes was in jail by using with him the method of a "salt shot" which produced a "heart attack", one of Castro's favorite methods to assassinate opponents. José Abrahantes knew too much and Castro could not allow him to live. These sentences differ completely of the treatment given to the case of Rolando Cubela, "AMLASH".

On June 27, 1991, I wrote the following letter to the editor of The Times Picayune:

Editor
The Times Picayune
3800 Howard Avenue New Orleans, La. 70140

Sir:
    I would like to take exception to the letter printed in your issue of June 15, signed by Jay C. Albarado, a member of the Orleans Parish Grand Jury at the time that Jim Garrison was District Attorney.
    As a witness to the so-called "Garrison Investigation" I have to agree with attorney F. Irving Diamond's statement. "I don't think he (Garrison) had any case: I think he knew he didn't have any case." Also I would have to agree with Iris Kelso and her opinion about how Oliver Stone was handling his movie.
    On the other hand I have to agree with Mr. Albarado in regard to the point that Garrison didn't acted alone. Yes, Mr. Albarado, like it happened in Germany during the Hitler era,

and in Cuba with Castro, an egotist man is not able to achieve so much power without the help of other people. Some were well intentioned people duped by the charisma of a leader that attract them in a Freudian way, some others are fellow travelers that join the wagon to fulfill their own ideological goals.

I know how the Jewish people had to be feeling when they were brought to gas chambers and at the same time some well-intentioned citizens of the Third Reich were taken over by the charisma of Adolf Hitler. Yes Mr. Albarado, history teaches us that dupes had existed during all eras, even during the Garrison's reign of terror.

In 1967, famous reporter Oriana Fallaci predicted to me that one day a movie will be made about Garrison and in it he would be portrayed either as a hero or as a clown, all depending in the outcome of Shaw's trial. I am sorry Oriana but you were wrong, now the villains are heroes and the heroes are villains.

But maybe we are not talking about the same Jim Garrison. The Garrison that I met was:

1) *One that brought several leftists to help him in his case. Even a person who was expelled from the State Department in 1948 because of his known associations with agents of the Soviet Union.*
2) *One who prostituted his office to achieve personal recognition.*
3) *One who had a complete disregard for the truth ignoring any fact that didn't help the case that was built for him.*

I could relay numerous instances where in my opinion Garrison violated some people's civil rights, even one when I was called as a translator but it will make this too long.

At that time I expected Garrison to end up in jail but I was too young and too naïve. How could I have expected the U.S. Attorney General to prosecute Jim Garrison for his activities when the person that occupied that post at that time was none other than Ramsey Clark, the same Ramsey Clark that just recently tried to stop our national hero Gen. Norman Schwarzkopf from marching through the streets of New York.

As far as I know three persons died as the result of Garrison's persecution: Clay Shaw, David Ferrie and a little baby girl, my own, (born dead who never had the opportunity to enjoy life.) Homicide is defined as the killing of a human being by another, whether by intention or not, and in my opinion those three persons were killed by Garrison's "investigation."

Now Oliver Stone could try to rewrite history and portrait to us the Garrison that is not. It is his right no matter the fact that he is wrong. What it is a crime is to be cynical to the point to accept that the end justify the means and what it is worst is to use fiction in regard to something so important in US history as the assassination of JFK. In my opinion the movie will be a "SCUD" movie, it will miss the point, and it will be inspired by the spirit of Ho Chi Minh.

Castro, Arafat and Sadam Hussein will love the movie but there is no question in my mind that it will be a travesty of history.

Sincerely.
Carlos J. Bringuier

As you can expect The Times Picayune never published this letter.

On Saturday. January 29, 1994, I presented my book "Operación Judas" at the offices of Ediciones Universal who published it. The person in charge of the presentation was Cuban newsman Agustín Tamargo, the same one that I had met for the first time in January 1, 1959 at the Cuban Embassy in Buenos Aires. A nice group of Cubans gathered there, among them I recognized a face that recently I had seen in a book purchased by me (another of the coincidences in my life).

When the questions and answers period ended, the owner of that face approached me asking if I knew who he was. I told him that he was Félix Rodríguez, the man who had captured Che Guevara in Bolivia. Félix congratulated me for my book and told me that I can rest assured that what I wrote there was the truth, that he had been a friend of Bobby Kennedy and he knew what he was saying. I told him that I envy him for having had the opportunity to capture Che Guevara, to having seeing Che Guevara pleading for his life and watching him die.

During these years there was another incident, very important, that could be turn into another book: The assassination of Martin Luther King, Jr. which occurred on April 4, 1968 was another way for Fidel Castro to move his pawns to bring a black and red revolution into the United States of America.

Martin Luther King Jr., had been surrounded by Communist agents who had tried to gain him to Communism but they never achieved that. Martin Luther King Jr., principal goal was to get equal rights for the black people not to bring a Communist takeover of the United States and Castro never forgave him for that. The Spartacist League, created and financed by Fidel Castro portrayed Dr. King in their pamphlets as a lackey of the white people [184]

Fidel Castro's ambition of taking over the African continent and to mobilize the black people into a revolution to overthrow the government of the United States confronted the problem that Dr. Martin Luther King Jr., was against his plans.

In August 1967 the Soviet Union Centre decided to replace Dr. King with a more radical leader and approved a plan by the deputy head of Service A, Yuri Modin to discredit King portraying him as an "Uncle Tom".[185] Fidel Castro had been leading the battle against King. Dr. King never accepted Castro's invitations to visit Cuba and Castro directed his weapons against Dr. King. Sometimes he used black Americans residing in Cuba like Robert F. Williams, a National Sponsor of the Fair Play for Cuba Committee[186] who was publishing there "The Crusader" a monthly newsletter in English been sent to the blacks and Communists in the USA. In "The Crusader" they were showing the blacks in the USA as slaves in the white kingdom.[187] Dr. Martin Luther King, Jr., had become expendable.

On November 22, 1963 Lee Harvey Oswald, with his three shots erased Fidel Castro's most dangerous enemy. Then the one who occupied that place of more dangerous enemy was Robert F. Kennedy. Bobby

---

[184] The Joint Legislative Committee on Un-American Activities, State of Louisiana Report No.9. July 14, 1967, page 51.

[185] "The Mitrokhin Archive", by Christopher Andrew and Vasili Mitrokhin, page 237.

[186] The Joint Legislative Committee on Un-American Activities, State of Louisiana, Report No.5, Part 2, April 13, 1964, page 17.

[187] The Crusader, Vol.34 No.8, May 1963.

Kennedy represented to Fidel Castro the danger of an intelligent man who was going to avenge the assassination of his brother, he could not be allowed to become President of the United States. On June 6, 1968 Sirhan Bishara Sirhan, another Castro's sympathizer took care that Robert F. Kennedy would never reach the Presidency of the United States. In the meantime, Fidel Castro had taken care that on April 4, 1968 his enemy inside the Negro movement in the United States, the one who never accepted his invitations to go to Cuba and embrace him, Dr. Martin Luther King, Jr., was also assassinated paving the way for the sending of 40,000 troops by Fidel Castro trying to conquer the African continent and trying to conquer the Negro movement in the United States of America.

CHAPTER XIII

MIAMI, NEW ORLEANS, ALABAMA (1995-2005)

On March 29, 1998 the El Nuevo Herald published a headline stating: **Pentagon: *Cuba is not a threat***, which moved me to write a letter to the editor accusing the Pentagon of idiotism. What I ignored at the time was that the Pentagon report was written by none other than Ana Belén Montes, known as the "Queen of Cuba" by her colleagues at the Defense Intelligence Agency (DIA) who finally was arrested as a Castro's spy on Friday September 21, 2001.

Coincidently the FBI's Miami field office arrested the 'Wasp' network on September 1998. The "Wasp" network was composed of Castro's spies working inside the United States against our government.

In January 10, 2000, moved by a sad incident of life I wrote the following letter to The Times Picayune:

Dear Editor:

It is sad to write a letter about a recently deceased person but when that person was not an ordinary person, when that person was a giant in any field he participated in, when that person was the Light of Hope for millions of people suffering oppression in the Captive Nations, then we have to put aside our sadness and realize that live goes on.

Dr. Alton Ochsner, Jr., was such a person. Anyone who new him has to remember him for his kindness, for his love for humanity but most of all for his love for freedom and for the United States of America.

In my name and in the name of all those that were born in the Captive Nations I will like to express our condolences to his family. If this City one day wants to erect a monument to Freedom there is no better choice than Alton Ochsner, Jr., who wanted freedom for humanity, without any distinction of race, gender or ideas. A good person has passed away.

The Times Picayune was kind enough and published my letter. A few days later I received the following letter:

Dearest Carlos,

I cannot thank you too much for the letter you wrote about Abby, He was so dear to us and we too appreciate all that he did for others and his love for his fellow man. Thank you and God Bless.

Barbara Ochsner
January 21, 2000

On January 13, 2000 my wife underwent surgery for breast cancer. The surgeon was Dr. David Treen, Jr., and thanks to God the surgery was perfect and after some months of radiation treatment my wife survived.

On April 25, 2000, fed up with the liberal bias of The Times Picayune I sent them the following letter:

Dear Editor:

For several weeks The Times Picayune has been engaged in a campaign to trash the Cuban-Americans living in this country. Seldom there have been a day where your paper has not brought a writer to smear us, been this writer from Arizona, Atlanta or New Orleans.

After the infamous violation of the rights of the Gonzalez family in Miami, orchestrated by Castro, Clinton and Reno, where they also violated the sacred right of Freedom of the Press,

I was expecting that you will have the minimum decorum and condemn such atrocity. But no, you came out today with an editorial justifying "Castro-Clinton-Reno" actions in Miami.

I came to the City of New Orleans, 39 years ago believing that the United States was a bastion of freedom and due process of law. My ancestors thought the same when they emigrated here in the 1870's. Now I feel betrayed, not by the American people, but by an amoral politician who occupy the Presidency of the United States.

As I consider that for years your editorial line have been anti Cuban-Americans, either by a racist misconception of reality or by differences in ideologies I have decided to terminate my subscription to your newspaper because I don't want your venom to infect my home. I hope that more freedom loving people will have the dignity of doing likewise.

Sincerely,
Carlos J. Bringuier

On March 1, 2002 I resigned my job at Radio Shack and became a retiree. We had planned to move to Fairhope, Alabama and buy our son's house which we did and we enjoyed the surroundings for three beautiful years.

While living in Alabama I was contacted by a German newsman, Wilfried Huismann, who was making a documentary about JFK's assassination. He went with his crew to Fairhope and he did the interview. I was impressed with Huismann because he appeared to me as a person searching for the truth. In my mind he was 180 degrees from Oliver Stone. My main concern was that in that field if you are not working against the United States, against democracy, you have almost no chance to come out in the winning side in Hollywood or with the liberal press. I have noticed that almost every time that an actor or writer come out shinning as a star eventually he/she will show his/her true colors to the left of the truth.

By the end of 2004, our daughter María Ellzey had convinced us to move close to her in The Woodlands, Texas. On January 14, 2005 we bought our new home in The Woodlands.

CHAPTER XIV

＊━━◆◆◆━━＊

THE WOODLANDS, TEXAS (2005-PRESENT)

On March 21, 2006 I wrote the following letter to President George W. Bush:

Hon. President George W. Bush
The White House
1600 Pennsylvania Avenue SW
Washington, D.C. 20500

Honorable President Bush:

I am writing this letter with a heavy heart. I voted for you in the last 2 presidential elections and I believe you have the best intentions for the American people and the whole world.

But you inherited a cancer named Fidel Castro and that cancer had done metastasis and has now spread to Bolivia, Argentina, Uruguay and Venezuela. Yesterday I was appalled hearing the vulgar insults against you spoken by Mr. Hugo Chávez.

Years ago my wife suffered breast cancer. It was diagnosed at the right time, surgery was done followed by radiation and today she is a healthy person. There are moments when we have to decide if we are going to do surgery or not. We took the right decision. I pray to God you do likewise.

American history showed me what meant "Remember the Alamo", "Remember the Maine" and "Remember Pearl Harbor." Now it have come the time to "Remember Kennedy". In January of this year laureate German newsman Wilfried Huismann produced a documentary "Rendezvous with Death" which clearly prove Fidel Castro's participation in the assassination of President John F. Kennedy. The axis Cuba-Venezuela-Iran is a very dangerous situation for the United States, the world and our descendants. Waiting for Castro to die of natural causes will be disastrous for us. The time has come to indict Fidel Castro for the assassination of John F. Kennedy. When the facts are shown to the American people, public opinion will be in our side. After Castro's demise this hemisphere will return to a peaceful place to live. It's your decision. I pray God you will do what it is right.

Respectfully,
Carlos J. Bringuier

Unfortunately President George W. Bush added his name to the long list of American Presidents unwilling to risk their lives confronting the Beast of the Caribbean. I hope I will never have to see George W. Bush arrested by a Communist government in the United States.

In September of 2005 Pochi and I took a 21 days trip to Spain. One of the places we visited was the city of Guadalupe, Cáceres province, a little west of Madrid were we met 3 third cousins. We had the opportunity to visit the home where my grandfather, Don Alonso Expósito, was born. I mentioned to almost everybody that I met there that what impressed me the most was how I was witnessing the "Reconquista"[188] in reverse. I could very clearly see how the Muslims were invading Spain and I had to agree with the feelings of Italian news lady, Oriana Fallaci that the world is going to be taken over by the Muslims.

A couple of years after our return from Spain one of my granddaughters, Lauren, insisted that I should find a job and she informed me that Border Books, in Market Square was looking for new booksellers. On May 20, 2007, I was interviewed by David Glover,

---

[188] Reconquista was when the Spaniards reconquered Spain from the Muslims.

Manager of that store and on May 22, 2007, I started working there as a bookseller. I cannot thanks Lauren much enough because I did found there a real heaven of work environment.

But right, for those who had claimed that the CIA was paying me $25,000 a month in 1963 (more than $100,000 in 2007's dollars) it would look strange that at 73 years of age I was going to accept a full time job, standing 7 or 8 hours a day, five days a week. For me it was more a matter of pride. The liberals kept spreading the word that the work situation was terrible, that people was losing their jobs and here I was 73 years old coming back to join the work force.

During these years I have seen the deterioration in the health of Dictator Fidel Castro and how he eventually decided to move aside and let his brother Raúl become the new Dictator. During decades it had been publicized all the extravagances and the squandering incurred by Fidel Castro during his dictatorship. It has been publicized his enrichment while the Cuban people starve.

But the liberal press, the same one that attacked Reagan and Bush while applauding Jimmy Carter and Bill Clinton, typically ignored those facts and instead kept attacking the embargo against Cuba established by John F. Kennedy without realizing that what is really hurting the Cuban people is the embargo implanted against them by Fidel and Raúl Castro.

Castro's cancer had suffered metastases and had already spread to Venezuela, Brazil, Chile, Nicaragua, Bolivia, Ecuador and Argentina. The Republican Party of the USA had become not the Party of Ronald Reagan but an amorphous entity moving away from the Conservative ideas. The Democratic Party has moved more to the left and Liberalism have been left behind to embrace a new form of Socialistic Fascism.

No matter the attacks of the Liberal press. They react against the interference in the lives of Barack Hussein Obama's daughters but for them it is fair to attack Sarah Palin by attacking her daughter. That same Liberal press attacks Sarah Palin accusing her of lack of experience to occupy the Presidency of the United States but they remains silent about the immoral behavior of President Bill Clinton with Monica Lewinsky inside the White House. The liberal press attacks Sarah Palin for writing in her hand some notes at a Tea Party conference but it is OK for Barack Hussein Obama to use the teleprompter to look good as a speaker.

Luckily for the world is that the United States of America is a great Country and if this Nation was able to survive the four years of Castro's friend Jimmy Carter and the eight years of Bill Clinton, I am sure that a new young Teddy Roosevelt will emerge from the ashes of the Republican Party and guide the world to a better future than the neo-socialist-fascists in the Democratic Party are trying to implant in order to destroy this Country and bring a Socialist World Government Tyranny.

In the meantime Fidel Castro has escaped to be indicted for the assassination of President John F. Kennedy, no matter the fact of all the credible and irrefutable evidence showing him as the mastermind of such evil act. The "Masters of Deceit", as John Edgar Hoover called them, keep lying to the American people and to the world.

CHAPTER XV

━━◦◦◦◦◦◦━━

COMMERCIAL ACTIVITIES

My first job in New Orleans was working for two days with the "California Redwood Produce Co.," owned by Mr. L. C. Levy, My income for those 2 days of work was $20.00.

Around April 1ˢᵗ 1961, I started working as a salesperson at Macy's Discount House, 714 Canal Street, New Orleans, La. Owner: Mr. Abe Glazer. Starting salary $40.00 per week (66 hours a week).

After New Year's Day 1962, Mr. Glazer closed the store at 714 Canal and opened another at 704 Canal Street. The new store had the name Ward's Discount House. I remained as a salesperson.

Around the middle of March 1962 I realized that it was good business selling to the merchant seamen arriving at the Port of New Orleans and I made a deal with Mr. Glazer who supplied me with clothes in consignment and on a Sunday morning I visited the first ship, a Greek one, by the name of "Protoclitos."

I had a good day of selling and in April 1962 I quit my job and my brother-in-law Rolando Peláez did likewise. We started peddling in the riverfront having some good days and some very bad ones.

On October 1, 1962 we started working as co-Managers of a new store, "Casa Roca", located at 107 Decatur Street. The owner of the store was Mr. Shepard (Shep) Zitler.

Around July 1964 I quit the work at "Casa Roca" and again went back to peddling in the riverfront.

On September 15, 1964, I opened my own store "Casa Cuba" at 115
½ Decatur Street. My wife thought that I was crazy, we did not have
any money but I had a lot of confidence in myself and I was foreseen a
bright future for us. The capital invested in the opening of "Casa Cuba"
was $300.00 which I got as a result of a piece of jewelry that my sister
Totó had brought from Cuba. She offered to me and I pawned it on a
Rampart Street pawn shop. The furniture at the store was free because it
was the result of me picking it up from the street, furniture thrown away
by merchants on Canal Street.

In the way that I started operating "Casa Cuba" was obtaining
merchandise in consignment from wholesalers, selling it, paying back the
wholesaler and getting more merchandise in consignment. When I was
able to put aside enough money then I was buying (not in consignment)
the merchandise from the wholesaler, in which way I obtained a larger
profit. Capitalism 101.

Calculators were very expensive and out of my reach and for that
reason I had to keep in my brain the cost of every piece of merchandise
and at night time, after closing, figure out my profit. For me the more
important part was not how much I sold but how much was my profit, in
that way I could determine how much of that profit would remain in the
business and how much I could use for myself. From the first day "Casa
Cuba" was a profitable business, I could not afford to be otherwise.

The first shipment of blue jeans that I placed with H. D. Lee, Co.,
was for $295.00 and I had to pay it COD because I was not able to
obtain credit from companies outside New Orleans. At the time the
salesman of H. D. Lee Co., was a very nice and patriotic American
Wesley Younger who all the time tried to help me as much as he could.
I would like to mention that years later H. D. Lee, Co., was selling me
over $30,000 a month to be paid in 30 days. I really could write a book
about my experiences in business, but this could give you an idea of how
I started and how I was *in God's hands.*

When my lease for 1 year was going to terminate and the owner
of the building had told me that he was not going to renew the lease,
another indication that I was *in God's hands* happened to me. I had a
Jewish business neighbor, Jules Greemberg who had a business named
"Greenberg's Costumes" at 111 Decatur Street. Mr. Greemberg asked me
to see him at his store and told me: *"Carlos, I am moving to a new building
on Rampart Street, there have been some merchants around here who have*

come to ask me to transfer the lease on the building to them, but I consider that you are the most honest person around here and I prefer, that if you like to have the building you take over my lease".

I don't have to tell you how I felt. I bought his furniture for $500.00 and went to the Real Estate Company of Leo Fellman and Co., and signed the transfer of the lease to my name. Then I moved "Casa Cuba" to its new location, a three stories building at 111 Decatur Street. To those so-called "historians" who keep placing Lee Harvey Oswald at "Casa Cuba" or at 111 Decatur Street, please don't get confused and don't confuse your readers, the store visited by Oswald was "Casa Roca" at 107 Decatur and I was not the owner of "Casa Roca", Mr. Shep Zitler was the owner of that store.

In 1974 I foresaw the downfall of the Port of New Orleans and I bought a building at 2048 Magazine Street just in case that one day I could lose my lease and in that way I had a place to move my merchandise and keep operating from there. The building consisted at the time on two small commercials downstairs, one small room behind the businesses, one apartment at the back and three rooms, a kitchen and a bath upstairs. A barber was the owner of the building.

I did some renovations to the building, using some Cubans friends. Eventually the building was converted to a large commercial in the front; an apartment in the back, and three apartments upstairs, each one with its kitchen and bathroom. I paid for the building $19,900 which I covered with a small down payment and a monthly mortgage of $115.00. When I sold that building the whole ground floor was a grocery store "Casa Cuba", which I eventually opened there, and the three upstairs apartments, each one rented for $200.00 per month. I sold the grocery to a Vietnamese couple who also bought the building. I did owner finance and the price of the building was $100,000. Capitalism 101.

Another thing that helped me was a visit to the store at 111 Decatur Street from a former friend of mine from Tarará Beach, Cuba. One night Fernando Salas walked into the store and embraced me. We had been friends at Tarará and he was one of the veterans of Brigade 2506. Now, Fernando had opened a business in Miami, "American Distributor and Book Sales, Inc.," and was distributing Spanish publications in the United States. Fernando was asking me to represent his company in the New Orleans area and distribute his magazines. Fernando explained that there was a lady distributing his magazines and she wanted to carry only four of them: Vanidades, Buenhogar (Good housekeeping), Cosmopolitan and Selecciones (Reader's Digest). Fernando needed to distribute more than thirty different ones. He then told me the name of the lady, Milagros Suárez, and I knew her. Mrs. Suárez was a widow and she had been bringing me those 4 magazines. I turned down Fernando's offer telling him that I would not take Mrs. Suárez's business away from her. Next day, Fernando showed up again, this time with Mrs. Suárez at his side. Mrs. Suárez told me that she could not do the work requested by Fernando, she had decided to resign as representative in New Orleans and that as somebody else would be taking over the distribution of the magazines, she knew me and she preferred that I was the one who continue with the business. It was something done, she was out, and as Mr. Greemberg before, she preferred me than others who wanted the distribution. I started a long relationship with "American Distributors Magazines, Inc.," that lasted for many years.

I foresaw the coming changes of the Port of New Orleans affecting my business. I knew that containerized ships would be taking the place over regular ships, which means less seamen aboard and shorter stays in port. As I had started without money, I had been operating like a centrifuge and I had to slow down the centrifuge in order to be able to get out without any harm. Capitalism 101. That was the main reason for me to buy the building at 2048 Magazine Street.

In 1979 I started my career in Real Estate working as an Agent with Stan Weber and Associates. For four consecutive years I was a member of the "Million Dollar Club"; I took and passed my exams as a Broker and GRI (Graduate of Realtor Institute) and as the Real Estate company was not handling the sale of businesses I opened my own company: "Best Business Consultants; Inc.," Capitalism 101.

As in 1984 I had opened a Grocery store at 2048 Magazine Street and the business was going so well, I quit Real Estate and dedicated my time to the Grocery store. That Grocery store "Casa Cuba" was a real moneymaker. Eventually, in 1986, after my wife had been hold up with a gun to her head, we decided to sell the grocery. Business was so good that my wife did not wanted to sell but I convinced her that it was the right time to do that. The store was at its peak and I was concerned that other people would try to open more groceries in the same block. Finally we sold the building and the business to a very nice Vietnamese couple. A year after I had sold the grocery, three more groceries had opened in the same block. My intuition proved to be right.

While owner of the Grocery store I had an incident which I consider one of the nicest things that could have happened to me in my life. At the beginning of our sole ownership, my wife and I were the only workers, with the assistance of one of my tenants, a former Catholic priest by the name of Carlos Catá. As the business kept growing, I put a sign at the front window asking for a cashier. Two ladies applied for the job. One was white the other was black. I gave a test to them and I hired the black lady. Later on she told me that she had been told not to apply for the job because for sure I was going to hire a white person, I told her that she had better qualifications and that that was the reason why I hired her.

We had long hours of conversations during the slow hours of the afternoon and I explained to her how important is for a person to try to improve. That if a person limit her/himself to live from welfare there were many things in life that the person will be missing and will never know about. Her name is Carmilla Moore and she was a good listener and a very good learner. One day she confronted the problem that her young son had contracted meningitis. Carmilla was worried because she could not come to work and when she explained the situation to me I told her that her son was the most important thing at the moment, that she should take care of him and not to worry about anything else, that as long as her son was sick she would continue to receive her full paycheck. When I sold the grocery the new owners kept her for a few months. One day she called me saying that she wanted to ask a favor from me. She was going to get married and she wanted that I would walk her to the officiating pastor at the ceremony. When the day of the wedding arrived my wife and I were the only white persons over there and I walked her very proud of her. Years later she contacted me while I was working in Miami and told me that she had become an executive with a pharmaceutical company and was working in Boston, Massachusetts. She and her husband were making a very good amount of money. As of this writing we keep in touch once in a while. I am very proud of her and satisfied that I did the right thing at the right time.

I would like to mention that I could not have done all the things that I did and achieved in business if it would not have been for the help of my wife who worked side by side with me, and very hard in order to help us.

With the stores on Decatur Street closed (I had opened another store in the second hundred block of Decatur Street) and with the grocery store sold I continued, from the garage in my house, with the distribution of the Spanish magazines. As a business owner I worked very hard, during some years, 15 hours a day seven days a week.

In 1989. In order to obtain medical insurance I filled an application at Radio Shack. I entered as a Manager Trainee working at the store at the Oakwood Mall in Gretna, Louisiana, less than one mile from my house. After six months I was appointed Manager of the Radio Shack at Westwego, Louisiana where I stayed less than a year been then transferred as Manager of the store at Carondelet Street in downtown New Orleans. After several months there, one night the District Manager called saying that he needed me to take over as Manager of the store on Williams Boulevard in Kenner, close to the airport. An emergency had happened when they apparently had discovered a large shortage of inventory at the store and he wanted me to straight the situation there.

I worked at the William Boulevard store for a couple of months and I felt physically burnt out. I resigned and continued with the distribution of the Spanish Magazines which I had been doing all along.

In 1994 I decided to move to Miami, Florida and I got a job as Case Manager with United Home Care Services, Inc. Six months later I was promoted as Supervisor of the Admissions Department. Later on I occupied different other positions like Supervisor of CCE (Community Care for the Elderly), Supervisor of Emergency Services and Supervisor of Fee for Service Services, the three at the same time. But as I was disillusioned with Miami I requested to cease as Supervisor and return to Case Manager, in the meantime that I prepare our return to Terrytown, Louisiana.

In 1998 we returned to our house at 319 Terry Parkway, Terrytown, Louisiana which we have not put for sale while we were exploring Miami. My first job, back in the New Orleans area, was at a Nissan dealership in the Westbank. Then around Christmas of 1998 I started working again with Radio Shack at the Oakwood Mall. I made the District Manager aware that I was not interested in a Management position, I just wanted to work as a salesperson. I was waiting for the right time to retire and my wife be covered by Cobra until she was able to be receive her Medicare. I worked there until March 1, 2002.

I enjoyed three years of retirement in Fairhope, Alabama very close to our son's home. In 2005 our daughter María Ellzey was begging us to move close to her and we sold our house in Fairhope and in January 14 bought a house in The Woodlands, Texas.

In 2007, my granddaughter Lauren thought that it was going to be good for me to return to work and she asked me to apply at Border Books. I was going to be more productive if I return to the labor force. It was a challenge to me and I would be challenging the system. I was 73 years old, a lot of liberals were shouting that the economy was bad and I wanted to find out myself if they were telling the truth or just lying.

I found three opportunities for work. The one that attracted me the most was with Border Books on Market Street in The Woodlands just 7 miles from my driveway. I had already undergone a drug test from another employer at 2:00 p.m. and I was going to be assigned in charge of a department in a Supermarket when, at 4:00 p.m., I had an interview with David Glover, Manager of Border. Immediately I opted for Border where I worked for years in a very nice environment surrounded by very congenial co-workers. To me was a great success having had three opportunities to work at 73 years of age and since them I have been working full time until I resigned before Border Books went into bankruptcy.

The above is my employment history in the United States of America. I have never collected welfare checks, food stamps, or unemployment checks. I never received any money from any intelligence agency of the United States government, contrary to what some distorters of the truth have stated. I never received any money from any anti-Castro organization including the DRE. I challenge all the liars to prove the contrary. It will be impossible because it never happened.

In my jobs, in my businesses since 1961 I had been *in God's hands* and in order to be able to succeed that is enough.

CHAPTER XVI

---◄●►---

LIES, LIES AND MORE LIES

We are at war against Communism and nobody, in his/her right mind, could deny that. War sometimes is conducted with bullets, some other times is conducted with words using words as bullets. In Cuba, Communism won the battle of words. It was completely one sided.

The great German military man Erich Ludendorff was right when he maintained that it was important in wars the continued and intelligent diffusion of ideas and facts, true or false, designed to damage the enemy and this is worth a lot more than military armed divisions.

Communism has been following Ludendorff's ideas enriching them with those of another German military man, Joseph Goebbels.

We are going to see some of the lies disseminated by our enemies. Alexander Dumas wrote that he did not like to have enemies, but that if he has an enemy he preferred him to be evil and not an imbecile. The Communists are evil and they use a lot of imbeciles.

My name has been mentioned, sometimes truthfully others wrongfully, among others in the following books:

> *A Heritage of Stone, by Jim Garrison*
> *Big Brother and the Holding Company, by Weissman, S.*
> *Case Closed, by Posner, Gerald.*
> *Coincidence or Conspiracy, by Fensterwald, B.*
> *Conspiracy, by Summers, A.*
> *Crime and Coverup, by Scott, P. D.*

Crossfire, by Marrs, J.

Deep Politics, by Scott, P. D.

Destiny Betrayed, by DiEugenio, J.

Fatal Hour, by G. Robert Blakey and Richard N. Billings.

First Hand Knowledge, by Morrow, R.

Government by Gunplay, by Blumenthal, S.

High Treason, by Groden R. and Livingston, H

Live by the Sword, by Russo, Gus.

Mafia Kingfish, by Davis, John H.

Man of a Million Fragments: The True Story of Clay Shaw, by Donald H. Carpenter.

Oswald and the CIA, by Newman, J.

Oswald in New Orleans, by Weisberg, Harold foreword by Garrison, J.

Oswald Talked, by LaFontaine

Penthouse, 1981-10

Portrait of the Assassin, by Ford, Gerald R. Rendezvous with Death, by Huismann, Wilfried

Spy Saga, by Melanson, P.

The Assassination of John F. Kennedy, by Duffy, J., and Ricci, V.

The Assassination: Dallas and Beyond, by Scott, P. D.

The Fish is Red, by Hinckle, W. and Turner, W.

The Garrison Case, by Brener, Milton E.

The Iran-Contra Connection, by Marshall, J.

The Last Investigation, by Fonzi, G.

The Man Who Knew Too Much, by Russell, D.

The Road to Dallas, by David Kayser.

The Ruby Cover-up, by Kantor, S.

The Torch is Passed, by The Associated Press.

The Unanswered questions about President Kennedy's assassination, by Fox, Silvan.

The Witnesses, The New York Times.

Ultimate Sacrifice, by Waldron, Lamar and Hartmann, Tom.

Whitewash, by Weisberg, Harold.

Whitewash II, by Weisberg, Harold.

ZR Rifle, by Furiati, C.

Now let's start doing some autopsies about the work of those who had lied, distorted the truth or just use faulty information fooling the American people and sometimes spreading false information about my person.

The House Select Committee on Assassinations:

Congressman Thomas Downing (D-VA.) joined forces with a Castro sympathizer, Congressman Henry Gonzalez (D-TX) to create a committee to investigate the assassinations of President Kennedy, Senator Bobby Kennedy and Martin Luther King, Jr. On September 17, 1976 the Downing-Gonzalez bill creating the HSCA passed in the House by a vote of 280 to 65 as Resolution 1540.

One of the first measures adopted by Downing in October 1976 was to appoint Richard A. Sprague as Chief Council of the HSCA. Unbelievably the person who recommended Sprague to Downing was none other than a lawyer associated with several pro-communist organizations and who had received money from the KGB: Mark Lane. Mark Lane, in my opinion, has been discredited as a serious and honest opponent of the Warren Commission and that the HSCA follow his recommendation speaks very poorly about the integrity of the HSCA.

After a few months the HSCA was embroiled in a prima-Donna controversy among Sprague and Representative Gonzalez. Gonzalez counted with the favor of Representative Thomas O'Neill, Jr., Speaker of the House, and Representative Jim Wright of Texas. Finally, Representative Gonzalez decided to bitterly resign his post at the HSCA.

During a meeting of the HSCA Mr. Robert Tanenbaum, Deputy Counsel for the HSCA, stated: *"We have found out that it was Bringuier who called the media to have this filmed."* Mr. Tanenbaum was referring to the incident of Oswald carrying on a demonstration on August 16, 1963 in front of the International Trade Mart in New Orleans, Louisiana.

This is another of the many lies spread by Castro's moles. I never called the television stations in regard to any Oswald's demonstrations for the Fair Play for Cuba Committee. In her book "Marina and Lee", Priscilla Johnson McMillan on page 351 explained how Oswald, himself, was the one calling the TV station:

"He had already called the local TV stations to tell them that there would be a Fair Play for Cuba demonstration that day in front of the Trade Mart building in downtown New Orleans."

Another "inaccurate facts" spread about me had been written by Jefferson Morley who I refused to receive in my home in The Woodlands, Texas after I found out his "type" of writing. Here is an example, read some paragraphs of the following Morley's article published in the Miami New Times on April 12, 2001:

> *"Bringuier called Borja to ask what he should do next. "Our answer to him was just "face him down," the former military-section chief recalls." Go out there and contest him. Talk to the press, uncover this guy." And Bringuier did just that. On August 16 another friend of Bringuier in the Directorate reported that Oswald was again handing out FPCC pamphlets. Bringuier sent the friend to Oswald's house posing as a Castro supporter to find out who was backing his work."*

In order to set the record straight I want to make it clear that I didn't call Isidro Borja, the person that I contacted was José Antonio González Lanuza. On August 16, 1963 the person that contacted me about Oswald's demonstration was Carlos Quiroga a friend of mine from Belén who never was a member of the DRE.

> *"Not long after Oswald was killed, the DRE laid off its efforts to link him and Castro. George Joanides continued to assist the group in ways large and small. He paid expenses, accepted intelligence reports, and helped "exfiltrated" Jorge Medina Bringuier, Carlos's cousin and the Directorate last remaining leader inside Cuba who wasn't in prison."*

Here I have to make another correction. Jorge Medina Bringuier was not my cousin as described by Morley but my nephew. At the time of Jorge Medina Bringuier's defection he was not in Cuba, as alleged by Morley, but in Leipzig, East Germany. I would like to make a brief history of this incident because Morley and others apparently don't know the facts of what they write.

My sister María del Carmen Medina had been writing letters and sending money to her son Jorge (Jorgito) Medina Bringuier who at the time was in East Germany. My father was living in Miami with my brother Julito and he received the visit of some federal agents who brought him to the offices in Opalocka, Florida to question him about those letters sent by his daughter to Leipzig, East Germany. No matter whatever bad his grandson could have done, for my father Jorgito was always his grandson. Jorgito had been writing letters to his mother insinuating that he was disillusioned with Communism, he had asked for permission to visit Paris but it had been denied and he requested not to let know anyone in Havana about his plans.[189]

On November 12, 1963 Jorgito wrote to his mother: *"You don't know how much I appreciate that the Cuban government gave me the opportunity that I have had to really know the socialist countries, to known them profoundly, if not personally but through the ones who are studying here. I have known a lot of things and I have accumulated a lot of experiences very interesting and useful."*

On November 24, 1963 Jorgito wrote the following to his mother: *"All the students from Socialist countries who are here when they feel confident they express their dissatisfaction and they speak of the differences in between the children of political persons and the children of the average people and you can even see this among us because they don't mix the children of the leaders with the average children. Ones receive abundant money from their parents the others had to conform with the stipend as student given to them. For example a Cuban who visited Bulgaria during his vacation returned shocked for what he saw and heard. And was told that in Cuba the people was enthusiastic about socialism as they were but that eventually they would find out and become as disgusted with socialism as they are now."* Jorgito continued referring to example of people from Poland and from Africa. The letter was a long one, 8 pages handwritten, and in it he is offering to help the United States government.

On December 3, 1963 Jorgito wrote another letter to his mother, his plan was that my sister visit Berlin and he was going to get a permit to visit her there and then defect.

The agents that questioned my father got an interest in Jorgito's possible defection because Jorgito could furnish intelligence information about Castro's agents infiltrated in the United States. My sister was contacted in New Orleans and she had to go to Miami. The CIA agent in charge of her case used the name "Bernard". Jorgito was asking her mother for money and he was thinking in traveling from Berlin to

---

[189] Letter from Jorge Medina Bringuier to his mother, dated November 8, 1963.

Switzerland and from there his intention was to continue to Sudan, the native country of his girlfriend Houda Alameddin.

The next day, December 4th., 1963 my sister went to the Pan American Bank of Miami and made a Foreign Money Transfer No. 480808 for the amount of $90.00 to Houda Alameddin SUDAN KONTO No.52121 WITH BERLINER BANK, 1000 Berlin 12, Hardenbergstrape 32, D. B. R.

Bernard, the CIA Case Officer had everything prepared for the trip of my sister to Berlin.

She was given an Ecuadorian passport, an Ecuadorian identity document No.825-904, an International Certificate of revaccination against smallpox showing that she was born on September 4, 1923 at Ecuador done at Guayaquil, Ecuador. My Cuban born sister entered Germany as an Ecuadorian born citizen. She was brought to a Hotel to wait for the arrival of her son who had promised to be there on December 13, 1963.

When my nephew arrived at the hotel room. CIA personnel bundled them in two large carpets, brought them out of the hotel and inside a waiting truck. From there they were brought to a U. S. Military airport and after several stops in different countries they finally arrived to the United States.

During this period the CIA had sent to a couple of different countries, one of them Italy, persons with a strong resemblance to my nephew so they could check the Castro government reaction to my nephew defection. Immediately after they suspected the defection, teams of assassins were sent by Castro's counterintelligence services to the locations were the impersonators were present.

My poor sister had accomplished her mission. She had helped her son to regain his freedom. She did what all good mothers in the world would do. But before her trip to Germany her brain was not acting well, I am not a psychiatric but I believe that she was in denial of accepting what his son had done in Cuba. For her he was a good boy. After the trip to Germany her mental deterioration increased and she never was the same until about a couple of years before her death on April 3, 2007.

I am sure that Jorgito's defection caused panic among the Cuban Intelligence Services. On December 21, 1963 Jorgito's sister Carmucha, sent a telegram to my brother Julio house in Miami, it read:

"Ruego informes esta via ciertamente donde y como está mami, Carmucha, Neptuno 1212, Habana"
"I beg you to send information this way where truly and how is mother"

My brother Julito obliged and sent the following telegram:

"Mami aquí y bien. No comprendo preocupación. Explica."
"Mother here and well. Don't understand your worry. Explain."

Was during this period in December 1963 that I met Bernard. We took a trip to Miami to expend Christmas with my parents and Julito and his family at Julito's house in Miami. At the moment Jorgito was sequestered in a CIA safe house in the Miami area. Julito and my father were allowed to visit Jorgito there. Bernard was consulted to see if I could go with them. The request was approved and one night I was brought with my brother to visit my nephew at the safe house.

There he was with exercise equipment to keep his body in shape. I told Bernard that I was going to visit Jorgito as his uncle not as a member of DRE. Jorgito for me was like my little brother, he had been born at the house in Calzada 255 and we had played together as brothers while we were children.

I was told that he had turn over the CIA, during his debriefing, a lot of information about Castro's spies in the United States. I also learnt that he had really betrayed the DRE in Cuba, as my friend Chilo Borja had wrote me in a previous letter. Apparently Jorgito had been directed by Castro's Intelligence Services and was under direct control of Raúl Castro. He moved up within the ranks of the DRE by entrapping members in higher positions and occupying their posts. He reached to the top of the DRE inside Cuba. He infiltrated in Cuba members of the DRE from Miami and he took them in tours of Havana showing them how the situation was controlled by him. I remember talking, after Jorgito's defection, with Luis Fernández Rocha who was one of those infiltrated in Cuba by the DRE and who Jorgito took under his wing. Luis told me how, while he was infiltrated in Havana, they had attended mass and had taken communion together and that he was glad that Jorgito didn't apprehend him. I was told that the plan created by Raúl Castro was for

Jorgito to lure the leaders of the DRE to infiltrate Cuba, their aim was to get Juan Manuel Salvat, the top leader of the DRE, to go to Cuba to have a meeting with Jorgito, at Salvat's arrival he was going to be arrested and Jorgito was going to "escape" to the United States and become the leader of the DRE working at the orders of Raúl Castro.

I had been told that there are hundreds of Cubans who went to jail because of the betrayal of my nephew and some who lost their lives for the same reasons. It is hard for my heart to write about these things but if it is the truth it has to be told. It is part of history and those who write inaccurate, misinformed or false events could not tell the true history.

During my Christmas trip to Miami in December 1963 I didn't go to visit the offices of the DRE. The CIA offered Jorgito to put him in the witness protection program, change his name and sent him to another city in the U.S. Jorgito refused the idea, he was in love with Houda and he wanted to return to Europe and marry her. That was what he did after the debriefing ended. I never saw Bernard again. The one who brought this to light for the first time was newsman Jack Anderson who as usual, as he did so many times tergiversated the facts and in one of his columns portrayed me as a CIA informant.

Jorgito and Houda got married, had a son and finally got divorced. With Houda I have only talked over the phone and I had been told that Jorgito's son had become a very intelligent and professional man. Jorgito remarried in Spain and had several other children whom I met in a trip that the children took to Miami while I was living there. They looked very intelligent and very nice persons.

My sister María del Carmen sacrificed her mental sanity to save her son. That tragedy in our family was due to the ambition of power of a sadistic pair of brothers: Fidel and Raúl Castro.

In his Miami New Times article Morley continued writing:

> *Fidel Castro and the majority of the American people don't often agree, but on the JFK conspiracy question they are like-minded. In December 1995 Fabian Escalante, retired chief of counterintelligence for Castro's security services, offered new details of the Cuban interpretation of Kennedy's assassination. As Castro had insinuated from the beginning, Cuban communists believed that certain exiles, working in league with CIA officials who loathed Kennedy's Cuba policy, were likely responsible*

for the crime. Speaking at a conference of JFK historians in the Bahamas, Escalante said that he had conducted to Cuban government's first full scale inquiry into the assassination in 1991 and 1992. He claimed he and a colleague had interview 150 people in Cuba and said he had reviewed relevant files.

Now Jefferson Morley is portraying Fabián Escalante as a historian in a group of "historians" in a Bahamas meeting. This is the same Fabián Escalante who was identified by Martin Underwood, a former JFK assistant and then Lyndon B. Johnson assistant, in a secret memo to Johnson as having flown from Mexico City in November 22, 1963 to the Red Bird airport in Dallas waiting at the airport until the news was broadcasted that Lee Harvey Oswald had been arrested and then Escalante flew back to Mexico City.

Morley continued in his article:

"I think that the people who had to do with (the assassination) are people in the DRE," he told the conference. But Escalante was another investigator who knew nothing about Joannides. He emphasized that he didn't think Juan Manuel Salvat or other military section leaders were the organizers of the plot. "When you are going to carry out an operation as complex as this one, you cannot put all your money on one single horse. You have to use different ways in order not to have any mistakes. He added, "Obviously the DRE was in on the whole plot against Cuba."

In this regard I would have to partially agree with Escalante because he was betrayed by what he knew. Fidel Castro didn't put all his money on one single horse, he had several teams working inside the United States to kill President John F. Kennedy. At the end Lee Harvey Oswald was the one who succeeded.

On January 14, 2008 I sent the following email to Chilo Borja:

Chilo: I am doing some research for my upcoming book and I found this article by Mr. Morley:

Revelation 19.63

For nearly four decades the CIA has kept secret the identity of a Miami agent who may have known too much too early about Lee Harvey Oswald.

By Jefferson Morley

"Miami Daily News" 4-12-01
Bringuier called Borja to ask what he should do next, "Our answer to him was just "face him down," the former military section chief recalls. "Go out there and contest him. Talk to the press, uncover this guy."

Chilo, I don't know from where he got the above information because with the only person with whom I communicated at that time was with José Antonio González Lanuza and I have copies of the letters that we interchanged at the time.
I would like to know if it is true you said to Morley that you and I talked at the time. I am inclined to believe that this is another invention of Mr. Morley.
Hope you are doing ok.

Carlos

On January 31, 2008, after returning from a vacation, Chilo Borja answered with the following email:

Carlitos
Morley is sneaky and he tries to lead you into a corner. What I told Jeff was a general statement about we (el Directorio) communicated with you" (I did not remember who but if you say it was Jose Antonio so be it) and probably asked you to keep an eye on Oswald, etc. At the time I did not even knew that you were the DRE representative in New Orleans.
Excuse my delay in answering you but I was out of Miami since January 6 until today.
I embrace you.

Chilo

As you can realize Chilo Borja's recollection, after 45 years, is kind of foggy. I never talked to Chilo in regard to Oswald. The person that I contacted, before the debate, was José Antonio Lanuza. Chilo's memory is foggy because in his email he stated: *"At the time I did not even knew that you were the DRE representative in New Orleans."* Chilo is forgetting his letter of February 1, 1963 where he wrote in the first paragraph:

> *I am happy of receiving your letter, and my feelings about you been in good health together with your family is reciprocal. Truly it was a real surprise to me to know you were helping us from New Orleans in the delegation of the DRE."*

And Chilo, after 45 years do not remember that it was he the one who in a following letter communicated to me the betrayal done to the Cuban cause by my nephew Jorge Medina Bringuier. That is in the way that many "historians", like Morley, present their "investigative works". I do not blame Chilo, he was my friend during my youth and I consider him my friend now. I think that he was used by Morley. I have in my possession both letters from Isidro "Chilo" Borja from February 1963.

In regard to Jefferson Morley I can say that some years ago he contacted me over the phone and I faxed to him a couple of letters to clarify his ideas. It was at the time that the internet was not what the internet is today. Around April of 2005 Mr. Morley contacted me again and tried to schedule an interview with me which I cancelled after reading in the internet some of his articles. If you want to know more about the subject I recommend you the name of Dale K. Myers, an Emmy Award winning animator and author. In 2008 he published a couple of very good articles in jfkfiles.blogspot.com the first one in February 27 entitled "The CIA vs. Jefferson Morley" and the second one on June 2, entitled "The Last Word: Bringuier, Joannides and the DRE".

One person, the "king of Liars," who had been at war against the United States since he was in the Sierra Maestra, "Maximum Tyrant," "Commander in Chief" Fidel Castro since November 22. 1963 had been lying about the assassination of JFK and about me. He lied to the "naïve" members of the HSCA; and he also lied when he offered the Cuban people elections in 18 months; he lied when he denied been a Communist and sent people to jail for "defaming" him in this respect; he lied when recently he denied that there had been Cuban interrogators in Viet Nam torturing American soldiers; he lied to the "gullible" members of the HSCA; and he lied on November 23, 1963 when trying to counter my accusation against him in national and international television he, after referring to me stated that there was not a "Fair Play for Cuba Committee" chapter in New Orleans and he will continue lying to any sucker who is willing to believe him.

On January 19, 2006, Castro's newspaper "Granma" carried a long article entitled "The anti-Cuban terrorism and the assassination of Kennedy". The article was signed by José A. de la Osa and Orfilio Peláez, but surely behind it had to be Fabián Escalate. In it one paragraph said:

"Even, he was filmed in some of these actions and he participated in a public altercation with a Cuban agent of the CIA Carlos Bringuier, with whom he engaged in a radio debate about Cuba." Another time they appealed to the same lie, they label me as a CIA agent something that I never have been. Castro has to lie, otherwise he would have to admit his guilt. At one time I dare him to allow me to debate the assassination of Kennedy in Cuban TV and he never responded. I challenge him again: let me debate with whomever you want on Cuban soil, on Cuban television the facts about the assassination of President John F. Kennedy. I am sure that as a guilty coward that Fidel Castro is he will not allow that to happen.

But I have seen outrageous lies from other people. Let's hear from Jim DiEugenio:

He's Baaack!
The return of Gerald Posner
By Jim DiEugenio

None of the reviewers mentioned another problem with Case Closed, the interview denials. Some of the people who Posner sources in his footnotes deny ever talking to him. For instance, when Peter Scott phoned Carlos Bringuier in New Orleans to confirm that he told Posner what Posner quoted him as saying, Bringuier said he didn't recall ever talking to the author. Gary Aguilar wrote a letter to the Federal Bar News & Journal noting this phenomenon (Vol.41 #5): (Jim DiEugenio).

Now, come on, author Gerald Posner with his lovely wife expend a whole day in our house in Terrytown, Louisiana. Posner, who I consider a very honest writer, no matter the fact that we disagree in the motivation of Lee Harvey Oswald, did a very complete interview and I ended it up ordering pizza for all of us.

In 1993 I received, around 46 pages from "Independent Research Associates", P.O. Box 2091, NY NY 10013-2091 with reports that have been recycled by distorters of the truth. In page marked 539 the Independent Research Associates wrote referring to me: *"He came to the United States on February 8, 1961 where he became associated with the FDR, and had ties with the CIA. Columnist Jack Anderson wrote about a CIA OS document that stated that Bringuier was a CIA informant. Several CIA Domestic Contacts Division documents indicated a close relationship between Bringuier and the CIA."*

The lied is recycled again. I never had any contact with a CIA agent until after the assassination of President Kennedy. They will never be able to prove differently because it never happened. I am sure that to what Jack Anderson was referring was to my first encounter with a CIA agent when while expending Christmas with my father in my brother's Julio house in Miami, in December 1963, my father, my brother Julio and I were taken to a CIA safe-house in Miami to meet my nephew Jorge Medina Bringuier who had just defected from behind the Iron Curtain. And this was AFTER November 22, 1963. In regard to the falsehood *"several CIA Domestic Contacts Division documents"*, I am sure that they cannot produce any documents indicating any relationship between me and the CIA before the assassination of President Kennedy. I am inclined to believe that the idea comes from the Intelligence Department of the Castro dictatorship. Not several, but it cannot be a single document stating that I had any kind of relationship with the CIA before the assassination of JFK. After the assassination I had two contacts with the CIA office in New Orleans to apprise them of Garrison's plans to smear the CIA implicating it in the assassination. Besides those instances not even Houdini would be able to produce legitimate prove showing any contact of me with the CIA before the assassination of President John Fitzgerald Kennedy.

On Pages marked 540 and 541 the same Independent Research Associates stated:

Howard Hunt and Carlos Bringuier presumably knew each one another in the early 1960's. Besides both being connected to the FRD and CRC—Howard Hunt described himself as involved in the propaganda effort of the CRC and Bringuier stated his title was press and propaganda secretary of the same organization—they shared many common ideas. Both men were afraid that Kennedy was going to replace Castro with another leftist, Manolo Reyes. Bringuier termed this "Operation Judas." Finally, Bringuier and Hunt both had connections to President Nixon. In 1972, Bringuier was the leader of Cuban-Americans for Nixon. Hunt was linked to Nixon through Watergate. John Caufield, a former member of the New York City Police.

Department's Intelligence Division who was also involved with Nixon in Watergate, was in charge of monitoring the activities of the DRE. Hunt was endorsing Bringuier by having Oswald stage an incident with him. Bringuier, like General Walker, would become an anti-communist hero after the Kennedy assassination, because of him been attacked by Oswald.

Again, we have here the same recycling of lies. Again, "presumably" the above was written by Dictator Castro's Intelligence Department, because it could not be so full of falsehoods and half-truths without the intervention of Castro's henchmen. I never in my life met Howard Hunt or had any kind of contact with him. My only contact with the CRC was when, for a couple of months, I worked as Secretary of Press and Propaganda for the NEW ORLEANS DELEGATION, having nothing to do with the CRC Miami office. Then the "historians" writers of the above falsehoods mistakenly identified the leftist leader as "Manolo Reyes" when in reality that person was "Manuel Ray" it could make you laugh at their ignorance but it is tragic how they confuse the people. In my book "Operación Judas" what I refer to with that title was to the agreement reached by Kennedy and Khrushchev to cool down the Cold War and get rid of Castro. Agreement that eventually cost Kennedy his life and ten months later Khrushchev lost his power.

In 1972 I was not the Chairman of Cuban-Americans for Nixon; in 1972, I was CoChairman of the Cuban-Americans for Nixon in the city of New Orleans, not nationwide. And I did so because it was well known that Senator George McGovern, Nixon's opponent, was another mole of the Castro's dictatorship. Hunt could not have been "endorsing" me in any way because I was an unknown person to Hunt. It is inconceivable how distorters of the truth lie and try to confuse the American people who deserve not to be lied upon.

FABIAN ESCALANTE

Fabián Escalante was born in Cuba in 1941. A supporter of Fidel Castro he joined the Department of State Security (G2) in 1960. It has been published reports that he was in Minsk, Soviet Union, when Lee Harvey Oswald was there, and that seven weeks before the assassination he was in contact with Lee Harvey Oswald in Mexico City.[190] At the time of the assassination of John F. Kennedy, Escalante was head of a counter-intelligence and was part of a team investigating a CIA operation called "Sentinels of Liberty." an attempt to recruit Cubans willing to fight against Castro.

The following are Escalante's description by Castro's sources:

In 1965 Escalante was part of the operational unit that "investigated" the involvement of Rolando Cubela in the attempt to assassinate Fidel Castro. During this period, one of G-2's agents, Juan Feliafel Canahan, had infiltrated the anti-Castro movement and was very close to Manuel Artime (Movement for the Recovery of the Revolution). He provided important information to G2, including the fact that David Sánchez Morales appeared to be working very closely with Cubela.

Fabián Escalante was appointed as head of the Department of State Security (DSE) in 1976. Later that year members of the US House of Representatives Select Committee in Assassinations visited Cuba and requested help with investigating the assassination investigation of John F. Kennedy and Martin Luther King. Escalante was asked to oversee this investigation. This involved studying the files of revolutionaries, terrorists and émigrés. The final report was sent to the House Select Committee on Assassinations (HSCA). However, it contained information that the HSCA did not want to hear and it was never published.

My reaction to that trip to Cuba is very simple. How do you think would be your reaction if John Edgar Hoover had asked Al Capone for his cooperation to investigate the Mafia? Stupidity 101.

---

[190] *The Dallas-Cuba Committee", by Gus Russo. "Secrets of a Homicide", by Dale K. Myers, August 6 2009.

In 1978 President Jimmy Carter arranged for a group of imprisoned exiles to be released. This included Tony Cuesta who was involved in an attack on Cuba on May 29th 1966. A member of his team, Herminio Díaz García, was killed during the raid. Cuesta, who always vowed that Castro would never take him alive, attempted suicide by setting off a grenade, which blinded him and blew off his right hand. Cuesta spent a long time in a hospital as result of his serious injuries.

Just before leaving Cuba, Cuesta asked to see Escalante. Cuesta allegedly told Escalante that he had been involved in the assassination of President Kennedy. He allegedly also named Herminio Díaz García and Eladio del Valle as being involved in the conspiracy. Cuesta allegedly asked Escalante not to make this information "public because I am returning to my family in Miami-and this could be very dangerous." All these according to Fabián Escalante.

In 1982 Escalante became a senior official in the Interior Ministry. By this time Escalante was considered to be Cuba's leading authority on the history of CIA activities against his country.

Escalante became head of the Cuban Security Studies Center in 1993. This allowed him to re-examine the assassination of John F. Kennedy. As he points out, along with "Colonel Arturo Rodríguez the available material and publications, consulted with former agents and Mendoza (now deceased), I studied all operatives, and investigated all the accessible documentation."

In a Cuban television documentary broadcast on November 26, 1993, Escalante named the gunmen who killed John F. Kennedy as three Chicago mobsters (Lenny Patrick, David Yaras and Richard Cain,) and two Cuban exiles (Herminio Díaz García and Eladio del Valle,) but said many in the CIA and elsewhere knew what was going to happen Tony Cuesta returned to Miami and died in 1994. The following year, Wayne Smith, chief of the Centre for International Policy in Washington, and whom my cousin José Enrique (Cucú) Bringuier had met in Cuba and described Smith to me as an admirer and follower of Fidel Castro, arranged a meeting on the assassination of John F. Kennedy, in Nassau, Bahamas.

Others in attendance were: Gaeton Fonzi, Dick Russell, Noel Twyman, Anthony Summers, Peter Dale Scott, John M. Newman,

Jeremy Gunn, John Judge, Andy Kolis, Peter Kornbluh, Mary and Ray LaFontaine, Jim Lesar, Russ Swickard, Ed Sherry and Gordon Winslow.

Some high level Cuban officials attended the conference. This included Fabián Escalante, Carlos Lechuga (former Ambassador to Mexico City and contact of Cuban spy Fernando Fernández Bárcenas and former liaison of Castro with the Fair Play for Cuba Committee) and Arturo Rodríguez, a State Security official. Escalante revealed details of Cuesta's confession. Cuesta was dead and could not refute his claim. Escalante also informed the group that they had a spy in the anti-Castro community in Miami who knew about the plot to kill Kennedy.

Fabián Escalante is the author of several books, including *The Secret War: CIA Covert Operations Against Cuba, 1959-62 (1995)* and *CIA Targets Fidel: The Secret Assassinations Report (1996)*. As usual Fabián Escalante always portrait me as a "CIA agent". He did so also while interviewed by Wilfried Huismann in *"Rendezvous with Death."*

In his books Fabián Escalante never explain what he was doing in Minsk or what he was doing in November 22, 1963 when he flew in a small airplane from Mexico City to the Red Bird airport in Dallas, Texas and waited there until Lee Harvey Oswald had been apprehended, returning then to Mexico City and flying back to Havana.[191]

[191] "Rendezvous with Death", by Wilfried Huismann.

Dr. Alton Ochsner, Sr., New Orleans Mayor Victor
M. Schiro and Dr. Carlos J. Bringuier

413

ROLANDO CUBELA

There is a NODULE (www.ajweberman.com/modules) in the internet with the following information:

> *As early as March 1952 Rolando Cubela was working against Batista. That year with student friends he reinstituted the Student Directorate (DRE). In October 1956 Rolando Cubela assassinated Blanco Rico, Fulgencio Batista's Chief of Military Intelligence. Fleeing to the U. S., he became involved in military planning and purchasing arms until February 1958, when he and sixteen other students returned clandestinely to the Escambray. He led a famous military column, and became the overall military leader of the DRE. The DRE refused the military leadership of Che Guevara, fighting only under Rolando Cubela's orders. They occupied the Presidential Palace on January 1, 1959, and initially declined to turn it over to Fidel Castro. BRINGUIER was in Rolando Cubela's group.*

First the DRE was not formed until 1959 to fight against Castro at a time when Rolando Cubela was already a henchman of the Castro government. I never was in any group with Rolando Cubela who I never met. I could not have been occupying the Presidential Palace with Rolando Cubela on January 1, 1959 because I was in Buenos Aires, Argentina and I did not return to Cuba until January 26, 1959 when I found my house occupied by militiamen of the Ministry of Recovery of Misappropriated Properties.

Rolando Cubela was AMLASH participating in Castro's plan to get information about what John F. Kennedy was willing to do to get rid of him.

In 1973, ten years after the assassination of President Kennedy, Rolando Cubela was assigned another intelligence job by Fidel Castro. His assignment was to kidnap Fulgencio Batista in Spain and bring him to Cuba where Fidel Castro wanted to try him and execute him. Batista avoided this kidnapping by Rolando Cubela when Batista died on August 6, 1973 in Guadalmina, near Marbella, Spain.

After that the Cuban government "accused" Cubela of participating with the CIA to try to kill Fidel Castro and no matter the fact that the accusation was one that deserved the death sentence Cubela was only "sentenced" to a jail term. In August 1978, I was *in God's hands* because while I was in my house I decided to hear in my shortwave radio Radio Havana Cuba something that I rarely was doing. To my surprise they were broadcasting an event going on in Cuba entitled: "The Cuban Youth Tribunal Accuses the U.S. in JFK killing." To my surprise the one that was testifying was Rolando Cubela, supposedly in jail, who was accusing the CIA for the assassination of President John F. Kennedy. I had some reports that while Cubela was supposedly in jail he was seeing in restaurants and night clubs in Havana together with Intelligence officers.

Fidel Castro has executed people who had never conspired to kill him, but Rolando Cubela was spared. Eventually Cubela was "pardoned" and now is living in Madrid, Spain.

Another thing that had come out to light is that Rolando Cubela was the intelligence Case Officer from the Castro government in charge of taking over the case of Lee Harvey Oswald when Oswald returned to the United States. Another interesting item that has come to light is that Cubela's name was in a file that the CIA have about George De Mohrenschildts the man who was surprised that Oswald had failed to kill General Walker.[192]

There are some other characters that had been lying about the assassination of President Kennedy and, in my opinion, had been giving aid and support to the enemies of this Country. Let's review some of these new Ananias:

Harold Weisberg

On September 21, 1947 the Washington Times Herald published a list of ten discharged employees of the State Department, among them was Harold Weisberg.[193]

The House Committee on Un-American Activities Chairman, Rep. Willis, brought out to the House of Representatives some of the background of Mr. Weisberg. He stated:

---

[192] "The Dallas-Cuba Connection" 2009 Update by Gus Russo, "Secrets of a Homicide", by Gale K. Myers.
[193] "Blacklisted by History", by M. Stanton Evans, page 172.

"According to press releases of the Special Committee to investigate Un-American Subversive Activities, January 30, and 31, 1940, Harold Weisberg paid $100.00 for forged letters which were used in an attempt to link then Chairman Martin Dies to the militant Silver Shirts, an extremist group. The Silver Shirts Legion of America was a Klan hate-type organization which adopted a policy of depriving certain ethnic groups and individuals of their constitutional rights. Weisberg, after obtaining this forged correspondence, used it on January 27, 1940, issue of **The Nation**. *Additionally, according to the press releases, Weisberg allegedly used the bogus letters to write a speech for a Congressman who opposed Dies and his Committee and who placed the misinformation in the Congressional Record.*

Weisberg was earlier, in 1938, discharged from his investigative post on the LaFollette civil liberties committee "for giving confidential matter to the **Daily Worker**, *the leading Communist newspaper in the country."*

In the summer of 1947, Weisberg was fired from his post with the U. S. Department of State, along with nine others, for known associations with agents of the Soviet Union.

Weisberg has appeared several times before the New Orleans Grand Jury investigating the Kennedy assassination plot alleged to have occurred in that city. His latest book on the assassination carries a foreword by District Attorney James Garrison.

On December 16, 1966, Harold Weisberg discussed his book on "the Militant Forum," a program conducted by The Militant, official organ of the Trotskyite-Communist Socialist Workers Party.[194]

When Harold Weisberg was assisting New Orleans District Attorney Jim Garrison he showed up in front of my store "Casa Cuba" with one of Garrison's assistants. When I noticed that Weisberg started to take pictures of my store I went outside, with my camera, and started to take pictures of both of them. I gave Mr. Weisberg the opportunity to prove

---

[194] Congressional Record, 2/29/1068. Pgs. H1560-1-2.

his lies when I sued him in New Orleans. Unfortunately for him the truth proved to be on my side and so ruled the Judge.

Bernard Fensterwald

Bernard Fensterwald, the son of a wealthy clothing merchant, was born in Nashville, Tennessee, on August 2, 1921. From 1951 to 1956 Fensterwald worked for the State Department as an Assistant Legal Advisor. This job included defending State Department employees accused by Sen. Joseph McCarthy of being members of the American Communist Party. Fensterwald served in the US Navy during the Second World War.

Fensterwald graduated from Harvard Law School in 1949. He entered the Georgetown University school of Advanced International Studies, a private institution, and received an M. A. in 1950.

Fensterwald became involved with Jim Garrison and his investigation of the John F. Kennedy assassination. In January 1969, Fensterwald joined forces with Richard E. Sprague to form the Committee To Investigate Assassinations, which was mainly concerned with finding the people responsible for killing Kennedy. As a result of the investigation Fensterwald and Michael Ewing co-authored: *Assassination of JFK: Coincidence or Conspiracy.*

Fensterwald employed Lou Russell as a private detective to help him with some of his legal cases. One of Russell's first tasks was to investigate the journalist Jack Anderson. Russell also purchased $3,000 in electronic eavesdropping equipment from John Leon of Allied Investigators. Russell's friend Charles F. Knight, was told that this equipment had been purchased for James W. McCord. At the time, Russell also did part-time work for McCord. This equipment was used to tape the telephone conversations between politicians based at the Democratic Party National Committee and a small group of prostitutes run by Phillip Mackin Bailey that worked their trade in the Columbia Plaza.

On June 16, 1972, Lou Russell spent time at his daughter's house in Benedict, Maryland. That evening Russell traveled to Washington and spent between 8:30 until 10.30 p.m. in the Howard Johnson's Motel. This was the motel where those involved in the Watergate burglary were staying. However, Russell later told FBI agents that he did not meet his employer, James W. McCord, at the motel. Russell then said he drove back to his daughter in Maryland.

Soon after midnight Russell told his daughter he had to return to Washington to do "some work for McCord" that night. It was estimated that he arrived back at the Howard Johnson's Motel at around 12.45 a.m. At 1.30 a.m. Russell had a meeting with McCord. It is not clear what role Russell played in the Watergate break-in. Jim Hougan has suggested that he was helping McCord to "sabotage the break-in."

Later that night Frank Sturgis, Virgilio González, Eugenio Martínez, Bernard L. Baker and James W. McCord were arrested while in the Democratic Party headquarters in Watergate. McCord employed Fensterwald as his lawyer On December 21, 1972 James W. McCord wrote a letter to Jack Caulfield: "Sorry to have to write you this letter but felt you had to know. If Helms goes, and if the WG (Watergate) operation is laid at the CIA's feet, where it does not belong, every tree in the forest will fall. It will be a scorched desert. The whole matter is at the precipice right now. Just pass the message that if they want it to blow, they are on exactly the right course. I'm sorry that you will get hurt in the fallout."

In April 1973, Lou Russell suffered a heart attack. However, despite being unable to work, James W. McCord continued to pay him as an employee of Security International. Russell did not have a bank account and Fensterwald paid him checks into his Committee to Investigate Assassinations.

Another of Fensterwald famous client was James Earl Ray, the man who had been found guilty of killing Martin Luther King. In June 1974 Fensterwald filed a motion to grant Ray a new trial on the basis of alleged collusion between his former attorney and the author William Bradford Huie. In 1976 Ray dismissed Fensterwald as his lawyer.

On April 2, 1991, Bernard Fensterwald, 69, died of a heart attack at his home in Alexandria, Virginia.[195]

The Communists had been diligently working, first they physically assassinated President John F. Kennedy, then sent us in a socialist whirlpool during the Johnson's years and after that they committed the political assassination of Richard M. Nixon.

---

[195] All above information taken from "Google".

Joan Mellen: "A Farewell to Justice"

This book could also had been written by Castro's State Security. One of those giving praise to this book is non-other than Fidel Castro's ideological lover Oliver Stone.

On her book Ms. Mellen portray me as a FBI or CIA informant and tried to associate me with George Joannides, according to her and others, as a CIA operative. I heard the name Joannides for the first time while researching some of Jefferson Morley's allegations and this was after Mr. Joannides had passed away. I never met, talked or had any direct or indirect contact with Mr. George Joannides but these recyclers of lies keep repeating the same lies. Ms. Mellen then compares Oswald's attempt to infiltrate the DRE in New Orleans and our confrontation on Canal street saying that it closely resembles Phillip's masterminding the overthrow of Jacobo Arbenz in Guatemala and that *"in Oswald's case, the ultimate goal of making public future <assassin> Oswald's pro-Castro sympathies was to blame Castro for the assassination, precipitating a ground war in Cuba."*

What Ms. Mellen achieved with her words was to convince me of Castro's emotional situation when I forced him, with my accusations of November 22, 1963, to go to a public meeting on November 23, to denounce me as a liar because he was cowardly afraid that with Lee Harvey Oswald in prison it could be discovered his hand behind the assassination.

I am not sure if Ms. Mellen also accuses Oswald's widow as a CIA agent because Marina had made statements about Oswald's infatuation with Fidel Castro and Oswald's idea of hijack an airplane from New Orleans to Cuba. Ms. Mellen also forgets the use, by Oswald, of the alias "Hidell" (for "Fidel").

I repeat what I have said before, when I see a book about the assassination of President Kennedy the first thing that I do is read what the author writes about me. When it is inaccurate or a lie, I don't buy the book. I didn't buy Ms. Mellen book. Oliver Stone could continue endorsing her, but I know the truth.

David Kaiser: The Road to Dallas

Bingo! Another recycler. On pages 190 and 191 of his book, Kaiser wrote:

> *"In early August Oswald appeared at the store of Carlos Bringuier, head of the New Orleans branch of the militant anti-Castro student organization DRE, and a day or two later he became involved in a street altercation with Bringuier and two other Cuban exiles over the FPCC handbills, which outraged them."*

What Kaiser don't mention is that the store was "Casa Roca" owned not by me but by Sheppard Zitler. Showing his total disregard for historic truth and for his readers he just mention "early August" instead of August 5, and he put the incident on Canal Street at "a day or two later" when it was on August 9th, four days later. That is the historical truth. But, who cares?

On page 192, Kaiser writes:

> *"The DRE's New Orleans Delegate Bringuier, was a young, very anti-American who had settled in New Orleans in 1961, joined the Cuban Revolutionary Council in early 1962, and become head of the DRE's New Orleans branch in July of that year. Twelve months later, during the third week of July 1963, the FBI discovered a plan to bomb Cuba from a staging area near New Orleans. The operation involved both the DRE members and organized crime elements with connections to Havana and the New Orleans area.'*

I believe that anyone expending money buying this book could sue Kaiser for fraud. He lies and defames me when he calls me "very anti-American". He cannot tell that to the "Daughters of the American Revolution", "Christian Crusade", "INCA" and many other American organizations who praised me. I was, and I am very anti-Communist either Russian, Cuban, American, Chinese, Vietnamese etc., One of my grandmothers was American, a father with one of his names "Teodoro" in honor of "Theodore Roosevelt", and part of a family that always looked at the United States as part of our roots likes France and Spain, only an oxymoron, or someone following the line of my real enemies could write such a lie. Then, by implication, he tried to connect me with a plan of bombing Cuba which I was never aware of until a Castro spy was discovered there.

In the same page 193, Kaiser writes: *"But the key man in this latest plot to bomb Cuba turned out to be Victor Espinosa Hernandez, who had a long history as a revolutionary. He had worked with Rolando Cubela and José Luis Echeverria of the original DRE in 1957-58, acquiring arms for assassination attempts on Batista officials."*

Here again Kaiser is wrong, first he should be referring to "José Antonio Echevarría" no Jose Luis Echeverria, and second, the DRE was not formed until 1959. It was not in existence in 1957-58 as this supposed "historical writer" writes.

In page 196, Kaiser mention the camp of the Christian Democratic Movement across Lake Pontchartrain and the capture of Castro's spy Fernando Fernández Bárcenas ending with this paragraph: *"This incident evidently came to the attention of Bringuier, indicating that the New Orleans branch of DRE was in contact with the training camp as well."* This is another falsehood from Kaiser. I became aware of the identity of the spy by reading the Miami newspaper Diario Las Americas to which I subscribed. How I got knowledge of the training camp has been previously detailed in this book.

In page 200 he writes: *"Carlos Bringuier told the New Orleans Times Picayune that Ferrie had worked with the New Orleans DRE, but the organization dropped him because of his homosexuality."*

I checked this out because I never said such thing. I could not have said so because it is not true. David Ferrie never worked with the DRE in New Orleans. I am inclined to believe that Mr. Kaiser obtained this information from a memo dated February 19, 1967 from CIA Agent Lloyd A. Ray in which memo Mr. Ray stated that in an article of February 19, 1967 on The Times Picayune I stated that Ferrie was affiliated with the Cuban Student Directorate (DRE) until the connection was terminated because of Ferrie's homosexual activities,

When I discovered that memo from CIA Agent Lloyd A. Ray I was intrigued because I have never said such thing because Ferrie was never a member or had any kind of affiliation with the Cuban Student Directorate. Therefore, on July 21, 2009 I mailed by certified mail the following letter to the Central Intelligence Agency:

July 21, 2009
Central Intelligence Agency
1700 Chain Bridge Rd
McLean, VA 22101

Sirs:

I am enclosing copy of a memo from your New Orleans office dated 29 February 1967 (Exhibit A) stating that in an article in the New Orleans Times Picayune of February 19, 1967 I stated that David Ferrie was affiliated with the Cuban Student Directorate and that I expelled him for his homosexual activities.

I am enclosing copy of an article from the New Orleans Times Picayune dated February 19, 1967 (Exhibit B) in which no such statement appears.

As I am writing a book "How Castro Assassinated JFK" and I want real facts to be known and as David Ferrie was never a member of the Cuban Student Directorate I would like to know from where your agent Lloyd A. Ray obtained such inaccurate information.

Sincerely,
Carlos J. Bringuier

The above letter was refused and returned to me by the United States Postal Service.

On August 4, 2009 I mailed a similar letter to the CIA this time I addressed it to: Central Intelligence Agency, Information and Privacy Coordinator, Washington, D.C. 20505.

On August 31, 2009, Delores M. Nelson, CIA Information and Privacy Coordinator mailed the following response:

"This is a final response to your 4 August 2009 Freedom of Information Act (FOIA) request, received in this office of the Information and Privacy Coordinator on 14 August 2009, in which you asked the following:

"I would like to know from where your agent Lloyd A. Ray obtained such inaccurate information."

The FOIA was enacted to provide a means for the general public to access government records. Under the provisions of the FOIA, federal agencies are not required to answer questions posed as FOIA requests. Since your request does not constitute a request for records, we must decline to process it."

From where CIA Agent Lloyd A. Ray got that wrong information? The CIA refuse to divulge it but one thing that I am sure of is that my New Orleans Delegation of the DRE never worked with David Ferrie, Ferrie never was a member of it or in any way was affiliated with the Delegation. If an Agent of the CIA wants to lie I don't have any control about it but I can set the record straight and say that Mr. Ray was wrong when he wrote that. His purpose? I don't know.

Mr. Kaiser on page 215 brings the following: *Letter dated August 1, from Oswald to V.T. Lee.*

In regard to my efforts to start a branch F.P.C.C. in New Orleans I rented an office as I planned and was promptly closed three days later for some obscure reasons by the renters. They said something about remodeling, etc., I am sure you understand. After that I worked out of a post office box and by using street demonstrations and some circular work have sustained a great deal of interest but no new members.

Through the efforts of some Cuban-eli (sic) "gusanos" a street demonstration was attacked and we were officially cautioned by police. This incident robbed me of what support I had leaving me alone.

Nevertheless thousands of circulars were disturbed (sic) and many, many pamphlets which your office supplied.

We also managed to picket the fleet when it came in and I was surprised by the number of officers who were interested in our literature.

I continued to receive through my post office box inquires and questions which I shall endeavor to keep answering to the best of my ability.

Thank you,
Lee H. Oswald

I am inclined to believe that in this letter Oswald was totally referring to the incident that he had with other Cubans, among them Rafael Aznarez when Oswald was demonstrating in a wharf close to a U.S. Navy ship. Oswald only referred to been "cautioned" by the police which happened according to Mr. Aznarez. If he would had been referring to our incident of August 9, in a letter dated August 1, Oswald had to have had mental abilities unknown to the world.

Later on I will quote the letter written by Oswald on August 12, 1963, the day of the trial and three days after our encounter of August 9 on Canal Street and you can see how he tried to gain the goodwill and sympathy of the FPCC.

On page 217 Kaiser wrote: *"Just three days later, on August 8, according to Bringuier's account, a Cuban friend of him, Celso Hernandez, came into his store during the afternoon to report that a young American was standing on Canal Street handing out leaflets . . ."*

Kaiser's historical facts had gone down the drain again. Now he places the Canal Street incident taking place on August 8, when in reality was August 9. In the future it is possible that other recyclers of errors would quote August 8 as an accurate historical day, but who cares about historical accuracy?

On Pages 217 and 218 Kaiser wrote: *"Bringuier later ran into journalist Bill Stuckey and told him that he had discovered a pro-Castro activist. He gave Stuckey Oswald's address."*

Another Kaiser's inaccuracy because when I encountered Bill Stuckey in the morning of August 12, I did not give him Oswald's address but just related what happened and that we were going to have a trial at the Second Municipal Court. I furnished Oswald's address to Stuckey when he called some day after the trial because he wanted to interview Oswald and it was when I presented to him the idea of the debate.

On page 220 Kaiser copied the following letter from Oswald, dated August 12, the day of the trial, and addressed to V.T. Lee Chairman of the Fair Play for Cuba Committee:

Dear Mr. Lee:

Continuing my efforts on behalf of the F.P.C.C. in New Orleans, I find that I have incurred the displeasure of the Cuban exile "worms" here. I was attacked by three of them as the copy of the enclosed summons indicates I was fined ten dollars and the three Cubans were not fined because of "lack of evidence" the judge said.

I am very glad I am stirring things up and shall continue to do so. The incident was given considerable coverage in the press and local. E.B. news broadcast.

I am sure it will be to the good of the Fair Play for Cuba Committee.

Sincerely yours,
Lee H. Oswald"

Here Oswald is talking about the incident with me and not with the previous one that he had with Rafael Aznarez, and it is dated August 12 the same day of the trial.

On page 220 Kaiser continues writing:

"During the next week Bringuier, with a little help from Bill Stuckey and Ed Butler, managed to use Oswald to pursue the mission the DRE had been giving by their sponsor organization, the CIA: to propagandize against Castro all over the Americas."

Here David Kaiser is trying to portray me as a tool of the CIA. I was just a Delegate in New Orleans of the DRE, I was not receiving instructions or orders from the CIA, I never received any money from the CIA, if others in the DRE at the Miami office were receiving money from the CIA that was not my case. I was working very hard as a salesman as comanager of "Casa Roca" to bring food for my family. I never received any money from the Miami DRE office or any other office of the DRE, on the contrary my delegation was sending small amounts of money to Miami headquarters. That is the historical truth.

In 2005 another distorter, Lamar Waldron, came out with a book entitled "Ultimate Sacrifice." Until August 2007, I did not became aware of his false statements about me. I wrote an article about it and I sent it to my friends and contacts over the internet. Here is my article:

"ULTIMATE SACRIFICE or more lies about JFK's assassination.
By Carlos J. Bringuier

A recently published book "Ultimate Sacrifice" caught my eyes and as I do with all the ones that deals with the assassination of President John F. Kennedy I perused its pages to find out what it says about me. If what it said is true I buy it, if is one that lies about me I discard it as a science fiction political book or as a Communist propaganda book.

Two authors get credit for its writing: 1) Lamar Waldron, producer of programs for Discovery Channel; 2) Thom Hartmann, whose national program, syndicated by Air America Radio is carried on more than eighty stations across the US and draws some three million listeners.

On the back cover appear four endorsements for the book:
1) "IT'S FINDINGS ARE REMARKABLE. An important news analysis, with incredible new disclosures . . . Waldron and Hartmann report that our government had a secret plan for a Cuba insider"—named in this new edition for the first time—to kill Fidel Castro in December 1, 1963—just days after JFK's assassination. It would be followed by an invasion of Cuba by Cuban exiles aided by the U.S. military. It was managed of the books by Robert Kennedy and a select group of government officials . . . The Mafia learned about it . . . Had (Kennedy) killed in Texas. Knowing that our government could not disclose the real facts without admitting its own provocative plans and risking nuclear retaliation."—San Francisco Chronicle (from review by Ronald Golfarb, Mafia prosecutor for Attorney general Robert Kennedy.)

2) 'Until the CIA and Kennedy papers are all finally released in 2017, this book will do as 'the last word'—Liz Smith, Syndicated columnist.

3) 'A truly remarkable book . . . There is no doubting the compelling logic of its conclusion.' The Sunday London telegraph.

4) 'Compelling, often breathless reading.' The Dallas Morning News.

As I mentioned at the start I always read what it is written about me in a book. When I read it, I was shocked. How can a writer write so many falsehoods and inaccuracies. How can the writers write so many lies but immediately came to my mind Section A of the Cuban Department of State Security (Departamento Cubano de Seguridad del Estado, Sección A.)

Section A of the KGB was the one in charge of discrediting anti-Communist individuals. Section A of the KGB was the one in charge of planting in the world media the falsehood about John Edgar Hoover's transvestite experiences and the liberal press bit the lie and spread it all over the world. Section A of the KGB was the one in charge on November 22, 1963 of manufacturing lies about anti-Communists involvement in the assassination of JFK and the liberal press took as a holy duty to spread the lies all over the world.

Now I was reading something that could have been manufactured by Section A of the Cuban Department of State Security as a response to the enlighten documentary "Rendezvous with Death" by laureate German producer Wilfried Huismann. By the way this excellent documentary has been shown in more than 40 countries but not in the USA.

On page 539 I read: *"Bringuier as a friend of David Ferrie."*
Truth: I was never a friend of David Ferrie.

On page 540, I read several of the most incredible lies about me:

> *"As noted earlier, by August 1963 the CIA was resuming contact with Bringuier's old colleague from the original DR student group and the Cuban Revolution, Rolando Cubela (AMLASH). Since storming the Cuban Presidential Palace together, Bringuier and Cubela followed different paths, with Bringuier becoming anti-Castro exile with the DRE while Cubela remained in Cuba, an increasingly irrelevant mid-level official who was able to travel freely throughout the world. However since 1961—when Cubela had contacted the CIA about helping them against Castro—both Cubela and Bringuier had essentially been in the same side."*

Truth: A) I have never in my life met Rolando Cubela.

B) I never stormed the Cuban Presidential Palace, even more I never set a foot inside the Cuban Presidential Palace (I was very little when my great uncle Dr. Federico Laredo Brú was President of Cuba). I never participated in the storming of the palace in any form. At that time I was an Officer of the Court at the Fifth Criminal Court of Havana.

C) I became a member of the Cuban Student Directorate (Directorio Revolucionario Estudiantil) in mid-1962 not in 1957 (year of the storming of the Cuban Presidential Palace) as charge by the authors.

But for Ronald Golfarb these are "credible new disclosures." For Liz Smith this book is "the last word." For the Sunday London Telegraph "A truly remarkable book." And for the Dallas Morning News is "Compelling, often breathless reading." I don't know if you can put these four with all the useful idiots mentioned by that great Cuban writer, Humberto Fontova, in his books but I believe that Section A of the Cuban State Security could have had a hand behind the book and his endorsers.

There was a Cuban say: "El papel lo aguanta todo" which freely translated means "you can put in paper anything." But I want it to come out an expose these lies and I will continue to do so as long as I am alive.

August 12, 2007

Note by the author: On a day like today in 1959 was executed in Matanzas, Justo Díaz. In 1963 were executed in Havana, GE Saturnino Gallardo y Marcelo Valle. In 1969 was assassinated at sea Carmelo Morales.

That was the article that I sent to my friends and contacts over the internet. I want to clarify that after writing the above article I found out other recyclers that had specified the storming of the Presidential Palace occurring at the beginning of January of 1959 and I want to clarify that in the history of Cuba there are two storming of the Presidential Palace: 1) On March 13, 1957 when the DR and other anti-Batista organizations attacked the Presidential Palace, that day I was working in my courtroom and I didn't have anything to do with it. If I am not wrong I believe that Rolando Cubela did not participate in it. 2) The storming of the Presidential Palace in the first days of January 1959. At that time I was in Buenos Aires, Argentina from where I returned in January 26, 1959 finding my house occupied by Castro's militiamen which mean that it was impossible for me to have taking part in that "storming of the Presidential Palace."

Another book written presenting wrong "facts" about me is the one written by a person known as David Talbot. The title of Talbot's book: "Brothers." Mr. Talbot is identified as a "liberal" writer and he bring into scene a person to his book who tries to defame me. The whole incident portrayed in "Brothers" appears, most probably, to have been written by Castro's Intelligence Department. According to Talbot, a Cuban and ex-member of the 2506 Brigade, Angelo Murgado (real name Angel Murgado who apparently later on changed his name to Angelo Kennedy) told him that he went in the summer of 1963 to New Orleans to do a surveillance job and there he ran into Lee Harvey Oswald and watched him distributing proCastro propaganda in the street (he doesn't say what day or which street.) Murgado later claimed that he saw "stacks" of Oswald's pamphlets in the office of Carlos Bringuier, one of the local DRE delegates. Murgado, according to Talbot, reached the conclusion that Oswald was a FBI informant.

Fabián Escalante, Chief of Castro's Intelligence Department would have been delighted writing something like that. The only Oswald's Fair Play for Cuba Committee pamphlet that I ever had in my hands was the one left in "Casa Roca" by a Cuban on August 16, 1963. After Oswald had left New Orleans I cut the pamphlet by the part which read 'Hands Off Cuba" and then above it I wrote with a color marker the word "Russians" and stapled it to the sign, the same sign that I had used when I was trying to located Oswald on August 9, 1963. If Murgado said that he saw a "stack" of those pamphlets in my office then Murgado was lying.

I bought Talbot's book at Border Books, in The Woodlands, Texas when they put it for sale for $1.00. As I never met Mr. Murgado I inquired from a couple of friends who were members of the 2506 Brigade. The first one to answer said to me, over the phone, that Mr. Murgado was known in Miami as a "dialoguero" which means a traitor to free Cuba and who was in good terms with the Castro government. The second person emailed me that he was going to investigate Murgado who he remembered from the time that they spent in jail in Cuba and who at that time was a good person. This same ex-member of the 2506 Brigade later sent me another email stating: *"Carlos, I spoke with some members of the brigade, and the news are not good, he changed his name to Angelo Kennedy, and is a non-grata person among the Cuban circles, he went to Cuba some time ago but I don't know his motivation, and he was expelled of the community of the Brigade."*

I didn't have to read anymore of Mr. Talbot's book, it is enough. In his acknowledgments he thanks among others, Jefferson Morley and Peter Dale Scott.

But this is how History is distorted. You can put in a pot the works of Mark Lane, Harold Weisberg, Jim Garrison, Oliver Stone, Bernard Fensterwald, Anthony Summers, J. Marrs, Robert Tanenbaum, Lamar Waldron, Gaetano Fonzi, G. Robert Blakey, C. Furiati, Jefferson Morley, Jim DiEugenio and hundreds of others and you will have a melting pot of lies, falsehoods, misrepresentations, errors, etc., but not the truth.

CHAPTER XVII

———◦(◦)◦———

THE VERDICT

In any criminal investigation the authority in charge of it have to accumulate the evidence that the prosecutor will end presenting to the jurors at the time of the trial. At the end of the trial it is in the hands of the Jury to render its verdict. I will assume the role of the prosecutor.

One of the first things that a prosecutor have to prove is that the accused was able to commit the crime. Is Fidel Castro a normal politician or a conniving sadistic assassin? You can be sure that if Fidel Castro would be only a leftist and corrupt politician like Cristina Fernández, President of Argentina, the situation would have been different. Cristina Fernández could be corrupt and leftist but I don't have any prove that she had personally assassinated or order the assassination of anyone. The case of Fidel Castro is different.

1) In February 22, 1948 Fidel Castro participated in the assassination of his political rival Manolo Castro in Havana, Cuba.

2) In April 1948, Fidel Castro participated in the riots in Bogotá, Colombia after the assassination of Jorge Eliécer Gaitán. Fidel Castro was spotted talking, hours before the assassination, to the person identified as the assassin. Fidel Castro was arrested by the Colombia police at the Colón Theatre and this show the

complicity of Fidel Castro in the assassination of Gaitán as it was investigated by Scotland Yard in 1948.[196]

3) For years Fidel Castro was a member of a gangster "revolutionary" organization named "Unión Insurreccional Revolucionaria" (UIR) which organization conducted a series of assassinations in Cuba during the democratic governments of Ramón Grau San Martín and Carlos Prío Socarrás prior to Fulgencio Batista taking over with a coup in March 10, 1952.

4) During his preparation for his landing in Cuba he ordered the assassination of at least one person, reported as an informer, in Mexico.

5) After his arrival to Cuba for his revolution he had been reported as ordering the "execution" (assassination) of several Cubans during his campaign.

6) After the triumph of his Revolution he ordered the assassination, only in Oriente Province, and only during the first days of January 1959 of more than 500 Cubans. Thereafter he implanted an assassination platform, "executions" to get rid of possible rivals, among them Commanders Jesús Carreras, William Morgan, Humberto Sorí Marín and Arnaldo Ochoa, among others.

7) After the triumph of his revolution he ordered the assassination in Buenos Aires, Argentina of Cuban labor leader Eusebio Mujal, assassination which he was not able to accomplish because my intervention saving Mujal's life.

This show how Fidel Castro has his hands stained with blood as a result of assassinations. But now let us study the mind of this assassin and show how he disguise his acts with premeditated lies. Lies that the House Select Committee on Assassinations was gullible enough, or accomplice, to swallow in presenting him as innocent party in the assassination of President Kennedy.

My good friend Miguel Uría, member of the 2506 Brigade and son of an honest Chief of the Cuban Police before the Batista's coup in 1952, had recompiled some of the lies of Fidel Castro and I copy some of them:

---

[196] El Nuevo Herald, April 10, 2001.

"And I want to tell the people and the mothers of Cuba, that I will resolve all the problems without spilling a drop of blood. I said to the mothers that never, because of us, they would have to cry."

Now, this words show what a liar he is. Thousands of Cubans murdered and executed, hundreds of thousands that had suffered jail, families divided among those over two million who went into exile and those who had to remain in the island. Over one million Cubans dead in exile and Dictator Castro telling the Cuban people and to the Cuban mothers that they would not have to cry anymore and that not "a drop of blood" will be spilled.

"In respect to Communism, I can only say to you one thing, I am not a Communist, neither the Communists are strong to be a determining factor in my Country."

The above lie don't need any explanation. He, himself, has proven how he lies.

"I am not interested in power and I don't foresee assuming it at any moment."

Now, only the HSCA, Jimmy Carter, Rev. Jesse Jackson, Jr., Charles Rangel or other oxymoron can believe a liar like this. Fifty years of Dictatorship, the largest one in the history of this hemisphere and he was not interested in power.

"Who say freedom of the press, says liberty, says liberty of assembly and the right to freely elect not only the President, but also the worker to elect their leaders. Rights that could not be snatched away."

After more than 50 years of dictatorship there have not been free elections in Cuba to elect a President. The workers had lost even the right to strike and their leaders are imposed by the Communist Party. Fidel Castro snatched those rights from the Cuban people.

"When a right is suppressed it end up suppressing all other rights, disregarding democracy. Ideas are to be defended with reasons, not with arms. I am in love with democracy." Fidel Castro ended up suppressing all rights and democracy was assassinated in Cuba.

"I don't know in what form we could speak. It is possible that somebody could think that we hide obscure designs? It is possible that someone could affirm that we have lied to the people? It is possible that someone could think that we are hypocrites? Then when we say that our revolution is not

Communist, why they insist in accuse our revolution of what she is not? If our ideas were Communists we would say it here.

Fidel Castro lied and hid his obscure designs for the Cuban people.

"There is not Communism or Marxism in our ideas, but representative democracy and social justice."

Fidel Castro lied when he said that and had brought to Cuba not "representative democracy" but a feudal dictatorship where he and his henchmen destroyed social justice and owns the whole island. In the meantime the Cuban people continue to suffer for more than 50 years.

"We have said that we will convert Cuba in the most prosperous Country in the Americas, we have said that the Cuban people will reach the highest standard of living of any other Country in the world, because as the great powers have to invest a great percentage of their efforts in producing weapons, we are going to invest everything in producing riches, in building schools, in establishing industries, in make our land produce more, in developing the riches that we have in this marvelous land which besides been rich is the most beautiful."

Now after fifty years, Cuba is in a battle with Haiti to see which one is the one with more poverty. The Cuban people had to revert to prostitution in order to survive while Castro reach one of the top positions as one of the richest men in the world, according to Forbes Magazine. For the first time in its history Cuba had been forced to import sugar when the sugar industry had been decimated by the policies of the Communist government.

"In ten years we will achieve a higher standard of living than the United States."

"Our desire for Cuba is to establish a true democracy, without any resemblance to Fascism, Peronism or Communism, We are against any kind of totalitarianism."

I don't have to explain these lies, if you don't understand it you are in need of mental therapy.

Again I want to thank my good friend Miguel Uría for this recompilation of some of Dictator Fidel Castro's lies. These lies shows to you the character of the person in question. We have proved that he is an assassin, now we have proved that he is a liar. Now let us analyze his character, is he a valiant hero or is he is just a coward assassin?

During his time as an assassin before his Revolution he was cowardly carrying on his assassinations waiting in hiding for his victims. When he carried on the attack on July 26, 1953 of the Moncada Barracks he was not in the front line of the attackers but he was inside a car waiting to see if they would succeed. When they were defeated he escaped and begged to Archbishop Pérez Serantes to protect him and save his life. During his years in the Sierra Maestra he was always in the rearguard protecting his life.

When Colonel Orlando Piedra Negueruela, chief of Batista's Bureau of Investigation detained him at the Havana airport when Castro was trying to board an airplane with a false passport a few days after the assassination of Manolo Castro, Colonel Piedra remember how Fidel Castro cried when he thought that the police was going to kill him.[197]

That is the history of Dictator Fidel Castro, an assassin, a liar and a coward. Oliver Stone, maybe under the influence, could try to present him as a hero but history proves that he is not a hero but a vulgar criminal.

Now let us see how it would look like a verdict reached by a jury of his peers.

Whereas, it has been proved that on March 1961, Cuban Major Rolando Cubela establishes contact with the CIA.

Whereas, it has been proved that on June 1962, Lee Harvey Oswald left the Soviet Union to return to the USA.

Whereas, it has been proved that on July 18, 1962 Vladimir Kryuchkov of the KGB sent a secret telegram to Ramiro Valdés, Chief of Cuban Intelligence, apprising the Cubans to contact Lee Harvey Oswald.

Whereas, it has been proved that on November 1962 Cuban G2 established contact with Lee Harvey Oswald and assigned as his case officer Mayor Rolando Cubela.

Whereas, it has been proved that on April 10, 1963 Lee Harvey Oswald carried out his attempt to assassinate General Edwin Walker in Dallas. Texas.

Whereas, it has been proved that there are witnesses who saw Lee Harvey Oswald's file at a Cuban Intelligence Department.

*Whereas, it has been proved that Fidel Castro pronounced a speech to the press on September 7, 1963 where he threatened President John Fitzgerald Kennedy when he said: "**Kennedy is the Batista of these times . . . And***

---

[197] "Habla el Coronel Piedra", by Daniel Efraín Raimundo, pages 33, 34.

the most opportunistic American President of all times. He is fighting a battle against us they cannot win. Kennedy is a hypocrite and a member of an oligarchic family that controls several important posts in the government. For instance, one brother is a Senator and another Attorney General . . . and there are not more Kennedy officials because there are not more brothers . . . We are prepared to fight them an answer in kind. The United States leaders should think that if they are aiding terrorist plans to eliminate Cuban leaders, they themselves will not be safe."

Whereas, it has been proved that on September 27, 1963 Lee Harvey Oswald established contact in Mexico City with Valery Kostikov, KGB agent in charge of assassinations and reportedly with Cuban Secret Service General Fabián Escalante who has been reported as having been studying at Minsk.

Whereas, it has been proved that at his return from Mexico City Lee Harvey Oswald went underground using an alias, O. H. Lee, to rent an apartment in Dallas.

Whereas, it has been proved that on September 23, 1963, in order to gain intelligence about John F. Kennedy's intentions about Cuba and Dictator Fidel Castro, Major Rolando Cubela met in Porto Alegre, Brazil, with Néstor Sánchez of the CIA.

Whereas, it has been proved that Fidel Castro delivered a speech on September 28, 1963 where he attacked U. S. imperialism and threatened its leader (President John Fitzgerald Kennedy) when he stated: **"They are our enemies. And we will know how to deal with our enemies."**

Whereas, it has been proved that Major Rolando Cubela met on October 29, 1963, in Paris, France, with Desmond FitzGerald in charge of CIA Special Affairs staff. At which meeting Major Cubela requested "a high powered rifle with a telescopic sight that could be used to kill Castro from a distance."

Whereas, it has been proved, according to a secret memo of President Lyndon B. Johnson's adviser Martin Underwood, that on the morning of November 22, 1963 General Fabián Escalante, Chief of the Cuban Intelligence Department, flew in an small airplane from Mexico City to the Red Bird airport in Dallas, Texas where he stayed waiting until the evening when it was made public that Lee Harvey Oswald had been arrested.

Whereas, it has been proved that on November 22, 1963 Lee Harvey Oswald fired three shots from the sixth floor window of the Texas School Book Depository Building killing President John F. Kennedy.

Whereas, it has been proved that after committing the assassination, Lee Harvey Oswald escaped from the Texas School Book Depository Building, went to the rooming house where he had rented a room using an alias, got his revolver and tried to escape, with enough money to reach the Red Bird airport, but was intercepted by Dallas Police Officer J. D. Tippit who was killed by Lee Harvey Oswald.

Whereas, it has been proved that Lee Harvey Oswald was arrested at the Texas Theatre after resisting his arrest and assaulting one of the arresting officers who Oswald also attempted to shoot.

IT IS HEREBY RESOLVED THA WE, THE JURY, FOUND DEFENDANT FIDEL CASTRO RUZ, GUILTY OF THE ASSASSINATION OF PRESIDENT JOHN F. KENNEDY, AS THE "INTELLECTUAL AUTHOR."

CHAPTER XVIII

CONCLUSIONS

This is the true history of the assassination of President John F. Kennedy. I thank God that he provided me with enough life to write it. I know that after a person die falsehoods could be written about that person, I have seen during my lifetime how distorters of the truth have not waited until I pass away.

I cannot imagine what horrendous lies they could invent after my death, but while I am alive I want to set the record straight: I have never worked for the CIA, the FBI or any other agency of the government of the United States; I have never received any money from any agency of the government of the United States; I have never received any money from the Cuban Student Directorate (Directorio Revolucionario Estudiantil—DRE-). The pro-Castro distorters of the truth or just ignorant will never be able to prove otherwise because it is impossible to prove something that never happened.

I know that distortions of the truth have been done. I know that History theft had occurred in the history of the United States like when in the 1990's, under the Clinton Administration and previously during the Carter Administration the genocide in Cuba was ignored.[198] My hope is that the Marxists would not be able to disappear all the documents that have not yet been released like they have done before.

---

[198] "Scrubbing History is a Marxist Tradition in the Democratic Party", by John Carlton, October 19, 2009.

I would like to remind so called "historians" that there is a difference in between "Casa Roca" 107 Decatur Street, "Casa Cuba" 115 ½ Decatur Street and "Casa Cuba" 111 Decatur Street. I would like to remind them that I was the only member in New Orleans of the Cuban Student Directorate (Directorio Revolucionario Estudiantil—DRE-) before the assassination of President John F. Kennedy, later on Celso Hernández became Secretary of the Delegation, Miguel Aguado became Treasurer and for a short period of time Elsita Valdés Fonte became in charge of the feminine section.

I would like to remind so called "historians" that Miguel Cruz is a different person than Miguel Aguado, some have been confused.

I would like to remind some so called "historians" that I never met George Joannides or Howard Hunt.

I want to make a point about a photograph been circulated in the internet, apparently originated in Section A of the Castro's Intelligence Services showing the driver of the Kennedy's limousine shooting the President. Only a super oxymoron could believe that. But that is how the Communists operate. They try, with this picture, to use the useful idiots to whom Oliver Stone appealed. It is so insulting to the intelligence that I was not going to mention it. But they are doing this in 2013, what they will be doing in 2020?

I want to call to the Historians attention Cuban stamp Scott #827 which came out on April 1964, a few months after the assassination, which shows the American Eagle killed by a telescopic sight. This stamp shows Castro super ego.

I want to thank my friends, Cubans and Americans alike who helped me with their friendship in New Orleans, Louisiana; Miami; Fairhope and The Woodlands, Texas.

I want to thank my wife for her patience; I want to thank my parents for all the love that they provided to me. I want to thank God for having me in his hands giving me the opportunity to take the right decision when I decided to leave Cuba in order that my children could live in a free country and use their own brains to achieve their happiness and well-being, I did my part, now it has been up to them to do theirs. It is in their hands.

I want to thank my daughters Maria Ellzey and Maria Elena Simon for all their help and support.

I also want to give public thanks to that great American that was the late Senator Jesse Helms who had the vision to send me the Senate Report No. 94-755 of the 94th Congress entitled: "THE INVESTIGATION OF THE ASSASSINATION OF PRESIDENT JOHN F. KENNEDY: PERFORMANCE OF THE INTELLIGENCE AGENCIES" BOOK V—FINAL REPORT OF THE SELECT COMMITTEE TO STUDY GOVERNMENTAL OPERATIONS WITH RESPECT TO INTELLIGENCE ACTIVITIES UNITED STATES SENATE, dated April 23, 1976.

The reader has been able to read, from memos of the CIA and other reliable entities, that Fidel Castro organized various groups in order to plot to assassinate President John F. Kennedy; that Lee Harvey Oswald was under the control of the Cuban Intelligence Services; that Lee Harvey Oswald assassinated President John F. Kennedy and tried to escape; that a high ranking Cuban Intelligence Officer was waiting for him at Red Bird Airport in Dallas; that the Fair Play for Cuba Committee in Tampa, Florida was also, through some of its members, very much involved in the assassinations plots against President Kennedy; that Jack Ruby was not a "patriotic mourner" but a friend of Mafia boss Santos Trafficante, a double agent working for Fidel Castro.

During all these years I had the doubt in my mind of who really was that CIA agent, "Bernard" that I met in December 1963 when my sister María del Carmen was brought to Germany to rescue her son. Finally in January of 2012, I was able to find out his real name.

One of my nieces called me about a book that had come out written by a former CIA agent. On January 4, 2012 I ordered the book from Amazon.com. The title of the book: "Hey Spic! The author: Barney Hidalgo. On page 95 I read how he described the escape of my nephew Jorge Medina Bringuier from Germany. "Bernard" is Barney Hidalgo. In the book I also learnt that he was born in Cuba. When I met him he disguised that part very well.

At this writing the assassination of President Kennedy was around 50 years ago, Dictator Fidel Castro converted in a cynical predator old man, maintains his power in Cuba in the longest dictatorship registered in this hemisphere. The United States of America is sliding rapidly into Socialism. Lee Harvey Oswald would have been feeling as great at this moment as he did when he shot those three bullets from the sixth floor window of the Book Depository Building in November 22, 1963.

Fidel and Raúl Castro are still alive in Cuba, the USA under the government of Barack Hussein Obama is reaching a financial and political cliff that could bring the destruction of the USA as a leader of the world.

Lee Harvey Oswald, Fidel and Raúl Castro accomplished the present dangerous situation, with three shots fired on Dallas on November 22, 1963 when they committed the crime of Assassinating John F. Kennedy without been punished for it.